25¢

dBASE IV™ QuickStart

Developed by Que® Corporation

Text and graphics pages developed by

Lawrence C. Metzelaar and Marianne B. Fox

QUE® CORPORATION

LEADING COMPUTER KNOWLEDGE

dBASE IV™ QuickStart

For information, address Que Corporation, 11711 N. College Ave., Carmel, IN 46032.

Library of Congress Catalog No.: LC 88-61787

ISBN 0-88022-389-8

93 92 91 90 89 6 5 4 3 2 1

Interpretation of the printing code: the rightmost double-digit number is the year of the book's printing; the rightmost single-digit number, the number of the book's printing. For example, a printing code of 89-1 shows that the first printing of the book occurred in 1989.

This book is based on dBASE IV version 1.

Trademark Acknowledgments

Que Corporation has made every effort to supply trademark information about company names, products, and services mentioned in this book. Trademarks indicated below were derived from various sources. Que Corporation cannot attest to the accuracy of this information.

COMPAQ DeskPro 286 and COMPAQ MS-DOS 3.31 are registered trademarks and COMPAQ DeskPro 386 is a trademark of COMPAQ Computer Corporation.

dBASE III Plus is a registered trademark and dBASE IV is a trademark of Ashton-Tate Corporation.

HP is a registered trademark and LaserJet is a trademark of Hewlett-Packard Co.

IBM PC AT and Personal System/2 are registered trademarks and IBM PC XT is a trademark of International Business Machines Corporation.

PFS:FILE is a registered trademark of Software Publishing Corporation.

Publishing Director

David P. Ewing

Acquisition Editor

Terrie Lynn Solomon

Developmental Editors

Kathie-Jo Arnoff
Kathleen Johanningsmeier

Editor

Ann Campbell Holcombe

Technical Editors

Joel Shore
Tim Stanley

Production

William Hartman
Dennis Sheehan
Cheryl English
Jennifer Matthews
Lori Lyons
Peter Tocco

Indexer

Sherry Massey

Composed in Garamond by

HARTMAN Publishing

Page Design by

William Hartman, Hartman Publishing

Acknowledgments

Que Corporation thanks the following individuals for their contributions to this book:

Larry C. Metzelaar and Marianne Fox, for their extraordinary discipline, energy, effort, and creativity as they developed this book.

Kathleen Johanningsmeier, for her work with the original manuscript and graphics concepts.

Ann Holcombe, for her ability to turn a neat phrase and her unfailing good nature as she coordinated the efforts of editors and authors.

Kathie-Jo Arnoff, for her superb editorial eye and for reviewing the final pages of this manuscript.

Bill Hartman, for making each page come alive and for interpreting editorial comments from three editors without losing his sense of humor.

Terrie Solomon, for her ability to keep mountains of paper flowing between authors and editors.

Tim Stanley, for his technical expertise and for the attention he gave to this project in the final stages.

Joanetta Hendel and Stacey Beheler, for their invaluable administrative support.

Dennis Sheehan, Cheryl English, and Jennifer Matthews, for making the book come together at the end.

Contents

To the Reader

dBASE IV QuickStart uses an exciting new approach to introduce the fundamental concepts of dBASE IV to beginning users. Throughout the book, each dBASE IV topic is presented in two or more pages of easy-to-follow text, followed by two or more pages of graphics. The graphics illustrate the topic discussed on the text pages.

This innovative book shows you how to use the dBASE IV Control Center and its panels to accomplish a variety of database management tasks. You learn to design and create a database, edit data, organize your data in various ways, search your files for particular data, and view data in various ways. You also learn to design custom data-entry forms, reports, and labels.

After you become familiar with dBASE IV's Control Center, menus, and options, you can use the graphics in *dBASE IV QuickStart* for reference when you need to be reminded of the sequence of steps you need for particular operations. Become productive with dBASE IV quickly with *dBASE IV QuickStart!*

Introduction

dBASE IV™ QuickStart is a unique "show and tell" approach to dBASE IV. This book teaches you to use dBASE IV by showing you how to perform dBASE tasks. As you thumb through the book, notice that the *QuickStart* approach uses graphic spreads between text spreads to involve you visually in active learning. *dBASE IV QuickStart* provides just enough information to get you going—*quickly.*

Who Should Use This Book?

dBASE IV QuickStart is designed for new dBASE IV users, but you will benefit even if you already know something about database management programs. This book is for you if you have tried, without success, to learn the basics of dBASE IV. If you are looking for a quick guide to dBASE IV, this book is for you. If you are looking for a more detailed guide to dBASE IV, refer to Que Corporation's *dBASE IV Handbook.*

This book presumes that the dBASE IV software is already installed on your hard disk system. You may refer to the Appendix or to the dBASE IV documentation for information on installing the program.

How Is This Book Organized?

Most traditional books demand that you must first visualize a concept as you read about it, and then decipher its meaning. With *dBASE IV QuickStart* the visualizing is done for you by using graphic spreads.

We learn by using as many senses (hearing, seeing, and touching) as we can. For this reason, this book combines text pages with graphic pages to highlight specific dBASE IV features and explain concepts and processes too abstract to be demonstrated with a picture alone.

Chapters don't begin on right-hand pages, as they do in other books. Instead, each *QuickStart* page begins on the left in a two-page spread. Each spread explores one topic. Often one text spread and one graphic spread are enough to discuss a topic fully. Of course, more complex topics often require more than two spreads.

Each chapter begins with an introduction, key words, and an overview of topics covered.

How Do You Use This Book?

You'll find chapter titles listed down the side of the right page, beginning with *Introduction* and ending with *Custom Programs.* Notice that a red rectangle marks the title of the chapter you are reading. The major topics of the chapter appear across the top of the right page, with the current topic highlighted. Right now, "Using This Book" and "Introduction" appear highlighted. Look for the title of the major topic at the upper left corner of the spread.

What Is Covered in This Book?

Chapters 1 through 6 in *dBASE IV QuickStart* are organized so you create, maintain (add, edit, and delete data), and use (index, search, print) the database. You should read chapters 1 through 6 before reading other chapters in the book.

Imagine creating a form on your screen that matches an existing form, or producing a report that extracts and lists the overtime hours from scheduling documents. dBASE IV makes these tasks easy. Chapters 7 through 9 explore custom-designing your own data entry screens, reports, and labels. You can read these three chapters in any order. Chapter 10 provides an overview of the dBASE IV Applications Generator. Because Chapter 10 deals with a more sophisticated dBASE feature, you should read the chapter last. Installing dBASE IV is covered in the Appendix.

Using This Book

dBASE IV QuickStart is designed to help you learn the basics of dBASE IV as easily as possible.

The *QuickStart* approach gives you the power to access whatever information you need by using the top and right margins to find sections and chapter titles. Use the margin information to confirm your location in the book.

Text and graphics are integrated to help you learn dBASE IV by more than one method.

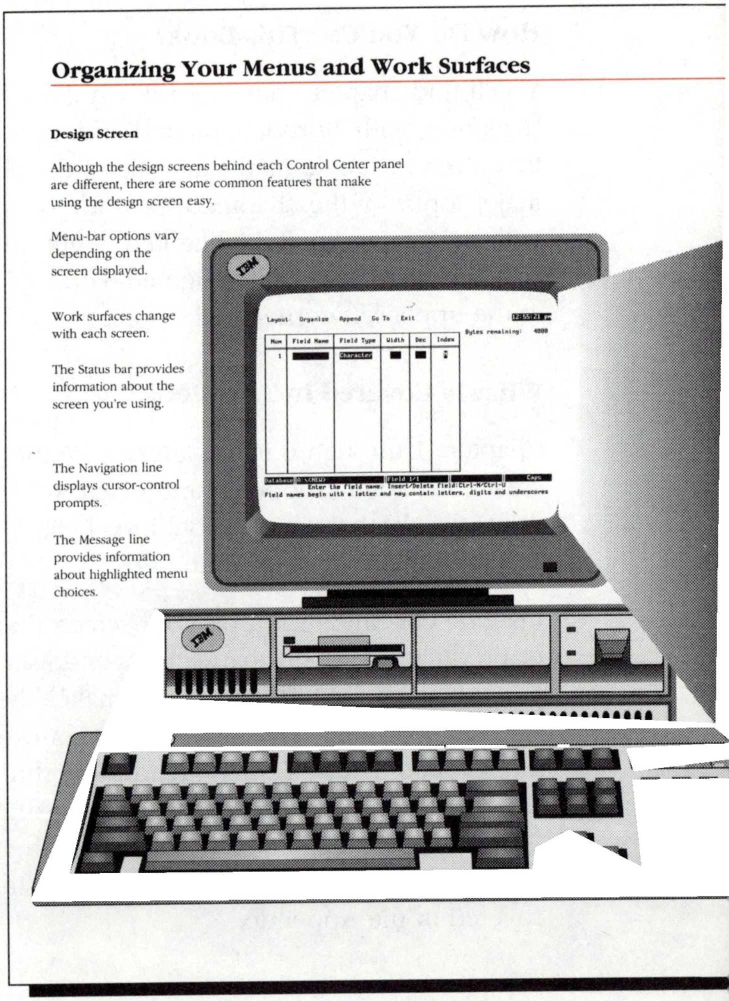

Organizing Your Menus and Work Surfaces

Design Screen

Although the design screens behind each Control Center panel are different, there are some common features that make using the design screen easy.

Menu-bar options vary depending on the screen displayed.

Work surfaces change with each screen.

The Status bar provides information about the screen you're using.

The Navigation line displays cursor-control prompts.

The Message line provides information about highlighted menu choices.

Topics

The topics within the current chapter are listed across the top of the right-hand page. You'll note as you flip through the book, the topics change from chapter to chapter. The red rectangle highlights the current topic.

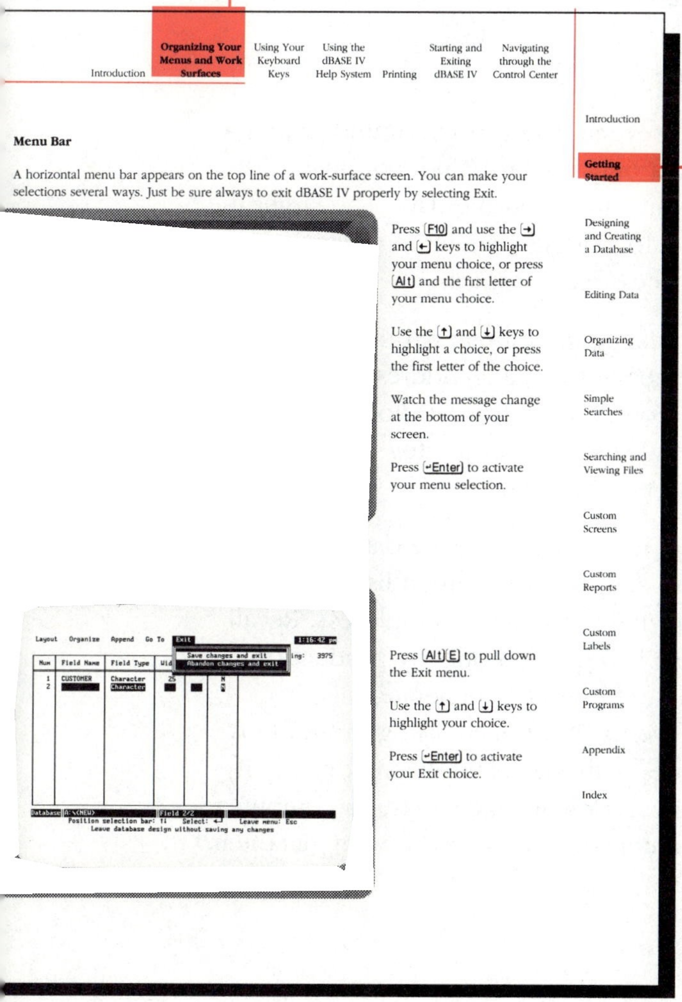

Introduction | **Organizing Your Menus and Work Surfaces** | Using Your Keyboard Keys | Using the dBASE IV Help System | Printing | Starting and Exiting dBASE IV | Navigating through the Control Center

Menu Bar

A horizontal menu bar appears on the top line of a work-surface screen. You can make your selections several ways. Just be sure always to exit dBASE IV properly by selecting Exit.

Press F10 and use the → and ← keys to highlight your menu choice, or press Alt and the first letter of your menu choice.

Use the ↑ and ↓ keys to highlight a choice, or press the first letter of the choice.

Watch the message change at the bottom of your screen.

Press ↵Enter to activate your menu selection.

Press Alt E to pull down the Exit menu.

Use the ↑ and ↓ keys to highlight your choice.

Press ↵Enter to activate your Exit choice.

Introduction
Getting Started
Designing and Creating a Database
Editing Data
Organizing Data
Simple Searches
Searching and Viewing Files
Custom Screens
Custom Reports
Custom Labels
Custom Programs
Appendix
Index

Chapters

Chapter titles are listed down the right margin.

The current chapter title is enclosed within a rectangle. As you move from chapter to chapter, the rectangle moves to reflect your location in the book.

What Is Database Management?

You gather, store, and access data every day of your life. For example, suppose you learn the birth date of a friend. If you want to keep that data, you are likely to store it with other birth dates in a date book or card file. Now you have related pieces of information.

In simple terms, a database is a collection of related data. Database management is the art of managing that related data—such as adding new birth dates, recalling birth dates in time to send greetings, and removing dates you no longer need.

Manual or Automated Database

You can store data in a database several ways: in your mind, on paper, or in a computer. If you store data only in your mind, you may not remember everything and only you can access the data. The larger the database, the more important it is to store its data in an organized manner and in a physical form accessible to others.

The yellow-pages directory is an example of a manual file—a database on paper. Most of us cannot memorize the name, address, and phone number of every business firm in our city. Instead, if those three data items are sequenced in the yellow-pages—first by category, then by company name, we can easily access the data.

Storing data in computer memory lets you manipulate data in ways not previously possible. For example, suppose you want a listing from the yellow-pages of all businesses having the same street address. Recall data in the yellow-pages database is organized only by product or service line and by company name. In order to generate a list according to street name, you have to check each listing in the book and manually write down the ones with the required street name. If, however, data items are stored in an organized database in computer memory, you can produce lists automatically—based on any data item you choose.

Consider another example. Suppose you work for an automobile dealership that keeps data about each automobile sold. The salesman records, on paper, information about each sale, places the paper in a folder marked with the customer's name, and stores the folder in a file cabinet. In database terminology, each data item in the folder—customer name, date of sale, and salesperson is a *field*. The collection of related data items about one sale is a *record* (in this case, the folder). All the sales folders (records) in the file cabinet comprise the sales *database*.

If you have the customer's name, you can easily find data in the file cabinet—the manual database. However, what if you want to know both the total sales for the month of January and the total sales made by a particular salesperson? In this manual database organized by customer name, you must physically look at every record, remove the ones meeting your search criterion, manually calculate the required totals, and refile the records in original order. Switching to a computerized database allows you to manipulate data based on any field to generate needed calculations.

An automated database-management system has other advantages when compared to a manual system. You can produce sales reports every morning; reports compiled right before the close of business late the night before. You can streamline your business operations by reducing the time and personnel costs associated with manual systems. Entering and editing data with a computer keyboard and monitor is faster and easier than entering and editing data by hand.

One added benefit of a computer database involves the security of the data. Few businesses keep a second copy of a manual (paper) database. In the event of a fire, the only sales records are destroyed. Using a computer database, you can copy data quickly to inexpensive disks or tapes and store these backup files in a separate, and safe, location.

What Is Database Management?

The Manual System

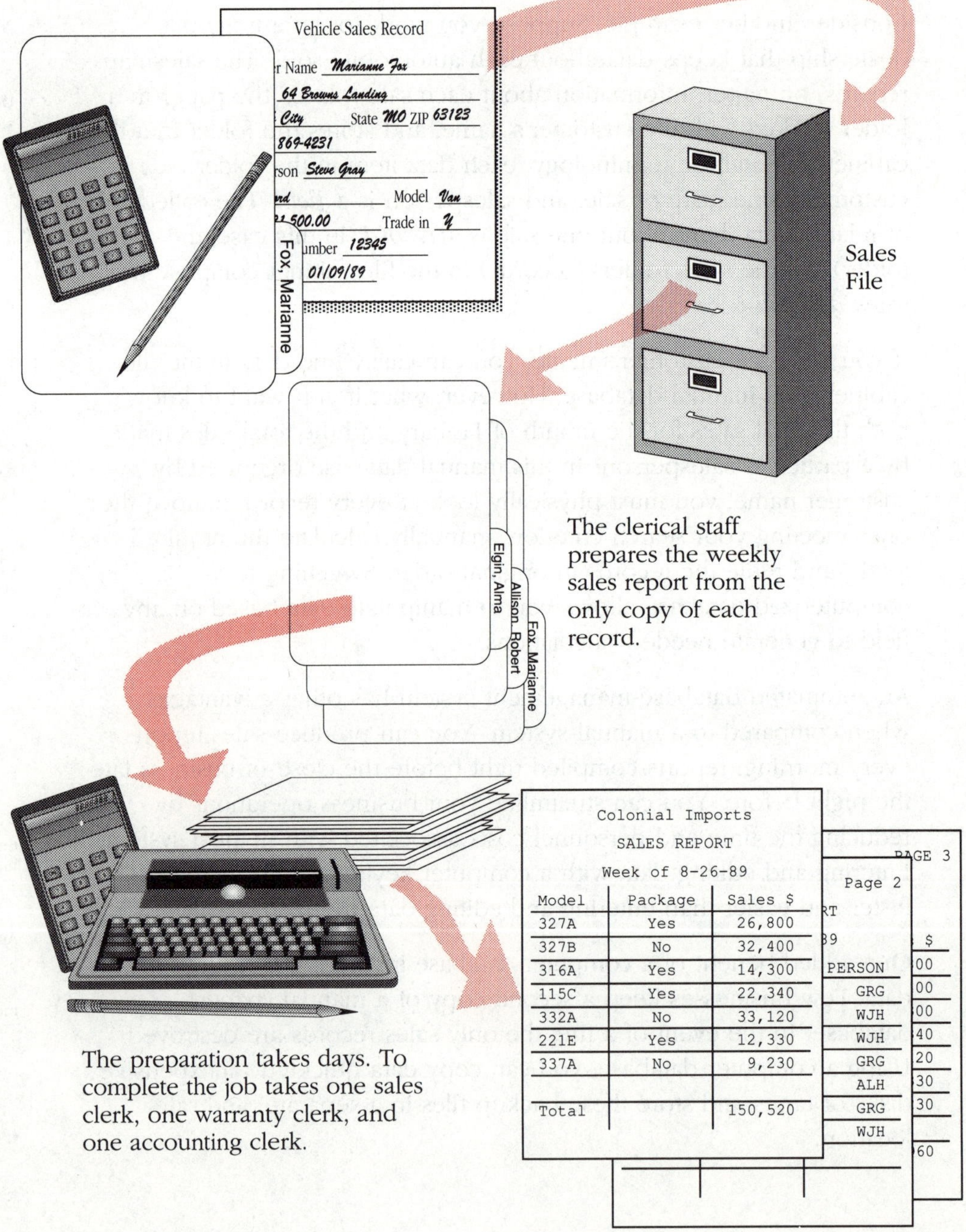

The Automated System

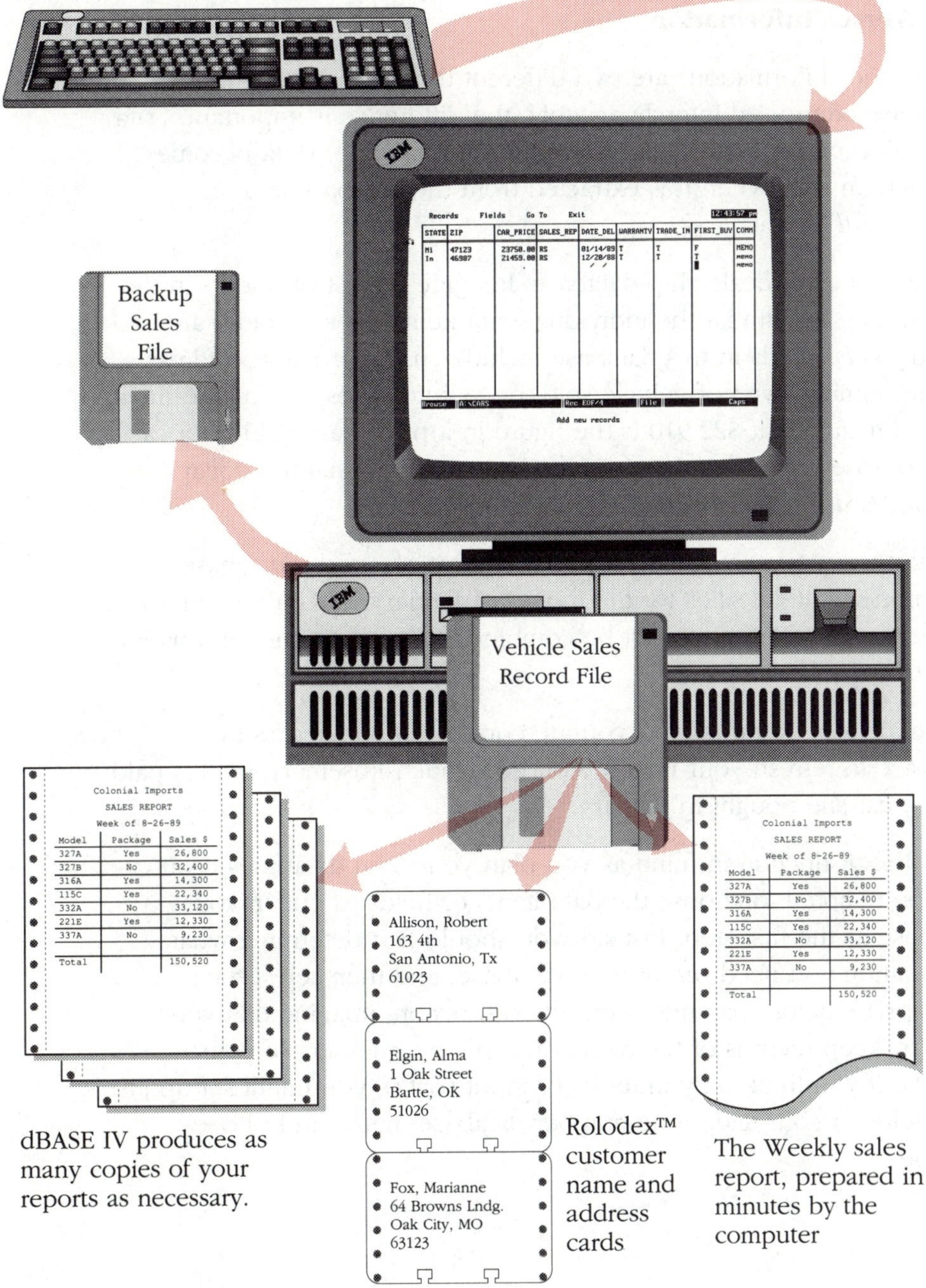

dBASE IV produces as many copies of your reports as necessary.

Rolodex™ customer name and address cards

The Weekly sales report, prepared in minutes by the computer

Data Versus Information

"Data" and "information" are two different things. Although the two terms are often used interchangeably, the difference is important. Data is a collection of facts that are stored in the database. Data becomes information only when it is extracted from the database in a *meaningful* format.

Consider the car-dealership database. Imagine the set of folders in the file cabinet. Recall that the individual data items in each folder are called *fields*. Fields in this database include customer name, address, phone number, type of vehicle sold, price paid, salesperson, and much more. Imagine that $22,910 is the figure in a price-paid field for a car sold to Rosemary Shanks in January. Do you think that the dollar amount is *data* or *information*?

If you answer "data," you are correct—*if* you access the database to determine the total sales for the month of January. Data about all sales in the month of January must be combined to produce the information about total sales.

If you answer "information," you are correct—*if* you access the database to refresh your memory on how much Rosemary Shanks paid for the car she bought in January.

Keep the distinction in mind as you plan your own databases. You may be tempted to choose the data items or fields to put *in* your database as the first step. Instead, you should first determine what information you need *out* of your database, and then select the appropriate fields. To understand the distinction, imagine that you want to keep records of the names and phone numbers of your friends. If you think only in terms of input (data), you might set up just two fields in your telephone-number database: name and phone number.

If instead you first concentrate on what you want from your database (output), you might decide you need an alphabetized listing of your friends as well as another listing by area code—to be used when you travel. To produce these lists, you need four fields, not two: last name, first name, area code, and seven-digit phone number. Always determine what information a database must provide before you determine what data to gather and maintain.

Multiple Databases

Although a single database may be quite useful, you can gain even more information by linking several databases. For example, each record in a dealership's sales database represents a new car sale to a different customer. Each record includes customer name, address, telephone number, price, and vehicle identification number of the car purchased. Assume also you want to track warranty work for each car. If you keep both sales and warranty information in the same database, the sales-related fields will be empty when a record concerns warranty work, and the warranty-related fields will be empty when the record concerns a sale. To avoid excessive blank fields that take up disk space, you'd keep the warranty database separate from your sales database.

You might use the warranty database to track maintenance and repairs made under a dealer-specific warranty to the original owner of the car. Each record represents service under warranty; a single customer may bring in a car several times. Fields in the warranty database might include vehicle identification number, date of service, and description of service. Because you decide to link the two databases by the common vehicle identification number field, you need not repeat the customer name, address, and phone-number fields in the warranty database. You can reach the warranty database by merely entering the vehicle identification number.

What Is Database Management?

Data or Information?

Although the terms are used interchangeably, data and information are different. Data are facts stored in your database. Think of data as pieces of a jigsaw puzzle. When the facts are organized and associated in a meaningful fashion, information results. The pieces of the puzzle form a picture!

Data Record

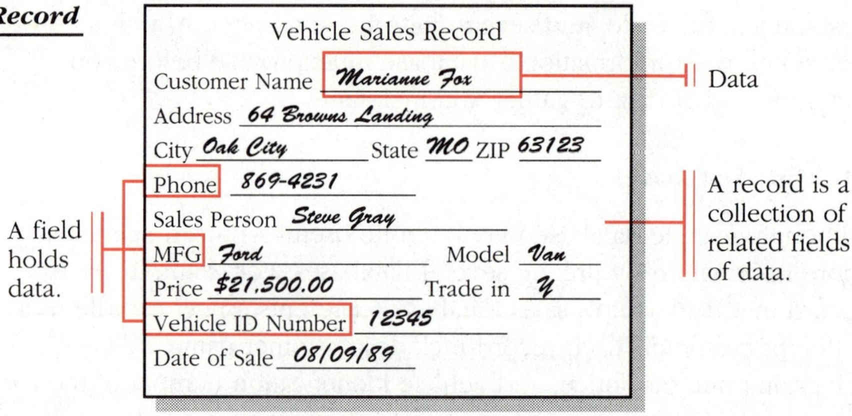

File

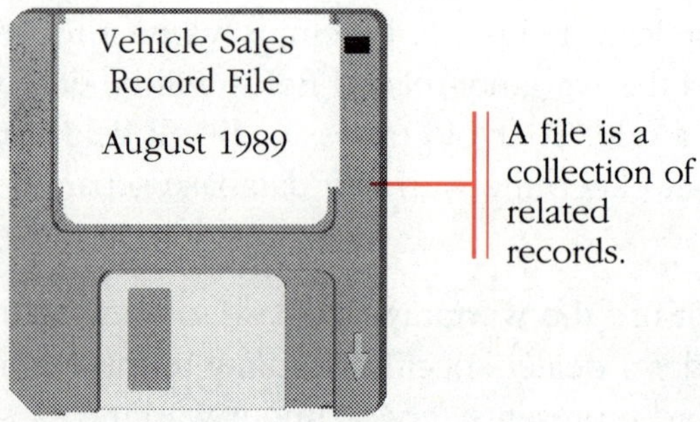

Information

Colonial Imports
SALES REPORT
Week of 8-26-89

Model	Package	Sales $
327A	Yes	26,800
327B	No	32,400
316A	Yes	14,300
115C	Yes	22,340
332A	No	33,120
221E	Yes	12,330
337A	No	9,230

Information is data that has been assembled, organized, and/or summarized for a specific purpose.

Multiple Databases

Many of your database requirements can be satisfied by using a single database; but there are times when you can link two databases to produce even more information.

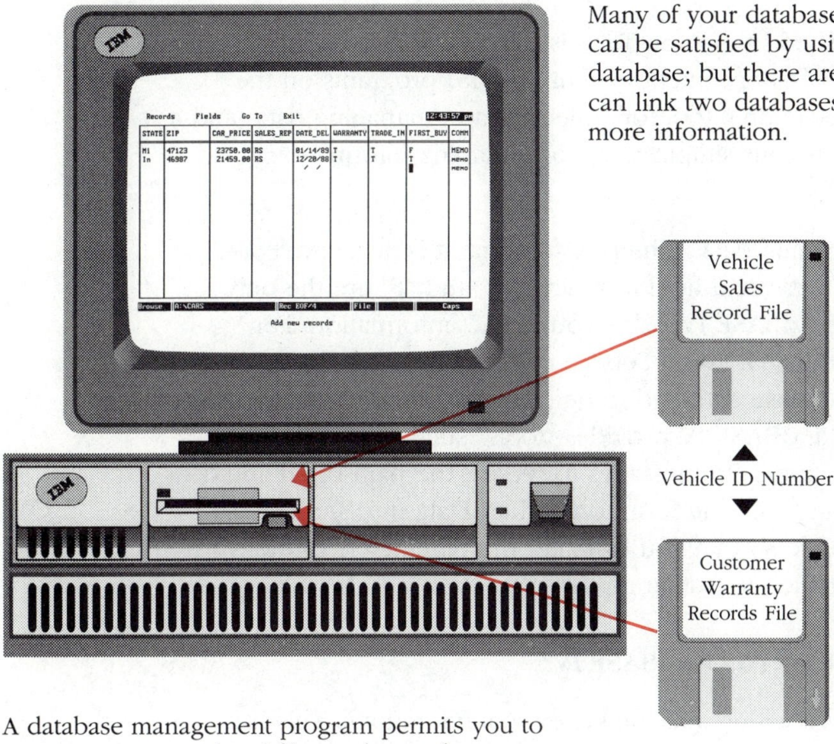

A database management program permits you to use two or more related files and treat them as one larger file.

Two database files are created to provide information about different aspects of dealership operations. The two databases are linked by a common field—in this case, the VIN (vehicle identification number).

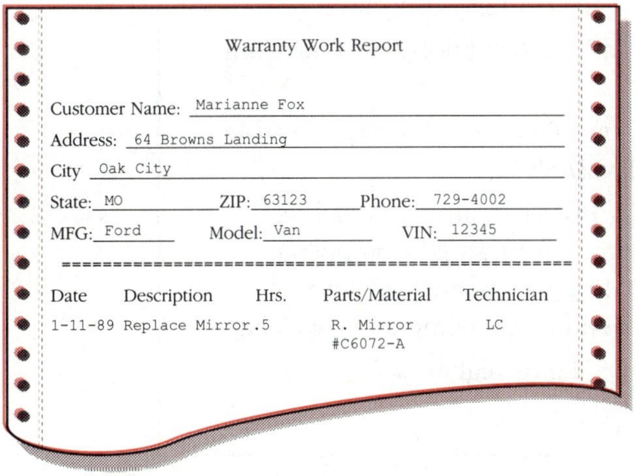

Warranty Work Report

Customer Name: Marianne Fox
Address: 64 Browns Landing
City Oak City
State: MO ZIP: 63123 Phone: 729-4002
MFG: Ford Model: Van VIN: 12345

Date	Description	Hrs.	Parts/Material	Technician
1-11-89	Replace Mirror	.5	R. Mirror #C6072-A	LC

dBASE IV, published by Ashton-Tate, is one of the most popular and powerful database management system (DBMS) programs on the market. It is an electronic tool for collecting and managing data, and it will help you with your simplest or most complex information management tasks.

dBASE IV can validate data to help ensure that it is accurate. For example, you can create a field in which "M" and "F" are the only acceptable entries. dBASE IV helps you extract information. For example, when the U.S. Postal Service converted its five-digit ZIP code to nine digits, database data had to be changed to increase the size of the ZIP-code field. dBASE IV provides "tools" such as pull-down menus, prompts, and help messages to reduce the pain of editing data or converting data from one form to another. Data in dBASE IV is adaptable to change so that you can alter the parameters of the database as your situations change.

What Do You Need To Use dBASE IV?

dBASE IV operates within specific system configurations. This list details the basic requirements that must be met before you can start using dBASE IV software.

- Your computer system must have a hard disk drive.
- Your computer must have at least 640 kilobytes of random access memory (RAM).
- You must have at least 3.5 megabytes of memory available on your hard disk to install dBASE IV.
- dBASE IV runs on IBM® AT, PC/XT™, and Personal System/2® (30, 50, 60, 70, and 80) Personal Computers. dBASE IV also runs on COMPAQ DeskPro 286® and Deskpro 386™ and on all IBM (100%) compatible systems.
- dBASE IV operates with DOS 2.0 or higher, and with COMPAQ MS-DOS® 3.31.

Creating and Maintaining Your Database

You'll use the **Data** feature to create instructions that provide dBASE with information about your database fields. These instructions are stored in a special file called a *database structure file*. For example, you can create a structure containing the first-name, last-name, and birthday fields in a birthday database.

Once the database structure is created, you can tell dBASE IV to open that file for use. In the file, you can add records to the database and edit or delete existing records.

You'll use the **Data** feature, to search your database to locate specific records. This search capability facilitates editing data and producing simple lists.

Querying Your Database

You'll use the **Queries** design screen to create a set of instructions to tell dBASE what records to access, and what fields within the records to use. dBASE stores these instructions in a special data file called a *query by example* file. The data that appears on-screen as a result of these instructions is called a *view*.

When you create a view, you tell dBASE IV what database to use, what records to select, and what fields to display or print. The set of instructions or query describes how the view should look. You can save queries on disk for use later.

Queries also can supply data for use with reports and labels. Browsing and editing databases becomes more efficient when you use queries to control which records and fields are accessed. You can even use queries to link (combine) two or more databases to create reports and mailing labels.

Generating Forms

dBASE IV provides two forms for adding, browsing, and editing data. You can display data using the *Browse* form in which each row represents a record and each column represents a field of data. Or you can display data using an *Edit* form in which only one record at a time appears on your screen.

You may also design your own screen display (used for entering or viewing data) called a *custom* screen. When you create your own screen, you can arrange data fields anywhere on the screen, add boxes and lines for emphasis, add comments for clarification, or create calculated fields.

Generating Reports

dBASE IV also provides two ways to generate reports: Quick Report and custom reports. A Quick Report needs no design work on your part. Just press two keys and you produce a listing of all data in your database, organized in columns by the type of information (last name, first name, Social Security number, etc.). If you want to design your own report, called a *custom* report, you do not have to start from scratch. dBASE IV provides a *Quick Layouts* option through which you can select one of several basic designs.

When you generate a report, you tell dBASE IV what database to use, what records to select, and what fields to print. The page number and date are placed at the top of each page. dBASE IV can link two or more databases to generate one report.

Creating Labels

dBASE IV also can create and print labels for mailers, name badges, invoices, stickers, or special tags. Using the Labels Design screen, you can create a set of instructions that tell dBASE IV how to print labels, even special label sheets for laser printers.

When you create a label, you'll tell dBASE IV what database to use, what fields to print, and how to print the data on the labels. The set of instructions, called a *label design*, describe how the label should look. The label design can be stored on disk for repeated use.

Additional Features

By using dBASE IV's on-screen Help feature you can avoid searching through bulky manuals for an answer to a question or an explanation of a dBASE feature. Context-sensitive help is just a keystroke away. You'll use the Help feature in this book.

As you become familiar with dBASE IV, you will be amazed by its powerful features. First, dBASE IV is menu-driven by a new feature called the *Control Center*. For those of you familiar with dBASE III® Plus, the Control Center replaces the old Assist menus. Even with little or no experience, you will find it easy to use the Control Center menus. Furthermore, you can use the new Control Center to accomplish many tasks without having to learn a complex programming language to communicate with dBASE IV.

If you are familiar with earlier versions of dBASE and want to use a programming language, you can still use the Dot Prompt mode. Or consider using the new Applications Generator. It uses a system of menus to create and test programs and menus quickly and easily. You can also code programs in the IBM standard Structured Query Language (SQL).

You now have a general understanding about how to use this book, what database management means, and about the overall capabilities of dBASE IV.

Understanding dBASE IV

The Control Center is your gateway to dBASE IV features and functions.

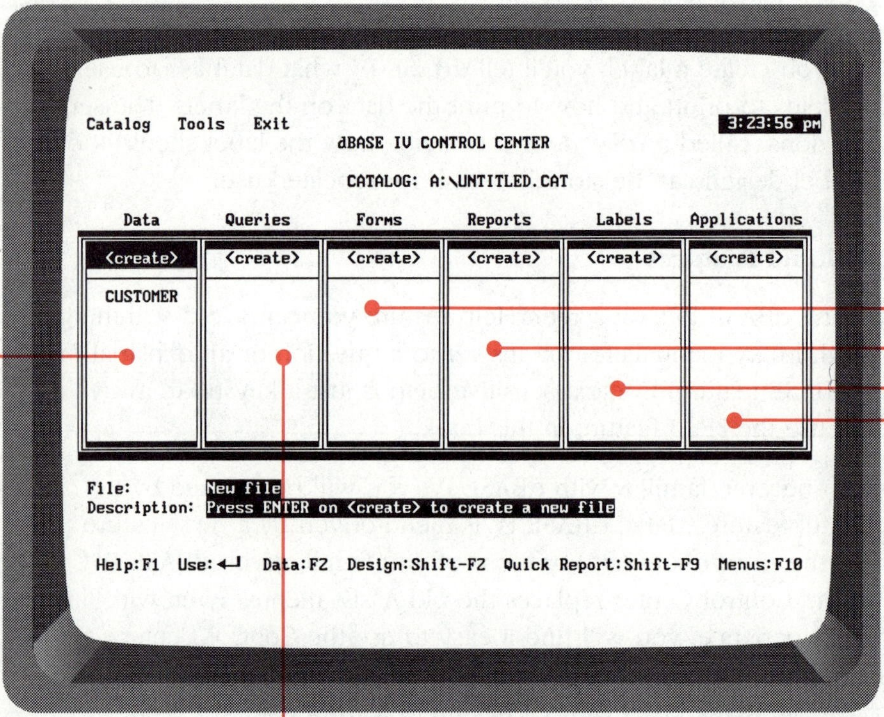

Use the Data panel to create, modify, search, activate, and deactivate your database.

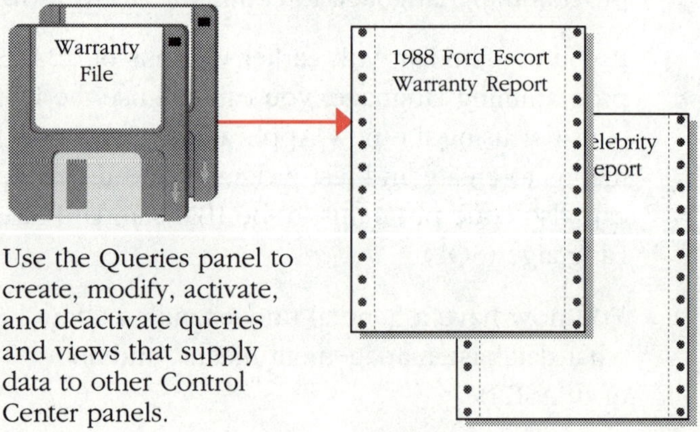

Use the Queries panel to create, modify, activate, and deactivate queries and views that supply data to other Control Center panels.

Use the Forms panel to create, modify, activate, and deactivate custom Input and Information screens.

Use the Reports panel to create, modify, and run Report Forms that produce custom reports.

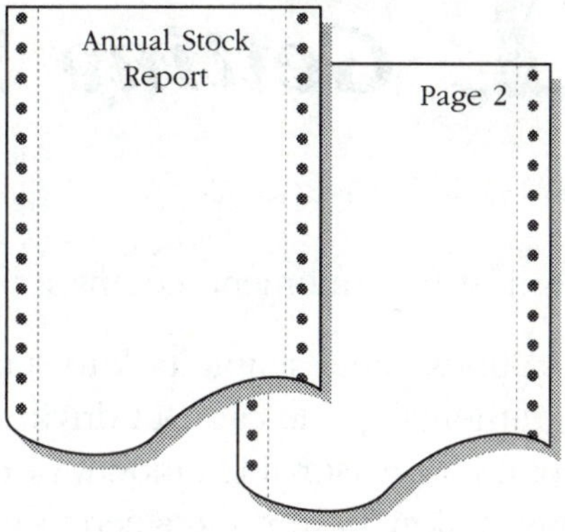

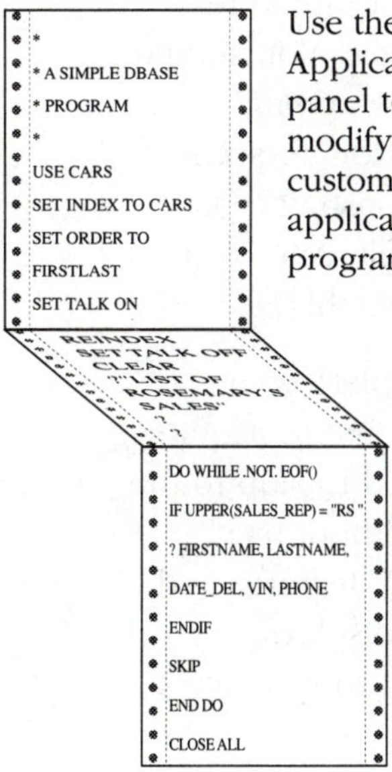

Use the Applications panel to create, modify, and run custom application programs.

Use the Labels panel to create, modify, and run Label forms that produce custom labels.

1 *Getting Started*

For just for a moment, compare using dBASE IV to driving your car.

It sounds like a simple task to start the car, drive to your destination, and then stop the car. But driving safely and reaching your stopping point in a reasonable amount of time requires knowing more than simply how to turn the steering wheel and insert the ignition key.

You must know the layout and operation of your car's features, such as the horn and windshield wipers. You must be able to interpret dashboard displays like the fuel gauge and speedometer. You should know how to call for help if needed. You must choose among options—taking the "quick" route via interstate or the longer scenic route. You must understand such requirements and constraints as carrying your driver's license and securing your seatbelt. And, you must know these items *before* you turn the ignition switch!

It can be a relatively easy task to start dBASE IV, complete your desired activity, and exit the program *if* you take the time to acquire some general knowledge in advance. Don't be tempted to skip to the end of this section and start the dBASE IV program without first understanding these topics: the layout of the dBASE IV features and the keys used to access them, the meaning of screen displays, the operation of the Help feature, and the procedure used to produce a Quick Report.

What Is Covered in This Chapter?

In this chapter, you learn about

- Organizing your work surfaces
- Moving your cursor and using function keys

- Using Help menu options
- Understanding general printing considerations
- Starting and exiting dBASE IV
- Navigating the Control Center

Key Words Used in This Chapter

Catalog	A group of related database file names. A catalog should not be confused with a *directory*. Catalogs do not contain the files themselves—only the file names.
Control Center	A dBASE IV screen display which provides access to a system of pull-down menus governing many dBASE features.
Control Center Panels	Six menu options from which you can create and maintain files (Data, Forms, Reports, Labels) and run Queries (searches) or Applications.
Menu bar	A horizontal menu appearing on the top row of a work-surface screen.
Navigation line	The space at the bottom of the screen which displays the keys you use to move the cursor for that particular task or file.
Pull-down menu	A menu on which the options are listed one after another in a single column.
Work surface	The actual work surface takes up most of the screen, excluding small areas devoted to primarily informational items such as the Navigation line, Status line, and Menu bar.

Organizing Your Menus and Work Surfaces

You'll use the dBASE IV menu system to accomplish your database management tasks. The menu system is a collection of work surfaces and menus. At the heart of the menu system is the Control Center. The Control Center itself is both a work surface and menu that serves as a gateway to all of dBASE IV's other work surfaces and menus. If you take time to understand the common work-surface features and how to use the work surface and menus, you can reduce any anxiety you might have about learning dBASE IV.

When you work with the menu system in dBASE IV, your entire screen display can be considered a work surface. Technically, a work surface is the entire screen with the exception of any horizontal Menu bar appearing at the top and any Status bar, Navigation line, and Message line at the bottom.

Menu Bar

A horizontal Menu bar appears on the top line of your screen. Its options are arranged across the line. When your cursor is in the work-surface area, you can access the Menu bar two ways.

- F10 — Press the F10 key, and the cursor moves to the first choice on the Menu bar.
- Alt-letter — Press the Alt key, and while holding down the Alt key, press the letter that corresponds to the first letter of your Menu bar choice. The cursor moves to that choice in the Menu bar. For example, press Alt-T to choose the Tools menu option.

After the cursor moves to the Menu bar, you can select options by moving the cursor highlight along the Menu bar, using the left arrow (←) and right arrow (→) keys. As an option is highlighted, a pull-down menu appears in a window on-screen just below the Menu bar.

The pull-down menu contains a series of options arranged one after another in a row. When any window first appears, one of the menu choices is highlighted. A message appears at the bottom of the screen explaining what the highlighted menu choice does. The option that is highlighted depends on what you were doing at the time you activated the menu.

You may make a menu choice from the pull down-menu in one of two ways:

- Highlight your menu choice, using the up arrow (↑) and down arrow (↓) keys, then press Enter.

  The advantage of highlighting your menu choice first is that a message appears on the bottom line describing the choice you highlight.
- Press the first letter of your menu choice.

Status Bar

The Status bar appears immediately below the work-surface area of the screen. The bar consists of a single row of five highlighted bars or sections. Status-bar information from left to right includes the following sections:

- Section 1 displays the current screen. For example, the message **Database** appears when you are using a work surface to create fields in a database structure.
- Section 2 displays the current file and its path. For example, **C:\DB4\DATA** appears as you create a database structure to be stored in the DATA subdirectory of the DB4 directory on hard disk drive C.
- Section 3 displays the cursor location or points to the current record, depending on the work surface in use. For example, **Rec 2/35** appears if you are editing record 2 out of 35 records in a database, or **Line:12 Col:0** appears if you are setting up a report and your cursor currently rests at the beginning of line 12.
- Section 4 displays information about the file supplying data to the current operation. For example, **File:Names** appears if you are setting up a report based on the contents of the data file NAMES.
- Section 5 displays toggle-key status. Toggle keys include the Insert, Num Lock, and Caps Lock keys. The section can be blank or any combination of the following toggle keys might appear.

  Num displays when you use the Num Lock key so that the numeric keypad functions as a simple calculator. When Num Lock is off, you can use numeric keypad arrow keys to move the cursor.

  Caps displays if you use the Caps Lock key to uppercase all the letter characters you type.

  Ins displays when you press the Ins key. When you type in insert mode, previously existing text shifts to the right.

You can turn off the Status bar during certain tasks such as editing. When the Status bar is off, the toggle-key indicators appear on the top line of the screen. The Status bar does not appear on the Control Center display.

Navigation Line

The Navigation line across the bottom of the screen displays information about how to perform activities such as moving the cursor or exiting a task. Navigation information refers to the screen in use. This is the Navigation line information that displays when you create a field in a database.

> **Enter the field name. Insert/Delete field:Ctrl-N/Ctrl-U**

The line instructs you to enter your choice of a name for the field. The Navigation line also tells you to insert a field between two existing fields by holding down the Ctrl key and then pressing the letter N. You are told to delete a field by holding down the Ctrl key and then pressing the letter U.

Message Line

Screens do not always contain a Message line. If a message does display, it provides instructions about the current operation and appears as the last line on the screen. For example, look at the Message line that appears when you name a database field.

> **Field names begin with a letter and may contain letters, digits and underscores**

The general format of a dBASE IV screen display remains the same whether you're using the Data, Queries, Forms, Reports, Labels, or Applications features. The Menu bar appears at the top; the Status bar, Navigation line, and Message line display at the bottom; and the work surface occupies the remaining area.

Organizing Your Menus and Work Surfaces

Design Screen

Although the design screens behind each Control Center panel are different, there are some common features that make using the design screen easy.

Menu-bar options vary depending on the screen displayed.

Work surfaces change with each screen.

The Status bar provides information about the screen you're using.

The Navigation line displays cursor-control prompts.

The Message line provides information about highlighted menu choices.

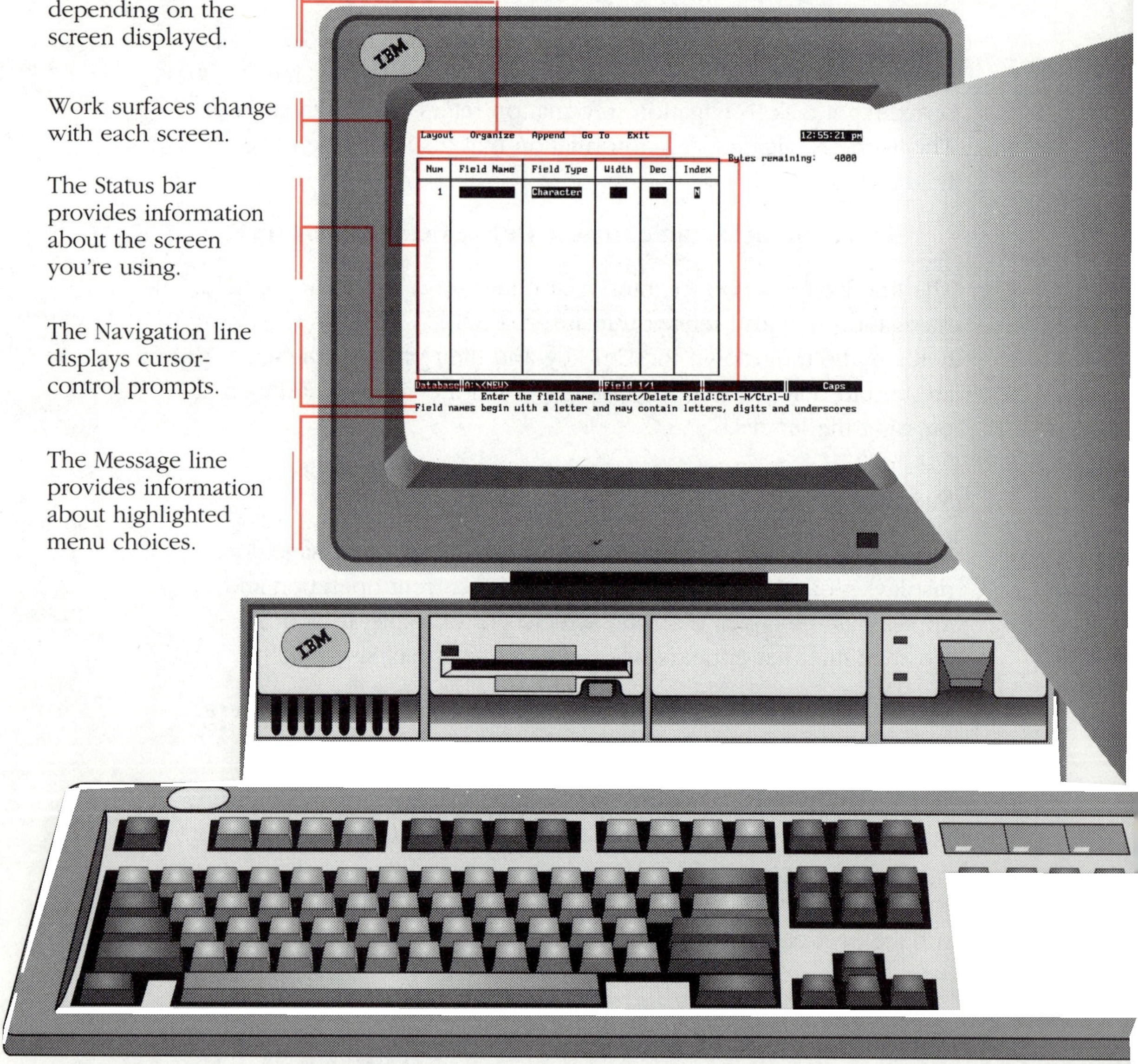

Menu Bar

A horizontal menu bar appears on the top line of a work-surface screen. You can make your selections several ways. Just be sure always to exit dBASE IV properly by selecting Exit.

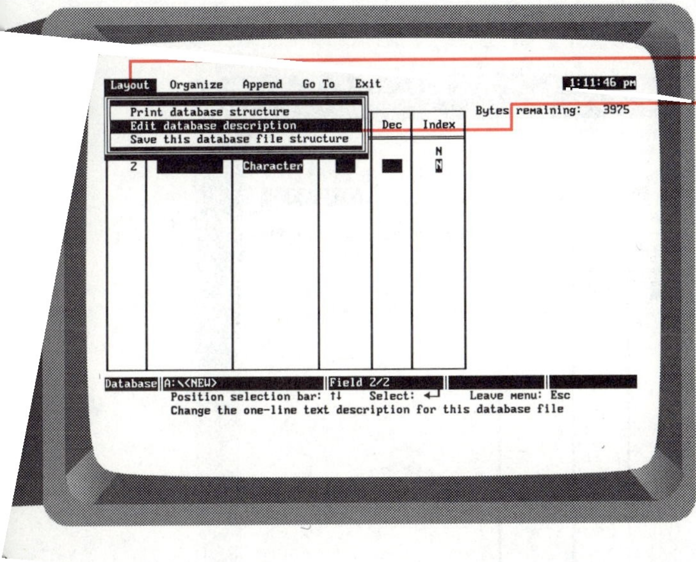

Pull-down menu

Highlighted choice

Press F10 and use the → and ← keys to highlight your menu choice, or press Alt and the first letter of your menu choice.

Use the ↑ and ↓ keys to highlight a choice, or press the first letter of the choice.

Watch the message change at the bottom of your screen.

Press ↵Enter to activate your menu selection.

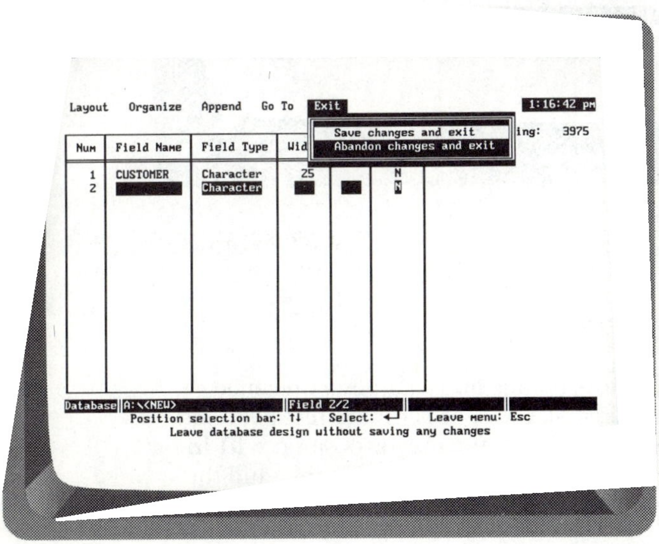

Press Alt E to pull down the Exit menu.

Use the ↑ and ↓ keys to highlight your choice.

Press ↵Enter to activate your Exit choice.

Status Bar

The Status bar tells you what screen, database, and view are displayed, where the cursor or current record pointer is located, and what keys are toggled on.

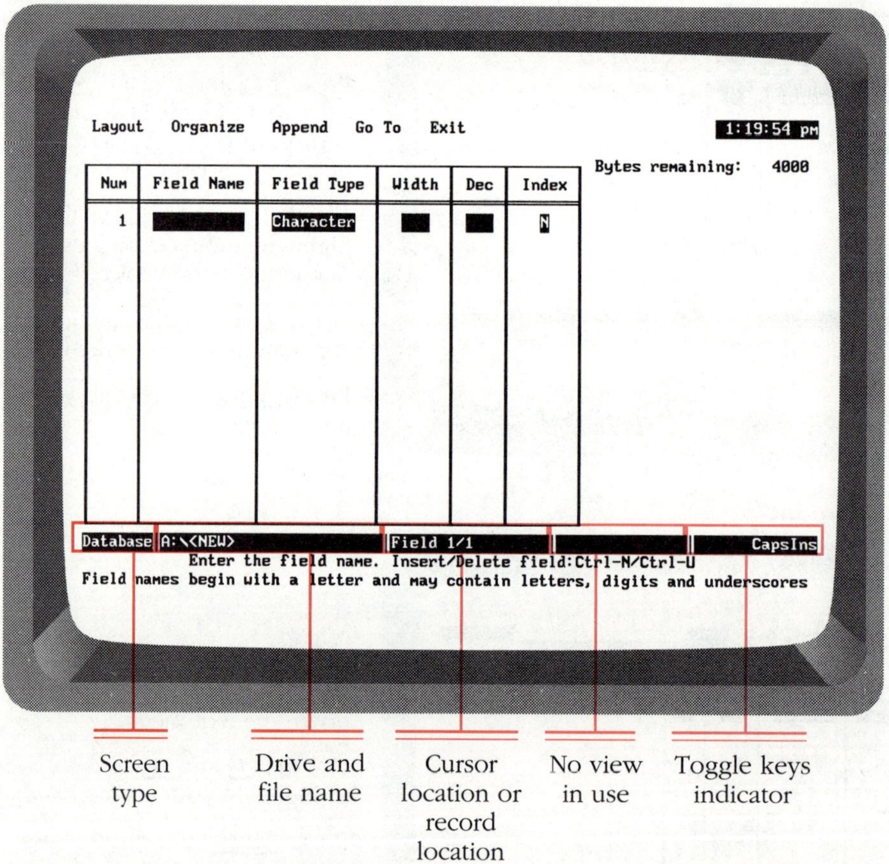

This Status bar tells you the database screen is in use; a new, unnamed file is being created on the A disk drive; the cursor is on the first field out of a total of 1 field; (Note: it does **not** tell you the cursor position **within** the field, such as the "field type" column.); no View file is in use, and the Caps Lock and Insert keys are toggled on.

Navigation Line

The Navigation line tells you what to do next. That is, the line indicates how to use the keys associated with the displayed screen.

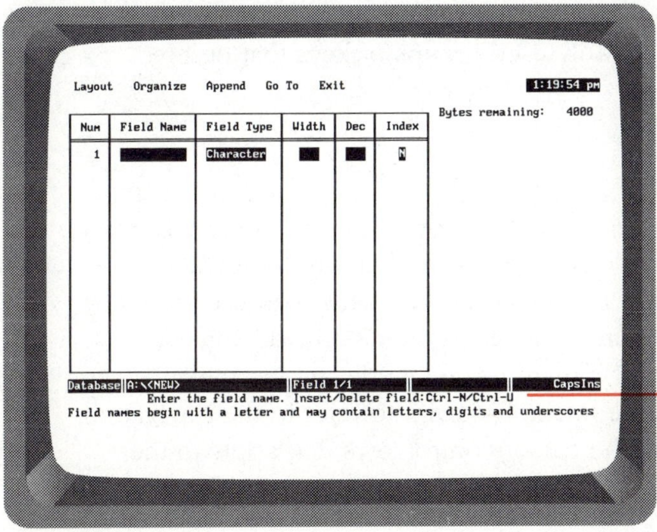

This Navigation line instructs you to enter a field name, press Ctrl N to insert a field, or press Ctrl U to delete the highlighted field.

Message Line

The Message line displays additional information about the menu choice currently highlighted. Not all screens display message lines.

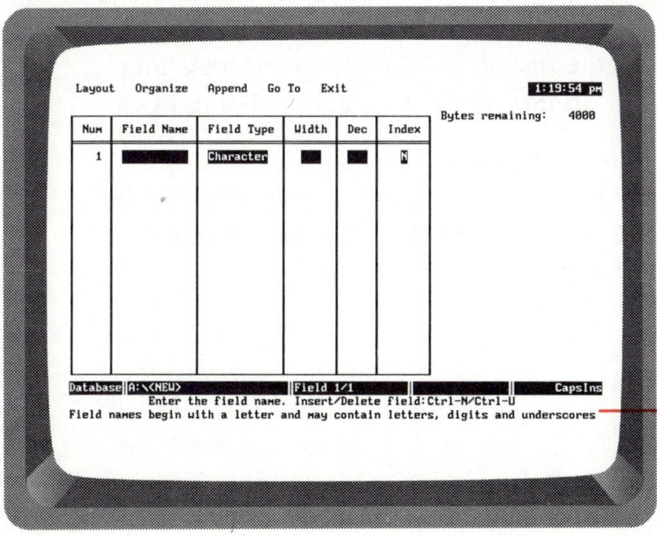

The Message line in this example tells you how to format the field name when creating a database.

Using Your Keyboard Keys

You use many keys and key combinations to move around work surfaces and menus and to execute specific dBASE IV functions, but you do not need to memorize all the keys. Remember, you can find information about using the correct keys by looking at the Navigation line. There are a few commonly used groups of keys that deserve discussion.

Cursor-Control Keys

Cursor-control keys are used to navigate on the work surface. The keys cause different movements or actions depending on the work surface in use. For example, if you press the Tab key while you use the Edit screen work surface, the cursor moves to the next field. However, pressing the Tab key while you are using Queries moves the cursor to the next column. To be safe, make it a habit to refer to the Navigation line for instructions about the cursor-control keys that apply to the current action.

Function Keys

Function keys appear on all keyboards. You may have a set of 10 function keys (F1 through F10) at the left side of your keyboard, or you may have a set of 12 functions keys (F1 through F12) across the top of your keyboard. Only the first 10 function keys are programmed to perform a specific task in dBASE IV. For example, pressing F1 activates on-screen Help.

You can also press each of the 10 function keys as you press the Shift key, and activate 10 additional programmed actions. For example, pressing Shift-F9 accesses the Quick Report feature.

Menu Control Keys

Always keep in mind that what happens when you press a key can vary with your current position in the dBASE program. Each of the following key actions describes the result of pressing a key(s) when you are selecting menus.

Key Actions To Select Menus

Key	*Action*
F10 (Menus)	Access the Menu bar
Alt + first letter of option	Access a specific option on the Menu bar
Right arrow (→) or left arrow (←)	Highlight the next choice or the previous choice on a horizontal Menu bar
Down arrow (↓) or up arrow (↑)	Highlight the next choice or the previous choice on a single-column, pull-down menu
Enter	Activate a highlighted option
First letter of option	Select and activate a pull-down menu option
Esc	Exit menu or list
Ctrl-End	Accept certain fill-in menus
End	Move to the last menu option
Home	Move to the first menu option
PgDn	Display next window of choices
PgUp	Display previous window of choices

Using Your Keyboard Keys

Keyboard layouts vary from one computer to another. Three common key arrangements are depicted on these pages. Even though slight differences do occur, all keyboards have function keys, alphanumeric keys, cursor (arrow) keys, and numeric keys.

IBM PC and XT Keyboard

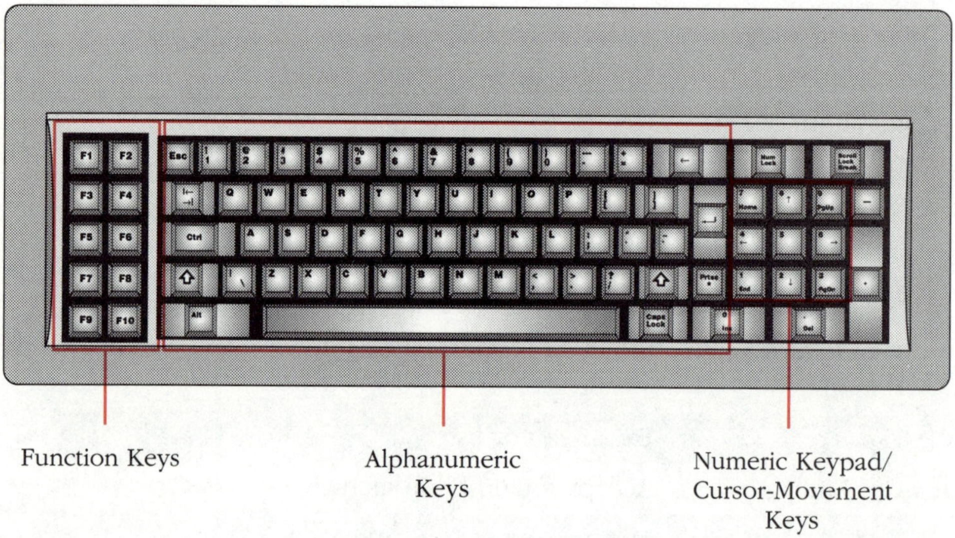

IBM AT Keyboard

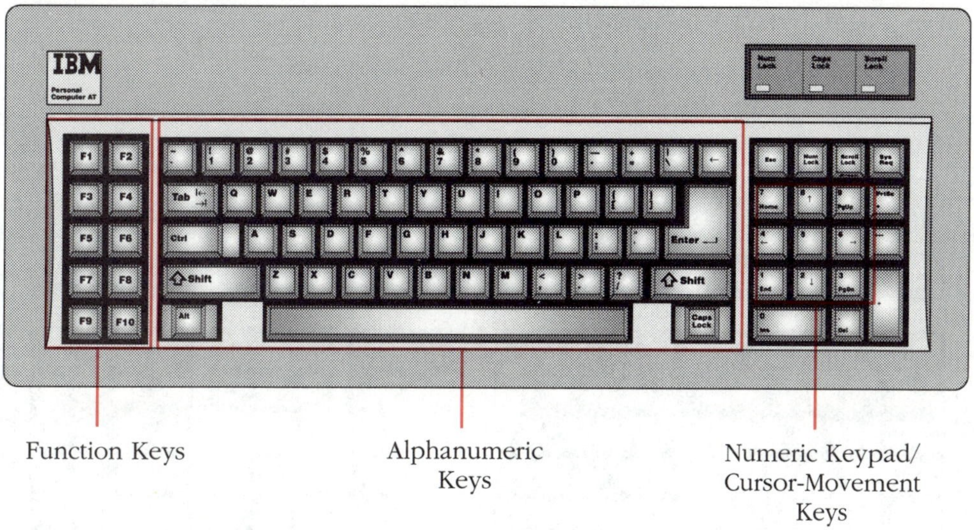

IBM Enhanced Keyboard

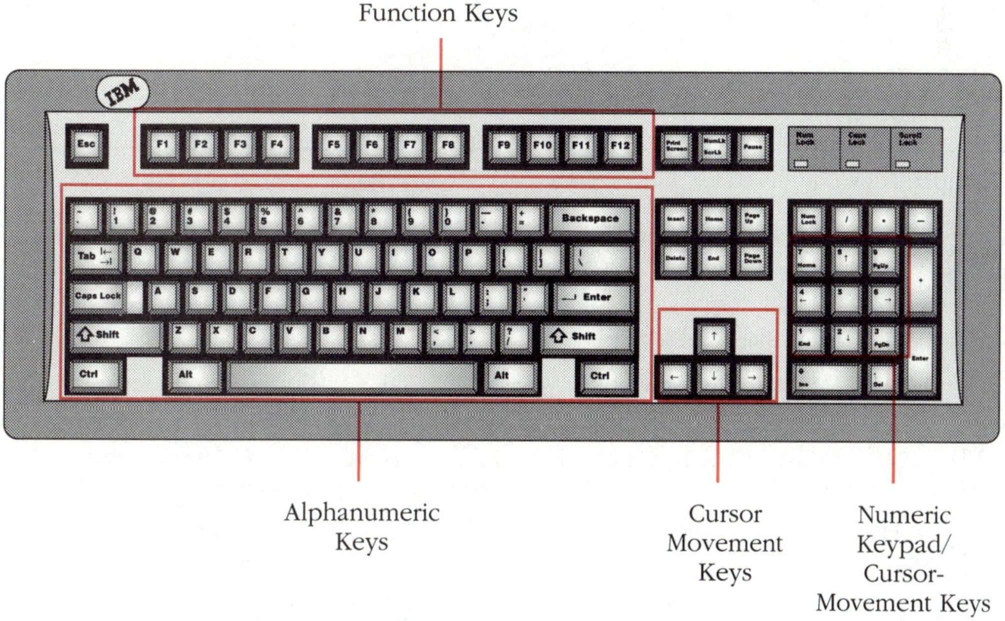

Using Your Keyboard Keys

Many dBASE IV functions are activated by pressing two keys.

For example, to activate Quick Report, you must press both the ⇧Shift and F9 keys.

Hold down the ⇧Shift key.

Press the F9 key once.

Function Keys

Key	Name	Function	Key	Name	Function
F1	HELP	Display on-screen Help	F6	SELECT	Select contiguous text and fields
F2	DATA	Toggle between Browse and Edit screen display	F7	MOVE	Move selected text and fields
F3	PREV	Move to the previous field or page	F8	COPY	Copy selected text and fields
F4	NEXT	Move to the next field or page	F9	ZOOM	Enlarge/Shrink items such as Memo fields
F5	FIELD	Add or modify a field	F10	MENUS	Access menus for the current screen

Shift Function Keys

Shift F1	PICK Display list of items to choose from
Shift F2	DESIGN Display Design screen
Shift F3	FIND PREV Find last occurrence of search string
Shift F4	FIND NEXT Locate next occurrence of search string
Shift F5	FIND Find search string
Shift F6	REPLACE Replace search string with another string
Shift F7	SIZE Change size of design and column width
Shift F8	DITTO Carry data forward from corresponding field in previous record
Shift F9	QUICKRPT Print Quick Report of data in current database
Shift F10	MACRO Call macro prompt box

Menu Keys

F10	Pull-down menu
Alt + letter	Pull down a menu using Alt plus the menu's first letter
← →	Highlight next/previous option on the Menu bar
↑ ↓	Highlight an option from pull-down menu
Esc	Back out of menu/list
Enter	Select menu option
End	Move highlighter to bottom of menu/list
Home	Move highlighter to top of menu/list
PgDn	Display next group of choices
PgUp	Display previous group of choices

Using the dBASE IV Help System

dBASE IV offers three help levels:

- Routine information display in Navigation and Message lines
- Automatic error-box display in certain problem situations
- User-activated, on-screen Help

In all cases, Help is *context sensitive*, which means that Help messages and screens refer to the task or command you are performing when you request Help.

Navigation and Message Line Help

You read about Navigation and Message lines earlier in the chapter. These lines offer continuous information about the task you are performing. These lines require no action on your part; they are simply helpful instructions about actions you are taking and choices that you can make.

Error Box Help

An Error box appears on the screen when you make an error or incomplete entry. The boxed message names the error and offers options for correcting the problem.

Suppose you attempt to execute a command that is not valid for what you are doing. You might get the message **Command only valid in programs** in an Error box, along with a display of the menu options **Cancel**, **Edit**, and **Help**. **Cancel** terminates the current operation so you can begin again. **Edit** permits you to correct the erroneous entry and continue. **Help** calls a Help screen to provide you with additional information.

Consider another example. If you attempt to exit from your current operation without saving your work properly, dBASE automatically offers Help in the form of the Error box message **Are you sure you want to abandon operation?** You must then select the appropriate menu choice **Yes** or **No**.

User-Activated Help

Imagine you see the **Page dimensions** option on a Print menu, and you don't understand what purpose the option serves. dBASE provides user-activated Help screens that display context-sensitive answers to your questions. To activate a Help screen, press F1. Once the screen appears, you have four choices.

- **Contents** — Provides access to a table of contents of Help subjects. From this list, you can choose any subject and access its Help screens.
- **Related Topics** — Provides access to a list of subjects related to the current Help screen. From this list, you can choose a subject and access its Help screens.
- **Backup** — Returns you to the previously displayed Help screen. It provides a quick way back to the original Help screen after you have moved through several layers of contents or related topics. The Backup option appears on all but the first screen in a series.
- **Print** — Causes the contents of the current Help box to print. You can also print the Help screen display by pressing the PrtSc key. Using PrtSc causes the entire screen to print including content outside the Help box.

As you begin to use dBASE IV, practice accessing the Help menu system. Press the F1 function key, select the Contents option, select a topic, and read the Help screen. If you have a printer attached to your system, turn it on and print the Help menu. When you are through using a user-activated Help box, exit by pressing the Esc key.

Using the dBASE IV Help System

dBASE IV offers three Help levels: help information routinely displays on the Navigation and Message lines; an Error box offers Help when you enter a command or respond to a prompt incorrectly; and you can activate context-sensitive Help screens.

Navigation and Message Line Help

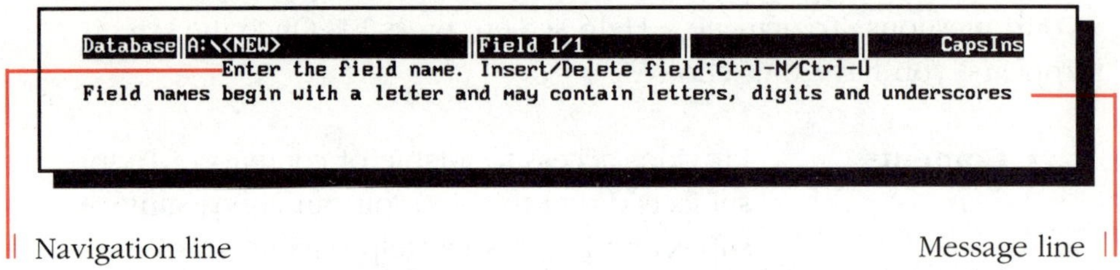

The Navigation line and Message line are the first Help level automatically provided. Line information changes to tell you what is happening and what action you must take for the task at hand.

Error Box

An Error box appears on the screen when you make an error or an incomplete entry. One Error box provides YES or NO options. The other allows you to cancel the task, correct the error, or view related Help screens.

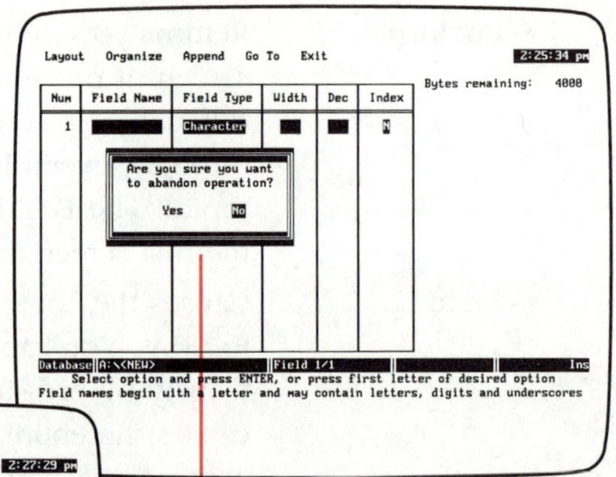

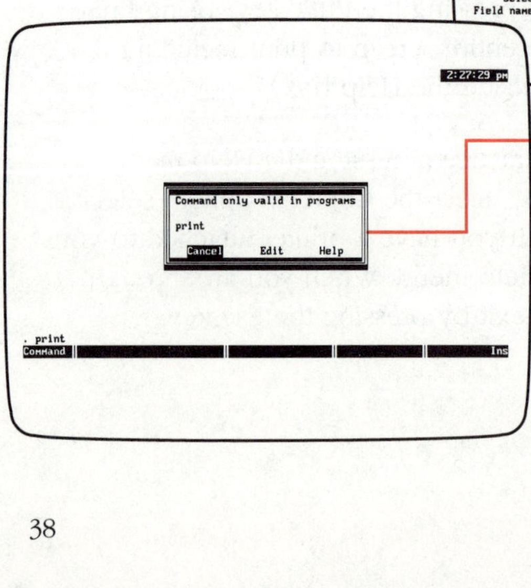

Error box

To access the Help system:

Highlight the Help option and press [↵Enter].

or

Press [F1], Help.

Help Box

The Help box is a sophisticated context-sensitive Help system. When you press F1 a Help box appears which contains information about the current task.

Use the ← and → keys to move to your selection. When you've highlighted your selection, press ↵Enter.

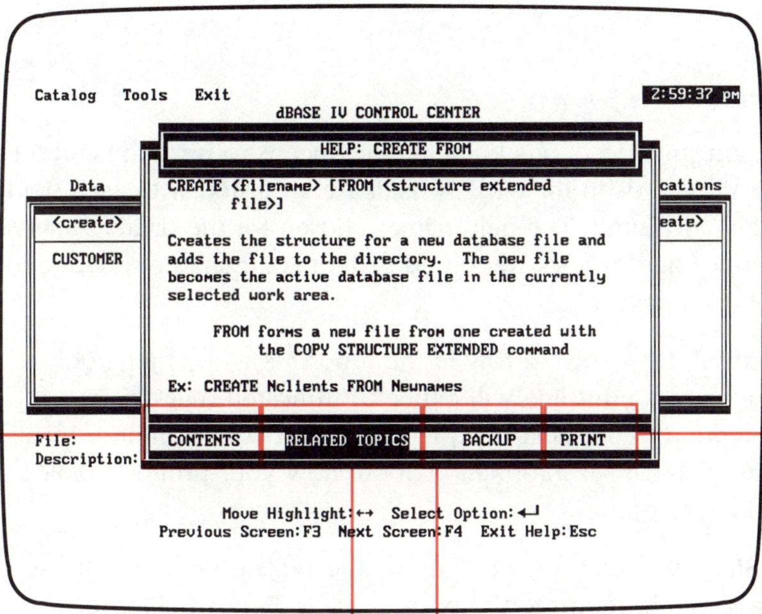

Select CONTENTS to display a table of contents in the Help box. Select a topic, and a new box appears.

Select PRINT to print only the contents of the displayed Help box. PrtSc prints the entire screen.

Select RELATED TOPICS to display a list of related topics on the screen. Select another topic, and a new Help box appears.

Select BACKUP to display the previous Help screen. If there is no previous screen, this option does not appear.

Press Esc to leave Help.

Printing

Printing in dBASE IV is simple. You can print Quick Reports to display the contents of Data or View files one record after another in a row and columnar format. You can also access a Print menu to produce custom reports and mailing labels. You'll refer to this section as you learn more about dBASE IV.

Quick Report

Quick Report provides a quick and simple means to print the current database. All records in the current database are listed with each field appearing in a column. The field names chosen for the database serve as column headings. Quick Report adds the page number and date to the top of each page.

If the width of the record (a row in the report) is wider than your printer, the excess print line will either be truncated (cut off) or wrapped around to the next line, depending on your printer. Consult your printer manual for information about how your printer handles lines too long to print.

Pressing Shift-F9 activates Quick Report and pulls down the Print menu. To send the report to the printer, select **Begin printing**. To view the report on your monitor, select **View report on screen**.

Print Menu

If you want more control over the printing process than Quick Report provides, you must access the Print menu. You can access the Print menu from several places in the Control Center as shown in subsequent chapters.

The Print menu contains several menu choices that tell dBASE IV where to print and how to control the printer. You can direct printing to the screen, to the printer queue, or a disk file for printing later. You can even store print specifications, such as number of print lines per page, and use them again. Your Print menu choices include:

- **Begin printing** Causes printing to begin, using currently set specifications. Press Ctrl-S to interrupt printing temporarily. Press Esc to stop printing entirely.
- **Eject page now** Causes the printer to eject paper and begin printing at the top of the next page.
- **View report on screen** Causes printing to appear on-screen. This message changes to **View labels** when you access the Print menu from the Labels design screen.
- **Use print form** Causes a set of printer specifications stored on disk to be loaded and used when you print a file.
- **Save settings to print form** Causes the currently selected printer specifications to be saved to disk for later use.
- **Destination** Causes output to be directed to a DOS file for later printing.
- **Control of printer** Determines the quality of printer output such as pitch (characters per inch), page eject, and pausing between pages (for single sheet paper feeding). This option lets you send special printer control codes to the printer before and after printing.
- **Output options** Causes printing to begin and end on specified pages; indicates the number of copies.
- **Page dimensions** Determines paper size, left margin, and line spacing.

Quick Report

Quick Report prints the current database. All records are listed, and each field appears in columnar format. The field names you've selected for the database appear as column headings. The page number and date automatically appear at the top of each page.

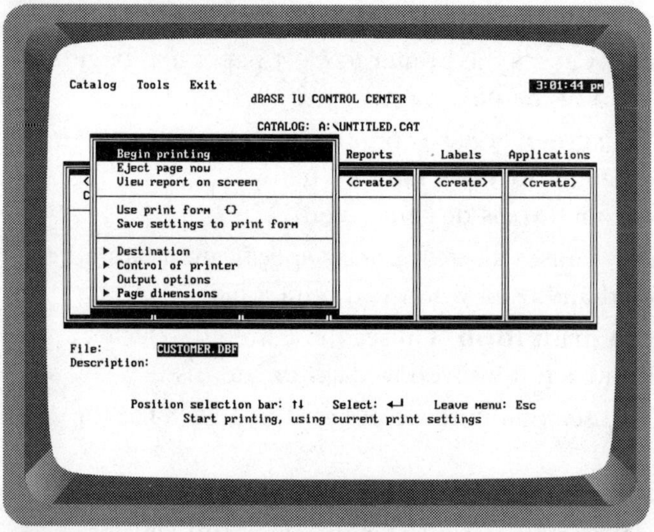

Press ⇧Shift F9.

Select **Begin printing** by highlighting the option, and then pressing ↵Enter.

Press Ctrl S to stop the printer temporarily.

Press Esc to stop the printing operation altogether.

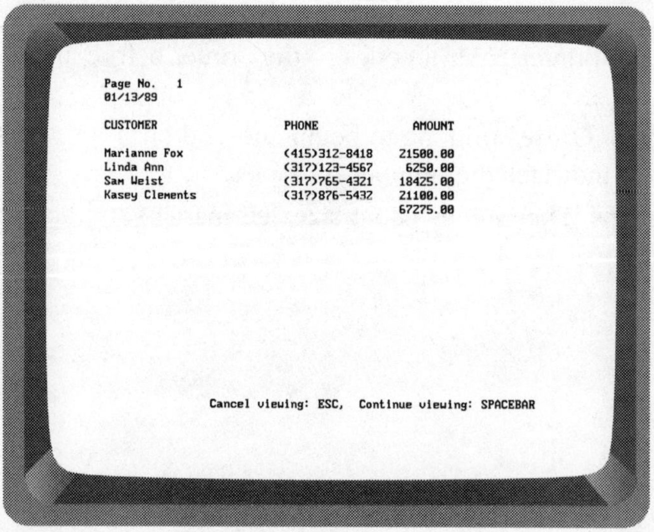

Select the **View report on screen** menu option to see the Quick Report of your customer database.

Print Menu

When you select Print from anywhere in the Control Center, you will see the same Print menu.

Print Menu Choices

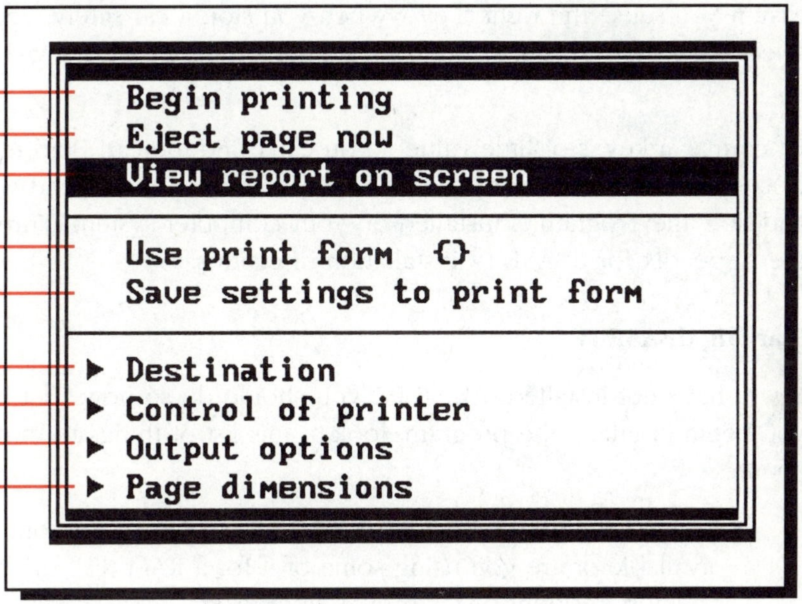

Result

Specifies placement of text on the page.

Specifies pages to be printed and number of copies to be printed.

Specifies size, quality, and paper movement.

Selects where the output is to be sent.

Saves the current print settings for repeated use.

Selects a set of print specifications stored on disk.

Displays output on the monitor.

Causes the printer to eject paper and positions the printhead at the top of the paper.

Causes printing to begin, using currently set specifications.

Starting and Exiting dBASE IV

Do you remember the comparison we made, at the beginning of the chapter, between operating a car and using dBASE IV? You have only to turn the key in the ignition to start a car. Starting dBASE is just as easy if you select the right "key." When you stop a car safely, you select park. Stop dBASE safely by selecting Exit to close and save your files.

Of course, a key is of little value if you can't find the car! Before discussing how to start or exit dBASE IV, you must understand where and how the program is installed on your computer system. Turn to the Appendix for dBASE IV installation directions.

Starting dBASE IV

If you have not installed dBASE IV, you should do so now. But before you begin installing the program, look at this list of things to think about:

- Is all of the required 640K of RAM memory on your computer available or are you using some of it for a RAM disk or memory-resident program like SideKick®?
- Do you have a hard disk with 3.5 million bytes of unused memory? Try to leave at least 25 percent of your disk space free after dBASE IV is loaded.
- Is a previous version of dBASE already installed on your system? If so, you might want to transfer files to the new program and erase the older program.

- The dBASE IV program is packaged on 14 disks. You may not, however, need to install all 14 disks on your computer. Think about the ones you are likely to use in the near future and only load those into appropriate subdirectories.

  For example, you may wish to install the "Samples" files in a subdirectory separate from your data subdirectory. The "Samples" files are provided to accompany the "Learning dBASE IV" booklet that is part of the dBASE IV documentation.

Accessing dBASE IV

If, when you turn on your computer, a menu of program names appears (such as a word-processing program, a spreadsheet program, and dBASE IV), you need only select the number of the dBASE IV option to access the dBASE program.

However, if you see an operating system prompt (perhaps **C>**) when you turn on your computer, you must set the current directory to the location of your dBASE program. Then type *dbase* and press the Enter key. The Control Center work surface appears and you are ready to begin using dBASE IV.

Exiting dBASE IV

Exiting dBASE is simple. From the Control Center work surface, press F10 to access the options in the Menu bar. Use the → or ← keys to highlight the Exit option, use the ↑ or ↓ to highlight the **Exit to DOS** option, and press Enter.

If you want to use a shortcut to the Exit menu, press Alt-E, highlight the **Exit to DOS** option and press Enter.

Starting and Exiting dBASE IV

System Requirements

To install and run dBASE IV, your system must be in this minimum-requirement configuration.

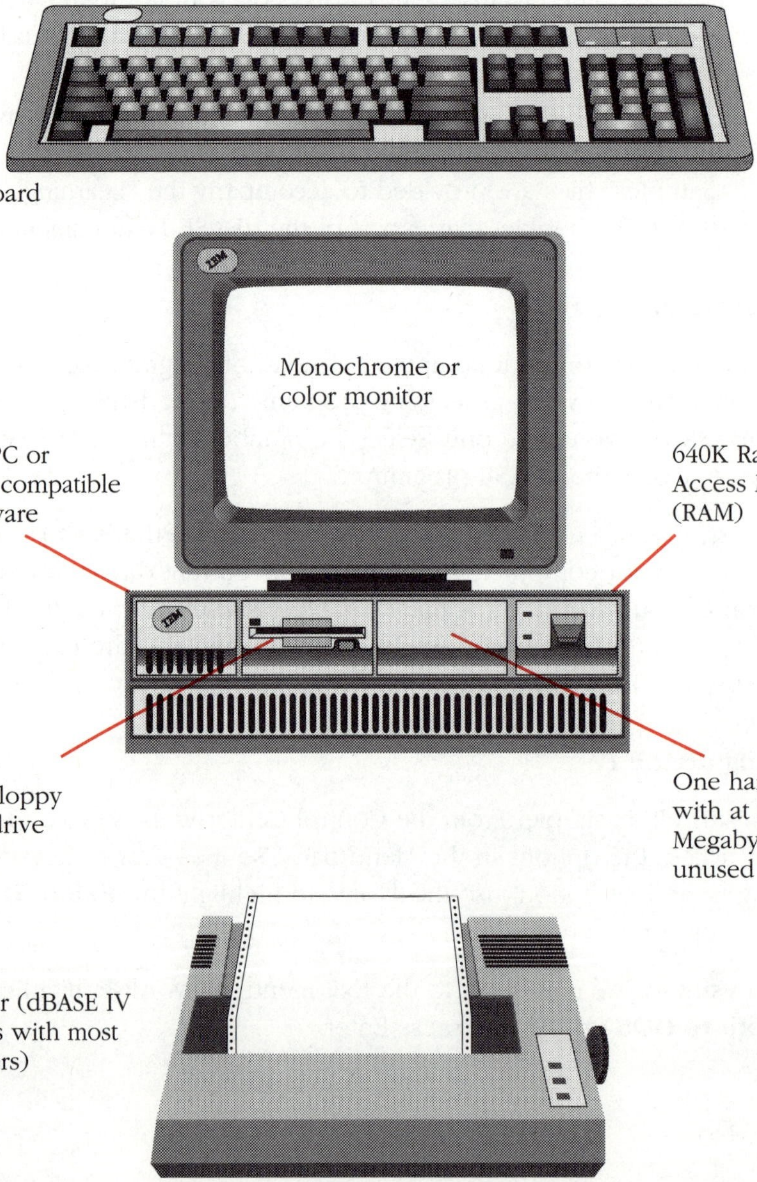

Starting dBASE IV

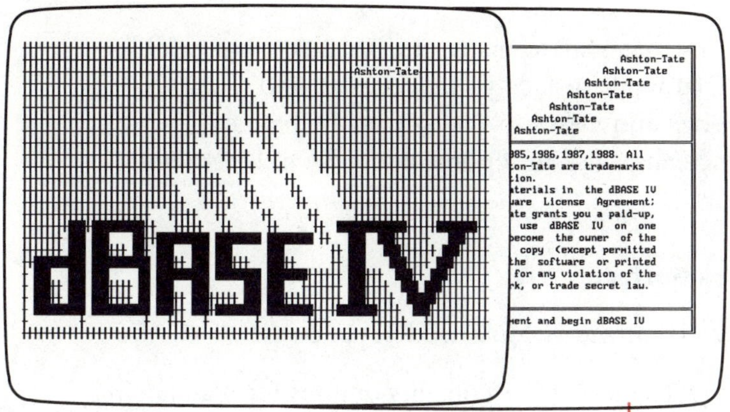

Turn on your computer.

At the **C>** prompt, type DBASE.

Press [↵Enter].

The dBASE logo and copyright screens display.

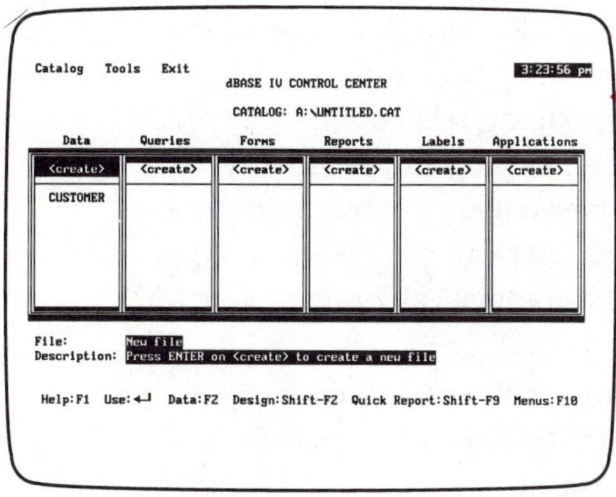

Press [↵Enter] to display the Control Center screen.

Exiting dBASE IV

Never turn off your computer before exiting dBASE IV.

Press [F10] and highlight the Exit option. (Pressing [Alt][E] serves the same purpose.)

Highlight **Quit to DOS** and press [↵Enter].

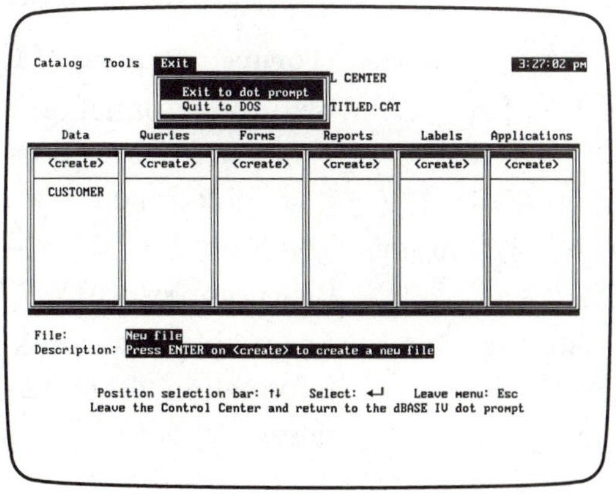

Navigating through the Control Center

The Control Center is the gateway to many of dBASE IV's powerful features. From this initial work surface you can create and maintain databases; design queries and views to access exactly the data you want; create custom screens, custom reports, and custom labels; and write custom programs.

Control Center Work Surface

The Control Center work surface is comprised of six parts:

- Menu bar — The Menu bar contains options for maintaining files and catalogs.
- Catalog name — The catalog name identifies the name of the active catalog. Catalogs are a dBASE IV technique for grouping related files. Only files listed in the open catalog can be displayed in the Control Center panels. If you do not open a catalog to keep track of the files you are using, dBASE IV automatically opens a catalog called UNTITLED.CAT.
- Panels — Six panels represent the dBASE operations you perform through the Control Center. Each panel's name appears at the top of the panel in the following order:

  Data Queries Forms Reports Labels Applications
- File — Two file information lines display the file name and description of the currently highlighted file.
- Navigation line — The Navigation line identifies the keys you use to accomplish dBASE IV tasks.
- Message line — As you begin to work in the Control Center, information about each task appears on this line.

The first entry in each panel is **<Create>**. A line appears under the **<Create>** option; and under the line, you see a listing of any files associated with the specific panel. To access a panel, use the (←) or (→) keys. To access a file within a panel use the ↑ or ↓ keys. To select the **<Create>** option, highlight **<Create>** and press Enter. To select a file, highlight the file name and press Enter. When a file name is selected, it moves above the horizontal line in the panel. The remaining chapters in *dBASE IV QuickStart* deal specifically with the Control Center panels, starting with four chapters on the Data panel and a chapter about each of the five remaining panels.

Control Center Menu Bar

The Control Center Menu bar contains three options: **Catalog**, **Tools**, and **Exit**. The first choice on the Catalog menu allows you to select a different catalog. The Catalog menu also contains options permitting you to add and remove files from the current catalog or change the name and description of the catalog or its files.

Tools menu options include importing data from (or exporting data to) software programs other than dBASE, setting up macros (capturing keystrokes for reuse), using passwords to protect data, and a number of more advanced features.

Navigating through the Control Center

Work Surface

The Control Center work surface is the heart of dBASE IV.

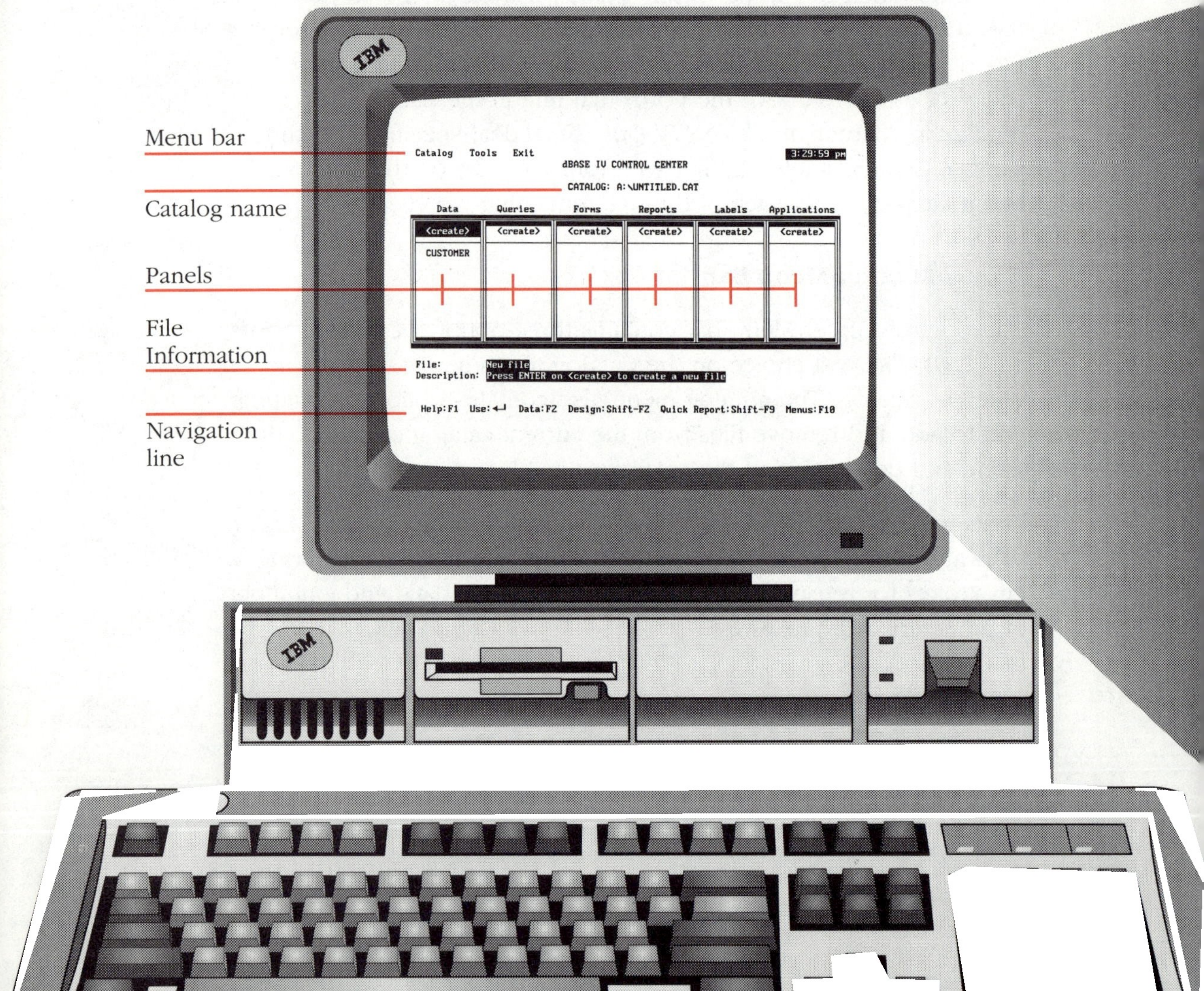

Menu Bar

The Control Center Menu bar displays three menu choices.

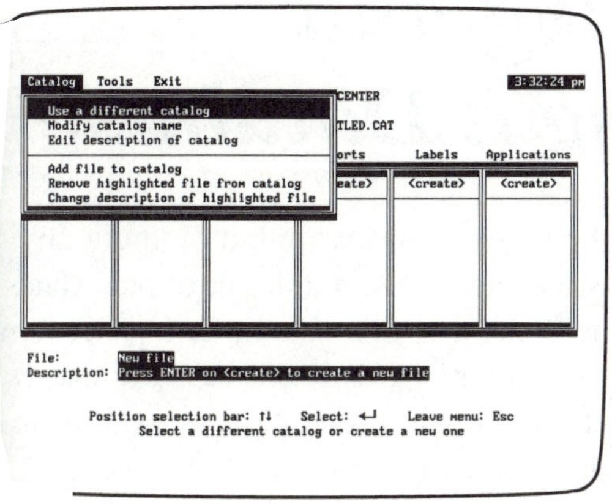

The Catalog menu offers six catalog-management options.

Use ↑ and ↓ to highlight your menu selection, and then press ↵Enter. dBASE IV displays a new menu.

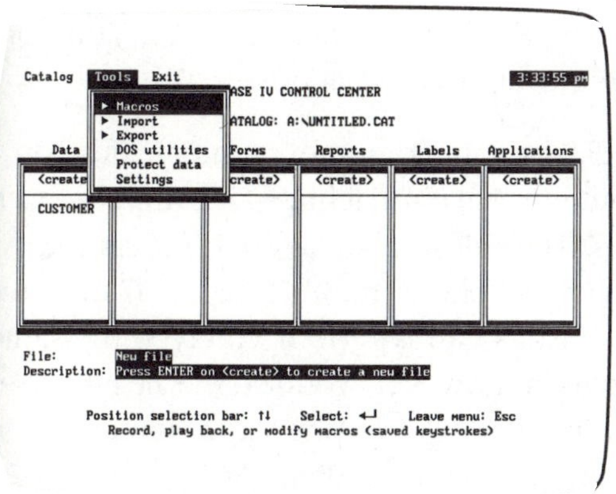

The Tools menu offers options that permit you to create time-saving programs called Macros, to import data from other software packages, to export dBASE IV data to other software packages, to use DOS commands from within dBASE, to secure your files by assigning passwords, and to change default settings.

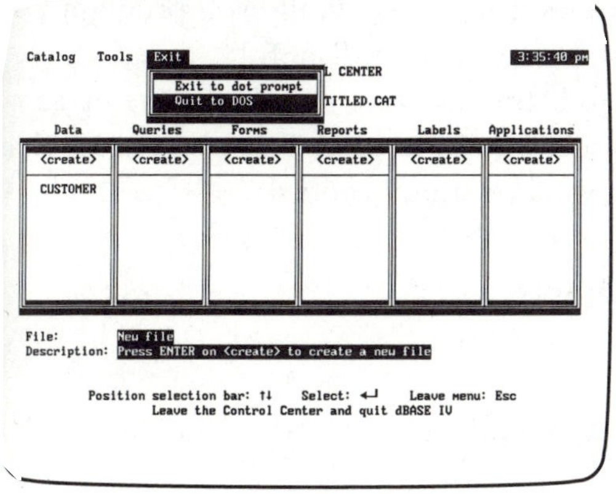

The Exit menu ensures that you will leave dBASE IV properly. If you don't use the Exit option, you risk damaging your files and wasting hours of work.

2 Designing and Creating a Database

You work with a database all the time—your own mind! Without any apparent structure, your mind stores an amazing amount of data (facts or assumptions). You, however, don't have to organize input to your mind in fixed categories, such as names, numbers, dates, places, and events. Somehow, if *Columbus* comes to mind, you know whether you mean Columbus, the capital city of Ohio, or Columbus, the man who supposedly discovered America. You know automatically whether 26450 is your ZIP code or the price you just paid for your new van. You don't have to plan input of data or retrieval of information.

You can maintain a powerful database in computer memory. But you must remember that the computer is only a machine—it cannot work for you without structure and rules. The rules vary from one program to another. For example, if you type the phone number 123-4567 on a word processor, the number appears just as you type it. If you type the same number into a spreadsheet program, however, you see the negative number `-4444`. A spreadsheet interprets the hyphen as a minus sign and subtracts the last four digits from the first three digits.

You must take the time to learn the rules for data in each program you use. As you will discover, the rules for data in dBASE IV, a database management system, are easy to learn. The first step in the life cycle of any database is to create the structure of the data. This process involves telling dBASE IV how the data is to be stored on disk.

What Is Covered in This Chapter?

In this chapter, you learn about

- Organizing the data-design work surface and Menu bar

- Determining types of dBASE IV fields: character, numeric, float, date, logical, and memo
- Determining the requirements for setting up each field: indicate name, type, width, number of decimal places (if appropriate), and whether or not you want the field indexed
- Using basic database design techniques
- Recognizing the elements of database structure: creating, editing, saving, and printing

Key Words Used in This Chapter

ASCII — A standard set of characters, which includes the letters, numbers, and other symbols available on your keyboard, such as a dollar sign and an asterisk.

Catalog — The mechanism in dBASE IV to group the user's related database file names.

Database — A collection of related records, such as the record information about items in an inventory.

Field — A portion of a database record that contains a specific item of data. For example, every inventory record might contain part number and unit price fields.

Index — A means to display or print database contents in a specified order. For example, use one index to list inventory records in order of primary supplier; use another to list the same records in order of description.

Record — A collection of related fields. For example, all fields (such as part number and description) concerned with one item in inventory constitute a record.

Introduction

The human mind retains a collection of facts and assumptions, which it organizes by using a set of intuitive rules. Most of the time, the process works just fine.

But when you need to share a vast amount of information with many others or to project the information from the shortcomings of the human memory—the electronic database management system becomes a very useful tool.

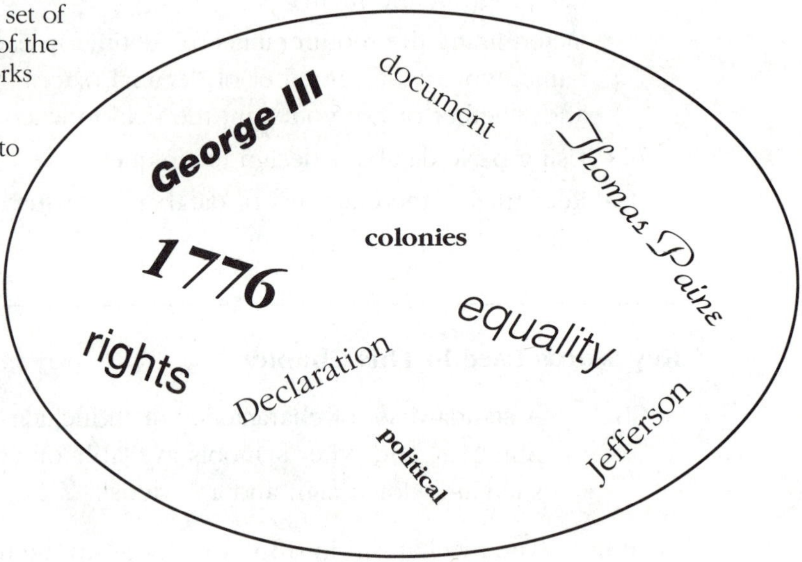

"Library of Congress"

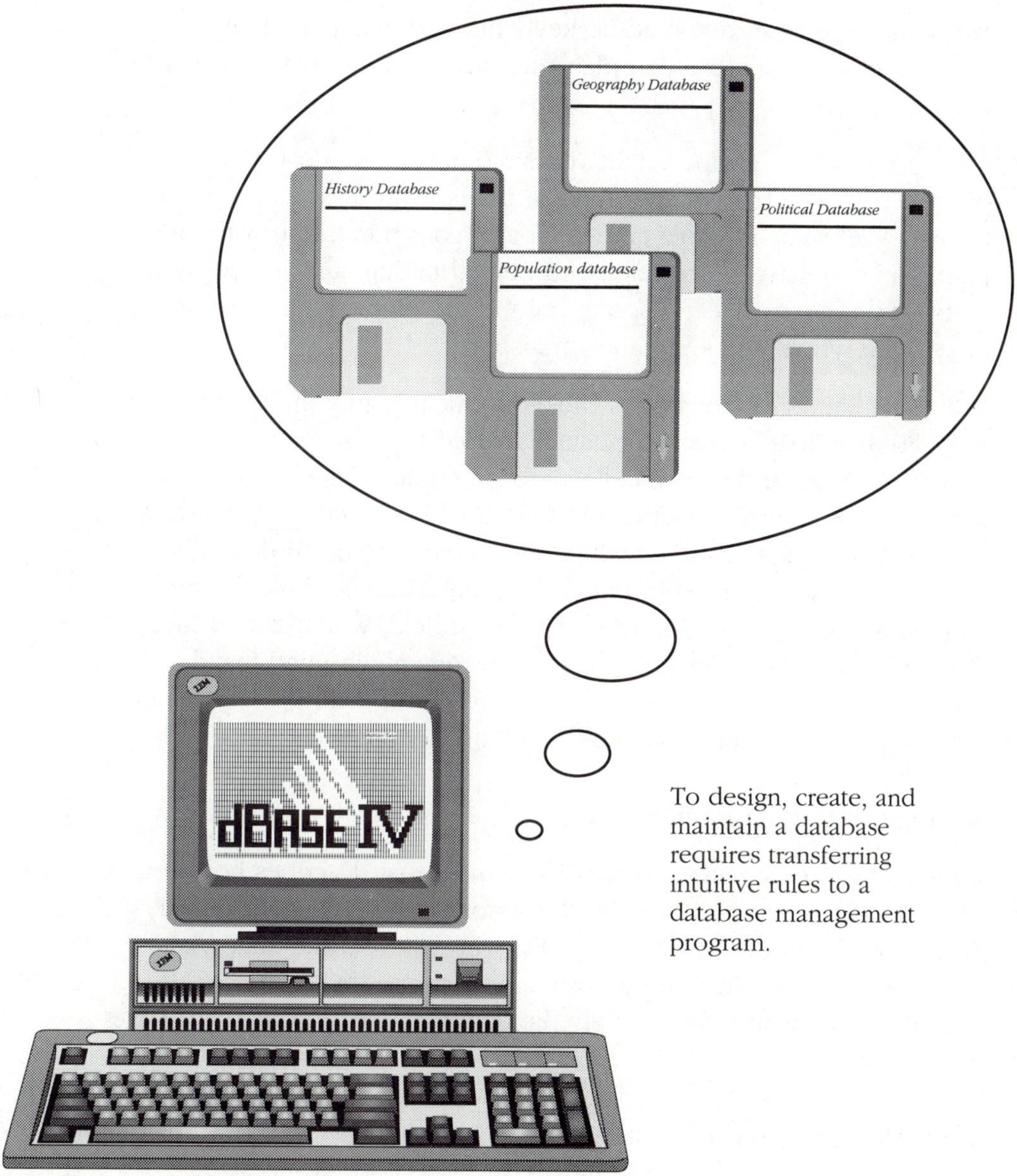

To design, create, and maintain a database requires transferring intuitive rules to a database management program.

Designing a Database

Resist the urge to sit down at the keyboard and begin creating the database structure before you plan carefully what you want to do with the data!

Just for a moment, suppose that you set out to build a car. Certain parts to complete the car are obvious: doors, windows, tires, and an engine. The car as a whole takes shape in your mind; but, without a plan, you may have problems if you begin building just yet. Suppose that you build a two-seater sports car and then remember that you have three school-age children to transport.

You can think of obvious parts (fields) to include in your databases as well. For example, a customer database used to track credit sales, prepare billings, and record collections on credit sales obviously would include fields of names, addresses, and amounts billed or received. Yet other not-so-obvious fields might come to mind if you thoroughly analyze what you want your database to do. You could, for example, include in the database a last-purchase-date field, which would trigger the mailing of promotional material to customers who had failed to make a purchase in the last 90 days. Some useful techniques can make planning easy and help you avoid omitting anything.

Setting the Database Objective

Write a clear and concise objective statement that describes how you plan to use the database. That's all; try not to describe specific data, databases, or output reports. Then, list who will use the data, what information needs must be met (remember not to dwell on specific data items or reports), how timely the data must be, and how available the data is.

Analyzing the Current System

If you already are using a paper or computer database system, use it as a starting point. A system already in place can indicate what information, expected outputs, and data fields you must have in your dBASE IV database. Your task may be as simple as automating a manual system with dBASE IV or converting from an old computer or software to dBASE IV. Remember, begin your dBASE IV application error-free by making sure that your old system does what you want before you make the move. If it doesn't, you probably should just redesign the old system from scratch.

Working Backward: Determining Inputs from Outputs

The easiest way to know what data fields should be in a database system is to figure out what you want your database to produce. First, create a list of the reports you want to receive from the database. Writing a brief objective statement about each report can be helpful. Ask yourself in what order the information should appear, what totals and subtotals are necessary, and which database records you need.

Next, make a written list, sometimes referred to as a data dictionary, of each data field that should be in the new database. Include a field name, description of data, type of data, size of field, number of decimal places, and an indication of whether or not the field can be used for sorting, totaling, or controlling a report. One other useful tool is a cross-reference list. Make a list of all outputs (screen and printed) across the page and all data fields down the side. Next to each data field, check which reports use each field's content.

Now you are ready to create the database. Don't worry if you have to adjust what you have done. One final word of warning: resist the "everything-but-the-kitchen-sink" approach of building in more data than you need. Any extra data takes up space, makes the system run slower, and costs money to maintain. dBASE IV allows you to add, delete, and change data fields whenever necessary and with little effort.

Designing a Database

Resist the urge to sit at the keyboard and begin creating a database structure before you plan carefully what you expect the database to do—that is, what information is the database expected to provide? Use these simple planning techniques to design your database management system.

Stating Your Objectives

Create a brief statement about what you want the database to do for you. Refer to this statement as you design the database structure.

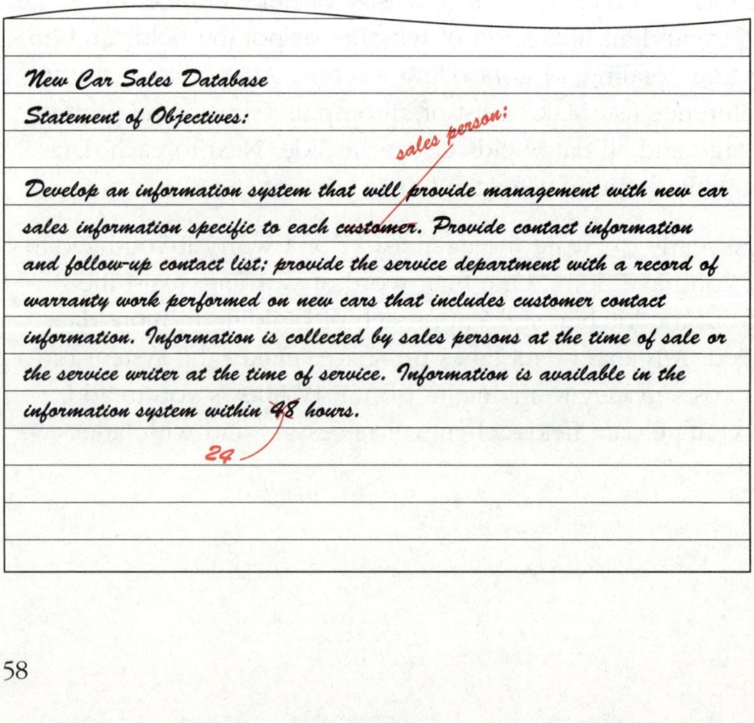
New Car Sales Database

Statement of Objectives:

Develop an information system that will provide management with new car sales information specific to each ~~customer~~ sales person; Provide contact information and follow-up contact list; provide the service department with a record of warranty work performed on new cars that includes customer contact information. Information is collected by sales persons at the time of sale or the service writer at the time of service. Information is available in the information system within ~~48~~ 24 hours.

Creating a Report, Lists, and Labels Checklist

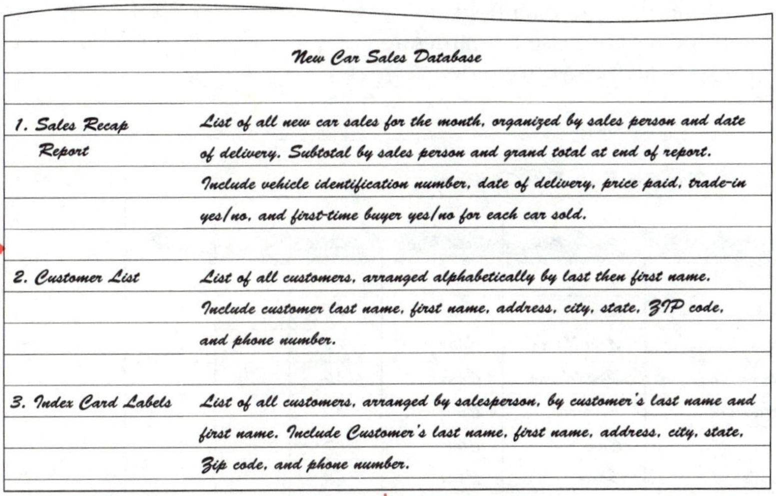

First create a list of the reports and labels that will be produced from the database. Include brief objective statements for each.

Designing the Document Layout

Next, design the layout of each report, list, and label so that you can visualize your data fields.

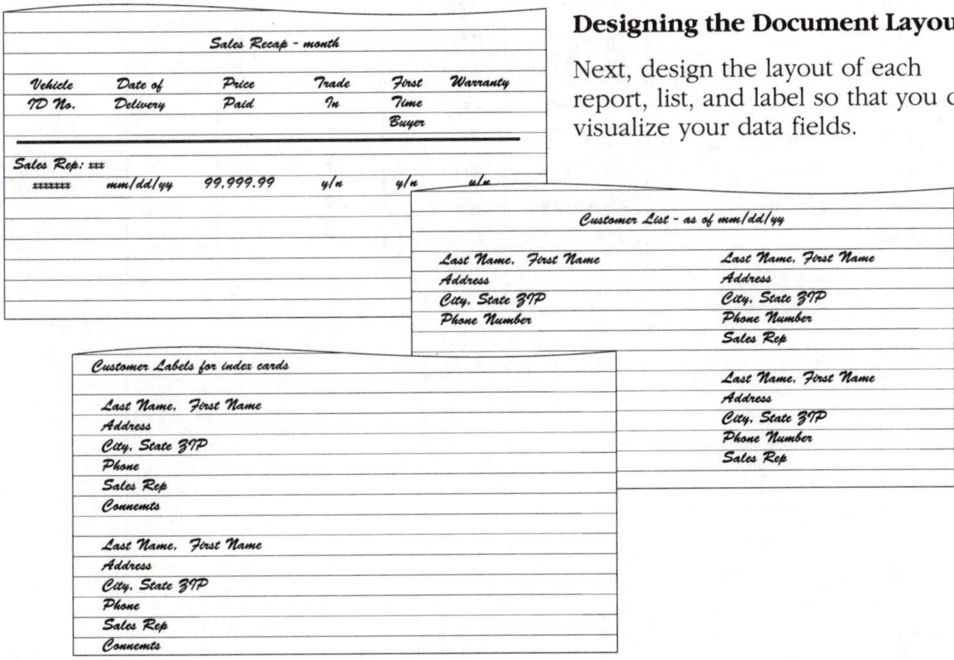

Designing a Database

Creating a Data Directory

Now create a list (data dictionary) of all data fields to be included in each document's database. Use the structure displayed on the data-design screen as your guide.

New Car Sales Data Dictionary

Num	Description	Field Name	Field Type	Width	Dec	Index
1	Vehicle ID Number	Vin	Char	10		×
2	Customer Last Name	LastName	Char	15		
3	Customer First Name	FirstName	Char	10		
4	Customer Street Address	Address	Char	30		
5	Customer City	City	Char	15		
6	Customer State Code	State	Char	2		
7	Customer ZIP Code (10 digits)	ZIP	Char	10		
8	Price of Car	Car_Price	Num	8	2	
9	Sales Rep Initials	Sales_Rep	Char	3		
10	Delivery Date	Date_Del	Date	8		
11	Warranty Purchased	Warranty	Log	1		
12	Trade-in Allowed	Trade_In	Log	1		
13	First-Time Buyer	First_Buy	Log	1		
14	Sales Rep Comments	Comments	Memo	10		
15	Phone	Phone	Char	14		

Creating a Cross-Reference Checklist

Finally, create a data and report cross-reference file that shows in which reports each data field appears.

New Car Sales Data and Report Cross Reference

Field Name	Sales Recap	Customer List	Customer Label
Vin	x		
LastName		x	x
FirstName		x	x
Address		x	x
City		x	x
State		x	x
ZIP		x	x
Car_Price	x		
Sales_Rep	x	x	x
Date_Del	x		
Warranty	x		
Trade_In	x		
First_Buy	x		
Comments			x
Phone		x	x

Access the data-design screen from the Data panel in the Control Center. Use the data-design screen to create and modify database structures, enter and edit data, and organize data. You also can browse through your data and print the database structure from this work surface. The data-design screen displays all the work-surface features, such as the Menu bar, Status bar, nNavigation line, and Message line.

Data-Design Work Surface

You must provide detailed instructions about each field of data to be stored in the database. You use the design work surface to type information about fields when creating a database. The design work surface contains six columns. dBASE IV uses column one, starting with the number 1, to number fields in the database structure. The other five columns, left to right, contain instructions for each field, including the following: choice of *name*, *type* of data, how much room (*width*) the data field needs, the number of decimal places (*Dec*) if the data is numeric, and whether or not the field automatically should be used to control the order of listing the database (*index*). Be sure that you know the rules involved with each of the 5 columns.

Choosing a Field Name

Choose a name for each standard data item (field) in your database. You need these names to refer to data stored in fields when you use the Control Center's work surfaces. Names can be from 1 to 10 characters long and contain letters, numbers, and the underscore character. The first character must be a letter.

Although N is a valid name for a field, the single-character name makes remembering what data the field contains difficult. Try to choose a field name that describes the data in the field. As an added suggestion, insert the underscore to improve readability of what a name represents. For example, you might name inventory part number INV_NUM instead of INVNUM. Do not include any blank spaces.

Selecting a Field Type

The field type tells dBASE IV the classification of data stored in the field. You may select one of six data types: character, numeric, float, date, logical, and memo. Select **Character** as the field type if one of the other five categories, described in the following text, is not appropriate.

Numeric: Use the *Numeric* data type for all numbers to be used in calculations (except for those numbers described in the float data type). Caution: If data looks numeric but is not used in calculations (phone number, ZIP code, Social Security number), select the character data type.

Float: Use the *Float* data type for scientific applications which use very large or small numbers that are frequently multiplied. For example, use float for a number using five or more digits or decimal places, such as pi or the speed of light.

Date: Use the *Date* data type for all dates.

Logical: Use the *Logical* data type for fields that contain a value representing true or false. You can type the value as upper- or lowercase *T* (True), *F* (False), *Y* (Yes), or *N* (No), as appropriate. For example, you might keep an out-of-stock (yes or no) field in an inventory database in order to maintain an up-to-date listing of unavailable items.

Memo: Use the *Memo* data type to attach narrative about the current record when you do not want a limit (other than the inevitable limit of available memory) to the amount of the data in the field. The other five field types have width constraints on content discussed in the next section. For example, in a person's credit record, you are required to maintain a 500-word rebuttal if one is submitted. A memo is ideal for this data.

Specifying a Field Width

Use the field width specification to indicate the maximum number of characters or digits a field can hold. You must specify widths for three types of fields (character, numeric, float); dBASE supplies the widths for three others (date, logical, memo).

Character: Enter a field width as narrow as 1 or as wide as 254; field content can include any ASCII characters.

Numeric/Float: Enter a field width between 1 and 20.

Date/Logical: dBASE IV supplies a date field width of 8 and a logical field width of 1. Dates appear in the format dd/mm/yy (day/month/year), such as **01/09/44**.

Memo: dBASE IV supplies a field width of 10. Although the field in the record displays only the word `Memo`, dBASE IV can store a large document at another location.

Specifying Decimal Places in the Field

You must indicate the number of decimal places (**Dec**) for two types of fields: *numeric* and *float*. The number of decimal places must be at least two less than the specified width of the field. For example, if the largest unit price in your inventory record is 8 digits (6 digits and 2 decimal places), set the width at 10 to reserve space for a period (.) and a sign (–).

Establishing a Field as an Index

You must indicate whether or not to index each field. If you type Y, you create an index that marks the field as one on which to organize records for display to screen or printer. When creating an inventory, you can specify Yes if you plan to print reports showing inventory listed alphabetically by description. Specify No if you don't intend to list name and address database records by street address. You can have up to 47 indexes per database.

Data-Design Menu Bar

The horizontal data-design Menu bar, which appears above the data-design work surface, allows you to save and print the database structure, organize data by sorting data or creating indexes, append data to the database from the keyboard or other files, position the record pointer at a particular field, and exit the data-design screen. You can use the Menu bar options described in the text that follows.

Use **Layout** to print the database structure, edit the structure description stored in the catalog, and save the database structure. Save each structure with a different name.

Use **Organize** to arrange data in a meaningful sequence, such as a list of students arranged by Social Security number.

Use **Append** to add records to the current database. You can add records from the keyboard, another dBASE IV file, or a non-dBASE IV file, such as one created by the PFS®:FILE program.

Use **Go To** to position the cursor on the first field description, the last field description, or a specific field number.

Use **Exit** to leave the data-design feature. You can save or abandon your database structure. If you abandon the database structure, no changes are written to disk. If you were editing a database structure that exists on disk and you select **Abandon changes and exit**, the original database structure remains unchanged. If you are saving a structure for the first time, dBASE IV asks you for a file name. The name is added to the current catalog and appears on the Data panel.

Data-Design Work Surface

You use the data-design screen to create and modify your database structures. You use it also to enter, edit, and organize data. The work surface is a table with rows that represent database fields, and columns that contain field attributes.

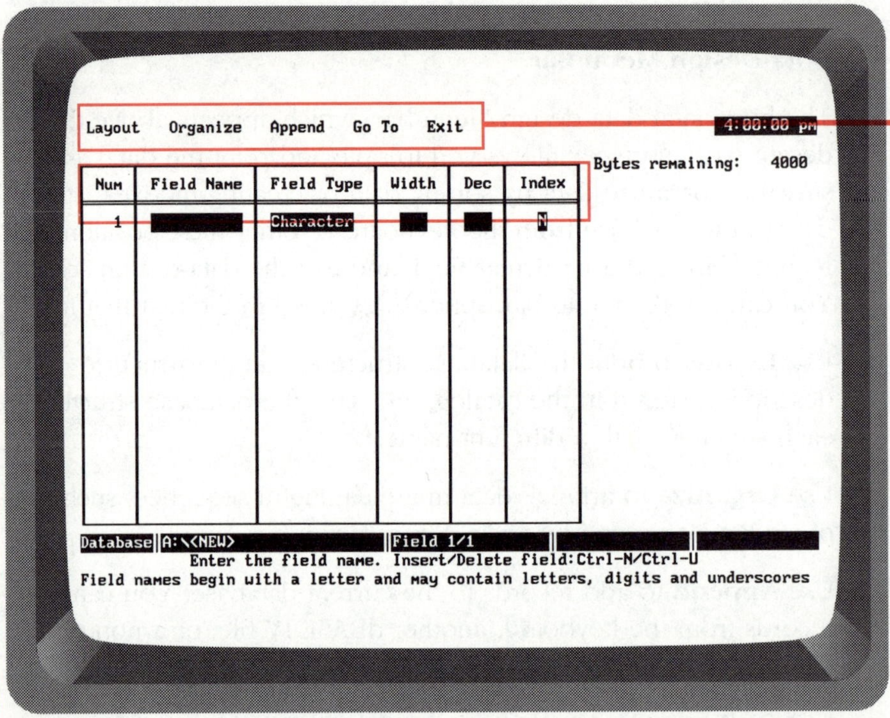

Num	A reference item that identifies the field's position in the database file structure.
Field Name	The name you assign to the data field.
Field Type	A classification you assign to describe the kind of field. The type can be character, numeric, float, data, logical, or memo.
Width	A numeral that defines the number of characters or digits the data field can contain.
Dec	A numeral that defines the number of decimal places in a numeric or float field.
Index	A Y/N designator you assign to indicate whether the field will be used to index (organize) the database.

Menu Bar

The data-design Menu bar contains the Layout, Organize, Append, Go To, and Exit menus.

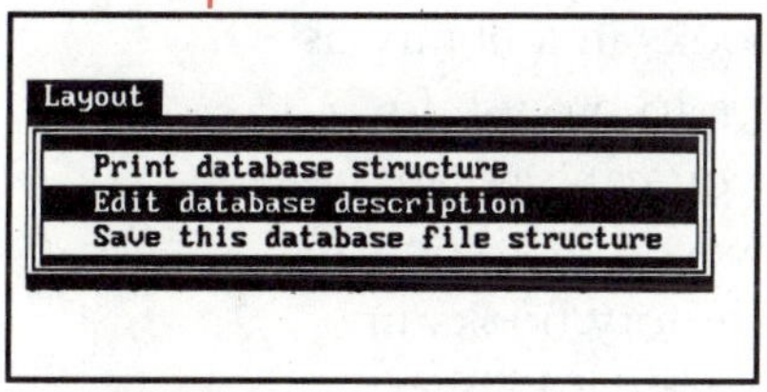

Use the Layout menu to save and print your database structure file.

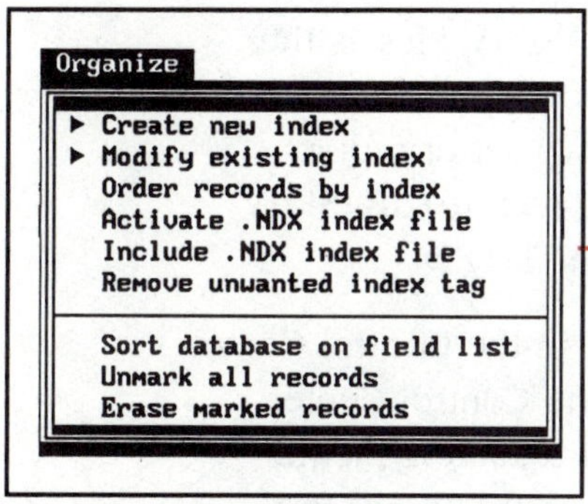

Use the Organize menu to arrange records in a meaningful sequence.

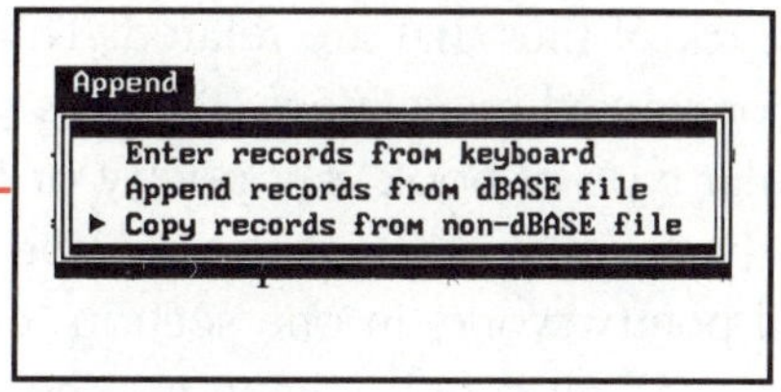

Use the Append menu to enter, append, and copy records to your database file.

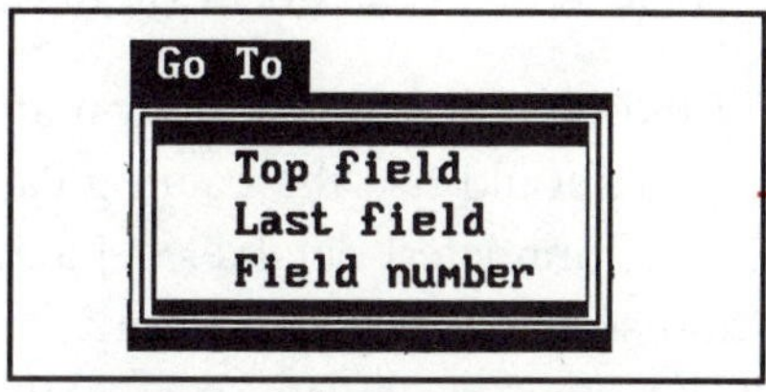

Use the Go To menu to move quickly to specific fields on the data-design screen.

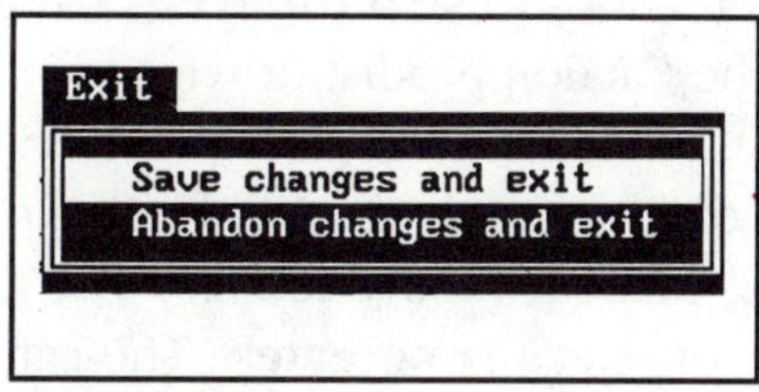

Use the Exit menu to leave the data-design screen.

Creating the Database Structure

After you decide what fields to include, creating the database structure is primarily a matter of typing. You specify a catalog, select **<create>** on the Control Center Data panel, enter up to five items for each field, and save the database structure.

Choosing a Catalog

To build your database structure, you first must choose a catalog to keep track of files that are related. Think of the books in a library as being organized by catalogs. Perhaps you just want to browse for a particular type of book, say poetry or history, or you can't remember the author or title of a cookbook. You know, however, that you can find all poetry works in one section (catalog), all history books in another, and all cookbooks in another. Using the standard library coding system, all related books are grouped in a section. Imagine the time you would lose checking for all poetry books if the only form of book storage was alphabetical by title or author.

Think of the disk directory that contains your dBASE IV files as the library. You should use the catalog capability if you are likely to have a number of unrelated databases, each with its own set of reports, labels, and so forth. If you do not use the catalog feature, dBASE IV puts all files that you create in a catalog called UNTITLED.

You create or select a catalog from the Menu bar in the Control Center Catalog. To create a new catalog, press Alt-C at the Control Center, and then choose **Use a different catalog** from the Catalog menu. From the Catalog picklist (a window in the upper right corner of the screen), select **<create>** and press Enter. At the message **Enter name of new catalog**, type the name of your catalog. To select an existing catalog, choose the name of the catalog from the picklist instead of selecting **<create>**. The catalog you create or select becomes the current catalog. Any files or forms you create will appear in the current catalog. Similarly, you see and access only file names in the current catalog.

Accessing the Data-Design Work Surface

After you have created or selected a catalog, you must access the data-design work surface. To create a new database structure, highlight **<create>** on the Control Center Data panel and press Enter. The next screen you see is the data-design work surface containing six columns headed **Num**, **Field Name**, **Field Type**, **Width**, **Dec**, and **Index**.

Specifying Field Characteristics

When you access the data-design work surface, the cursor rests in the **Field Name** column next to the number **1**. You are ready to type the first field name in your database structure.

The procedure for entering field names is simple. Type the first field name and press Enter. **Character** automatically appears in the **Field Type** column. If you want the field to be a character field, press Enter. Otherwise, select the field type by pressing the space bar until the appropriate data type (**Numeric**, **Float**, **Date**, **Logical**, or **Memo**) appears and press Enter.

Depending on the field type you specified, you may be required to enter information about the width and decimal places. The index is automatically **N[o]** unless you change it to **Y[es]**.

Keep the following guidelines in mind as you enter fields on the data-design work surface:

- Use the left-arrow (←) or right-arrow (→) keys to move the cursor within a field. If the cursor is at the beginning of a field when you press the left-arrow key or at the end of a field when you press the right-arrow key, the cursor moves to the preceding or next field, respectively. Use the up-arrow (↑) or down-arrow (↓) key to move up or down one field description.
- For efficiency's sake, fields used for indexing should be near the beginning of the record.

- Use the Tab and Shift-Tab keys to move the cursor to the next or preceding fields, respectively.
- Make corrections using the Ins and Del keys as necessary.
- Use Ctrl-N to insert a field at the cursor location or Ctrl-U to delete the current field.

Continue to type field characteristics until you have defined all data fields. Review the entries in your structure and correct any errors you may find.

Saving the Database Structure

After entering your field-type characteristics, you can save your newly created database structure in either of two ways from the data-design work surface. To save the structure and continue working, press Alt-L to access the Layout menu, select **Save this database file**, type a file name, and press Enter. To save the structure and return to the Control Center, press Alt-E to access the Exit menu, select **Save changes and exit**, enter a file name if prompted, and press Enter. To exit without saving your changes, select **Abandon changes and exit** from the Exit menu.

Closing and Using the Database Structure

You must tell dBASE IV what database you want to use. When you are finished using the database, you must tell dBASE IV that you are finished. This process is called *opening* and *closing* the database. Only one database will appear open on the Control Center Data panel. The name of the open database appears above the horizontal dividing line in the Data panel on the Control Center work surface. Closed database names appear below the line.

To close the database, highlight the database name in the Data panel, press Enter, select **Close file**, and press Enter once more. If you want to use a closed database structure (the name appears *below* the dividing line in the Data panel), highlight the appropriate database name, press Enter, select **Use file**, and press Enter once more. Notice that the name of the now-open file moves to the top of the panel above the dividing line.

Editing the Database Structure

After you create and save a database structure, you can edit it easily—even after data is stored to the database. For example, you may find a design error, such as a field size being too small. Or, in the future, you may need to add another field of data. To access the structure to edit, highlight the database name in the Data panel and press Shift-F2. As an alternative, you can highlight the database name in the Data panel, press Enter, select **Modify structure/order**, and press Enter once more.

The structure you selected appears in the background of the work surface; the Organize option from the Menu bar appears in the foreground. Press the Esc key to restore the full screen display of the structure. Use the cursor keys to access the fields to be changed, and enter the changes. When all changes have been made, save the changed structure. Select **Exit** from the Menu bar and choose **Save changes and exit**. To exit without changing the structure, select **Abandon changes and exit.**

Printing the Database Structure

After you create your database structure, you should print the structure so that you have a working copy for documentation. The process is simple. To print a copy of the structure, press Alt-L to select the **Layout** option from the Menu bar of the data-design work surface, select **Print database structure** from the Layout menu, and then select **Begin printing** from the Print menu.

You can stop the printer temporarily by pressing Ctrl-S. Press Esc to cancel the printing operation.

The terms *database* and *structure* are used almost interchangeably. The database that was created on disk is divided into two parts: the area containing the structure (fields and field characteristics) and the area containing the data for each field. Now that you can create a database structure, the next chapter discusses adding, changing, and deleting data.

Creating the Database Structure

Creating the structure of a dBASE IV database is easy: choose a catalog, select **<create>** on the Control Center Data panel, complete specifications for all fields, and save the file structure.

Choosing a Catalog

Catalogs organize your database files, reports, and forms by grouping files that have something in common. For example, the catalog called SALES might include the file names NAMES, SALES, WARRANTY, and COLDCALLS—with various three-character extensions assigned by dBASE, such as .DBF (database file) and .QBE (query file)..

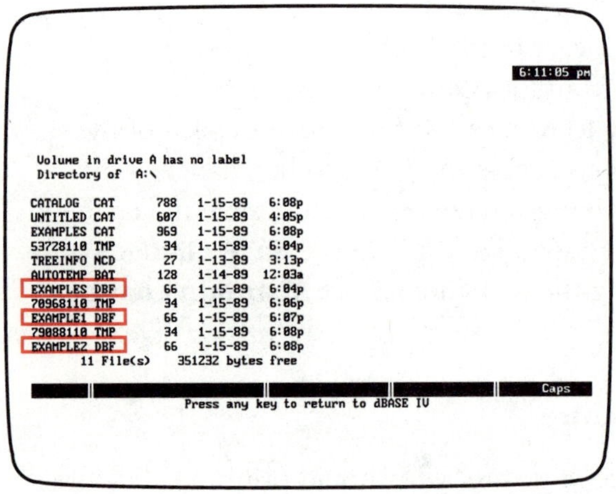

Think of the disk directory that contains your dBASE IV files as a library. Your database files are listed among the many files in the directory.

A catalog contains lists of related files. The same file can be listed in several catalogs. You can use as many catalogs as you need to organize your database files. dBASE IV limits which files from the disk directory are shown in the Control Center.

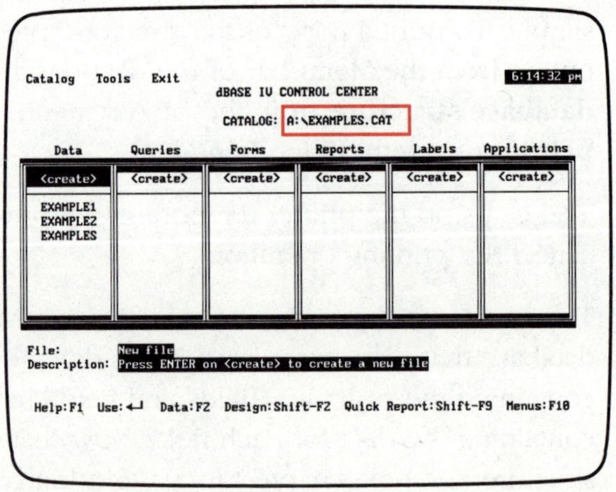

Creating a New Catalog

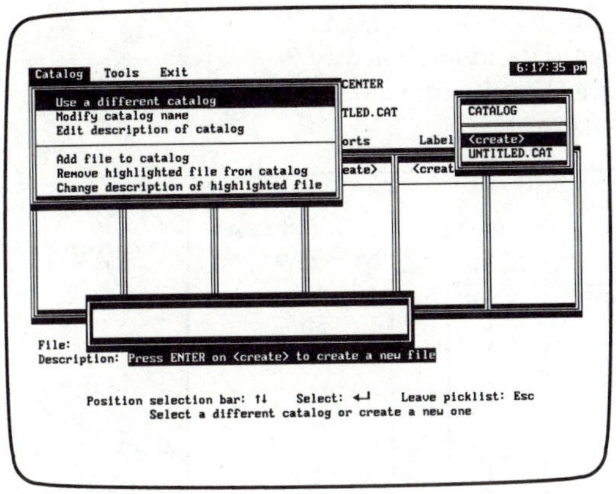

To create a catalog, press Alt C from the Control Center, highlight the **Use a different catalog** option on the pull-down menu, and press ↵Enter.

Highlight the **<create>** item that appears in the list at the upper right portion of the work surface.

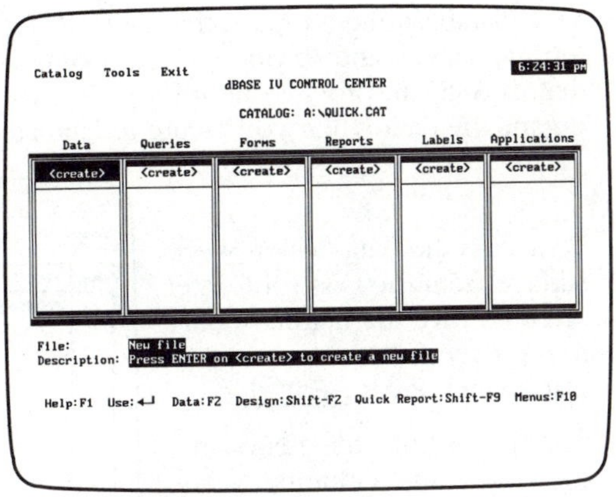

Press ↵Enter, type the name of your catalog (such as QUICK) when prompted to do so, and press ↵Enter again.

Selecting an Existing Catalog

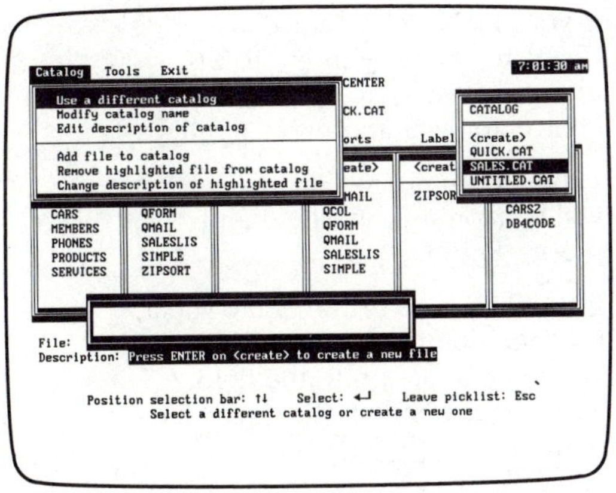

To select a catalog that already exists, highlight the name of the existing catalog from the list in the upper right corner of the screen and press ↵Enter.

Note: If you do not use the catalog feature, dBASE IV groups your files in a catalog called UNTITLED.

Creating the Database Structure

Entering Field Specifications

Your database files contain the data dBASE IV uses to produce forms, reports, labels, and so on. You must organize that data in such a way that dBASE can provide the information you want. You begin organizing data when you create a database structure file.

To access the data-design work surface from the Control Center screen, move the highlight bar to the **<create>** marker on the Data panel. Press [↵Enter]

dBASE positions the cursor in the Field Name column. Remember, each row represents a field.

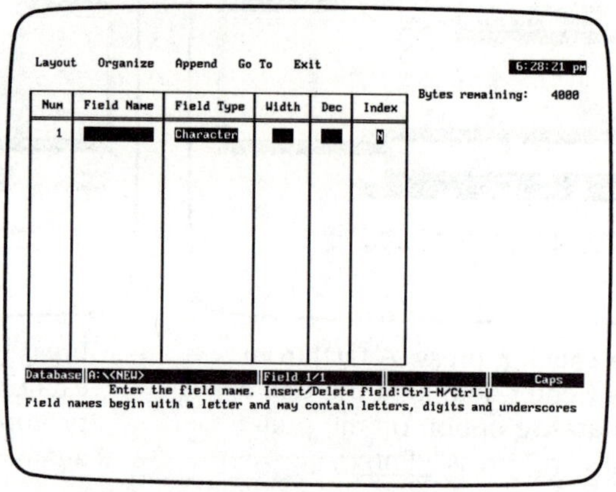

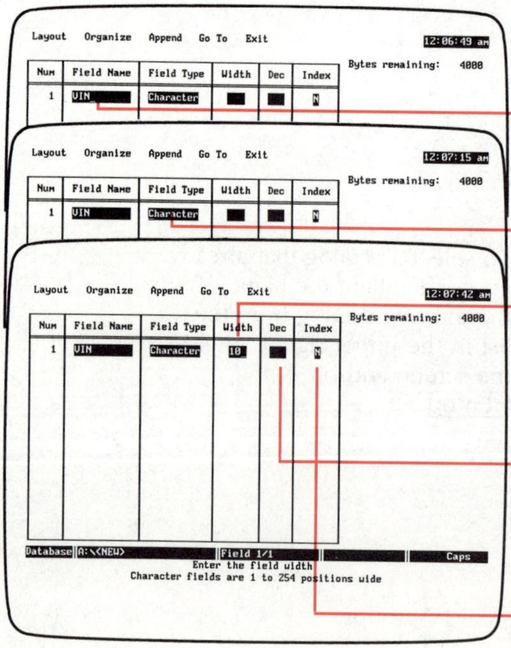

Type the field name. The first character you type must be a letter. You may use as many as 10 characters. Press [↵Enter]

If your Field Type choice is Character, press [↵Enter]. If it is not, press the space bar until your choice appears and press [↵Enter].

Type the number of characters that will be stored in this field and press [↵Enter].

If the field type is numeric or float, type the number of decimal places you want to assign to the field. Remember to count the decimal point. Press [↵Enter].

Type [Y] if you intend to create an index on this field and press [↵Enter].

If you do not plan to index on this field, press [↵Enter].

When you finish entering the specifications for the first field and press ↵Enter at the Index column, dBASE IV returns the cursor to the Field Name position in row two.

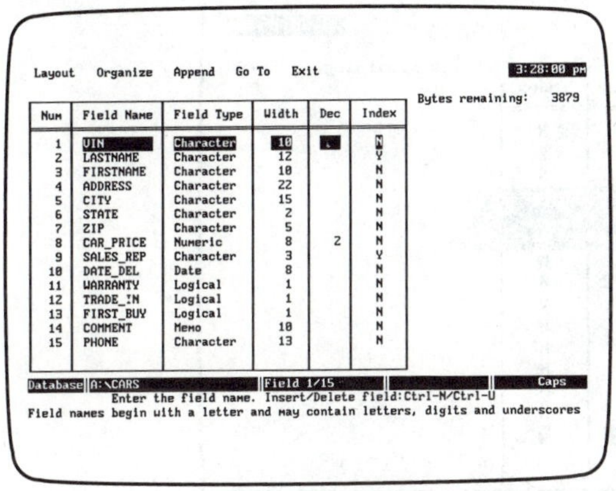

Continue defining your data fields. Remember to use the data directory you created in the planning phase. Don't overlook any important fields.

Hints for Entering Specifications

1. If you make a mistake in a field specification, position the cursor on the field and enter the correct information.
2. Watch the Navigation line and Message line for help in entering field specifications.

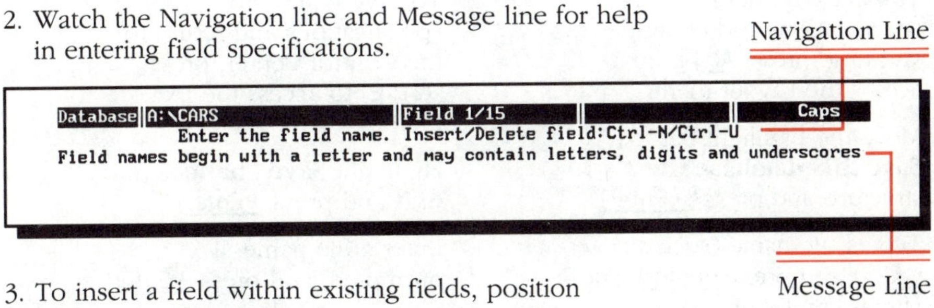

3. To insert a field within existing fields, position the cursor on the line where you want to insert a field and press Ctrl N.
4. To delete a field, position the cursor on the line containing the field specifications you want to delete and press Ctrl U.
5. To move a field, first insert the field in its new location and then delete it from its old location.

Creating the Database Structure

Saving the Database Structure

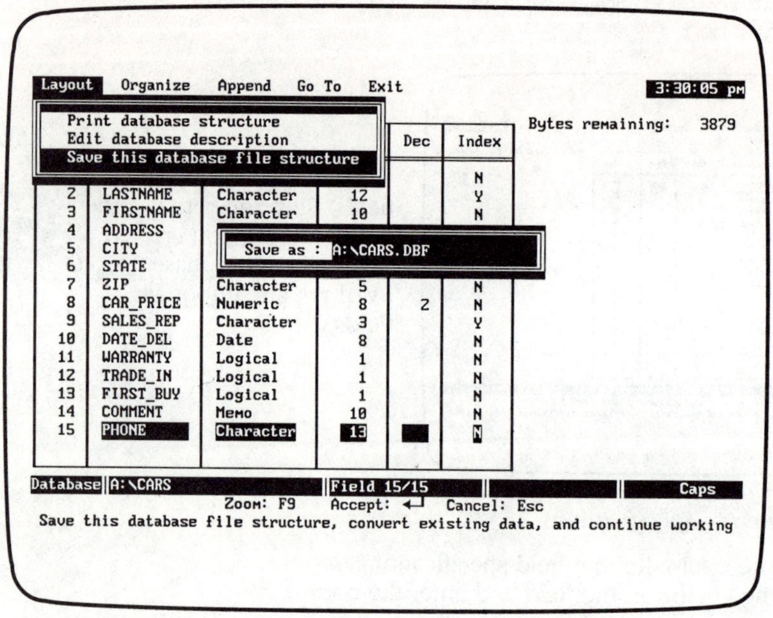

To save your field specifications and continue working, press Alt L to access the Layout menu.

Move the highlight bar to **Save this database file** structure and press ↵Enter.

Type a file name (such as CARS) and press ↵Enter. File names can be up to 8 characters in length and should not contain spaces.

To save your field specifications and return to the Control Center, press Alt E to access the Exit menu.

Highlight **Save changes and exit** and press ↵Enter.

Enter a file name, if prompted, and press ↵Enter.

Note: To exit without saving your changes, highlight **Abandon changes and exit** and press ↵Enter.

Printing the Database Structure

Page # 1

Structure for database: A:\CARS.DBF
Number of data records: 13
Date of last update : 02/24/89

Field	Field Name	Type	Width	Dec	Index
1	VIN	Character	10		N
2	LASTNAME	Character	12		Y
3	FIRSTNAME	Character	10		N
4	ADDRESS	Character	22		N
5	CITY	Character	15		N
6	STATE	Character	2		N
7	ZIP	Character	5		N
8	CAR_PRICE	Numeric	8	2	N
9	SALES_REP	Character	3		Y
10	DATE_DEL	Date	8		N
11	WARRANTY	Logical	1		N
12	TRADE_IN	Logical	1		N
13	FIRST_BUY	Logical	1		N
14	COMMENTS	Memo	10		N
15	PHONE	Character	13		N
** Total **			122		

To print your database, press Alt L from the data-design work surface to access the Layout menu.

Move the highlight bar to **Print database structure** and press ↵Enter.

Position the highlight bar on **Begin printing** and press ↵Enter.

You can stop the printer temporarily by pressing Ctrl S. Press Esc to cancel the printing operation.

Editing the Database Structure

After you create and save a database structure, you can edit the structure. Highlight the database name in the Data panel and press ⇧Shift F2. Press Esc. Then make the necessary changes.

3 *Editing Data*

Imagine going to a physician's office for the first time. You fill out forms listing your name, address, employment, insurance, and medical history. The office needs this data to add to the patient database. Each question on each form is a *field*; your response is the *data* in the field.

You "collect data" in several ways. Some data you hear and trust to memory. Other data you receive already written or you write it down yourself before entering it in your computerized database. If you have determined what fields you want in your database, you know what standard information you must have to enter records in your database.

After you design your database and collect your data, you can begin entering records. Recall that a record is a set of related data, in this case, a patient database. dBASE IV allows you to store a maximum of one billion records in a database. Of course, the actual number of records you store depends on the amount of disk space available on your computer.

Adding records is only the first step to *maintaining* a database. You must be able to rely on the accuracy of your database information; a database is useful only if you update its contents regularly. In a patient database, addresses, insurance providers, and places of employment change frequently. The doctor can lose time and money sending bills to the wrong address or billing an insurance carrier that no longer provides patient coverage. dBASE IV makes it easy to update data; making required changes and deleting unnecessary records promptly is up to you!

As you enter your first data, keep in mind that data *accuracy* and data *security* go hand in hand. No matter how carefully you update your data, you must be able to get to, or access, the data. Follow good documentation techniques by printing your data files periodically and backing up your data files to floppy disk or tape on a regular basis.

What Is Covered in This Chapter?

In this chapter, you learn about

- Entering records in Browse or Edit mode
- Changing the content of records, undoing changes, and deleting records
- Adding and changing memo fields
- Using the Browse Fields options

Key Words Used in This Chapter

Browse mode	A screen displaying up to 17 records with fields organized horizontally across the screen
Edit mode	A screen displaying one record with fields organized vertically down the screen
Memo field	A type of field used to add remarks or notes within a record. The contents of a memo field cannot exceed 64,000 characters.
Quick Report	A structured printout of the contents of all fields in the data file; the field names serve as column headings.
Text Editor	The limited dBASE IV word processor. (You can use it to enter narrative in a memo field.)

Browse/Edit Work Surfaces and Menu Bar

To help you update records, dBASE IV offers you two work surfaces where you can add and edit data. The Edit work surface allows you to see one record at a time on-screen. Browse permits you to see one record per line and 17 records per screen. (You can access the Browse work surface only if you have records in the database.) You can toggle between Browse and Edit mode by pressing F2 (Data). In addition, a Menu bar appears above each work surface. The Menu bar provides access to a series of menu choices to help you add and edit data. Take a few moments to learn the general characteristics of the work surfaces and Menu bar before you work with a specific database.

Edit Work Surface

The Edit work surface displays one record at a time. Data is displayed one field per line using as many screens as necessary to display the record. A record structure may have as many as 255 fields. As you scroll down (or up) the screen, fields move off the top (or bottom) of the screen and others move on the screen—much as you look through a movie camera as it pans a view of a tall building.

Each field appears in the order that it was defined in the database structure. The field name appears first, followed by an area to enter the data. This area for entering data appears in color (or inverse video if you have a monochrome monitor).

Browse Work Surface

Use the Browse work surface when you want to see and edit more than one record on-screen at one time. The Browse work surface is organized into rows (*records*) and columns (*fields*). Fields appear from left to right across the screen in the order each was defined in the database structure. Most records are too long to fit on-screen from left to right; furthermore, most databases have too many records to fit on a single screen, top to bottom.

In Browse mode, your screen becomes a window, panning left and right or up and down the database. The Menu bar, Status bar, and cursor-control keys help you move around the database and find records. For example, you can press PgUp to move the cursor to the previous record in Edit mode or the previous screenful of records in Browse mode.

The structures of the Browse and Edit work surfaces—17 records in row-and-column format, or 1 record with each field below the previous one—are built into dBASE IV. Most of your source documents (forms from which you draw data to enter in the database) will not match the Browse or Edit layout on the screen. Chapter 7 discusses creating custom data entry screens that allow you to arrange the field layout on your screen to look like the paper forms on which you collect data.

Browse/Edit Menu Bar

The Browse and Edit Menu bars contain similar options. The Browse Menu bar contains four options (**Records**, **Fields**, **Go To**, and **Exit**). The Edit Menu bar lists three options (**Records**, **Go To**, and **Exit**). These menu choices help you add, blank, and mark records as well as control the screen. (Recall that you can reach these menu options by pressing F10 [Menu], and selecting the option you want or pressing Alt and the first letter of the option.) Each time you enter a menu, the highlight bar appears on the last choice you made from that menu. Let's take a general look at each of these Menu bar options.

Records Option

Four commonly used options on the **Records** menu include undoing changes just made to a record, adding new records, marking records for deletion, and blanking a record. The undo option is handy when you want to reverse the changes you just made to a record. However, if you move the cursor off the current record (to another record), your changes are filed on disk and cannot be undone with the **Undo change to record** menu selection.

If you want to add new records when you are in the Edit or Browse work surface, you can select **Add new records** from the Records menu or you can move the cursor past the last record in the database until you see the prompt **===> Add new records? (Y/N)**. Either way, the cursor moves to the first field in a new record.

Choose **Mark record for deletion** if you want to remove a record from the database. You can also mark a record for deletion by positioning the cursor on the record and pressing **Ctrl-U**.

Pick the option **Blank record** if you want to eliminate data in an entire record without removing the record from the database. If you need to change most of the data in a record, you may find it easier to blank the record and start over, filling in the fields instead of trying to edit the previous contents extensively. For example, if the street address of a new car buyer has changed, it is easier to blank the old address and type the new one than to edit the old address. If, however, a ZIP code should be 46220 instead of 46210, do not blank the field and retype the contents. In this case, it is easier to edit the single character.

Fields Option (Browse Mode Only)

Use the **Fields** option to control the screen when you are in Browse mode. You can keep fields on the edge of the screen from shifting off the screen, blank the contents of a field, freeze the cursor in one field for easier editing, and adjust the size of a field.

Select **Lock fields on left {0}** from the Fields menu in order to keep a specified number of columns (fields) on-screen. For example, consider locking in the name-related fields in the car sales database so that you can see the car sales associated with each field of data in a record that extends beyond the edge of the screen.

Choose **Blank field** to clear the contents of a field. You can also blank a field by positioning the cursor at the beginning of the field and pressing Ctrl-Y.

Use **Freeze field**, in Browse mode, to limit the cursor's movement to one field. Use this feature when you have many changes to make to just one field in the database.

Select **Size** to change the size of a column (field) on the screen. By narrowing the width of a column display on the screen, you can see more columns at one time. When you enter and edit data in the field, the field contents scroll left and right within the size of the column.

Go To Option

Use the **Go To** option to position the cursor at the top or bottom of the database, at a specific record number, or to skip forward or backward a specified number of records.

Exit Option

Select **Exit** to leave Browse or Edit mode and return to the Control Center. You can also exit to the query design screen, discussed in Chapter 6. You can use queries to limit the records (or fields in records) that you see on-screen; Chapter 6 discusses queries.

Browse/Edit Work Surfaces and Menu Bar

dBASE IV offers two work surfaces to help you maintain your data: the Edit work surface and the Browse work surface.

Edit Work Surface

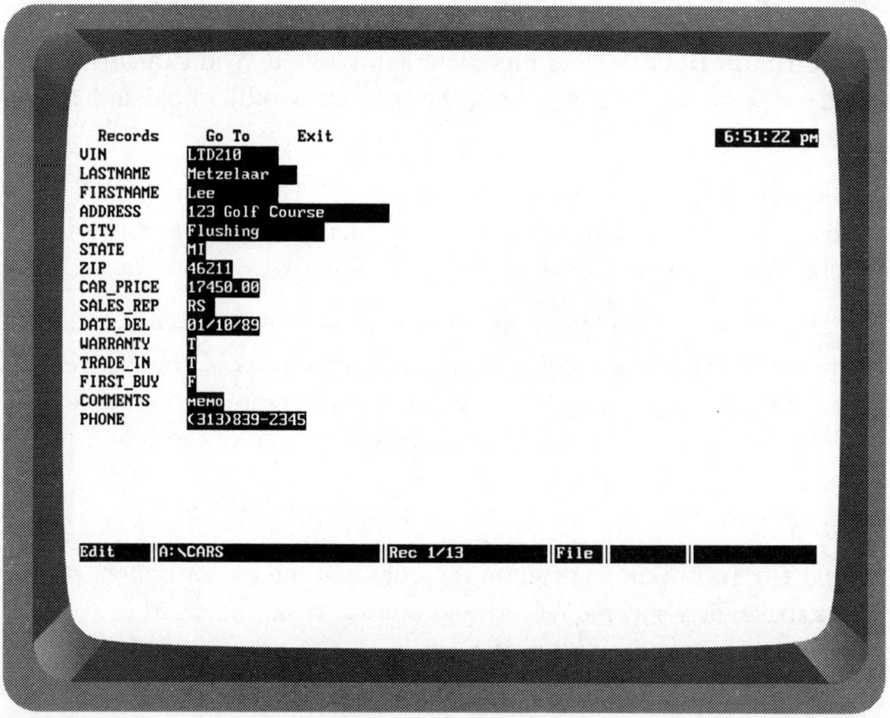

The Edit screen displays just one record at a time. Use the Edit screen to view field data and to enter data in a single record.

Access either the Edit or Browse screen from the Control Center by highlighting the file name and pressing F2. dBASE IV displays the work surface that was used last. If you do not see the screen display you want, press F2 again to access the alternate work surface.

Browse Work Surface

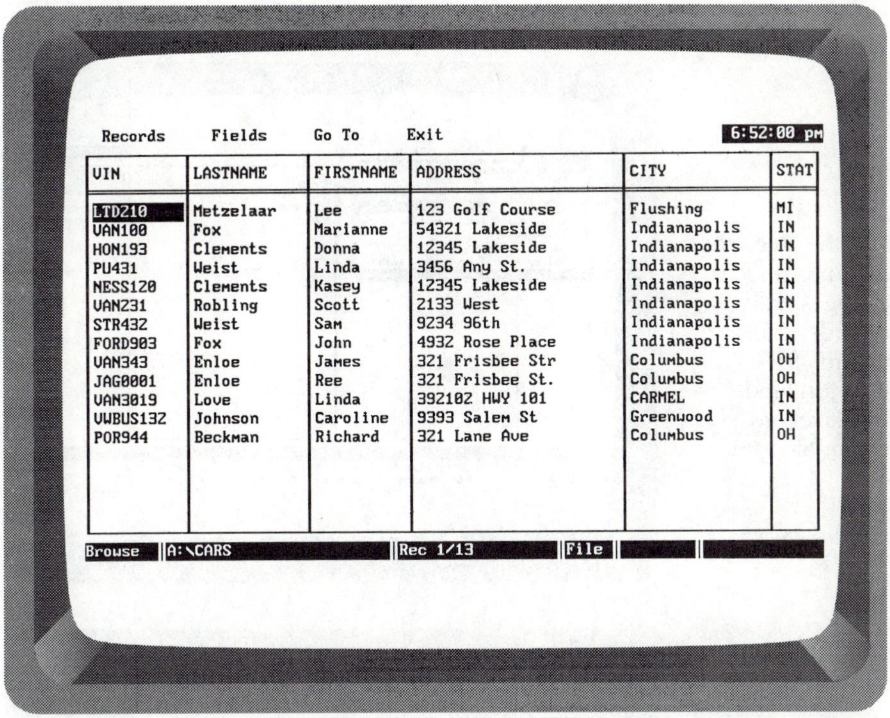

Records   Fields   Go To   Exit   6:52:00 pm

VIN	LASTNAME	FIRSTNAME	ADDRESS	CITY	STAT
LTD210	Metzelaar	Lee	123 Golf Course	Flushing	MI
VAN100	Fox	Marianne	54321 Lakeside	Indianapolis	IN
HON193	Clements	Donna	12345 Lakeside	Indianapolis	IN
PU431	Weist	Linda	3456 Any St.	Indianapolis	IN
NESS120	Clements	Kasey	12345 Lakeside	Indianapolis	IN
VAN231	Robling	Scott	2133 West	Indianapolis	IN
STR432	Weist	Sam	9234 96th	Indianapolis	IN
FORD903	Fox	John	4932 Rose Place	Indianapolis	IN
VAN343	Enloe	James	321 Frisbee Str	Columbus	OH
JAG0001	Enloe	Ree	321 Frisbee St.	Columbus	OH
VAN3019	Love	Linda	392102 HWY 101	CARMEL	IN
VWBUS132	Johnson	Caroline	9393 Salem St	Greenwood	IN
POR944	Beckman	Richard	321 Lane Ave	Columbus	OH

Browse | A:\CARS | Rec 1/13 | File

The Browse screen displays a number of records. Each record occupies a row. The field data is displayed in columnar format. Use Browse to view, edit, add, or delete data from several records. Access Browse from the Control Center by highlighting the file name and pressing F2 until you see data in row and column format.

Browse/Edit Work Surfaces and Menu Bar

Browse/Edit Menu Bar

Use the **Records** menu to undo changes, add records, mark records for deletion, and blank record contents.

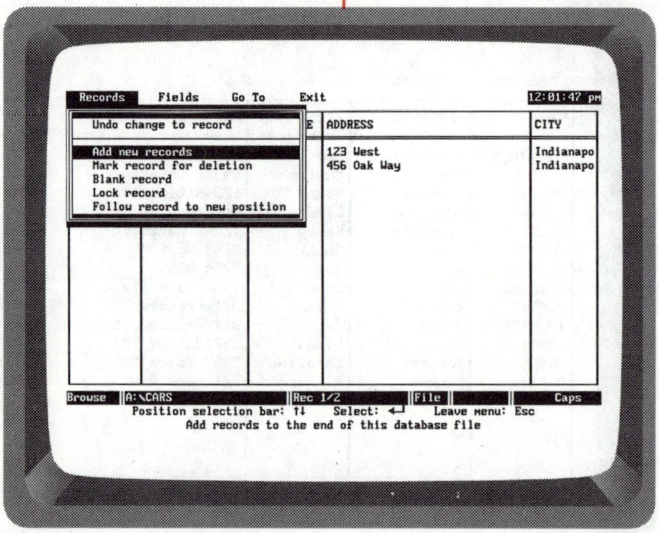

Use the **Fields** menu to control how fields are displayed in Browse mode. This option is not displayed on the Edit Menu bar.

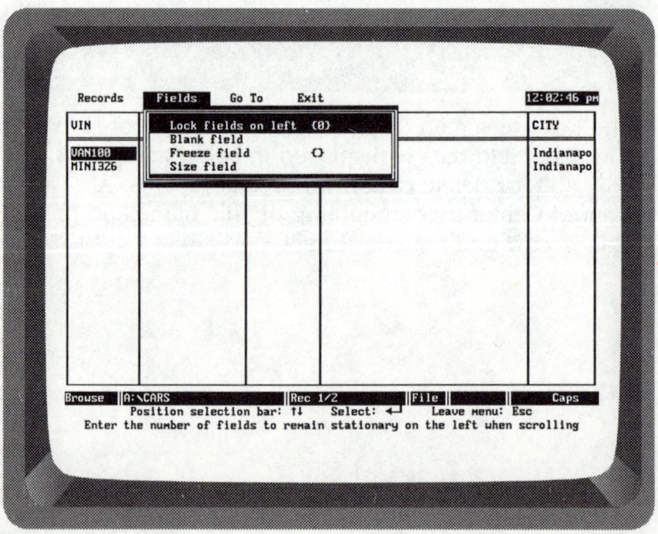

Go To Exit

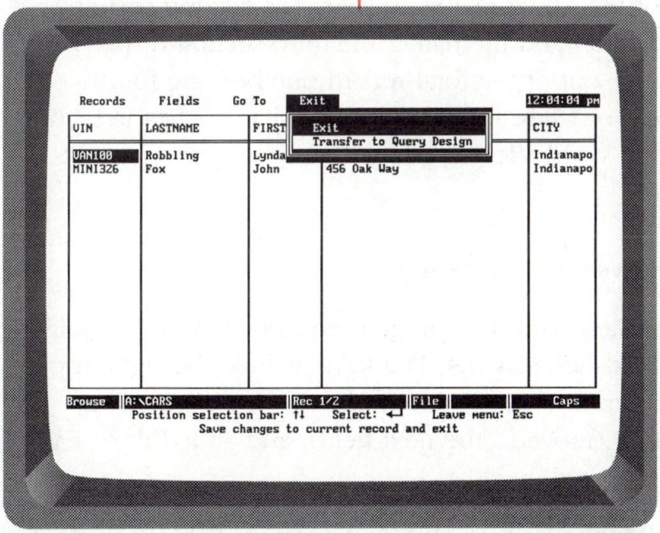

Use **Exit** to leave the Browse/Edit screen and return to the Control Center.

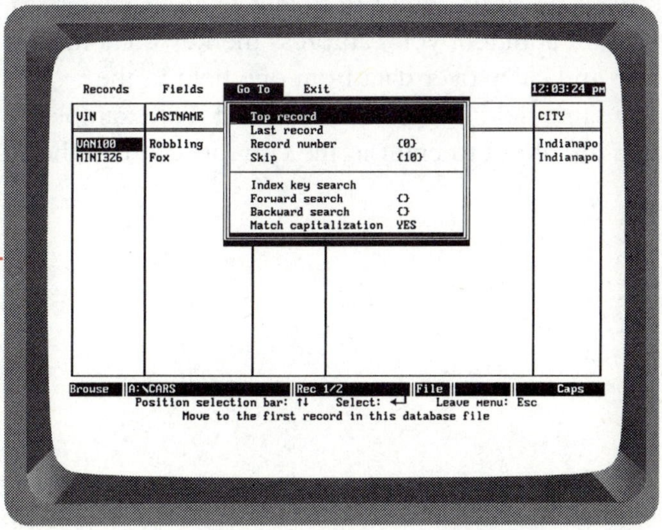

Use the **Go To** menu to move to specific records.

Using the Browse/Edit Status Bar

Recall that the Status bar displays information near the bottom of the screen, just above the Navigation and Message lines. The Status bar information changes to describe what you are doing. Whenever you use an Edit or Browse work surface, the words **Browse** or **Edit** appear in the first section of the horizontal Status bar. The second section contains the disk location and file name; the third section displays the current record number out of the total record number; the fourth section contains the word **File** if you can make changes to the record in the database or the word **View** if you can only see, but not edit, the contents of each file.

Keys To Use in Browse or Edit Mode

Use the cursor-movement keys to change the position of the highlight bar on the Browse and Edit screens. The keys include the right arrow (→), left arrow (←), up arrow (↑), down arrow (↓), PgUp, PgDn, Home, End, Tab or F4 (move to the next field), and Shift-Tab or F3 (move to the previous field).

You can use the following keys to edit field content: right arrow (→), left arrow (←), Del, Backspace, Ins, and Ctrl-Y (delete all characters to the right of the cursor). In addition, you can press the key combination Shift-F8 (the *ditto* key) and carry over data from one field in the previous record to the same field in the current record. For example, if the name of a city you are about to enter in the current record is the same as the name of the city in the previous record, you can press Shift-F8 to copy the city name and eliminate the keystrokes to type the name yourself.

Now that you know how your keyboard performs in dBASE IV, you are ready to begin filling your database structure with information. Begin by learning how to add records to new databases (and existing databases as well). Adding records is also known as *appending* records.

Accessing the Browse/Edit Work Surface

You can access the Browse or Edit work surfaces from the Control Center Data panel by highlighting the database you want to use, such as a car-sales database named CARS, and pressing F2 (Data). The database opens, and the Browse or Edit screen appears. You can also access Browse or Edit by highlighting the database name in the Data panel, pressing Enter, and selecting **Display data** from the menu.

If you access the Browse or Edit mode when the database is empty (the structure is created but no records exist yet), you see the Edit screen. If records are already entered in the database, you see the last screen in use. You can toggle between the Browse and Edit screens by pressing the F2 (Data) key.

Browse/Edit Work Surfaces and Menu Bar

Browse/Edit Status Bar

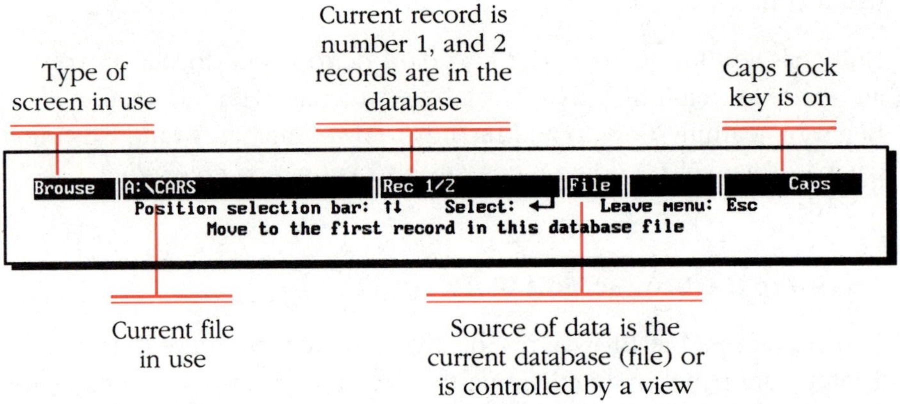

Keys Used To Navigate in Browse/Edit

Moves the cursor up or down

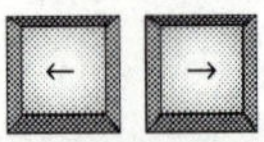

Moves the cursor left or right

Moves the cursor up or down one record in Edit mode or one screenful in Browse mode

Moves the cursor to the first character in the current field in Edit mode or the first field in Browse mode

Moves the cursor to the last character in the current field in Edit mode or the last field in Browse mode

Moves the cursor to the previous field

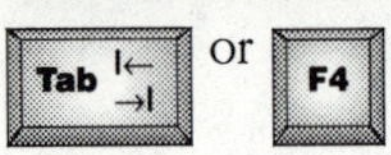

Moves the cursor to the next field

Keys Used To Add Data in Browse/Edit

Key	Action
Insert	Causes existing text to shift right one character for each new character typed
Shift F8	Copies data from a field in the previous record to the same field in the current record
Enter	Completes entry to a field and moves the cursor to the next field

Keys Used To Delete Data in Browse/Edit

Key	Action
Backspace	Removes the character to the left of the cursor
Delete	Deletes the character at the cursor
Ctrl Y	Deletes all characters to the right of the cursor
Ctrl U	Marks a record for deletion

Other Browse/Edit Keys

Key	Action
Esc	Leaves the current record without saving changes
F2	Switches between Browse and Edit mode
F10	Accesses menu options

Adding Records in Browse or Edit Mode

When the Browse or Edit screen appears, the cursor rests in the first field of the first record. If the database is new, you see an empty record. You can then begin to enter data.

If your database already contains records, you can add new records two different ways. You can select **Records** from the Browse or Edit Menu bar and **Add new records** from the Records menu. As an alternative method, you can scroll through (by pressing ↓ from the last field or PgDn) the existing records until the cursor goes past the last record. At the prompt **===> Add new records? (Y/N)** on the bottom of the screen, press Y to add new records.

Hint: When your cursor is at the bottom of the file, press ↓ to force the "add records" message. When your cursor is too far from the bottom of the file, use the Records menu and its **Add new records** option.

In Edit mode, you enter data one field after another down a column. In Browse mode, you enter data one field after another across a row. After each completed record, the cursor rests on the first field of a new record.

To enter data, position the cursor in the appropriate data field and type. There are, however, some rules or guidelines for entering data.

Guidelines for Entering Data in Fields

- To move automatically to the next field, you must fill the field. Typing a month-day-year combination in a date field or a Y (Yes) or N (No) in a logical field fills the field. A beep sounds when the field is filled, and the cursor moves to the next field.

Guidelines for Entering Data in Fields *(cont.)*

- To move to the next field if you have not filled the field, you must press Enter. When you type a 12-character city name in a field defined as 18 characters wide, you have not filled the field.
- To move the cursor within a field, use the left arrow (←) or right arrow (→) keys. If the cursor is at the beginning of a field when you press the left arrow (←), the cursor moves to the previous field; if the cursor is at the end of a field when you press the right arrow (→), the cursor moves to the next field.
- Press Tab or F4 to move the cursor to the next field. Press Shift-Tab or F3 to move the cursor to the previous field.
- Do not enter slashes in a date field (dBASE does it for you) or any punctuation (a $ sign or comma, for example) in a numeric or float field except the decimal point.
- Enter data in a memo field with the Text Editor (the Text Editor is discussed later in the chapter).

Saving Records

Be sure to quit entering records in a manner that saves your work. Do not turn off the computer without first exiting your current dBASE operation, or you risk loss of data. Choose **Exit** from the Browse or Edit menu and then select **Exit**.

When adding a large number of records, you should exit and save the database periodically and then reenter Browse/Edit mode to continue adding records. Periodic saving reduces the likelihood of work lost from a power failure.

Adding Records

You can begin to enter records in a database after you create and save the database structure. Enter your records in Browse or Edit mode.

Using the Browse/Edit Screen

Access the Control Center Data panel.

Highlight the database name.

Press F2 to access the Browse/Edit screen.

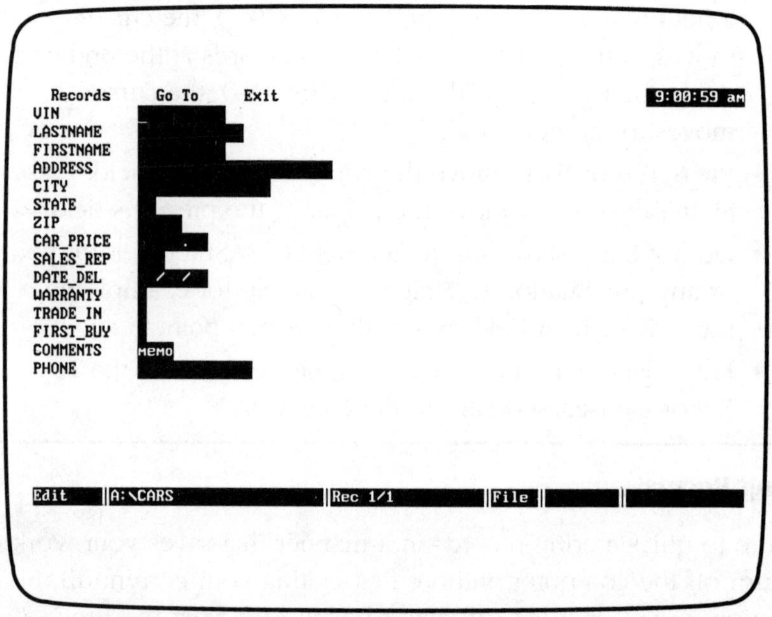

If there are no records in the database, this Edit screen displays, and you can begin entering data.

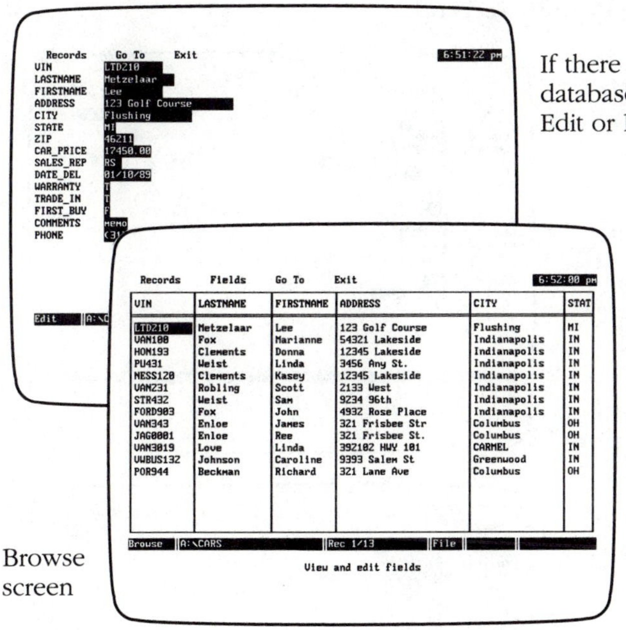

Edit screen

Browse screen

If there are records in the database, you see either the Edit or Browse screen.

dBASE IV remembers which screen was used last. That is the screen you see first.

The cursor appears in the first field of the first record.

To add a new record, press [Alt][R] to select the Records menu.

Press [A] to **Add new records**.

Enter the new record.

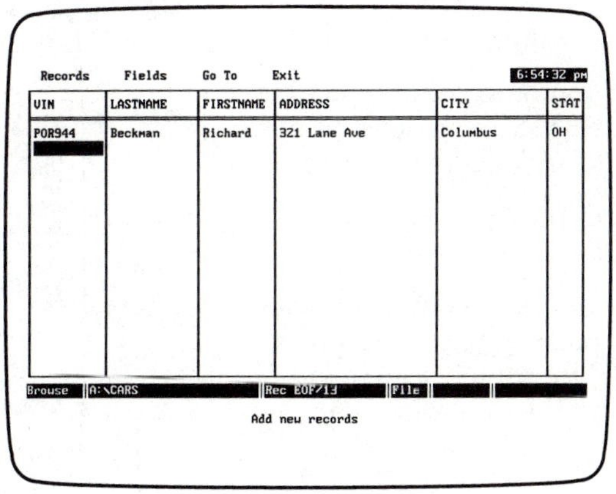

Adding Records

Adding a Record by Using the Edit Screen

In the Data panel, highlight the database file name that contains your records.

Press F2 until you access the the Edit screen.

From the Records menu, select **Add new records**.

Begin typing your data in the first field.

Press ↵Enter when you complete the entry. If you make a mistake, press the ←Backspace key and edit your error.

dBASE IV will beep and automatically move to the next field when you fill a field.

Continue entering data in the fields.

Press Tab or ↵Enter to skip fields you do not want to fill.

When you have completed all fields, dBASE IV moves to a new blank record automatically.

You can press PgDn to add another record as well.

When you have completed your work, press Alt E; then press ↵Enter to exit the screen and return to the Control Center.

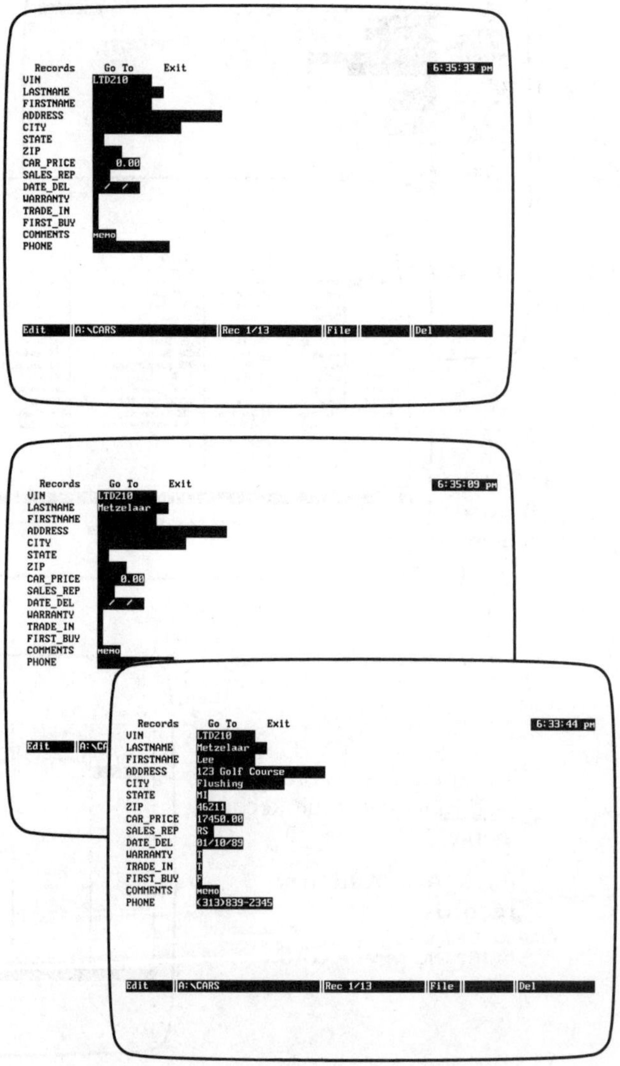

Adding a Record by Using the Browse Screen

In the Data panel, highlight the database file name.

Press F2 to access the Browse screen.

From the Records menu, select **Add new records**.

Begin typing data in the first field.

Press ↵Enter to complete the entry and move to the next field.

If the field is full, a beep will sound and the cursor will move to the next field automatically.

Continue entering data in the fields.

Press Tab or ↵Enter to move forward from field to field. Press ↓ to add another record.

To exit and save your work, press Alt E.

Press ↵Enter.

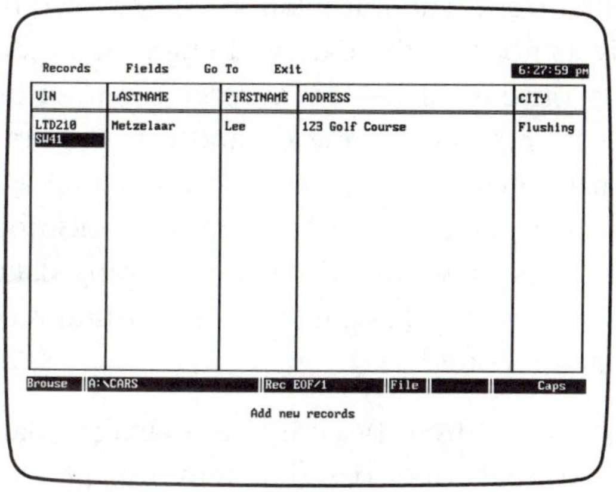

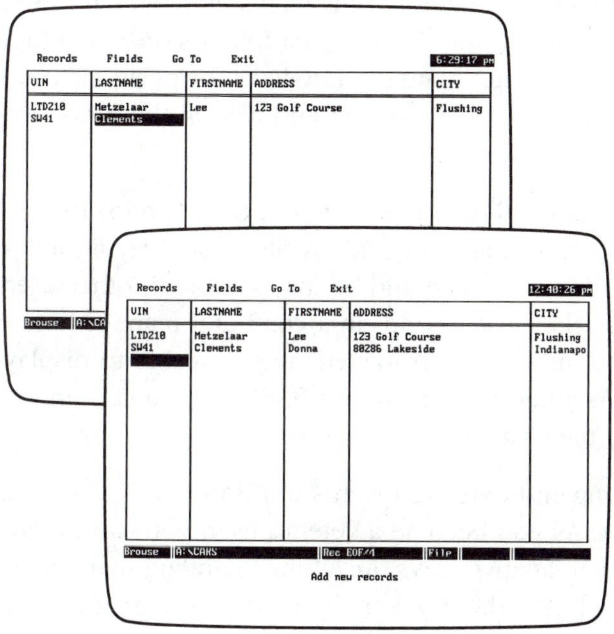

Changing and Deleting Records

Just entering data is not enough to maintain your database. You must keep its content current. The information you retrieve from your database is only as good as the data you enter. Some outdated information is inconsequential—if you reach a wrong phone number, you generally get a new listing quickly and can repeat the call. Other outdated information can be more costly—misstating a customer's balance because you fail to record a payment or distributing advertising brochures to wrong addresses. Keeping data current means constantly adding records, changing data in existing records, and deleting unwanted records.

Entering changes in a dBASE IV computer-managed database is much easier than in a manual paper-based system. Imagine working in a personnel department that maintains employee information on paper, with each employee's record in a folder stored in a file cabinet. If an employee changes name, salary level, or position, you must "white-out" or cross out the old data and type in the new—or add a revised form to the folder.

If you change the wrong item, you can't "undo" the damage without more white-out and retyping. A file folder can sit on a desk for hours waiting for an update and be inaccessible to other users. By contrast, a change takes just seconds in a computer-managed system, and the updated information is immediately available to display on-screen or print. As an added feature in dBASE IV, you can undo a change and restore the original.

Changing and deleting records in dBASE IV is as easy as adding records. As you become a veteran user, you can update your database in several creative ways, including changing many records in a single operation. For the moment, limit your changes or deletions to one record at a time.

Making Changes to One Record

To make a change to an existing record, first access the Browse/Edit mode. Recall that you can access the Browse or Edit work surfaces from the Control Center Data panel in one of two ways. You can highlight the database to use and press F2 (Data); or you can highlight the database name in the Data panel, press Enter, and select **Display data** from the menu.

Press the F2 (Data) key until your choice of Edit (one record per screen) or Browse (17 records per screen) mode appears. Use the cursor keys to navigate through your data records to the record that needs updating. Position the cursor in each field needing change, and type the changes.

You can save your revised record in two different ways: you can move the cursor away from the changed record to the preceding record or the next record, or you can select **Exit** from the Browse or Edit Menu bar. If you must look for just a few records throughout a large database, dBASE IV offers simple searches (described later in this book) to help you quickly find the records you need.

Undoing Changes

dBASE IV offers a new feature called **Undo change to record**. This option is helpful if you make an error while you are updating a record. For example, you might revise data in the wrong field, or blank the contents of the wrong record. In both cases, you need to restore the original field or record contents.

To undo changes, select the **Records** option on the Browse or Edit Menu bar, then select **Undo change to record**. The original record contents are restored.

Caution: If you move the cursor off the altered record, you cannot use the **Undo change to record** feature because your changes are saved in the database. Instead, you must reposition the cursor in the record and retype the changes.

Deleting Records

In dBASE IV, you can "delete" records and still maintain them in the database. The program recognizes that you may need to keep track of out-of-date records even after you move them from your "working" database. Suppose that you manage a physician's patient database. You can designate all patients not seen in two years as inactive and remove those patients' records from the screen display but not from the database itself. dBASE allows you to mark records for deletion and then "hide" them from view. You can then "undelete" a record should a patient return after a long absence.

As an alternative, you can mark records for deletion and then simply remove them, without "hiding" them, from the database. The two ways of moving records from the active database have both advantages and disadvantages.

If you mark and hide records, you can unmark and use them later. However, these hidden records remain in the file and take up space. Any searches run slower because dBASE IV must still read the records before ignoring them. To help you decide how you want to handle records to remove, consider the disk space available, the speed of your disk drive and processor, and the potential size of your database if you "hide" deleted records.

As yet another alternative, you can avoid the speed and space problems of hiding files by copying the deleted records to another database on the hard disk or a floppy disk. After safely copying the records, you can delete the original records. You now have a separate database of inactive records that you can access whenever you want.

Marking Records for Deletion

To *mark* a record for deletion, position the cursor within the record to be deleted and press Ctrl-U. The **Del** message appears next to the right end of the Status bar at the bottom of the screen. To unmark a record, use the same process—move the cursor to the record to be restored and press Ctrl-U. **Del** disappears from the Status bar.

Removing Marked Records from the Database

To erase all marked records from the database, you must access the data design work surface. After you return to the Control panel, highlight the database name, press Shift-F2, and select **Organize** from the Menu bar. Then select **Erase marked records**, and at the window prompt **Are you sure you want to erase all marked records?**, select **Yes**. Use this feature with caution—you cannot restore erased records.

Hiding Records Marked for Deletion

If you want to ignore some records in reports and searches, you can mark these records for deletion and hide them. dBASE IV uses switches called *Set commands* to alter its operating environment. You can set switches with the **Tools** option on the Control Center Menu bar.

One switch is **Deleted ON/OFF** which is normally **OFF**. This switch lets you access all records, including marked records. If you change the setting to **ON**, you cannot access marked records even in Browse or Edit mode.

To hide marked records, access the Control Center and select **Tools**, select **Settings**, choose **Options**, select **Deleted**, and press Enter until the word **ON** appears next to **Deleted**. Press Enter to "unhide" marked records, setting **Deleted** to **OFF**.

Changing and Deleting Records

Making Changes

You can change or delete records while in Browse or Edit mode. Use Browse mode when you want to see more than one record on the screen.

In the Data panel, press ↓ to highlight your database file name.

Press F2 to access the Browse screen.

Use ↓, ↑, PgUp, and PgDn to locate the record.

Position the cursor in the field to be changed using →, ←, Tab, and Shift Tab.

Type the change into the field. Use the Del key to remove extra or unwanted characters.

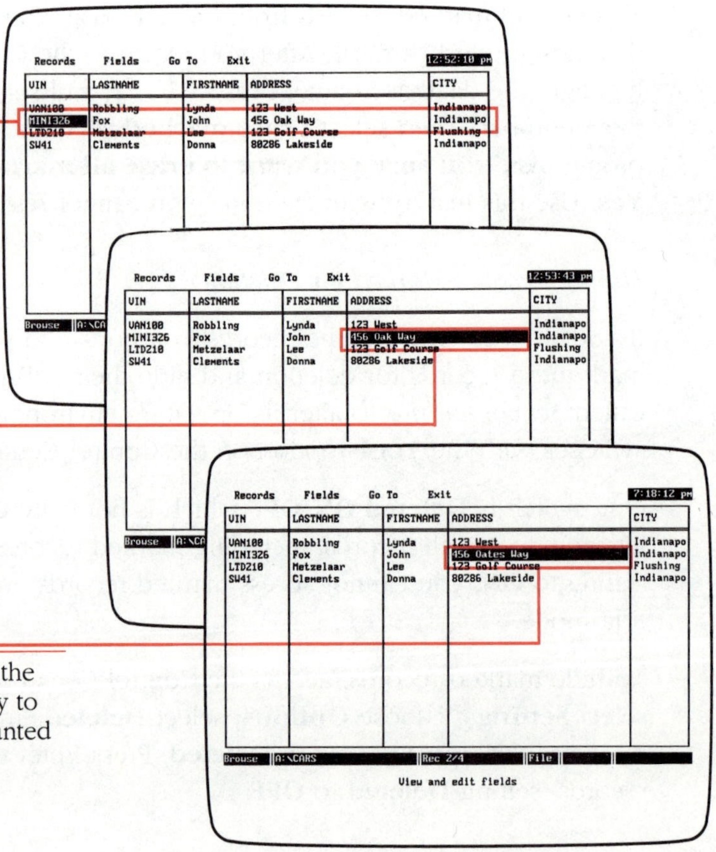

Undoing Changes

If you make a change and find that you need to "undo" it, do not move to another record, though you may move to other fields in the record.

From the Records menu, select **Undo change to record**.

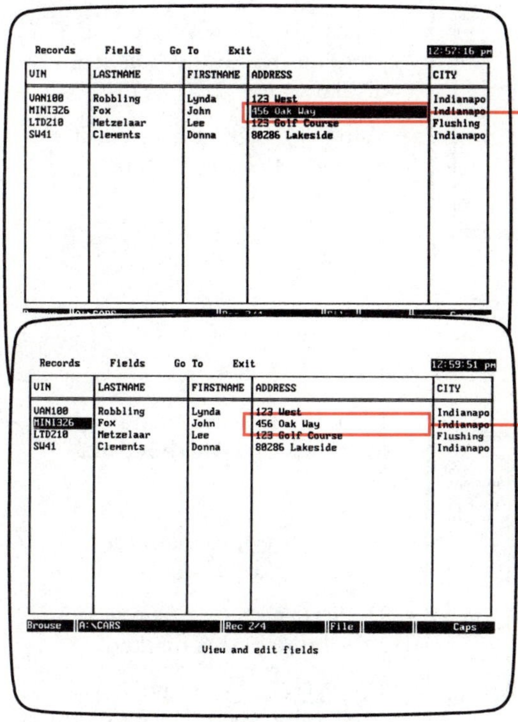

The changes have been replaced with the original data.

Go back and make the appropriate correction until you are satisfied that the entry is correct.

Undo works only if you remain in the record after making the initial correction. If you make a correction and move to another record, you cannot undo the correction using **Undo change to record**.

Select **Exit** from the Exit menu to return to the Control Center.

Marking Records

Records must be marked before they can be removed from the database or hidden from view. You can mark records from both the Browse and Edit screen. Because Browse displays several records, you may decide to work from the Browse screen if you have a number of records to mark.

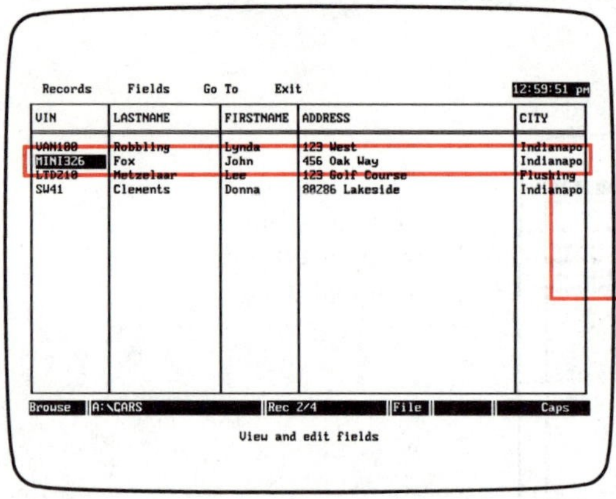

Access the Browse screen by pressing F2. If the Edit screen displays, press F2 again.

Using ↓, highlight a field in the record you want to mark.

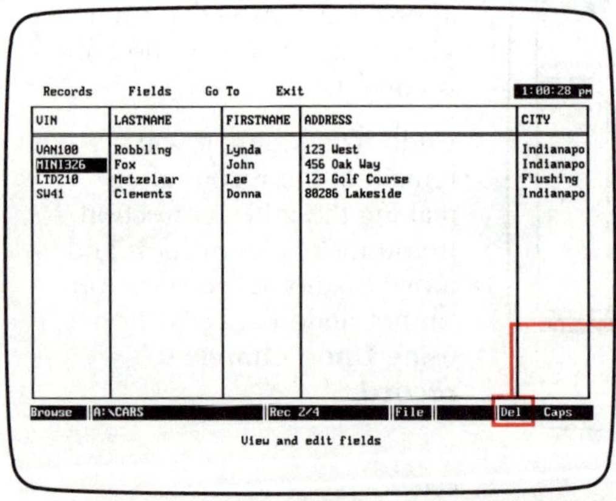

From the Records menu, select **Mark record for deletion**.

or

Press Ctrl U to mark the record for deletion.

Del in the status bar indicates that the record is marked.

Use PgDn or ↓ to move to mark other records for deletion.

Once records are marked for deletion, they may be removed from view or erased from the file.

Hiding Records

dBASE allows you to remove marked records from view but retain them in the database. If you merely remove records from view, but do not erase the records from the database, you are *hiding* the records.

For example, in a car sales database, you can mark for deletion all records for which the warranty has expired. To hide records marked for deletion, you must access the Tools option on the Control Center Menu bar and set the **Deleted** option on the Settings menu to **ON**.

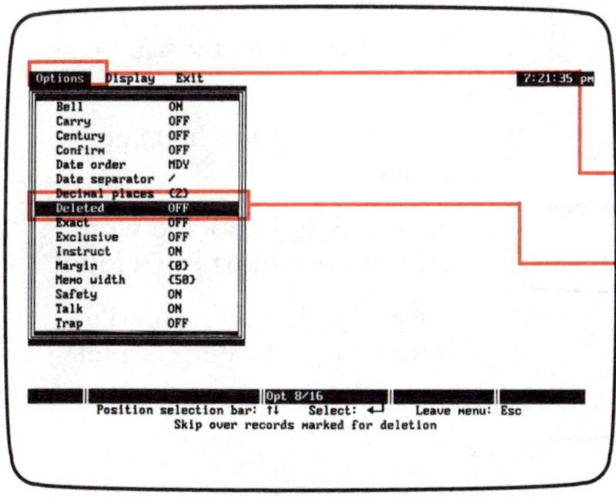

From the Control Center, press Alt T to access Tools.

Press S to select the **Settings** option.

The **Options** menu will be active.

Press ↓ or ↑ to highlight the **Deleted** option.

Press ↵Enter until the word **ON** appears next to the **Deleted** option.

Press Alt E and ↵Enter to return to the Control Center.

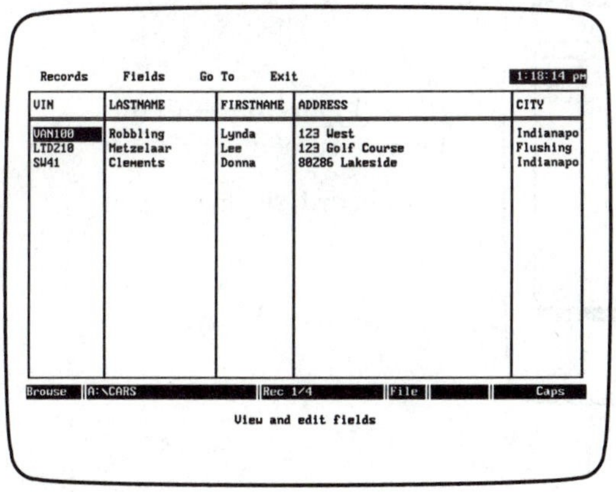

Press F2 to return to the Browse screen.

The marked record no longer displays on the screen, though the status line shows that the deleted record is still in the database.

Restoring Hidden Records

Hiding marked records removes the records from view on the screen and from reports or searches. However, you can restore hidden records to view if you set the **Deleted** option to **OFF**. For example, you might restore records concerning lapsed car warranties if owners purchase extended warranties.

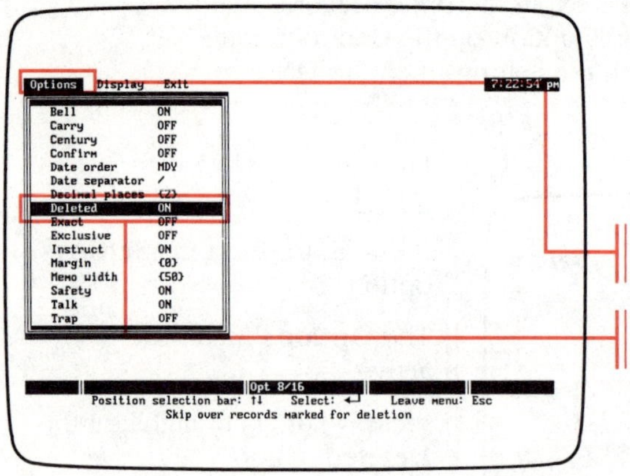

From the Control Center, press Alt T to access the Tools option from the Menu bar.

Press S to select the **Settings** option.

The **Options** menu will be active.

Press ↓ or ↑ to highlight **Deleted**.

Press ↵Enter until the word **OFF** appears next to **Deleted**.

Press Alt E and ↵Enter to return to the Control Center.

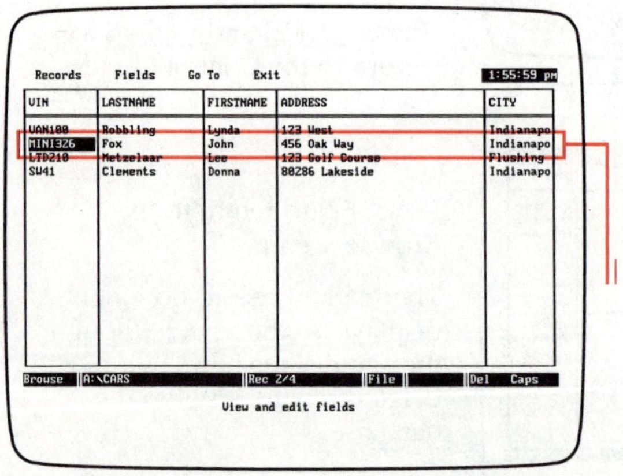

Press F2 to return to the Browse screen.

The record displays again.

Erasing Records

If you are absolutely sure that you no longer want marked records to be part of the database, you can erase the records. For example, you may want to remove all car sales records for sales that occurred more than 10 years ago. Keep in mind, however, that you cannot restore *erased* records as you can *hidden* records.

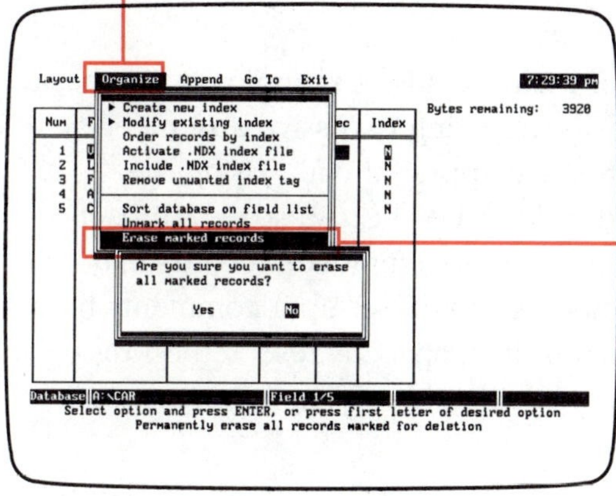

From the Control Center, press ⇧Shift F2.

The **Organize** menu will be active.

Press E.

Respond to the message **Are you sure you want to erase all marked records?**

Highlight **YES** and press ↵Enter to erase the marked records from your database.

or

Highlight **NO** and press ↵Enter to keep marked records in the database.

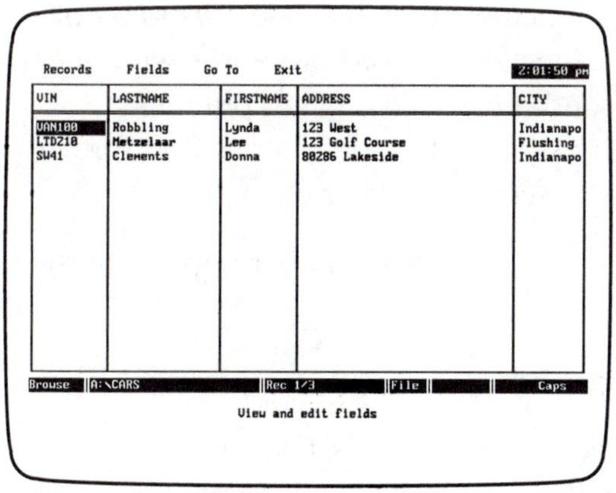

Press Alt E and ↵Enter to return to the Control Center.

Press F2 to return to the Browse screen.

Notice that the record is not in the database.

Using Memo Fields

Memo fields are unique types of data that deserve special discussion. A memo field in a database structure appears to have a 10-character width. dBASE IV, however, uses the field to locate a document associated with each record. Each document can hold up to 64,000 characters. For example, you can create the memo field COMMENTS in a car-sales database, and enter comments such as "first-time buyer" or "prefers blue" about a specific car buyer.

Records can contain any number of memo fields. An employee database might contain one memo field for documenting excessive absenteeism and another memo field for performance-appraisal data. Using the memo-field concept saves valuable disk space because space for each memo is reserved outside the database. Some employee records may not contain anything in a field for comments. If you set up a comments field as a *character* field instead of a memo field, space is reserved on disk for every record and you can waste considerable space if most records will *not* contain comments.

To enter data in a memo field, you must access the dBASE Editor. This section explains the general characteristics of the Editor.

Using the Editor Work Surface

The dBASE IV Editor work surface functions in two modes: *word wrap* and *layout.* Word-wrap mode functions like a word processor with lines that wrap around margins, search-and-replace capability, printing, display styling, and more. You can use layout mode to draw and format reports, labels, and custom screens discussed in later chapters.

Like other dBASE IV work surfaces, the Editor's Menu bar appears at the top of the screen:

Layout Words Go To Print Exit

The cursor is a blinking square when Insert mode is *On* and an underscore when Insert mode is *Off.* When Insert mode is on, the Status bar at the bottom of the screen displays **Ins**. (Recall that when you type a character in Insert mode, on-screen characters shift to the right of the current cursor position.) You can then type text at the blinking cursor on the work surface. When you complete a paragraph, press Enter before beginning the next paragraph.

To move, copy, or delete blocks of memo-field text in the Editor, use the F6 (Select) key to begin highlighting the block. You first position the cursor at the beginning of the block, press the F6 (Select) key, and use the cursor-control keys to highlight the text. You can use F6 to highlight text even more quickly: Press F6 once in word-wrap mode to highlight the first character, twice to highlight the word, and three times to highlight the entire paragraph. Press Esc to unhighlight text.

To move or copy a highlighted block of text, press F7 (Move) or F8 (Copy), position the cursor at the destination of the highlighted block, and press F7 (Move) or F8 (Copy) again.

To delete a highlighted block of text, press Del and respond *Yes* to confirm the deletion.

Entering and Editing Data in Memo Fields

Entering or editing data in memo fields is easy once you are familiar with the Editor. To edit a memo field from the Browse or Edit work surface, move the cursor to the desired memo field, press Ctrl-Home to access the Editor screen, and enter or edit the memo. Press Alt-E to access **Exit** on the Menu bar when you are through entering or editing the memo. Choose either **Save changes and exit** or **Abandon changes and exit** as appropriate.

Hint: As a general guideline, you can conserve disk space if you make short memo fields (less than 256 characters) into character fields.

Notice that in Browse or Edit mode, memo fields display the word **MEMO** instead of the data that appears in other types of fields. If the word **MEMO** is in capital letters, memo data is stored in the field. If the word **memo** appears in lowercase, that particular memo field has nothing in it.

Using Memo Fields

A memo field doesn't actually contain data. The memo field points to the Memo file in which the data is stored. The Memo file has the same name as the database except for the extension .DBT.

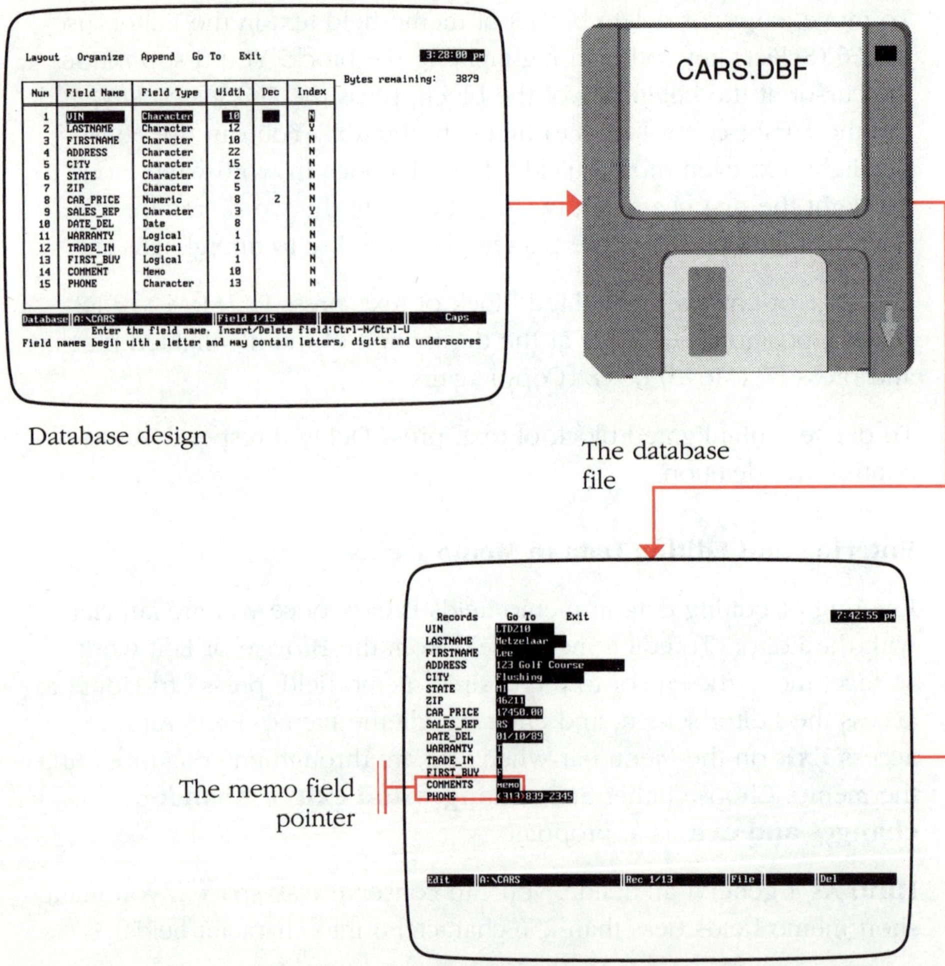

If you see **memo**, the memo field does not contain data. If you see **MEMO**, the memo field does contain data.

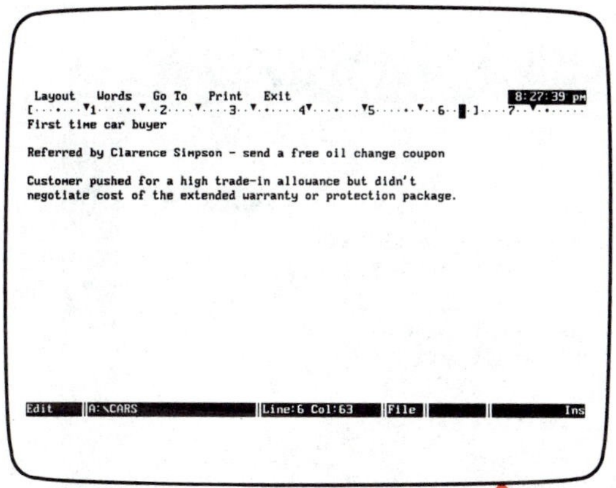

The memo field contents display on the Edit screen.

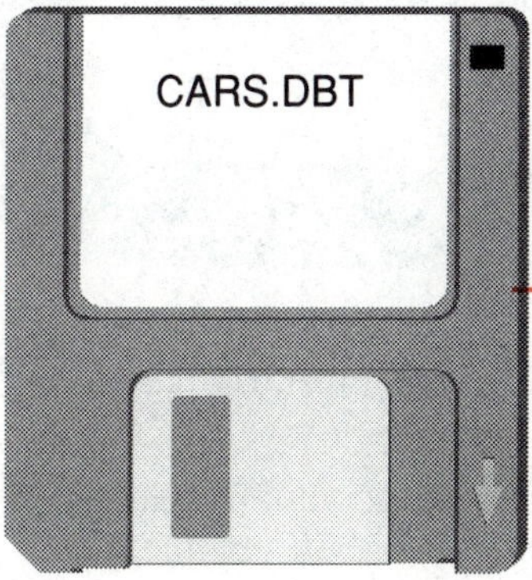

When you copy the database file, don't forget to copy the memo file too!

The memo file

Using the Editor Work Surface To Enter Data in a Memo Field

The dBASE IV Editor functions much like a word processor. To write in memo fields, you use word wrap and enter text in either insert or typeover mode. ↵Enter creates blank lines as it does in word processing programs. You press ↵Enter to end a paragraph or to add space between paragraphs.

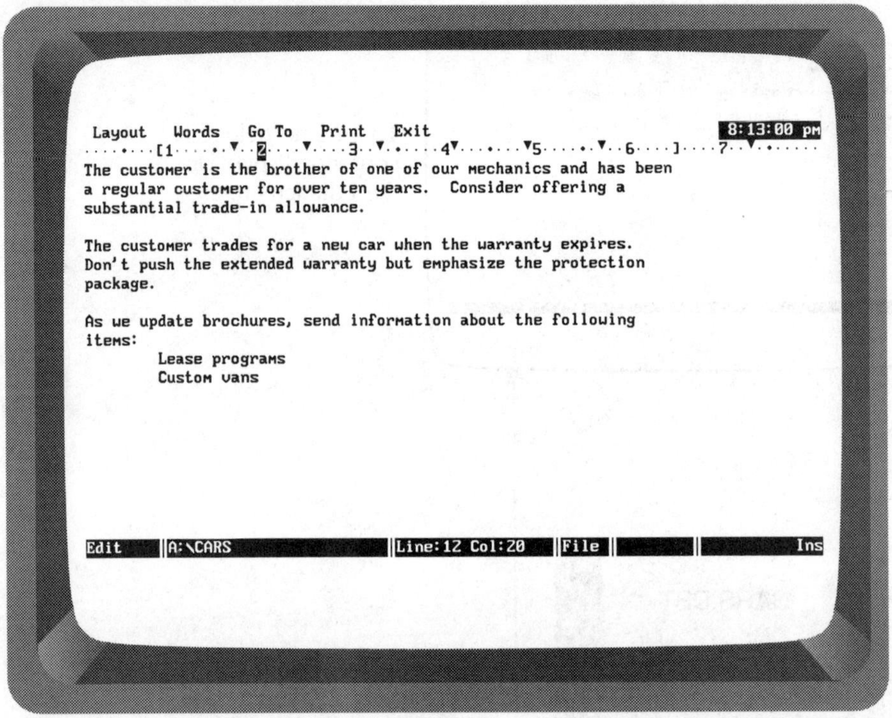

Word wrap automatically wraps your memo text to fit within the preset margins. Memo text scrolls up and down. Use →, ←, ↑, and ↓ to move through the text and Tab to indent text.

The Editor permits you to move, copy, and delete blocks of text; search and replace data; and write or read data to or from an ASCII text file.

Entering and Editing Data in a Memo Field

Access the Browse/Edit screen and locate the record containing the memo field for which you want to enter or edit data.

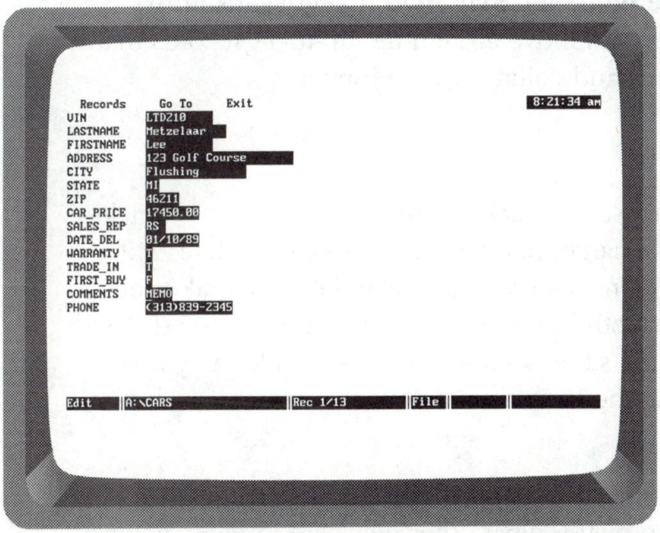

Press Tab or Shift Tab to position the cursor on the memo field to be edited.

Press Ctrl Home to activate the editor.

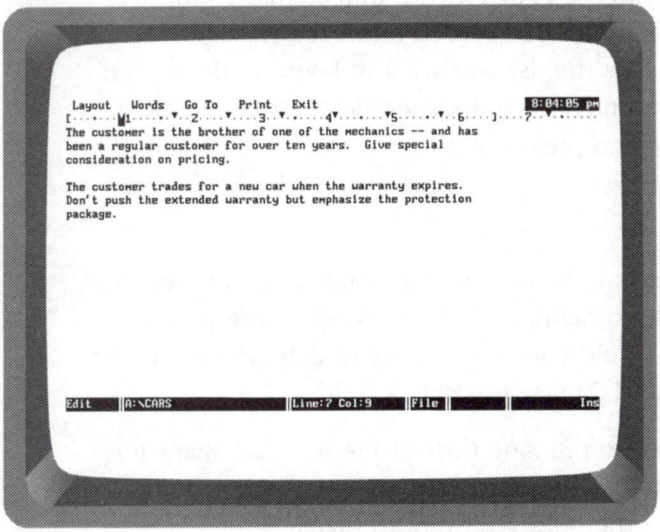

Enter the text in the Editor work surface.

Using either insert or typeover mode, make corrections or add data as necessary.

Press Alt E to Exit to the Control Center.

Your finished memo can be printed as a part of any screen or printed display.

Using the Browse Fields Menu

Recall that the Menu bars of the Edit screen and the Browse screen display three identical menu names: Records, Go To, and Exit. Only the Browse Menu bar offers Fields with its options—**Lock fields on left**, **Blank field**, **Freeze field**, and **Size field**. Using Fields in Browse mode, you can easily edit and move around the up-to-17 records that appear in the row (record) and column (field) format.

Locking Fields

Visualize a car-sales database in which the first nine fields are vehicle-identification number, last name, first name, address, city, state, ZIP, price of car, and salesperson. Assume that the address data takes up enough space to prevent both last name (field 2) and car price (field 8) data from appearing on the same screen in Browse mode. As you scroll to the right to bring the car price in view, the name data shifts out of view on the left.

To keep the vehicle-identification number and car buyer's last name on the screen at all times, no matter what other fields are in view, choose **Lock fields on left {0}** from the Fields menu. In response to the prompt **Enter number of fields to remain stationary:**, enter the number of left-most columns (fields) you want to keep on the screen (in this case, 2) and press Enter. To unlock the fields, select **Lock fields on left {2}**, type *0*, and press Enter.

Blanking a Field

As you enter or edit records in Browse mode, you may enter data in a field by mistake or decide to blank a field's contents before retyping. Position the cursor on the field you want empty of data. Press Alt-F to access the Fields menu, and then select **Blank field**.

You can also remove data by pressing Ctrl-Y to remove all characters right of the cursor. To use this key combination, you must position the cursor *at the beginning* of the field you want to blank.

Freezing a Field

Use **Freeze field** to limit Browse mode's cursor movement to one field. Suppose you need to make a number of changes to the insurance provider fields in a patient database. You can speed up editing if you restrict cursor movement to only the column needing changes. Press Alt-F to access the Fields option on the Browse Menu bar. Select **Freeze field** from the Fields menu and, at the prompt **Enter field name:**, type the name of the field (column) you want to freeze. When you finish the changes, you can cancel the freeze by selecting **Freeze field** from the Fields menu, pressing Backspace to remove the designated freeze field, and then pressing Enter.

Changing the Displayed Size of a Field

Use **Size Field** to change the amount of a field that appears on-screen. (With this option, you change only what appears on-screen, not the database structure itself.) You can see more columns on-screen at one time if you reduce the number of characters appearing on-screen. Suppose that you have established a 20-character width field for city data field. If you are familiar with your data, you can probably identify the name of the city from the first four or five letters. Remember, however, you cannot make the column any narrower than the width of its field name.

Position the cursor on the column (field) you want to "narrow." Press Alt-F to select Fields from the Browse Menu bar, and select **Size field**. The Navigation line at the bottom of the screen displays **Change current column width: ←→ End sizing: ↵** Repeatedly press the left arrow (←) until the column narrows to what you want on-screen, and then press Enter to end sizing. You can still edit data in a field that is too narrow to display the entire contents at once by using the arrow keys to scroll the field contents left and right within the size of the column. Use the same process to widen previously narrowed columns.

Using the Browse Fields Menu

When you use the Browse screen, all of your data fields may not fit on the screen at one time. The Fields menu permits you to control how fields display on the Browse work surface.

Locking Fields

Lock one or more columns on the left side of the screen to prevent the fields from scrolling off the screen as you move the cursor to the right. Use the **Lock fields on left {0}** option from the Fields menu.

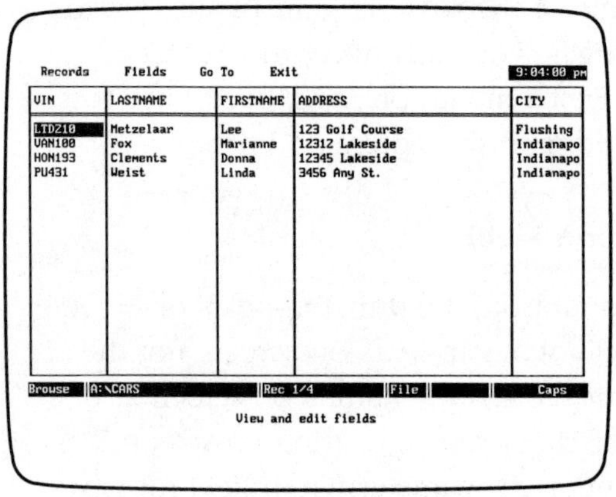

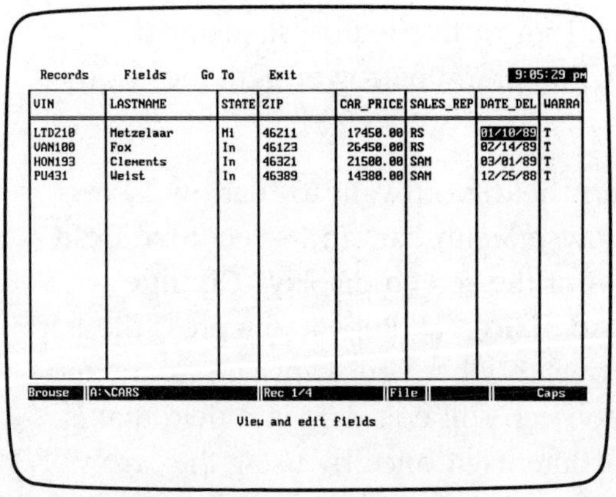

From the Browse screen, press Alt F to access the Fields menu.

Press L to select **Lock fields on left {0}**.

Press 2 and ↵Enter to lock two columns. The number 2 replaces the {0} on the menu. The screen appears normal for the moment, but you have locked the first two columns (fields) so that they will always appear on the screen—in this example, VIN and LASTNAME.

Press Tab repeatedly to move the cursor from field to field across the screen. Notice that as other fields move into view from the right, the VIN and LASTNAME fields stay on the screen while others, such as FIRSTNAME, ADDRESS, and CITY, move out of view on the left side of the screen.

Unlocking Fields

Press Alt F to access the Fields menu. Press L to select **Lock fields on left {2}**. Type 0 and ↵Enter to unlock the fields.

Blanking a Field

Use **Blank** to clear a field before entering new data. Blanking a field is faster than deleting text character by character.

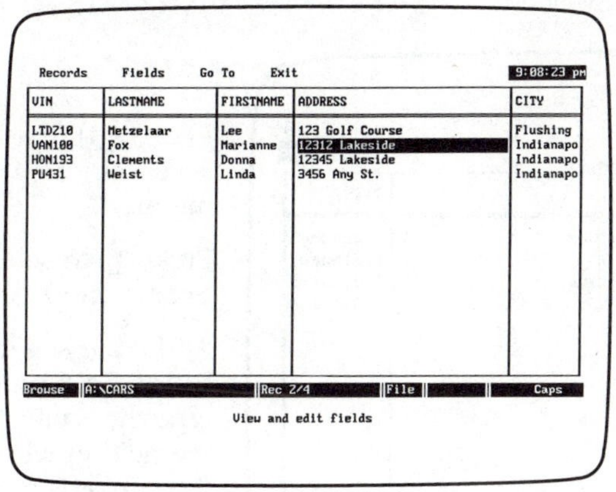

Position the cursor on the field to be blanked.

Press Alt F to access the Fields menu.

Press B to select **Blank field**.

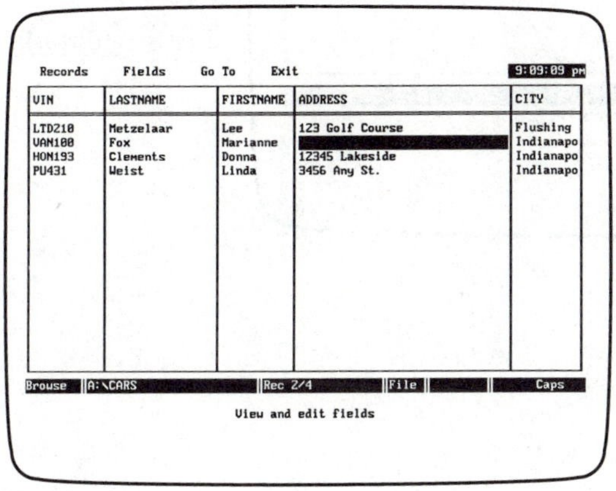

The highlighted field is now blank.

Freezing a Field

Use **Freeze field** to limit the cursor to a specific field. Freezing the field means you can move quickly through your records to edit the same field in many records. The cursor stops at only one field.

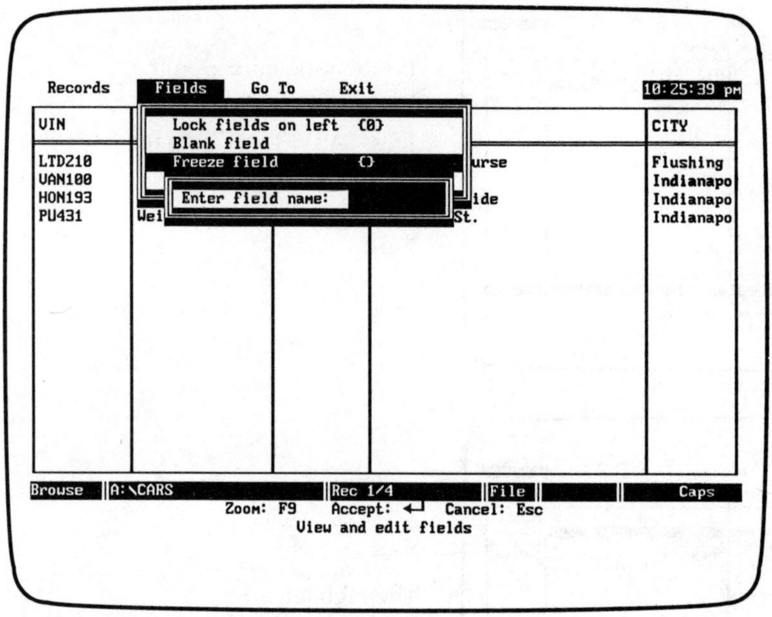

Press Alt F to access the Fields menu.

Press F to select **Freeze field**.

At the message **Enter field name**, type the name of the field in which the cursor is to be frozen.

Press ↵Enter.

To cancel **Freeze field**, press Alt F.

Select F.

Press ←Backspace to delete the field name.

Press ↵Enter.

Changing the Displayed Size of a Field

Size field changes the size of a Browse data field column without changing the field size in the database structure. Use **Size field** to compress the space a field column takes up on the screen. The field contents will scroll within the column size.

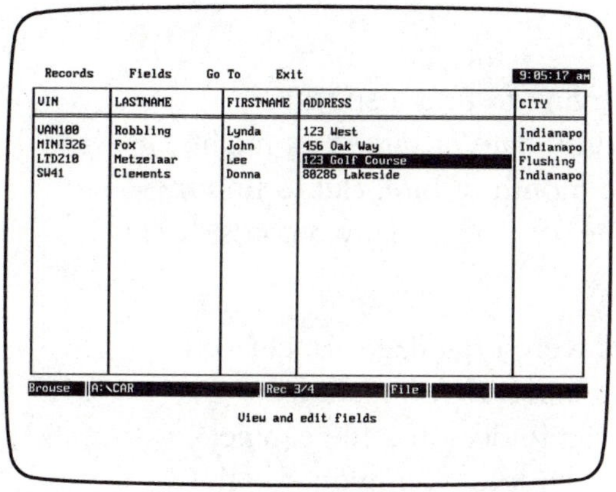

Move the cursor to the field you want to size.

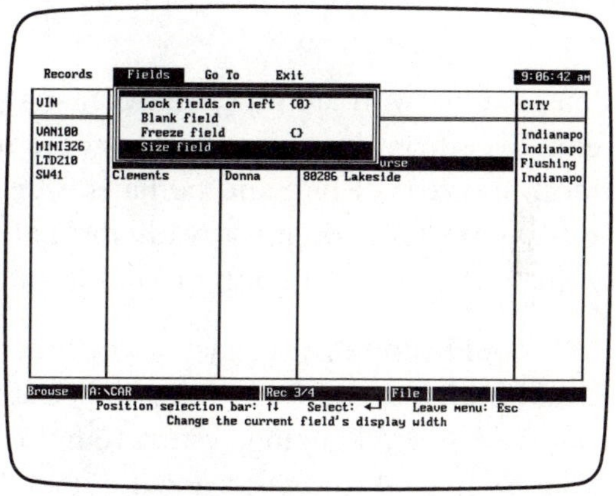

Press Alt F to access the Fields menu.

Press S to select **Size field**.

Press ← to decrease the column size.

or

Press → to increase the size of the column.

Press ↵Enter to exit the **Size field** option.

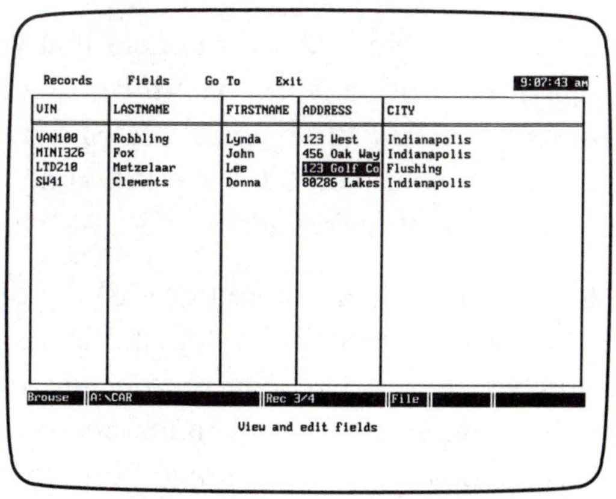

4 Organizing Data

Imagine that you are a personnel manager trying to find a specific employee from employee records organized by date of hire. You might recall the year of hire and perhaps even the month of hire. But to find the employee's file, you must wade through, one at a time, many records that contain the known month or year of hire.

You could shorten your task if your records were organized so that you could find an employee without all that searching. If you maintain a *manual* record-keeping system (employee file folders in a file cabinet), you are limited to *one* organizing field. For example, you might file the folders (records) by employee last name or by Social Security number.

If you maintain your database *electronically* on dBASE, however, you can rearrange records according to the contents of *any* field. For example, you can order records by employee last name and quickly change to a record arrangement based on date of hire or wage rate.

In database terminology, the field that your database records are organized around is the *record key.* Record keys indicate *what* to organize. In terms of *how* to organize, dBASE offers two choices: sorting and indexing. Both methods have the same result—arranging the database in a sequence that makes sense to you—but each method works differently.

Records are initially stored on disk by dBASE in the order you enter the records. Each record is automatically assigned the next highest record number. If you choose to reorder records by indexing, you do not physically rearrange the original records sorted on disk. The indexed records only appear rearranged on screen or in printed output. If, however, you choose to reorder records by sorting, you create a second database on disk in which the records are physically rearranged.

What Is Covered in This Chapter?

In this chapter, you learn about

- Sorting versus indexing
- Organizing data using an index
- Creating an index
- Modifying and removing an index
- Editing with an index in control

Key Words Used in This Chapter

Sort — The process of physically organizing each database record on disk according to the contents of a selected field (record key).

Index — The process of organizing each record by pointing to a tag for every record in the database. Tags (sometimes called index records) contain only the record key and instructions about the location of the complete record. Records are not physically rearranged when organized by an index.

Record key — A field on which to organize records. For example, use the LAST_NAME field in a membership database as the *record key* to organize records by member's last name.

Collating sequence — A built-in set of rules that dictate the sequence when records are sorted or indexed. The usual order places field contents beginning with blanks before field contents beginning with special characters, followed consecutively by fields beginning with numbers, uppercase letters, then lowercase letters.

Introduction

For information to be of value, you must be able to find the information and put it in a useful order. dBASE lets you sequence your data by any data field, or combination of data fields, using indexing and sort techniques.

This database has been organized by the MEM_DATE field. dBASE IV's index options permit you to arrange the data in many ways.

In database terminology, the key field that your database records are organized around is the *record key.*

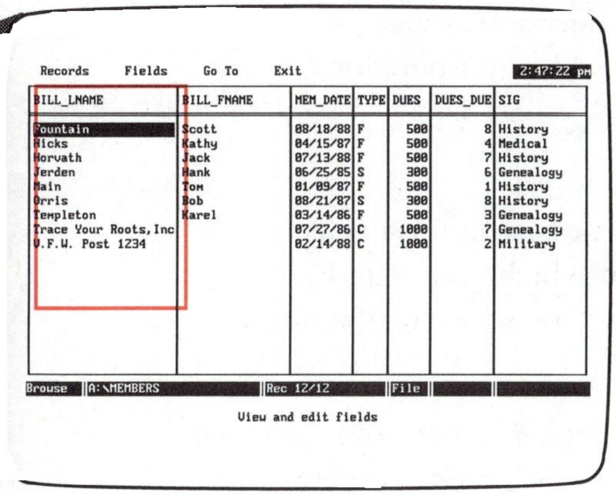

BILL_LNAME	BILL_FNAME	MEM_DATE	TYPE	DUES	DUES_DUE	SIG
Fountain	Scott	08/18/88	F	500	8	History
Hicks	Kathy	04/15/87	F	500	4	Medical
Horvath	Jack	07/13/88	F	500	7	History
Jerden	Hank	06/25/85	S	300	6	Genealogy
Main	Tom	01/09/87	F	500	1	History
Orris	Bob	08/21/87	S	300	8	History
Templeton	Karel	03/14/86	F	500	3	Genealogy
Trace Your Roots,Inc		07/27/86	C	1000	7	Genealogy
V.F.W. Post 1234		02/14/88	C	1000	2	Military

The record key is the member's last name.

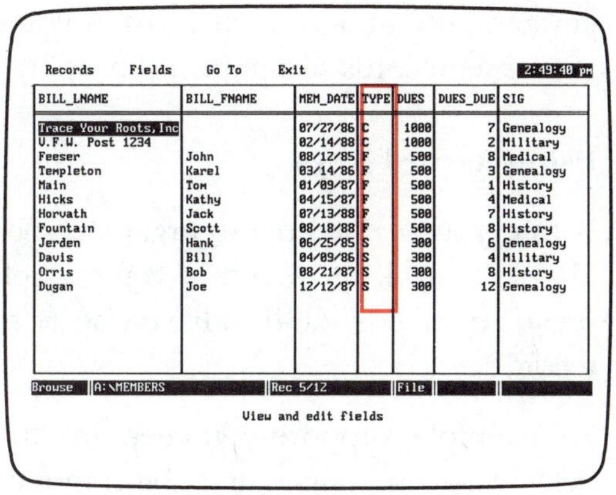

BILL_LNAME	BILL_FNAME	MEM_DATE	TYPE	DUES	DUES_DUE	SIG
Trace Your Roots,Inc		07/27/86	C	1000	7	Genealogy
V.F.W. Post 1234		02/14/88	C	1000	2	Military
Feeser	John	08/12/85	F	500	8	Medical
Templeton	Karel	03/14/86	F	500	3	Genealogy
Main	Tom	01/09/87	F	500	1	History
Hicks	Kathy	04/15/87	F	500	4	Medical
Horvath	Jack	07/13/88	F	500	7	History
Fountain	Scott	08/18/88	F	500	8	History
Jerden	Hank	06/25/85	S	300	6	Genealogy
Davis	Bill	04/09/86	S	300	4	Military
Orris	Bob	08/21/87	S	300	8	History
Dugan	Joe	12/12/87	S	300	12	Genealogy

The record key is the membership type.

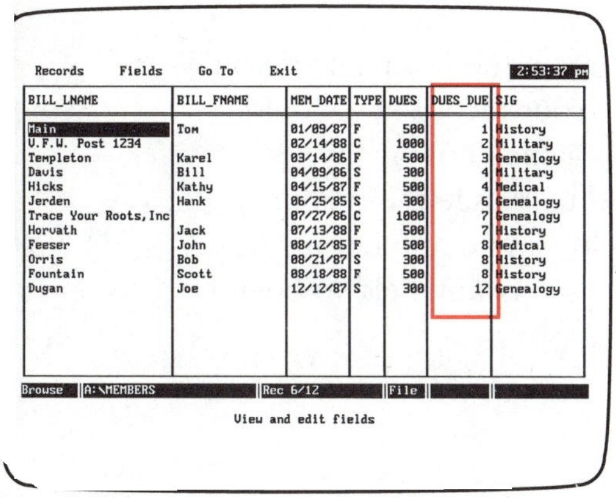

BILL_LNAME	BILL_FNAME	MEM_DATE	TYPE	DUES	DUES_DUE	SIG
Main	Tom	01/09/87	F	500	1	History
V.F.W. Post 1234		02/14/88	C	1000	2	Military
Templeton	Karel	03/14/86	F	500	3	Genealogy
Davis	Bill	04/09/86	S	300	4	Military
Hicks	Kathy	04/15/87	F	500	4	Medical
Jerden	Hank	06/25/85	S	300	6	Genealogy
Trace Your Roots,Inc		07/27/86	C	1000	7	Genealogy
Horvath	Jack	07/13/88	F	500	7	History
Feeser	John	08/12/85	F	500	8	Medical
Orris	Bob	08/21/87	S	300	8	History
Fountain	Scott	08/18/88	F	500	8	History
Dugan	Joe	12/12/87	S	300	12	Genealogy

The record key is the month when dues are due.

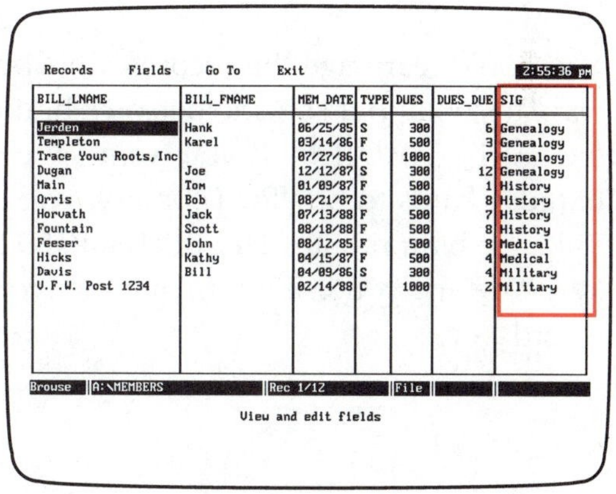

BILL_LNAME	BILL_FNAME	MEM_DATE	TYPE	DUES	DUES_DUE	SIG
Jerden	Hank	06/25/85	S	300	6	Genealogy
Templeton	Karel	03/14/86	F	500	3	Genealogy
Trace Your Roots,Inc		07/27/86	C	1000	7	Genealogy
Dugan	Joe	12/12/87	S	300	12	Genealogy
Main	Tom	01/09/87	F	500	1	History
Orris	Bob	08/21/87	S	300	8	History
Horvath	Jack	07/13/88	F	500	7	History
Fountain	Scott	08/18/88	F	500	8	History
Feeser	John	08/12/85	F	500	8	Medical
Hicks	Kathy	04/15/87	F	500	4	Medical
Davis	Bill	04/09/86	S	300	4	Military
V.F.W. Post 1234		02/14/88	C	1000	2	Military

The record key is the special-interest group.

Organizing Records in dBASE IV

You can rearrange your database on any field or combination of fields that you desire. You should first understand what is meant by record keys and collating sequence. Then you can decide whether to rearrange records using an *Index* operation or a *Sort* operation.

Using Record Keys

Before you decide how to organize your records, you must select useful record keys. A *record key* is a field on which you want to organize records. All files have one or more data items suitable for a record key.

For example, suppose you keep a birthday database that holds just four fields: last name, first name, birth month, and birth date. You enter names and dates as your family and friends come to mind—that is, no particular sequence—knowing that dBASE can later arrange the records in an order you specify. Before you try to pick the record key(s) for these birthday records, decide how you could use a rearranged set of records.

You could rearrange the records alphabetically on the last name if you want to look up a specific person's birthday. Your record key would be the LAST_NAME field. If you want to see at a glance how many birthday cards to buy for February, you could rearrange the original order by birth month. The BIRTHMONTH field can be another record key. Anytime you use your database, you can select any field to be a record key.

Understanding the Collating Sequence

After you pick the record key on which to organize your records, your computer operates with a built-in set of rules—rules that dictate the order of records after a sort or index operation. Suppose, for example, that you organize the records in an inventory database according to the part-number field. Further assume that one record does not contain a part number (blank), another record contains the part-number B025, another record contains the part-number 7803, and another record contains the part-number a456.

The records are rearranged according to rules that state whether blank fields should appear first or last, whether fields starting with *numbers* should precede or follow fields starting with alphabetic characters, and whether fields starting with uppercase letters should precede or follow those starting with lowercase letters. The rules determine the *collating sequence*. The usual collating sequence places blanks first, special characters next, followed by numbers, uppercase letters, and lowercase letters.

After you determine record keys and understand the rules for rearranging letters or numbers (collating sequence), you can decide whether you want to index or sort your records.

Indexing Records

Indexing records is generally preferred over sorting. Very simply, database records organized with an index are not *physically* sorted. The original database remains intact, and dBASE creates a user-specified index(es) within a separate file called a master index. Each separate index contains only the record key—just a small part of the whole record—and instructions (pointer) to locate each whole record. You can create up to 47 indexes within the master index.

One advantage of an index is the speed with which records are rearranged. An index reorders records because the contents are very small records. Unlike a sort operation, an index operation does not need to read each large record into dBASE IV (one character at a time). Instead, dBASE reads each shorter record key in the index and rearranges the record keys, and displays or prints the records in the order of the record number in the index. For example, if you create an index on last name in a database, the first four records in the index might appear in ascending order by last name along with the associated record number.

Anderson	12
Aster	77
Baker	32
Benton	57

When the last-name index controls the database, dBASE reorders the last names and then reads the first record number (pointer) in the index and finds the associated whole record (in this case, record number 12) in the original database. dBASE continues to find records for display or printing in the order of the pointers in the index.

You can create an index on a field at the time you create the field itself. You can also create or modify an index using the Organize menu accessed from the Data panel of the Control Center.

Sorting Records

Sorting involves physically arranging each record according to a selected record key. You might, for instance, sort on the date of a car sale in descending order (most recent date first) and the last name of the car buyer in ascending order. Mixing the Date field type and Character field type is fairly easy in a sort operation. (The same combination in an index operation would require converting Date to Character prior to rearranging records.)

Sorting a file requires more time than indexing it because entire records must be moved, often several times, before the sort is complete. The results of a sort are placed in a separate file, thus requiring much more disk space than an index. One advantage to a sort is that you can have several keys, mixing data types as well as ascending and descending options for each sort key. However, if you master dBASE IV's powerful index features, there are few occasions when you need a sort.

You can sort database records based on values in one or more key fields. You highlight the name of the database you want to sort in the Data panel of the Control Center and press Shift-F2. Then you select **Sort database on field list** and choose from the four available sort types: Ascending ASCII, Descending ASCII, Ascending Dictionary, and Descending Dictionary.

Organizing Records in dBASE IV

Using Record Keys

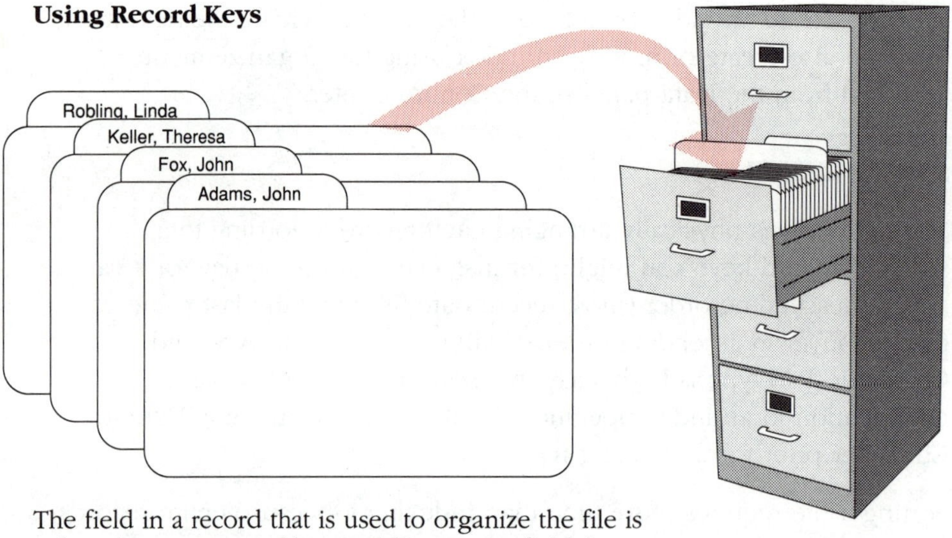

The field in a record that is used to organize the file is referred to as a *record key*. In this case, the field that serves as the record key is the last name.

Record keys can change. For example, you can arrange the file in order of Social Security numbers.

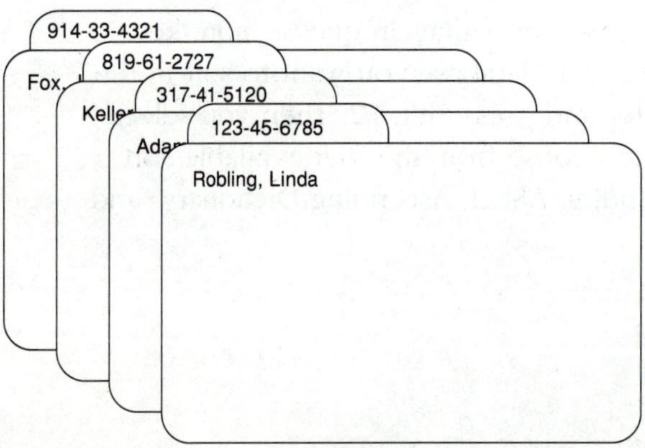

In a manual file, you can have only one record key. To change the record key, you must rearrange the records or create a second copy of all records and file the copies in a different order.

Understanding the Collating Sequence

After you pick the record key on which to organize your records, your computer operates with a built-in set of rules—rules that dictate the order of records after a sort or index operation.

The rules determine the *collating sequence.* The usual collating sequence places blank fields first, special characters next, followed by numbers, uppercase letters, and lowercase letters.

dBASE IV offers four alternative collating sequences for arranging your data. Notice how each of the four options sorts the same list of names.

Ascending ASCII	Descending ASCII	Ascending Dictionary	Descending Dictionary
A..Z a..z 0..9	z..a Z..A 9..0	Aa..Zz 0..9	zZ..aA 9..0
ALBERT	albert	albert	BOB
BOB	Bob	ALBERT	Bob
Bob	BOB	BOB	albert
albert	ALBERT	Bob	ALBERT

Indexing Records

The records in an indexed database are stored in the order each was added to the database. dBASE allows you to create a special file called an index. The index contains one small record for each record in the database. The index record (called a *tag*) contains a record key and a number that points to each record's location.

When the index controls the database, the records display in an organized format. dBASE allows you to create up to 47 indexes associated with one database; the indexes are automatically stored as one master index file.

The database contains records, including a LAST_NAME field.

The database itself is not organized in order by last name.

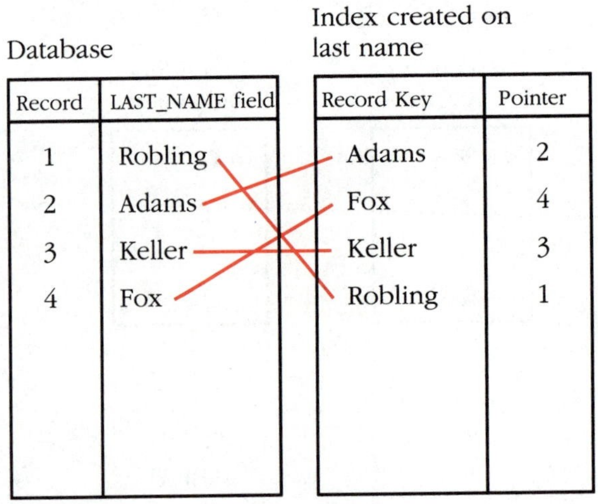

The index record contains only the record key (LAST_NAME field) and a pointer to the location of the complete record.

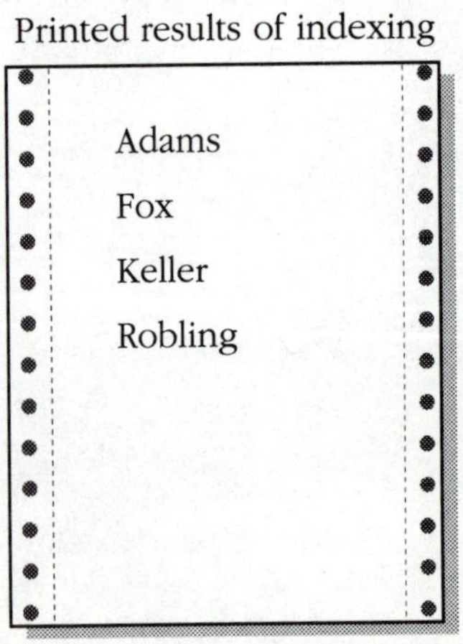

Although the printed copy is organized by last name, the database is not stored in order by last name.

Sorting Records

The records in a sorted database are physically rearranged and stored in a separate file. Records can be sorted from an original file and arranged in sequence by one or more fields.

Sorting a file requires more time than indexing, and the resulting file takes up more disk space than an index.

Unsorted records | Sorted Records

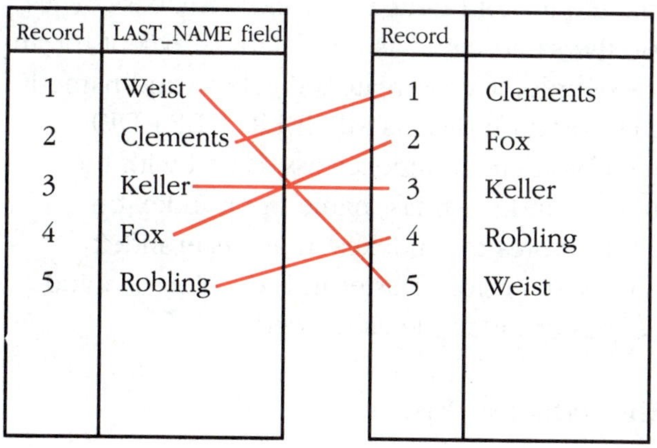

Records in the sorted database are renumbered.

Organizing Data with an Index

Using indexes to organize your data is simple. Create as many indexes as you need, either at the time you create the database structure or later, using the Organize menu. Forget about the indexes until you need to rearrange your database records for display to the screen or printer, and then tell dBASE IV to activate a specific index.

Only one index can be active (one that controls your file) at a time. However, you can have up to 47 indexes open (available) at one time. Although only one index controls the data organization, all indexes are updated when you add, change, or delete records.

dBASE IV creates a special file to hold indexes for each database. The file automatically takes on the same name as the database except for an .MDX file extension. For example, if you create a database and name it MEMBERS, the database is stored on disk as MEMBERS.DBF (.DBF stands for "database file"). If you create indexes associated with the members database (such as an index on last name or an index on membership date), dBASE IV stores the indexes in a master index called MEMBERS.MDX (.MDX stand for "master index"). You can add and delete indexes in the master index file as needed.

Creating an Index in the Database Structure

You can establish an index when you create or modify your database structure. The last column heading on the data design work surface is **Index**. If you indicate Y (Yes) to index any field in the database structure, dBASE IV creates the .MDX file when it creates the database file. If a database already exists, use the **Create new index** option on the **Organize** menu to create a new index.

You can access the work surface used to modify a database structure by highlighting your database choice on the Control Center Data panel and pressing Shift-F2. Locate the index entry for the field you want to index, change **No** to **Yes**, and exit, saving your changes. Your latest index is added to the .MDX master index file.

Using the Organize Menu To Create an Index

Access the Organize menu by highlighting the desired database on the Control Center Data panel and pressing Shift-F2. Use the first six options from the Organize option on the data-design Menu bar to create, modify, activate, and delete indexes.

Use the **Create new index** and **Modify existing index** options to establish and change an index. Select **Order records by index** to tell dBASE IV which open index in the .MDX file to activate. Always pick this option for all indexes defined in dBASE IV. Don't confuse this option with either of the next two options that handle indexes developed with older versions of dBASE.

Use the **Activate .NDX index file** if you want to use an index file created in dBASE III or dBASE III Plus; select **Include .NDX index file** to add an .NDX file to the current catalog. Do not confuse an .NDX file (separate file for each index in the dBASE III series) with an .MDX file (one master index, containing all the indexes in a database, featured in dBASE IV). Select **Remove unwanted index tag** to remove an index from the .MDX master index.

The Organize menu lists three other options. Select **Sort database on field list** if you want to rearrange the records physically in the database (which uses more disk space) over an index operation. You must specify a field or list of fields (sort keys) on which to sort the current database. dBASE IV copies the database to a new database in the sequence of sort keys you specify. Arrange the keys in the list in order of importance. For example, if you want to arrange the database records by city, then by last name within city, specify the city field first and last name field second.

Refer to the "Deleting Records" section in Chapter 3 to review the last two options on the Organize menu: **Unmark all records** and **Erase marked records**.

Organizing Data with an Index

If you choose to rearrange records using an index, dBASE keeps the original order of records in the database file (.DBF extension) and creates a master index file of the same name, but with an .MDX extension.

A master index (.MDX extension) contains as many as 47 record indexes (referred to as *index tags*). dBASE IV creates a master index the first time you create an index in the database structure or when you access the **Create new index** on the data-design work surface.

The master index MEMBERS.MDX and the associated database file MEMBERS.DBF

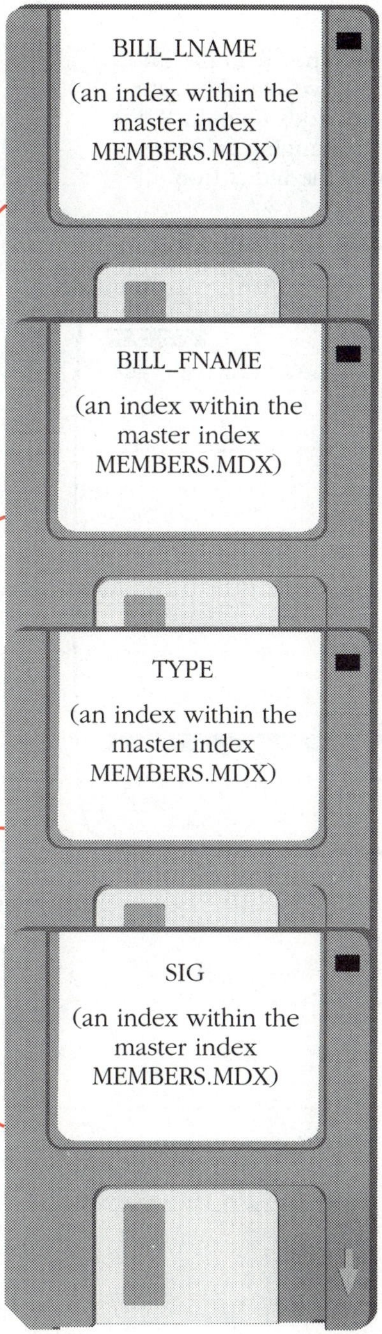

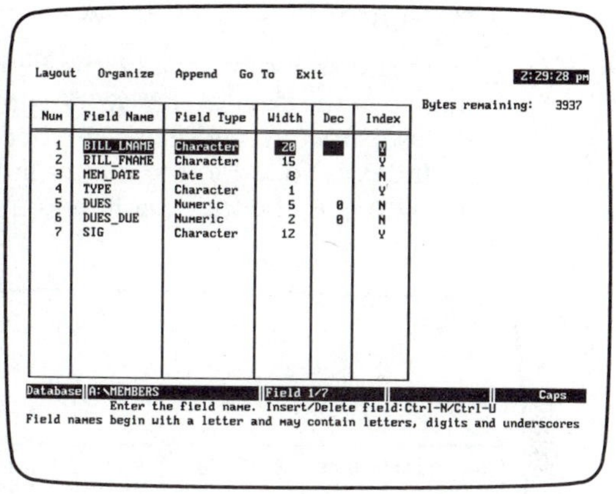

You decide which fields you want to control the arrangement of records printed or viewed on the screen, and set up an index on each of these fields.

To create an index, you specify **Y** in the Index column as you create a field.

You can also use the **Organize** menu on the data-design work surface to create, modify, and delete an index.

Creating an Index in the Database Structure

You create an index for a field when you type Y in the index column on the data-design work surface. If you modify your database structure and mark another field index column Y, the new index is added to the master index. Changing an entry from Y to N in the index column removes the index from the master index.

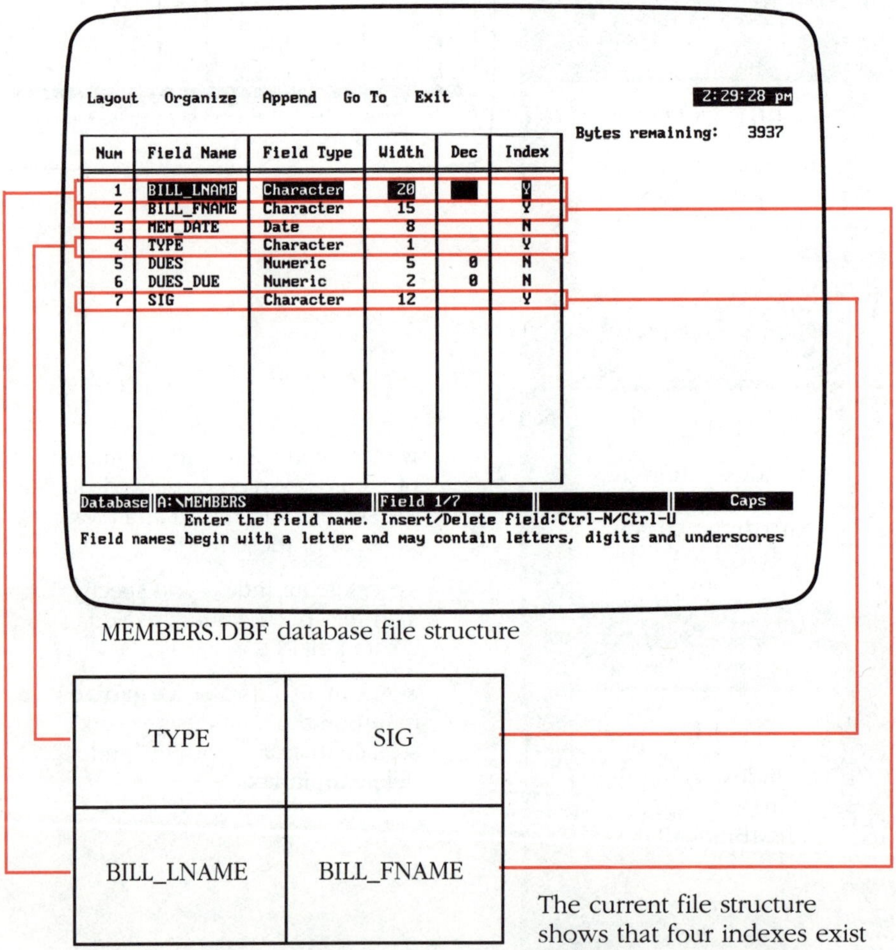

MEMBERS.DBF database file structure

MEMBERS.MDX master index file

The current file structure shows that four indexes exist within the master index.

Using the Organize Menu To Create an Index

Use the Organize menu on the data-design work surface to create, maintain, modify, and activate indexes.

Use this option to modify an index name, expression, or the order.

Activate a dBASE III index by using this option.

Use this option to create a new index. The index then becomes a part of the master index file for the current database.

Use this option to tell dBASE IV which index you want to be the master index.

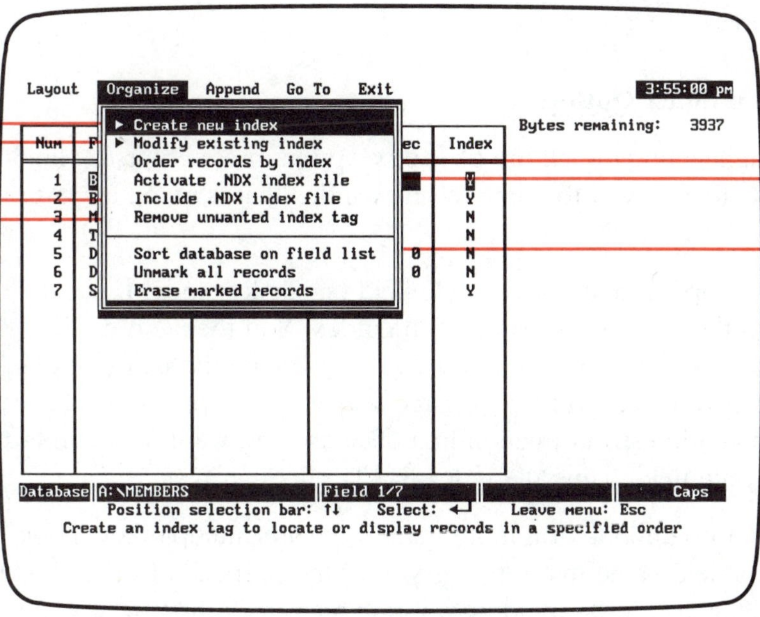

Use this option to remove indexes you no longer need from the master index file.

Use this option to copy data from the current database into a second sorted database.

Use this option to add a dBASE III index to the master index.

Creating an Index from the Organize Menu

If a database already exists, use the **Create new index** option on the Organize menu to create a new index. Complete up to four items on the **Create new index** menu to describe the index:

- Name of index
- Index expression
- Order of index
- Display first duplicate key only

You must enter your choices for the first two options on the **Create new index** menu. Respond to either of the remaining two options, if appropriate.

Name-of-index Option

After highlighting the **Name of index** option, press Enter. A blinking underscore asks you to name the new index that is saved as part of the master index.

If you set up an index on a single field (single-key index), use the name of the field as the name of the index. You then can easily remember the name of the index by just recalling the name of the field on which you want to rearrange records. For example, if you have name and address information in a database and want to set an index on the state field, name the index STATE.

If you set up an index on more than one field (multiple-key index), try to pick a field name that reminds you of the purpose of the index. For example, if you want an address listing rearranged first by state and then by city within state, name the index STATECITY.

Follow the same conventions to name an index as you do to name a field—the name can be 1–10 characters and include letters, numbers, and underscores. The first character of the name must be a letter.

Index-expression Option

The index expression is the field or field combination on which to base rearranging records. You must define the index expression when you create an index using the Organize menu. Highlight the **Index expression** option and press Enter; a blinking underscore prompts you to respond to the message at the bottom of the screen: **Specify the index expression or field by which to order this database file**. If you know the rules for typing the condition(s) for your new index and remember the field name(s) you want to use, start typing! Otherwise, watch the Navigation line for instructions.

The Navigation line displays **Enter an index expression. Expression builder:Shift-F1**. Press Shift-F1 to open a window containing three columns: **Fieldname**, **Operator**, and **Function**. The **Fieldname** column contains a list of fields in the current database. The **Operators** column lists operator symbols that let you combine keys for multiple-key indexes. The **Functions** column lists a special set of dBASE commands for manipulating data.

To reorder your address database based on only the ZIPCODE field, position the highlighted bar on **ZIPCODE** in the Fieldname column (use the down arrow [↓] to scroll any additional field names in view). Press Enter to transfer the name to the blinking underscore prompt. Press Enter again to complete specifying the index expression.

Order and Display-first-duplicate Options

Use the **Order of Index** option to specify that the record keys should be arranged in ascending (lowest to highest) or descending (highest to lowest) order. Select **Display first duplicate key only** to hide any duplicate keys. For example, suppose that you want a list of ZIP codes in your address database and you have the same ZIP code in 10 records. By setting the first-duplicate-only option to YES, you instruct dBASE to use only the first occurrence of each unique ZIP code.

Creating an Index from the Organize Menu

From the Control Center Data panel, highlight the database that contains the file for which you plan to create an index.

Press ⇧Shift F2 to access the data-design work surface.

Press Alt O to select the Organize menu.

Press C to select **Create new index**.

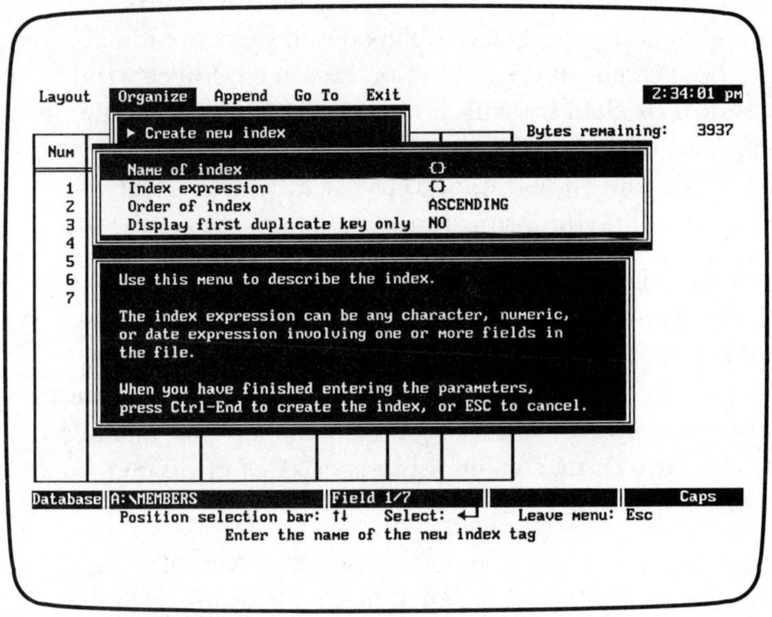

The **Create new index** menu displays four choices. You must complete the first two entries.

Name of index

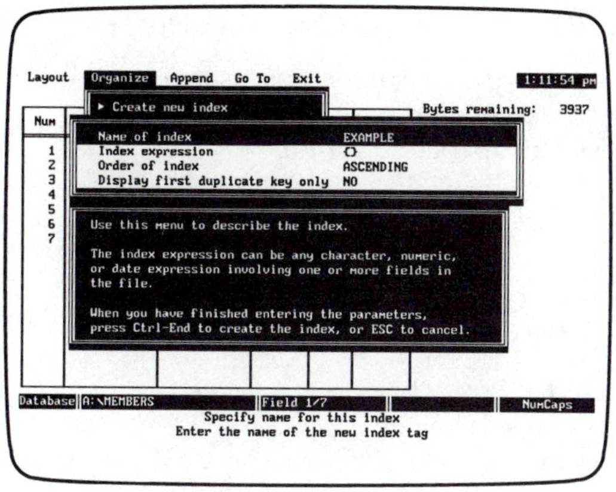

The **Name of index** option permits you to assign a name to the new index.

Press N to select **Name of index**. Type the index name.

The first character in the name must be a letter. After that, you can use as many as 10 characters (letters, numbers, and underscore symbol).

Press ↵Enter to complete your entry.

Index expression

The **Index expression** option defines how dBASE makes the new index. That is, the expression you define tells dBASE what field(s) to use when rearranging the records. For instance, you might select TYPE+BILL_LNAME as the index expression.

Press I to select **Index expression**.

You can press ⇧Shift F1 to display the expression builder. (Remember, you cannot use logical or memo fields to create your expression.)

Fieldname	List of field names from the current database structure
Operator	Used to join fields
Function	Used to manipulate data

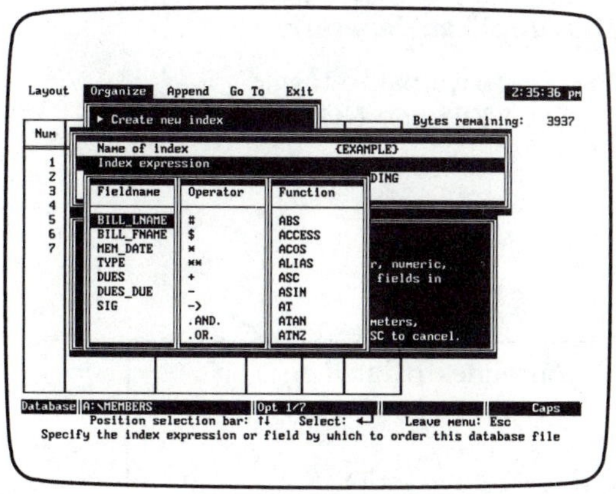

Highlight the entry and press ↵Enter.

or

Type the first letter of the new menu item and press ↵Enter.

If two items share the same first letter, the highlight bar will stop on the first occurrence. Move the highlighter to the item you want to use, and then press ↵Enter.

After you enter the expression, press ↵Enter.

Creating an Index from the Organize Menu

Order of index

Use **Order of index** to specify ascending (A to Z) or descending (Z to A) order.

In an ascending index, capital letters come before lowercase letters. For instance, in ascending order, *Drum* comes before *apple*. In descending order indexes, capital letters come after lowercase letters; *apple* appears before *Drum*.

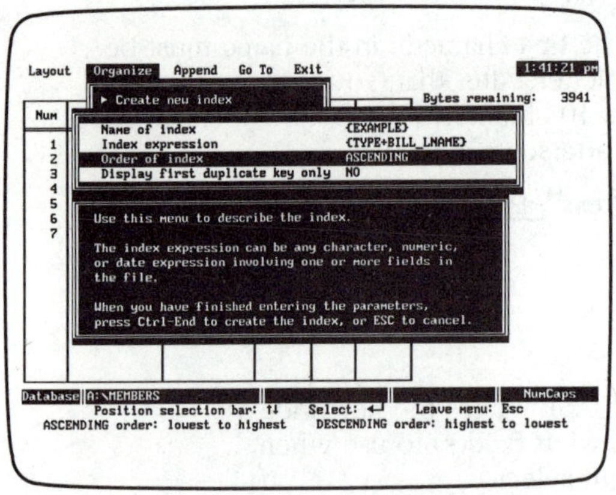

Press O to access **Order of index**.

Use the space bar to toggle between ascending and descending order of records.

Display first duplicate key only

Use the **Display first duplicate key only** option to tell dBASE IV to include only the first record (when duplicates exist) for each index expression.

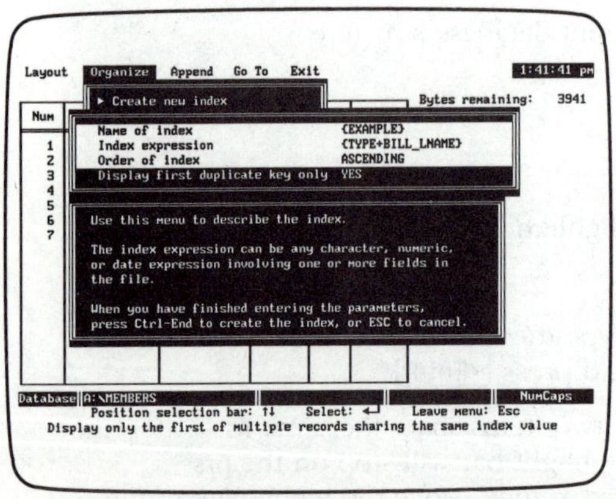

Press D to access **Display first duplicate key only**.

Use the space bar to toggle between **YES** and **NO**.

Press Ctrl End when you finish entering your index parameters.

or

Press Esc to quit, if you decide not to create the index.

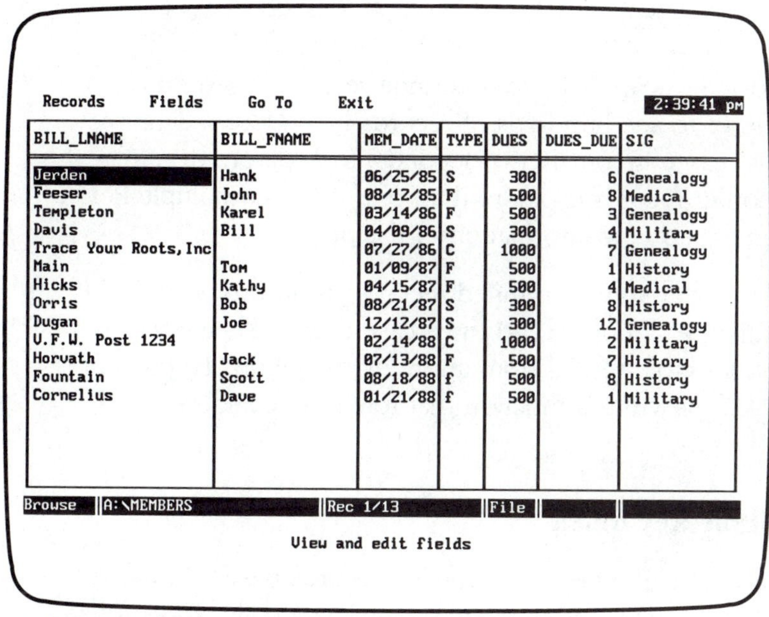

Records Fields Go To Exit 2:39:41 pm

BILL_LNAME	BILL_FNAME	MEM_DATE	TYPE	DUES	DUES_DUE	SIG
Jerden	Hank	06/25/85	S	300	6	Genealogy
Feeser	John	08/12/85	F	500	8	Medical
Templeton	Karel	03/14/86	F	500	3	Genealogy
Davis	Bill	04/09/86	S	300	4	Military
Trace Your Roots, Inc		07/27/86	C	1000	7	Genealogy
Main	Tom	01/09/87	F	500	1	History
Hicks	Kathy	04/15/87	F	500	4	Medical
Orris	Bob	08/21/87	S	300	8	History
Dugan	Joe	12/12/87	S	300	12	Genealogy
V.F.W. Post 1234		02/14/88	C	1000	2	Military
Horvath	Jack	07/13/88	F	500	7	History
Fountain	Scott	08/18/88	f	500	8	History
Cornelius	Dave	01/21/88	f	500	1	Military

Browse | A:\MEMBERS | Rec 1/13 | File

View and edit fields

MEMBERS database prior to activating an index

New index created from the Organize menu to rearrange records on BILL_LNAME

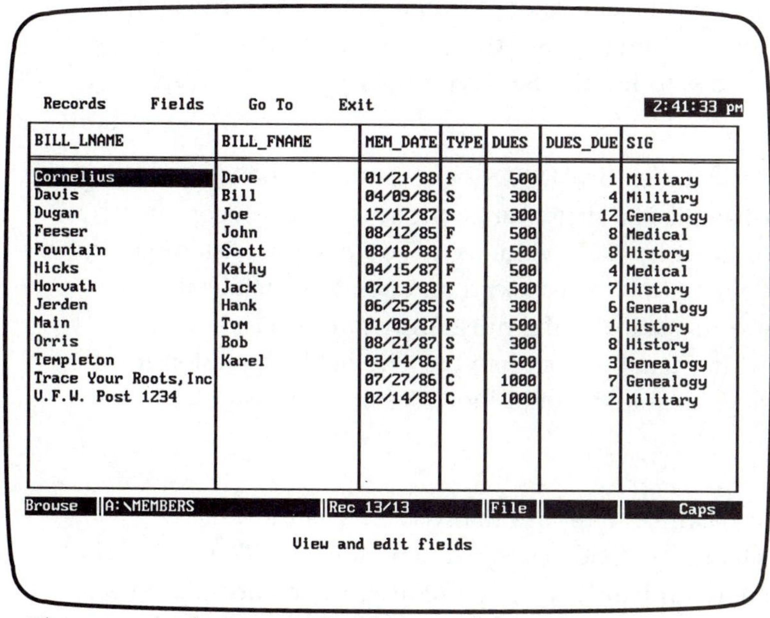

Records Fields Go To Exit 2:41:33 pm

BILL_LNAME	BILL_FNAME	MEM_DATE	TYPE	DUES	DUES_DUE	SIG
Cornelius	Dave	01/21/88	f	500	1	Military
Davis	Bill	04/09/86	S	300	4	Military
Dugan	Joe	12/12/87	S	300	12	Genealogy
Feeser	John	08/12/85	F	500	8	Medical
Fountain	Scott	08/18/88	f	500	8	History
Hicks	Kathy	04/15/87	F	500	4	Medical
Horvath	Jack	07/13/88	F	500	7	History
Jerden	Hank	06/25/85	S	300	6	Genealogy
Main	Tom	01/09/87	F	500	1	History
Orris	Bob	08/21/87	S	300	8	History
Templeton	Karel	03/14/86	F	500	3	Genealogy
Trace Your Roots, Inc		07/27/86	C	1000	7	Genealogy
V.F.W. Post 1234		02/14/88	C	1000	2	Military

Browse | A:\MEMBERS | Rec 13/13 | File | Caps

View and edit fields

The same database controlled by an index on the BILL_LNAME field

Creating Multiple-Key Indexes

You have seen dBASE's capability to rearrange records based on one field. It is impressive to see hundreds of records in a address database rearranged by last name in a matter of seconds. In addition, dBASE allows you to reorder records on more than one field—a multiple-key index—and even create new information in the process!

Always check to see that any rearranged records are in proper order. If, for example, a mixture of upper- and lowercase data exists in records, you might get undesirable results from an index operation. To prevent this mistake, dBASE provides a function that forces all characters to uppercase.

Creating a Multiple-Key Index

You can easily activate an index that reorders records based on more than one field. Think about student records kept by a college—including the data fields FIRST_NAME, LAST_NAME, MAJOR, SEX, AGE, and ENTER_DATE (enrollment date). Assume that the records in the database stored on disk are in the order of enrollment date. There are numerous useful ways to reorder the records for printing or display on the screen.

You can establish an index on MAJOR only. But think how much more information you have if you first arrange the records by major, then by SEX within major, then by AGE within sex. You can establish multiple-key indexes by joining field names with an operator, such as the plus sign (+). Specify your choice of the most important field, then the most important field within that field, and so on. The field expression for the multiple-key college example would look like the following:

```
MAJOR + SEX + AGE
```

Consider another example. Suppose that you keep an inventory database that includes the fields DESC (description), UNITPRICE, and ON_HAND (quantity on hand). You can reorder the records based on each item's total cost in descending order—yet total cost isn't even a field in the database! Just join the numeric fields UNITPRICE and ON_HAND with the multiplication operator (*) when indicating a field expression.

Until you are quite familiar with the format of typing an index expression, press the Shift-F1 key to access the Fieldname column, the Operators column, and the Functions column. To *concatenate* (put together) two or more fields to act as a single key, select the first field name from the Fieldname column and press Shift-F1 again to continue selecting the remaining field names and operators.

Indexing on Upper- and Lowercase Characters

Your computer's collating rules cause uppercase (or capital) letters to arrange before lowercase letters. dBASE IV is a case-sensitive database program because it treats upper- and lowercase letters differently. This can be a problem if, for example, names contain lowercase first letters, or a field containing a code, such as type of membership, accidentally contains both upper- and lowercase letters. Case problems can be prevented by using the **UPPER** function from the Shift-F1 Functions column.

At the **Index expression** option, press Shift-F1, select **UPPER** from the Function column by pressing U—or highlighting **UPPER**—and press Enter. You now see **UPPER()** on the expression list. To use the UPPER() function, place the name of the key field you want used without regard to case between the parentheses. To enter the key-field name, backspace the cursor to the right parenthesis, press Shift-F1, and select the name from the Fieldname column that you want added to the expression. The expression should appear as **UPPER(field_name)**.

The many other functions available in dBASE IV are discussed at length in Que Corporation's *dBASE IV Handbook*.

Creating a Multiple-Key Index

One advantage of creating an index using the Organize menu is that you can create complex reordering conditions. It may be useful, for example, to arrange your database records by first name as well as last name, or city as well as state. You may want your member list organized alphabetically by last name and further arranged by first name.

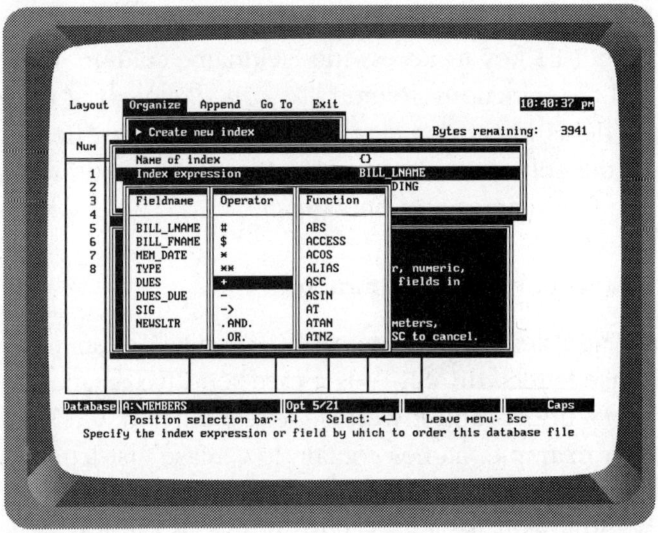

To create an index that sorts your database on more than one field, press C to access **Create new index** on the Organize menu.

Press N to access the **Name of index** menu.

Type the name for this index and press ↵Enter.

Press I to access the **Index expression** menu.

Press ⇧Shift F1 to activate the expression builder.

Select a field name from the Fieldname column.

Press ⇧Shift F1 and select an operator (such as plus [+]).

Press ⇧Shift F1 and select a second field name from the Fieldname column.

Continue to select all the field names and operators that will comprise the index expression. When you have finished creating the index, press Ctrl End.

Indexing on Upper- and Lowercase Characters

dBASE's expression builder offers you 130 functions with which you can effectively manipulate your data. Two of the functions are UPPER() and LOWER().

The UPPER() and LOWER() options cause the index to treat upper- and lowercase characters the same. Without changing the data in the database, UPPER() shifts the data in the index to uppercase. LOWER() shifts data to lowercase.

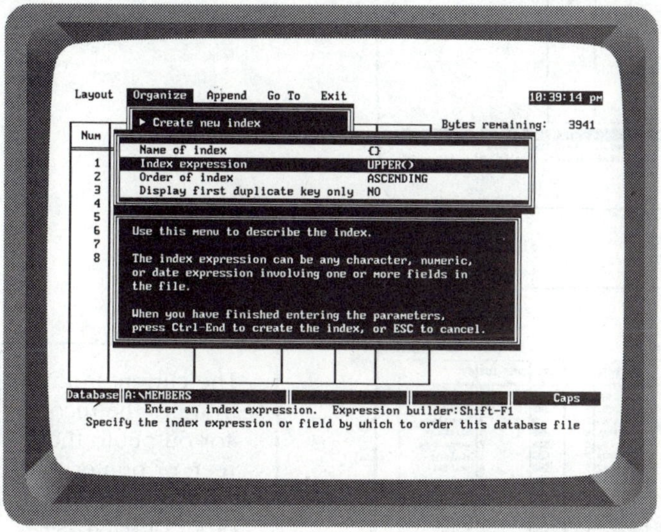

From the **Organize** menu, select **Create new index**, then choose **Name of index** to assign a name, and access the **Index expression** option.

Press Shift F1 to activate the expression builder.

Move the highlighter to the Function column and press U; press Enter to select UPPER from the Function column.

or

Press L O W and press Enter to select LOWER from the Function column.

Press ← to position the cursor on top of the right parenthesis.

Press Shift F1 and select the field name to be used with UPPER/LOWER.

The prompt **UPPER (field_name)** or **LOWER (field_name)** displays.

Finish creating the index.

Creating Multiple-Key Indexes

Indexes at Work

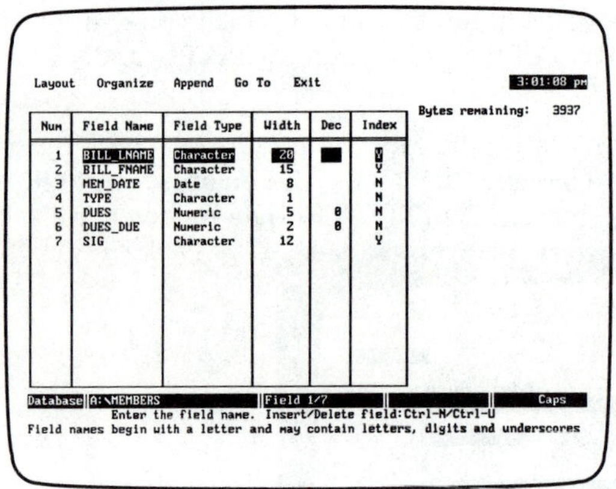

Database structure

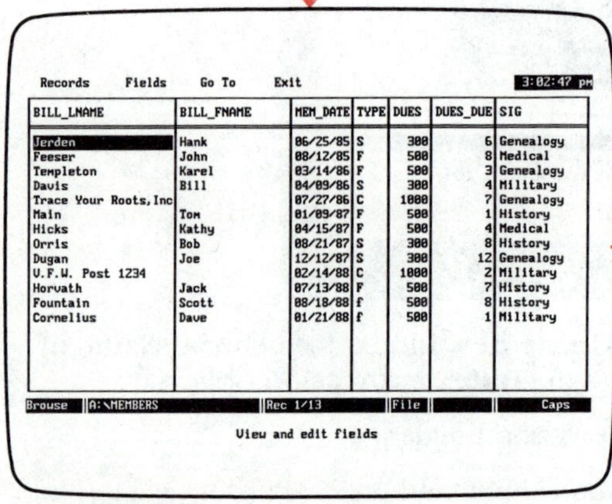

Database contents

The records remain in the order in which they were entered.

The current index rearranges the records for output to the screen or printer, but does not alter the order of database contents on disk.

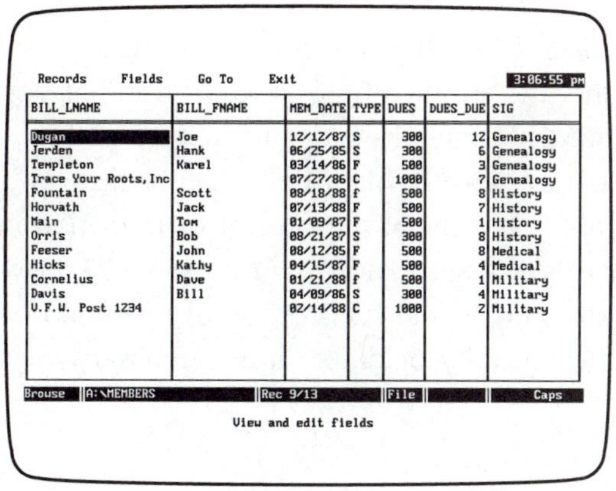

Records Fields Go To Exit 3:06:55 pm

BILL_LNAME	BILL_FNAME	MEM_DATE	TYPE	DUES	DUES_DUE	SIG
Dugan	Joe	12/12/87	S	300	12	Genealogy
Jerden	Hank	06/25/85	S	300	6	Genealogy
Templeton	Karel	03/14/86	F	500	3	Genealogy
Trace Your Roots, Inc		07/27/86	C	1000	7	Genealogy
Fountain	Scott	08/18/88	f	500	8	History
Horvath	Jack	07/13/88	F	500	7	History
Main	Tom	01/09/87	F	500	1	History
Orris	Bob	08/21/87	S	300	8	History
Feeser	John	08/12/85	F	500	8	Medical
Hicks	Kathy	04/15/87	F	500	4	Medical
Cornelius	Dave	01/21/88	f	500	1	Military
Davis	Bill	04/09/86	S	300	4	Military
V.F.W. Post 1234		02/14/88	C	1000	2	Military

Browse | A:\MEMBERS | Rec 9/13 | File | | Caps

View and edit fields

The index expression SIG+BILL_LNAME in control

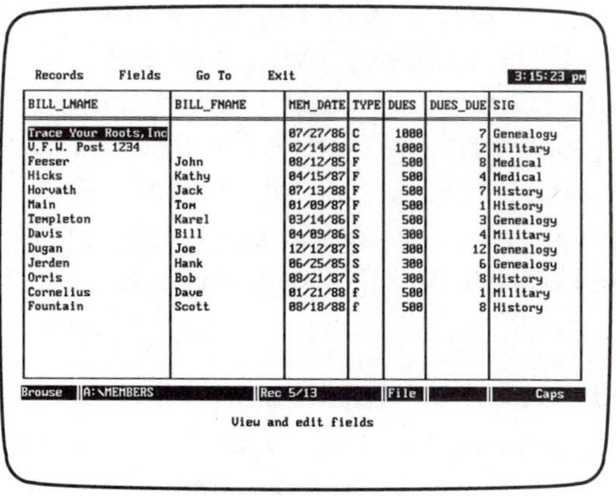

Records Fields Go To Exit 3:15:23 pm

BILL_LNAME	BILL_FNAME	MEM_DATE	TYPE	DUES	DUES_DUE	SIG
Trace Your Roots, Inc		07/27/86	C	1000	7	Genealogy
V.F.W. Post 1234		02/14/88	C	1000	2	Military
Feeser	John	08/12/85	F	500	8	Medical
Hicks	Kathy	04/15/87	F	500	4	Medical
Horvath	Jack	07/13/88	F	500	7	History
Main	Tom	01/09/87	F	500	1	History
Templeton	Karel	03/14/86	F	500	3	Genealogy
Davis	Bill	04/09/86	S	300	4	Military
Dugan	Joe	12/12/87	S	300	12	Genealogy
Jerden	Hank	06/25/85	S	300	6	Genealogy
Orris	Bob	08/21/87	S	300	8	History
Cornelius	Dave	01/21/88	f	500	1	Military
Fountain	Scott	08/18/88	f	500	8	History

Browse | A:\MEMBERS | Rec 5/13 | File | | Caps

View and edit fields

The index expression TYPE+BILL_LNAME in control

Upper- and lowercase characters are arranged differently. Notice the order of records containing "f" as opposed to "F".

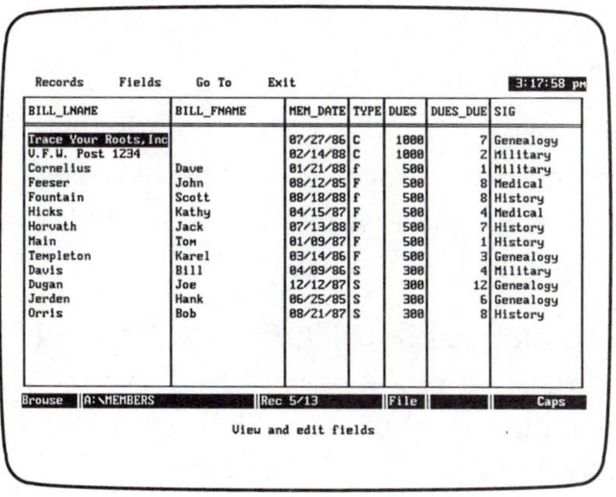

Records Fields Go To Exit 3:17:58 pm

BILL_LNAME	BILL_FNAME	MEM_DATE	TYPE	DUES	DUES_DUE	SIG
Trace Your Roots, Inc		07/27/86	C	1000	7	Genealogy
V.F.W. Post 1234		02/14/88	C	1000	2	Military
Cornelius	Dave	01/21/88	f	500	1	Military
Feeser	John	08/12/85	F	500	8	Medical
Fountain	Scott	08/18/88	f	500	8	History
Hicks	Kathy	04/15/87	F	500	4	Medical
Horvath	Jack	07/13/88	F	500	7	History
Main	Tom	01/09/87	F	500	1	History
Templeton	Karel	03/14/86	F	500	3	Genealogy
Davis	Bill	04/09/86	S	300	4	Military
Dugan	Joe	12/12/87	S	300	12	Genealogy
Jerden	Hank	06/25/85	S	300	6	Genealogy
Orris	Bob	08/21/87	S	300	8	History

Browse | A:\MEMBERS | Rec 5/13 | File | | Caps

View and edit fields

The index expression UPPER(TYPE)+UPPER(BILL_LNAME) in control

Upper- and lowercase characters are arranged as though they were all uppercase. Notice the order now of records containing "f" as opposed to "F".

Selecting, Modifying, and Removing an Index

Perhaps by now you are beginning to see the importance of the *creating* process in database software. It takes time to analyze what you need from your database—the information—in order to understand what you need to place in the database—the data fields. More time is necessary to create useful indexes that control the output of information to the screen or printer in a meaningful sequence. You must know how to activate a database to add, edit, and delete records. You must also be able to activate an index, and then modify or delete it as necessary.

Selecting an Index for Use

The newly created indexes appear in the .MDX master file with the same name as the database file (.DBF extension). When you put a database into use, usually from the Control Center Data panel, all associated indexes automatically open. As you update the database by adding, altering, or deleting records, all indexes update as well—automatically. If, however, you want to see your data in one of the indexed sequences, you must tell dBASE IV which index you want to control the order of the data.

To activate an index, select **Order records by index** from the Organize menu. Two windows appear in the upper right corner of the screen. The rightmost window contains a list of index names (tags) contained in the .MDX file. Use the up- and down-arrow keys to scroll the highlight bar through the list.

The smaller window to the left displays the index expression defined at the time the highlighted index name was created. Press Enter to select the index tag you want. After you select the Exit menu option **Order records by index**, your file is organized by the chosen index.

Be sure to activate the index you want before using Browse/Edit and printing reports (Quick Report or custom report) or labels. The just-activated index remains in control until you activate a different index or close the file at the Control Center Data panel.

Modifying an Existing Index

If an index already exists, use the Organize menu's **Modify existing index** option to change the index criteria. The option functions exactly like the **Create new index** option—with one difference. When you select the index to be modified, you can see current specifications in the fields. You must specify at least the first two of four index criteria:

- Name of index
- Index expression
- Order of index
- Display first duplicate key only

Access the four specifications and make any appropriate changes. You can edit the existing specifications, blank the contents of the field and retype them, or use the Shift-F1 lists of field names, operators, and functions. When you exit the data-design work surface, the revised index specifications are saved and the index rebuilt.

Removing an Index

As you examine your database structures, you may find an index that is no longer used. Because any index takes up space on disk and affects the speed of dBASE IV in Browse/Edit mode, remove indexes from disk that are not being used on a regular basis. Remember, you can easily create the index again. The more records your database contains, the more your database speed is affected by the number of indexes in use.

To remove an index, access the Organize menu on the data-design work surface, position the highlight bar on **Remove unwanted index tag**, and press Enter. You then highlight the index name (tag) to be removed and press Enter. The tag disappears immediately—without a warning message.

Selecting, Modifying, and Removing an Index

Selecting an Index

After you create an index, it is stored in the master index file (.mdx).

To select an index, select the database.

Access the **Organize** menu.

Press [O] to select **Order records by index**.

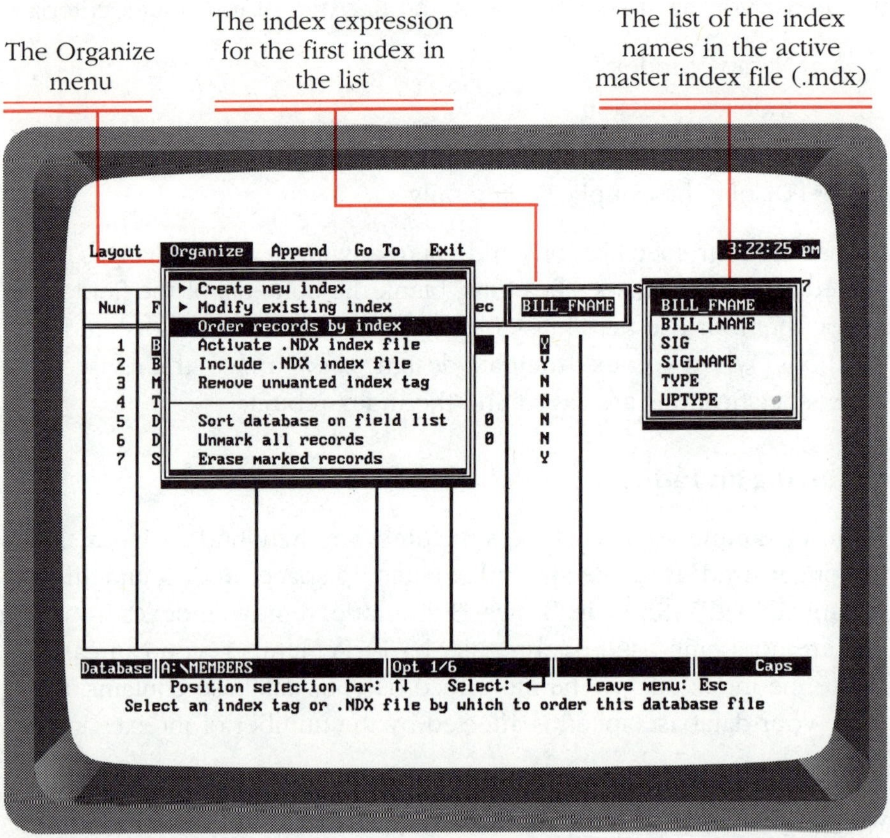

Select the index you plan to use.

The index name tag you select controls the database until you select another index or close the database.

Modifying an Existing Index

You use this procedure to change the information for existing indexes. The process is the same as for creating an index, with one exception—a list of index names (active in the current .mdx file) appears in the upper right portion of your screen, *and* a box appears next to the list, which contains the index expression for the index you've highlighted.

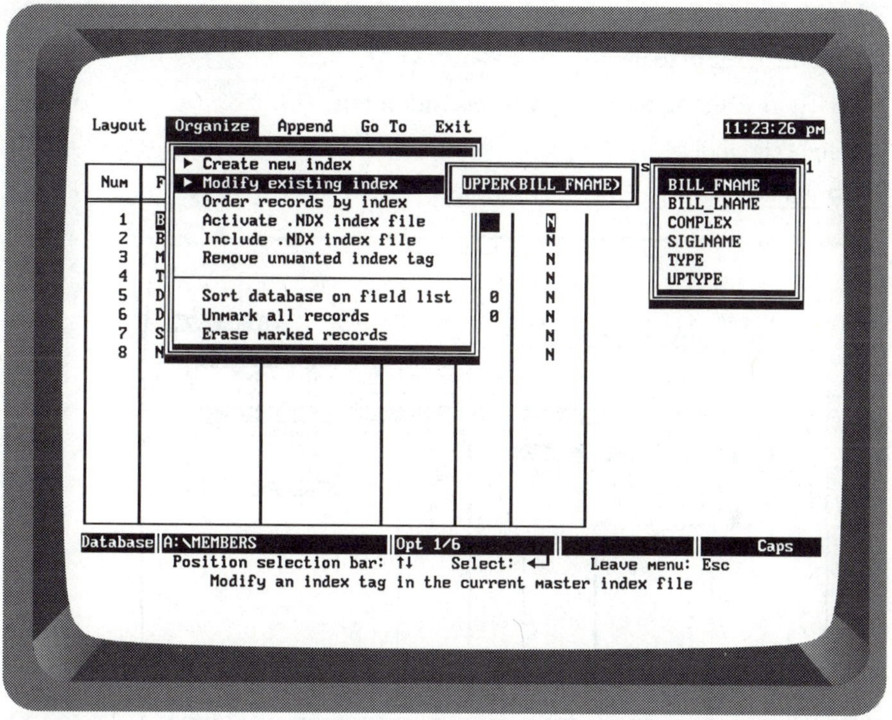

Select the database.

Access the **Organize** menu.

Press M to access the **Modify existing index** option.

Highlight the name of the index you plan to modify.

Press ↵Enter to display the **Index expression** menu.

Select and modify the settings.

Press Ctrl End to save your changes and exit.

or

Press Esc to exit without saving your changes.

Removing an Index

Because indexes use valuable disk space and slow dBASE processing time, you should remove indexes that aren't being used.

Select the database.

Access the **Organize** menu.

Press R to select **Remove unwanted index tag**.

Highlight the index tag you plan to remove.

Press ↵Enter.

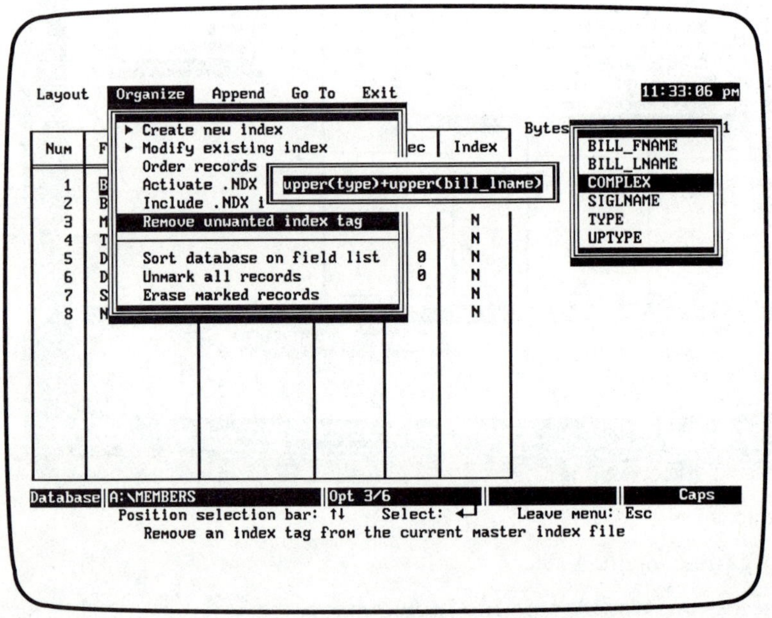

The index tag is immediately removed from the .mdx file.

Because the deleted index is not a DOS file, it cannot be "undeleted."

Managing Indexes

To recap, you use indexes to control the order in which your database records are arranged for printing or viewing on the screen. An index does not change the order of the records in the database stored on disk.

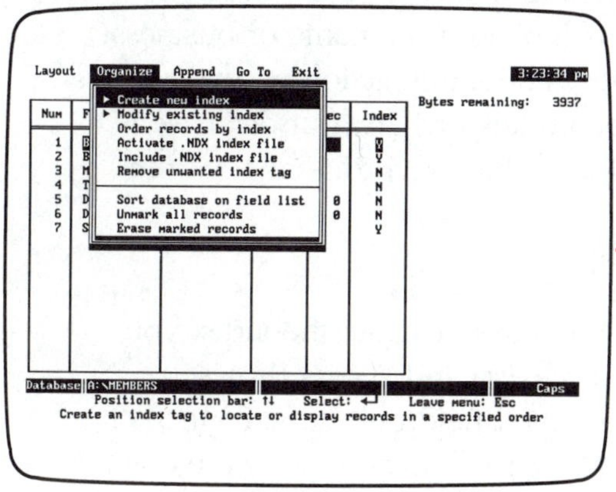

The **Organize** menu

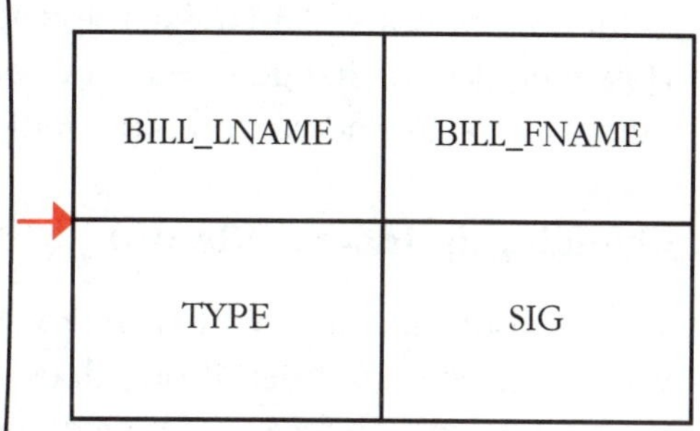

The master index file .mdx

By using the Organize menu, you can perform the following tasks:

- Create new indexes
- Modify existing indexes
- Activate an index to control your database
- Use dBASE III indexes or convert them to dBASE IV indexes
- Delete indexes that are no longer needed

Editing with an Index in Control

Browsing through a database editing records can be difficult when those records are not in any meaningful sequence. Recall that records in the database exist on disk in the order in which the records were entered. The last name *Mitchell* might appear after the last name *Simpson.* If you edit with an index in control, such as a last name index, you can find records as easily as looking up a name or business in the phone book. All indexes update without any action on your part. However, if you change one of the record keys when your database is running with an index, you must indicate which record is now current.

Changing an Indexed Record

To edit your database with an index in control, activate the index you want (or create an index if one does not exist) and access Browse mode. The only difference between editing a field under the control of an index and any other field involves the cursor location after the edit.

Suppose that you have an employee database under the control of an index on LAST_NAME, and you need to change only the DEPARTMENT information for several employees. Scroll through the alphabetical listing of names to find the first record that needs changing. To edit a record by changing any field except the controlling field, simply navigate in Browse mode to the record needing change and enter the change. The record you have just changed—the one on which the cursor is resting—is the current record. If you move the cursor from the current record by pressing the down arrow key, the next record becomes the current record, and you continue to browse your way through the alphabetical listing. The field being changed is not controlled by the active index, and you control cursor movement.

Suppose instead that you need to edit the LAST_NAME field for several employees after a rash of June weddings—the first change from **Fischer** to **Wilson**, and a second change from **Harless** to **Osborne**. Scroll through the records organized alphabetically on last name and change the Fischer record. As soon as you move the cursor off the record just changed, all indexes are updated and the changed record appears in its new location in the file—in this case, in the W's (for **Wilson**). The cursor follows the revised record to its new location and advances to the next record, such as **Wiltshire**. It's a long way back to the letter H for the next change, **Harless**!

Using the Follow-record-to-new-position Option

The cursor follows a record to its new location if the **Follow record to new position** option on the Records menu (the menu found on the Browse/Edit work surface) is set to **YES**. To prevent the shift in the cursor, access the Records menu, select the **Follow record to new position** option, and press Enter to switch the setting to **NO**. Now if you change the contents of a field controlled by the active index, the record moves to its new location, but the cursor does not follow.

You are in the process of learning a great deal about dBASE IV as a database management system (DBMS). The three basic elements to managing any database are creating, maintaining, and using it. At this point, you should feel comfortable about the first two elements because you have created both databases and indexes, and modified (or deleted) data, indexes, and database structures. The fun part is *using* the database—to either output your records in a meaningful sequence or selectively retrieve information. You explore rearranging your records with indexes in this chapter; you start searching for selected data in Chapter 5.

Editing with an Index in Control

When you edit in a field being used in the current index, you may change the indexed location of the records in the database file.

The records menu on the Browse/Edit screen permits you to make changes to your records. One of the change options is the **Follow record to new position**.

When the option is set to **YES**, the record appears in its new indexed position. If the option is set to **NO**, the records that previously surrounded the newly changed record continue to display.

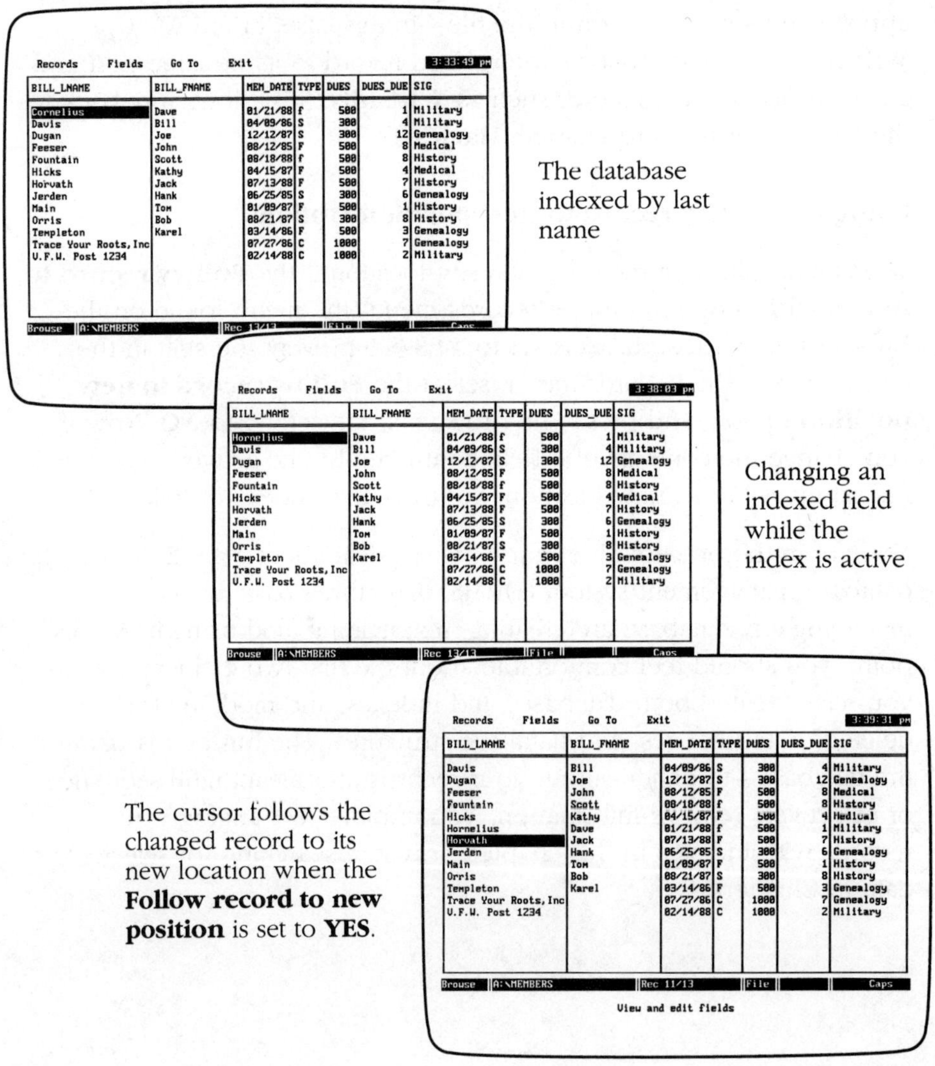

The database indexed by last name

Changing an indexed field while the index is active

The cursor follows the changed record to its new location when the **Follow record to new position** is set to **YES**.

To change the **Follow record to new position** option, press Alt R to select **Record** on the Browse/Edit screen.

Press F to select **Follow record to new position**.

The menu disappears. If the option had been set to **YES**, it is now set to **NO**. If the optioh had been set to **NO**, it is now set to **YES**.

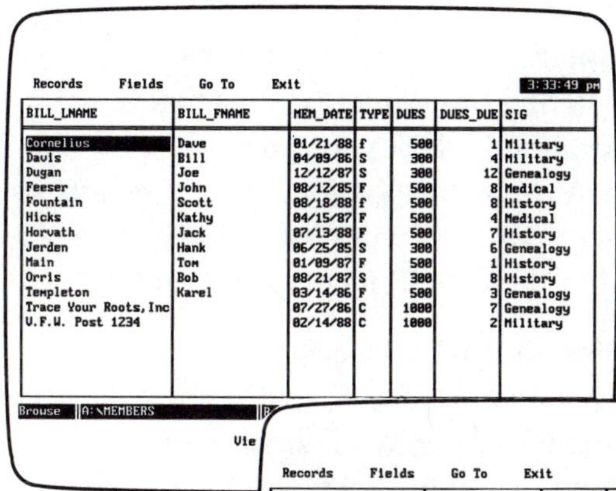

The database indexed by last name

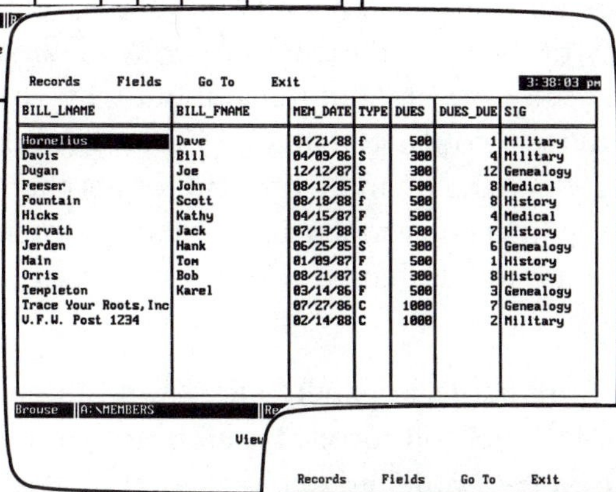

Changing an indexed field while the index is active

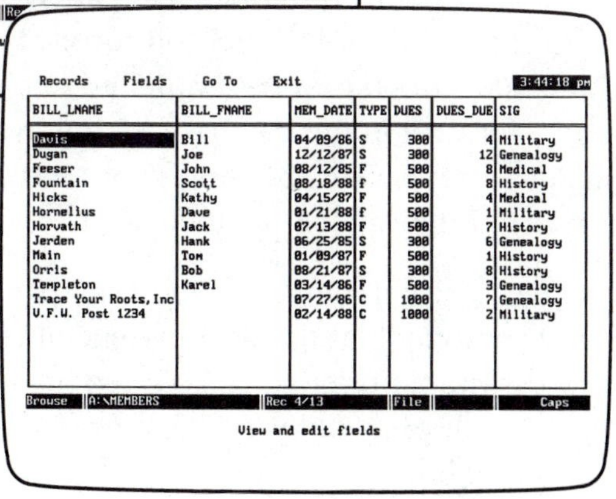

The cursor does not follow the changed record to the new location when the **Follow record to new location** is set to **NO**.

5 Conducting Simple Searches

You can spend much time setting up and maintaining a database—determining the file structure and entering or editing the contents of the records. Your efforts, though, are rewarded when you quickly rearrange your records in a meaningful sequence or successfully search your database. This chapter discusses *simple* searches, or those you complete using only the Data panel in the dBASE IV Control Center.

A wholesale mail-order firm maintains an inventory database—including data fields for catalog number, type, model, unit of measure, retail price, quantity on hand, and manufacturer. You already know that you can index database contents. But think about why you might want to search through these records: perhaps you need to update the retail price of one item, reduce the quantity on hand of another item, or find all items made by a particular manufacturer. Most database searches begin when you decide to edit records or find all records that meet specific criteria.

If you use options from the Data panel in the Control Center, you can go to specific records, based on record location or field contents. If you want, you can go to record number 500, skip to every 10th record, search forward in the database for any record in which the manufacturer is General Supply, or search backward for the record containing the catalog number AC415.

Think of a search limited to the Data panel as a maintenance search—you want to look at the data in general or make changes to selected records without printing custom reports or labels. Once you learn the basic search procedures possible from the Data panel of the Control

Center, you can try the expanded capabilities set up through the Query panel (see Chapter 6).

What Is Covered in This Chapter?

In this chapter, you learn about

- Positioning the record pointer
- Finding the first or last record, or locating a particular record by its record number
- Searching forward and backward through records
- Specifying search criteria that match field contents
- Searching an indexed database

Key Words Used in This Chapter

Match capitalization	The requirement that both upper- and lowercase letters must match in both field content and the search criterion
Record number	A unique number assigned by dBASE IV to a record as it is added to the database
Record pointer	An internal dBASE IV index file, separate from the database, which stores the sequence of numbers that point to where the records are stored in the database
Search string	A user-specified search condition for accessing selected records in a database
Wild card	One of two symbols used to represent a variety of characters. The asterisk (*) wild card stands for one or more characters; the question mark (?) wild card stands for any single character.

Introduction

You use the Data panel to create databases, enter records, and then edit those records. To edit records, you first must find them in the database. The Data panel includes the Go To menu, a tool for searching for and finding database records simply and easily. You can perform several types of searches using the Go To menu on the Data panel's Browse/Edit work surface.

Here are a few ways you can search your database from the Data panel.

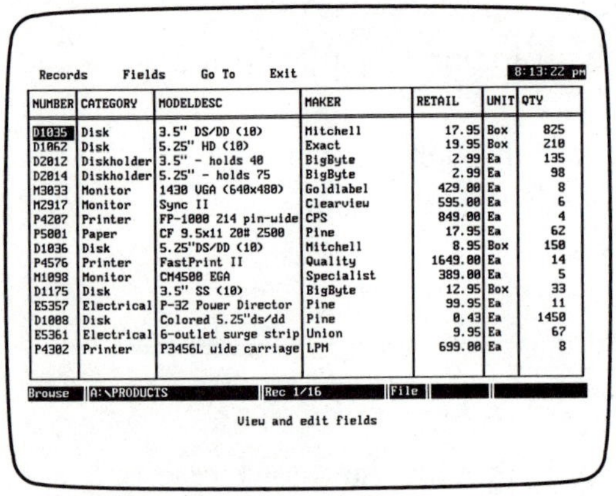

Access Browse/Edit mode from the Control Center's Data panel by pressing F2.

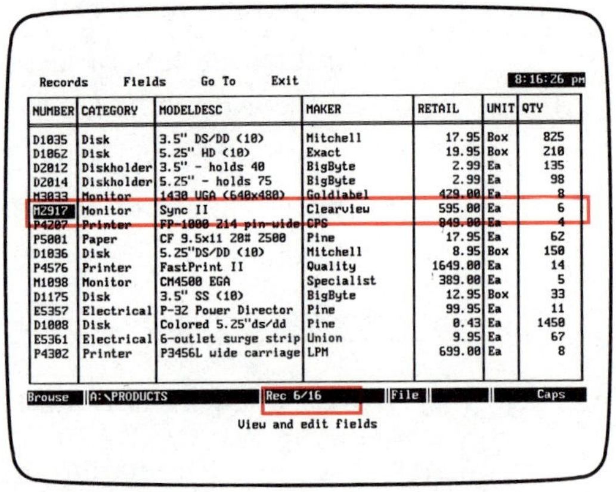

Find a specific record—in this case, record number 6.

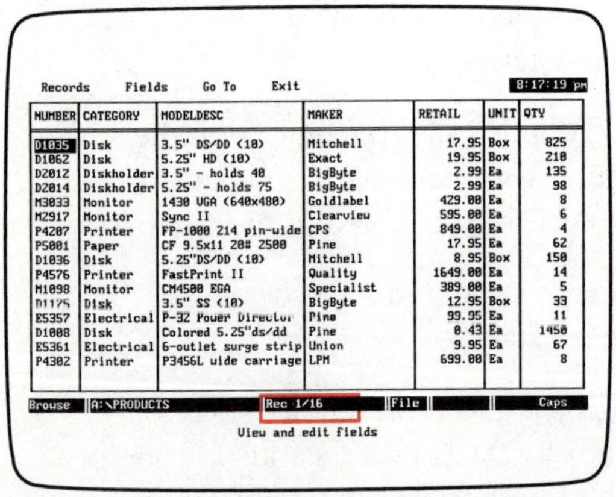

Find the first record in the database.

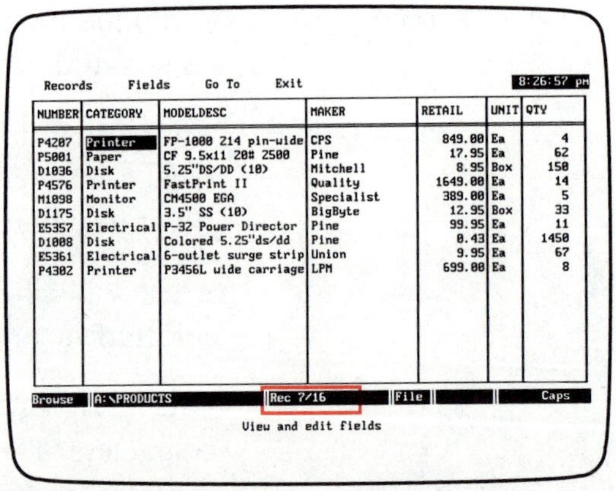

Search forward for a group of records. In this example, find the first occurrence of CATEGORY=Printer.

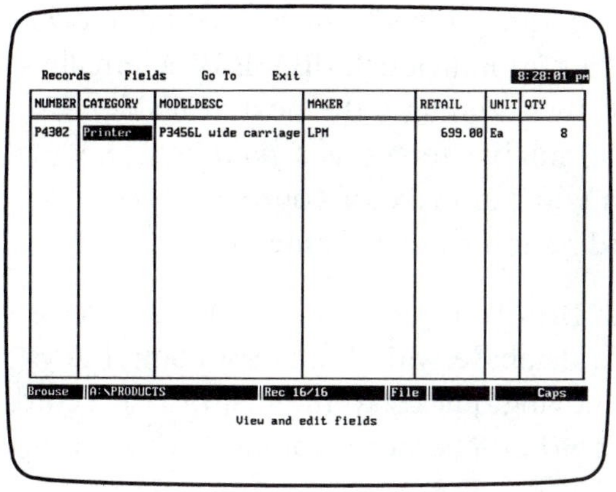

Find the last record in the database.

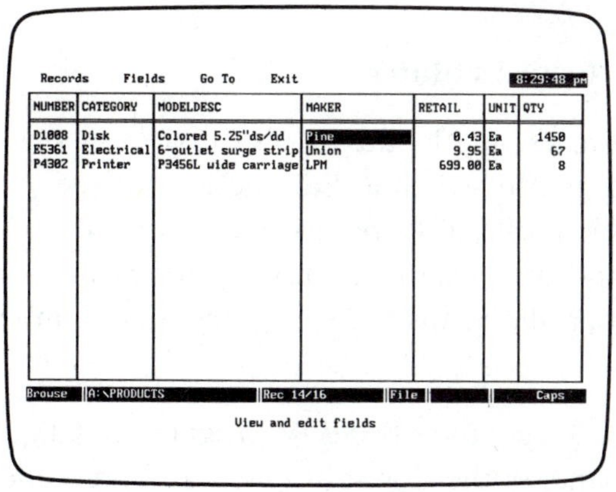

Search backward for a group of records. In this example, find the last occurrence of MAKER=Pine.

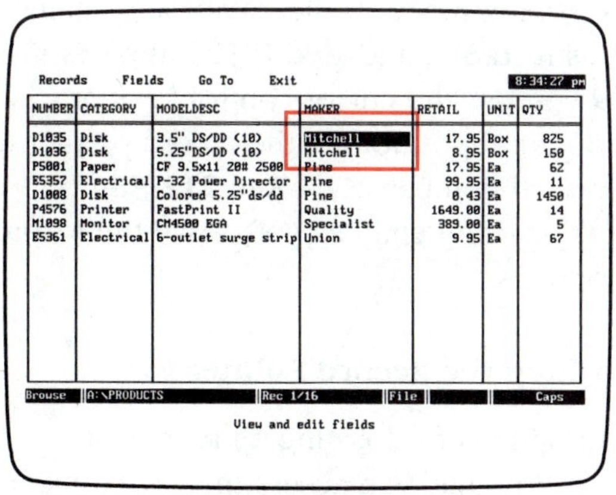

Use an indexed field to search for a group of records. In this example, search for MAKER=Mitchell.

Positioning the Record Pointer

A record number in a database uniquely identifies each record, much as a Social Security number identifies an individual. dBASE IV internally keeps track of each new record by assigning it the next available number in ascending order. The number serves as a *pointer* to the record. The most simple search you can make of your database involves finding a record according to its record number.

As you look at your database in Browse or Edit mode, you can access records by scrolling through the database with the cursor-control keys and the Go To menu options, moving quickly to the first or last record, going directly to a particular record number, or skipping over a specified number of records.

Understanding the Current Record Pointer

When you look at records in Browse mode, the highlight bar rests on one field in the *current* record. If you switch to Edit mode, you see only the *current* record on-screen. dBASE IV points to the current record by its record number, and displays that number in the Status bar. In addition to the record number, the Status bar shows the total number of records in the database.

Suppose, for example, that you access the dBASE IV program, highlight a database name in the Data panel of the Control Center, and press the F2 (Data) key to access Browse or Edit mode. If the database contains 580 records, the current record is record 1, and **Rec 1/580** appears in the middle of the Status bar. As you use the cursor-control keys or menu options to locate data, you are repositioning the record pointer to a new current record, such as record number 212 —**Rec 212/580** on the Status bar. Look at the Status bar frequently as you move the record pointer with the Go To menu options.

Using the Go To Menu To Position the Record Pointer

The Go To menu provides eight options for locating data, four of which merely reposition the record pointer. To access the Go To menu from the Browse/Edit work surface, press Alt-G. The first four options let you position the cursor at the top or bottom the database, move to a particular record number, or move the current record pointer backward or forward a specified number of records. The last four options are discussed later in this chapter.

Finding the First or Last Record

To move the current record pointer to the first or last record of your database quickly, select either **Top record** or **Last record** from the Go To menu. If no index is active, you see the first or last record in the database according to the record numbers. If an index is in control, you see the first or last record according to the way the records are indexed.

Finding a Record Number

If you know the number of the record you want to become the current record, select **Record number** from the Go To menu, enter the record number you want, and press Enter. You also can use this option to look around your database. For example, to look through records, you can indicate a record number, such as 300, and use the cursor-control keys to view surrounding records.

Skipping Records

You can move forward or backward, skipping a specific number of records. Select the **Skip** option on the Go To menu and enter the number of records you want to skip. A positive number moves the current record pointer forward; a negative number moves the current record pointer backward. For example, indicate –30 to make the record 30 records back from your current position the new current record; indicate 50 to make the record 50 records forward from your current position the new current record.

Positioning the Record Pointer

The Go To menu on the Browse/Edit work surface offers four options for merely positioning the current record pointer at the records you plan to access. You also can use four more sophisticated options on the Go To menu to tell dBASE IV to locate groups of related records.

Understanding the Current Record Pointer

dBASE IV uses an internal pointer system to indicate which record is currently available for use.

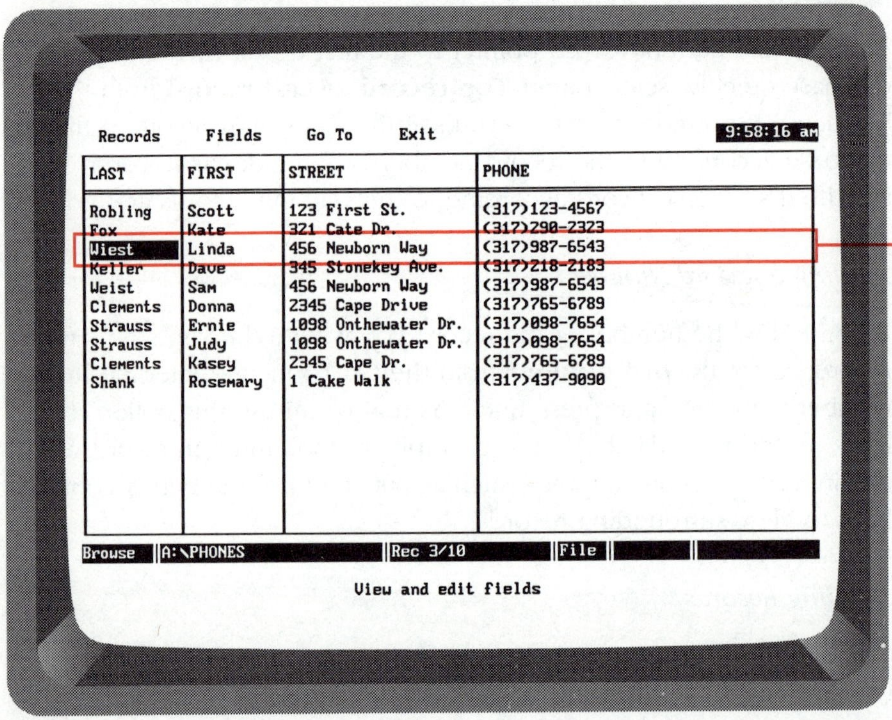

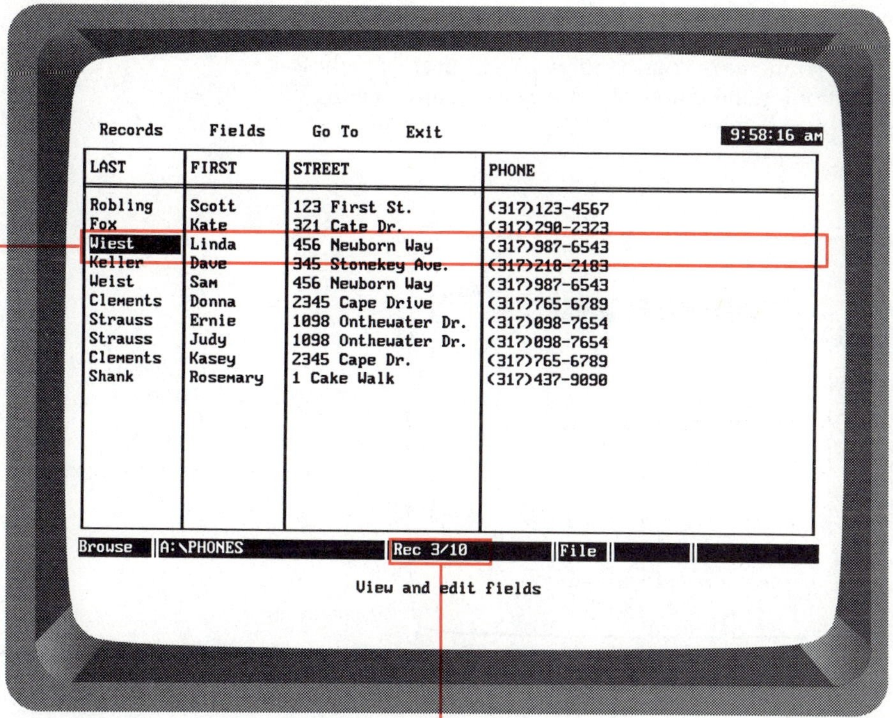

Rec 3/10

Current record pointer — Total records in the database

The Status bar keeps you informed about the current record by displaying the current record number and number of records in the database.

Positioning the Record Pointer

Using the Go To Menu To Position the Record Pointer

The Go To menu is your window to a variety of techniques for positioning the current record pointer and locating groups of related records.

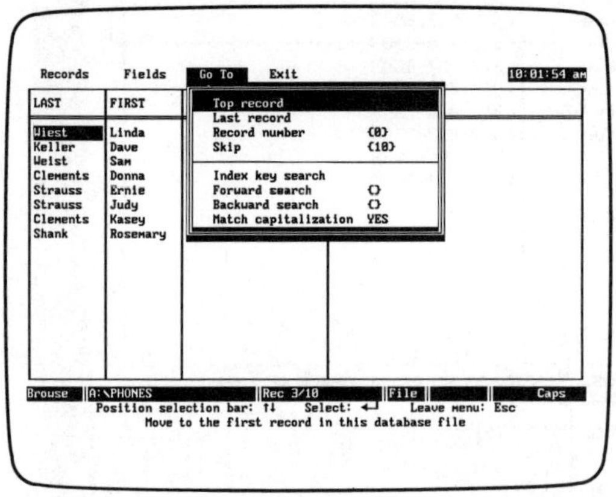

From the Browse/Edit screen, press Alt G to access the Go To menu.

Notice the options for moving the record pointer.

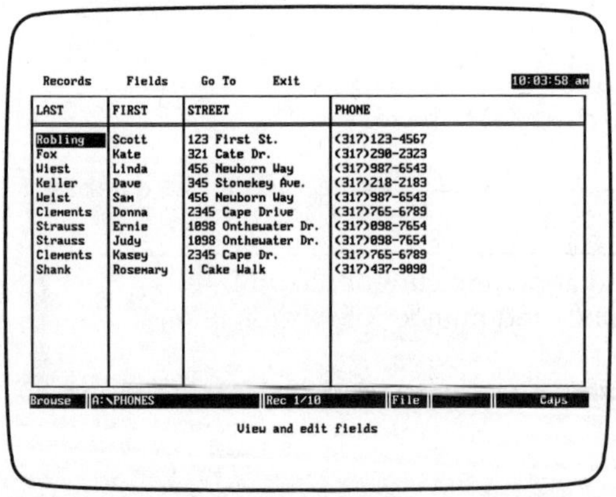

Finding the First Record

Press T to go to the **Top record** of the database.

Notice the record pointer in the status line.

After the record pointer is repositioned, the Go To menu closes.

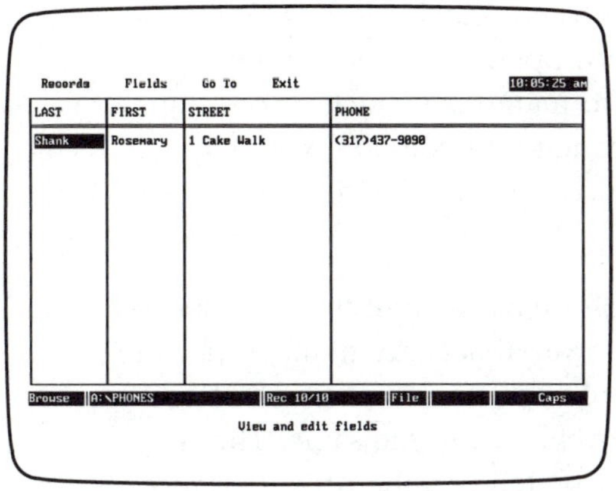

Finding the Last Record

Press Alt G again.

Press L to access the **Last record**. This time, the current record is the last record in the database.

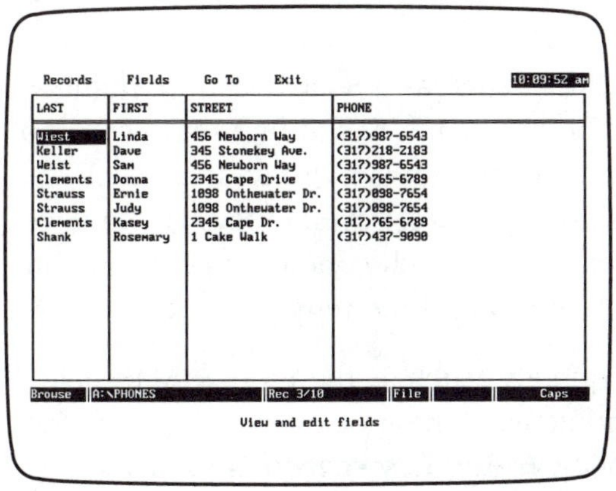

Finding a Record Number

Press Alt G.

Press R to select **Record number**.

When prompted, enter the record number by typing 3.

The current record number is 3.

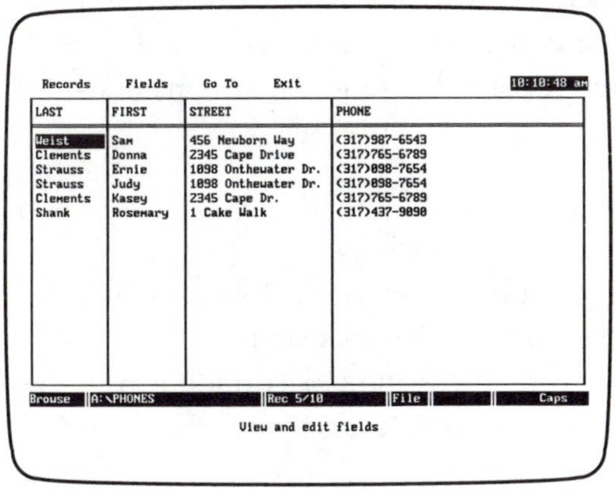

Skipping Records

Press Alt G.

Press S to **Skip** to a record.

Entering a positive number moves the record pointer forward *n* records, while entering a negative number moves the record pointer backward *n* records.

Type 2 and press ↵Enter to move to record 5.

Searching Non-Indexed Fields

Two problems can occur if you try to search for records in a large database using only Go To menu options to position the record pointer. First, you are unlikely to memorize which record number is associated with each record's content. In addition, you may find using only cursor-control keys a time-consuming way to move about when looking for a specific record.

If, however, you know some information about the record(s) you want to search for, such as a name or Social Security number, use the **Forward search** and **Backward search** options on the Go To menu. Both forward and backward searches work the same. The only difference is the direction of the search and the order that records are found.

You must furnish a search condition, such as a Social Security number. If your search condition is specific enough, you can find the record on the first try. However, if the search condition is more general, such as the last name *Smith*, you may find the first of several records. Once you find the first of the records meeting the search condition, keep pressing Shift-F3 (Previous) or Shift-F4 (Next) to find the remaining occurrences.

If you plan to search a field frequently (such as the LAST_NAME field), create an index on that field and activate the index before you use the Go To menu. If you do, the option **Index key search** is available. First you see the index expression used to create the index. Then you are asked to enter the data for which you want the index searched. The search is rapid, and you see each record whose index key matches the criteria you entered.

Searching Forward

Before you select the **Forward search** option, press Tab or Shift-Tab to position the cursor on the column you plan to search (for example, the LAST_NAME field). Press Alt-G to access the Go To menu from the Browse or Edit screen, select **Forward search**, and enter the *search* *string* of data. Type the string of data exactly as it appears in the database, including capitalization, or no match results. For example, if you are looking for the records in the database in which the last name is *Osbourne*, you must type the name exactly, not *Osborne* (spelled differently) or *OSBOURNE* (all capital letters). Later in this chapter, you will learn to use wild-card characters when you are unsure of the spelling of the field contents.

The forward search begins to check records when you invoke **Forward search** and continues to search each record until finding a record that matches the search string. Searching wraps around past the bottom of the database to the beginning (first record), and stops at the record where the search originated. Once you find the first record that meets the search condition, keep pressing Shift-F4 (Next) to find the remaining occurrences.

If dBASE IV cannot find a matching record, you hear a beep and see the message ** **Not Found** ** **Press any key to continue....** If you know that you correctly entered the search string, this message confirms that the record you want is not in the database.

When you invoke the **Forward search** command more than once, dBASE IV leaves the most recent search criterion on the screen and duplicates it in the **Backward search** option. You can type a new search condition or edit the old search string. Be sure to position the highlight bar in the field where you want to search before you select **Forward** (or **Backward**) **search**.

Searching Backward

The **Backward search** option performs much like **Forward search**. The difference is that the search moves backward to the top of the database, then wraps around to the bottom of the database and continues back to the starting point. Once you find the first of the records meeting the search condition, keep pressing Shift-F3 (Previous) to find the remaining occurrences.

Searching Non-Indexed Fields

The Go To menu offers four sophisticated options that let you search your database using search criteria to locate groups of related records while in Browse/Edit mode.

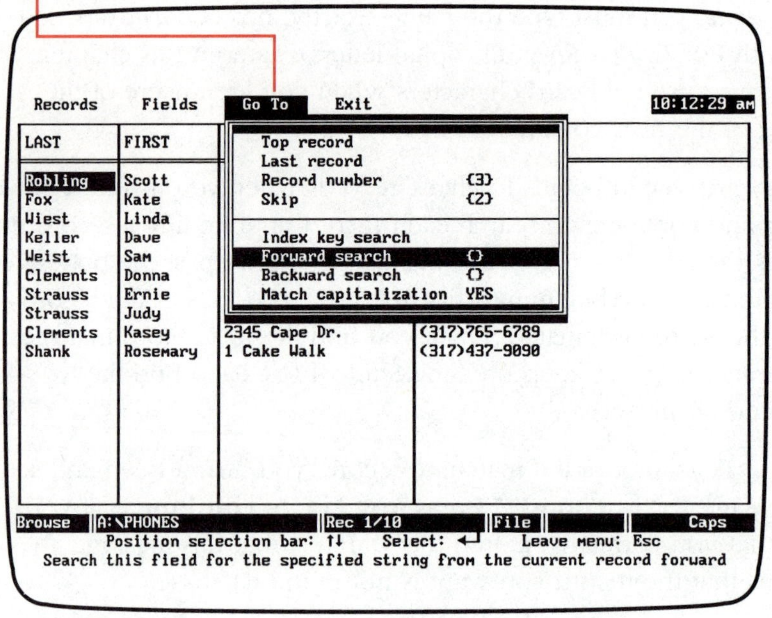

To use any of these four options, first press Tab or Shift Tab to position the cursor in the column to be searched. Then press Alt G to access the Go To menu.

Searching Forward

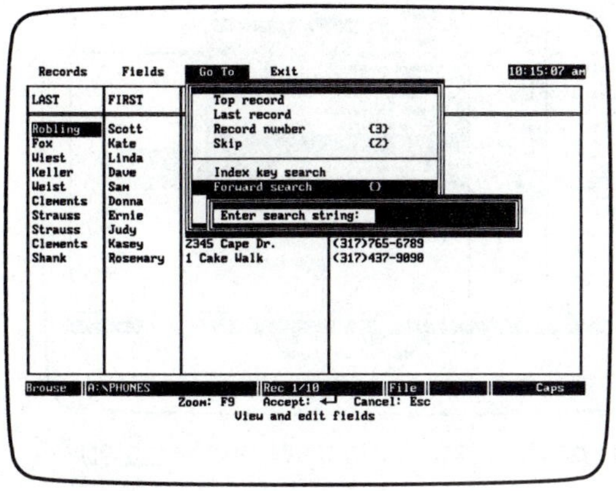

From the Go To menu, press F to select **Forward search**.

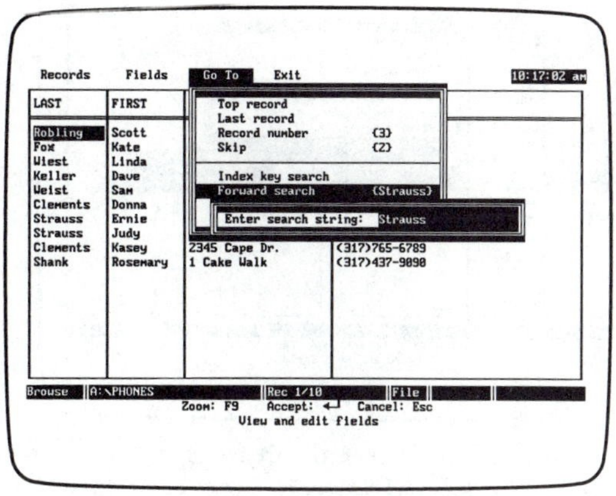

Enter the search string, and then press ↵Enter.

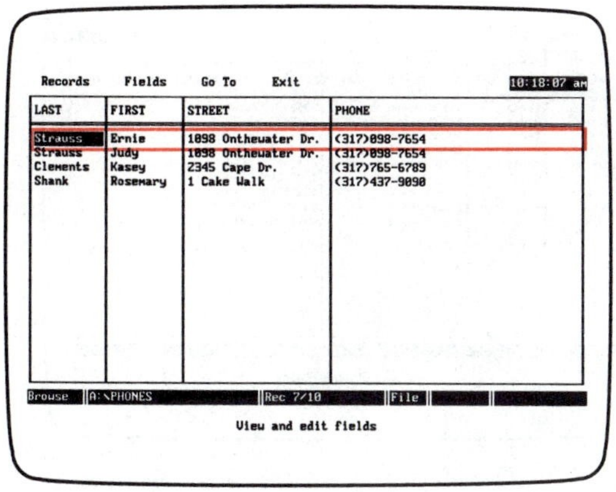

The current record is now the first record that meets the search criteria.

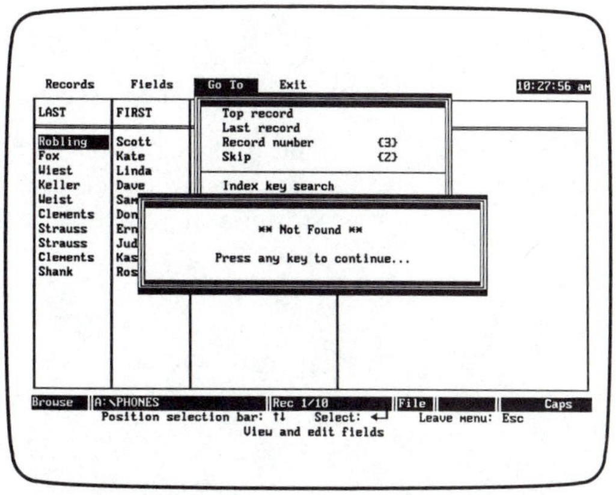

If no records are found, you will hear a beep and see the message **Not Found**.

Forward searches begin at the current record and move forward through the end of the database, around to the beginning, and back to the current record.

Searching Non-Indexed Fields

Searching Backward

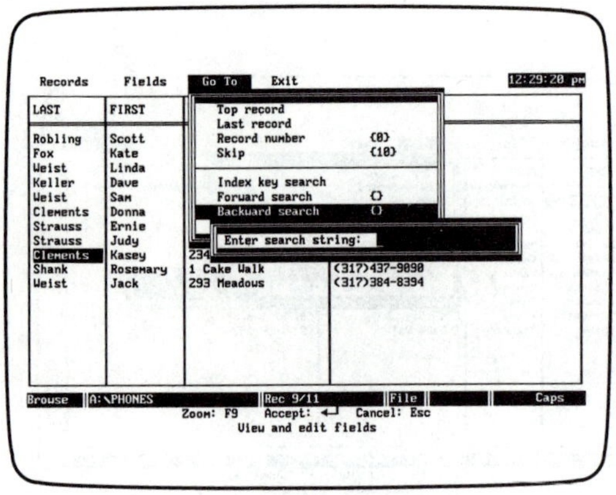

From the Go To menu, press B to select **Backward Search**.

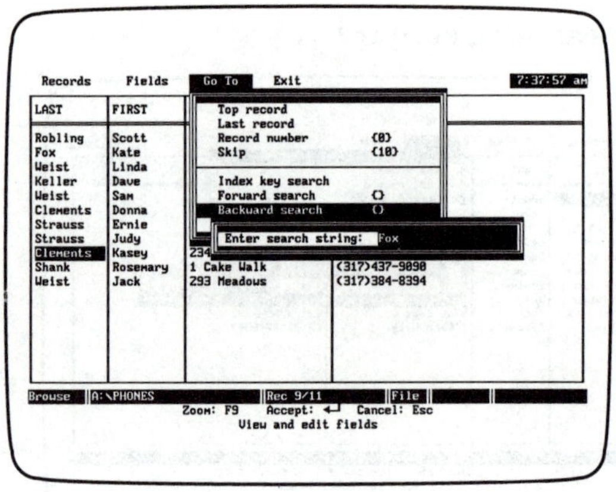

Type the search string and press ↵Enter.

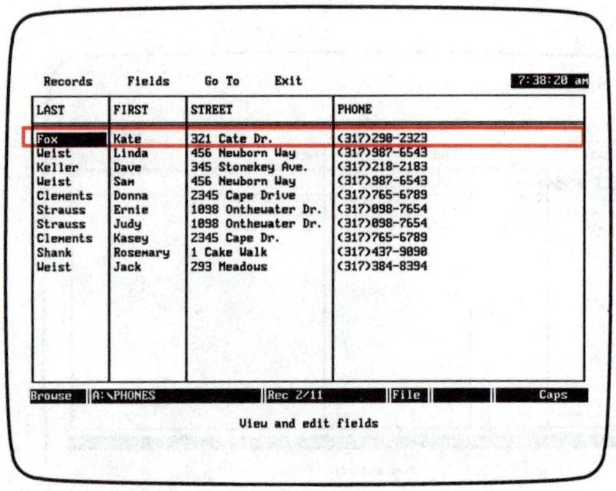

The first record to match your search string is the current record.

The search begins at the current record and moves backward to the beginning of the database, around to the end, and back to the current record.

Finding the Next Occurrence of a String

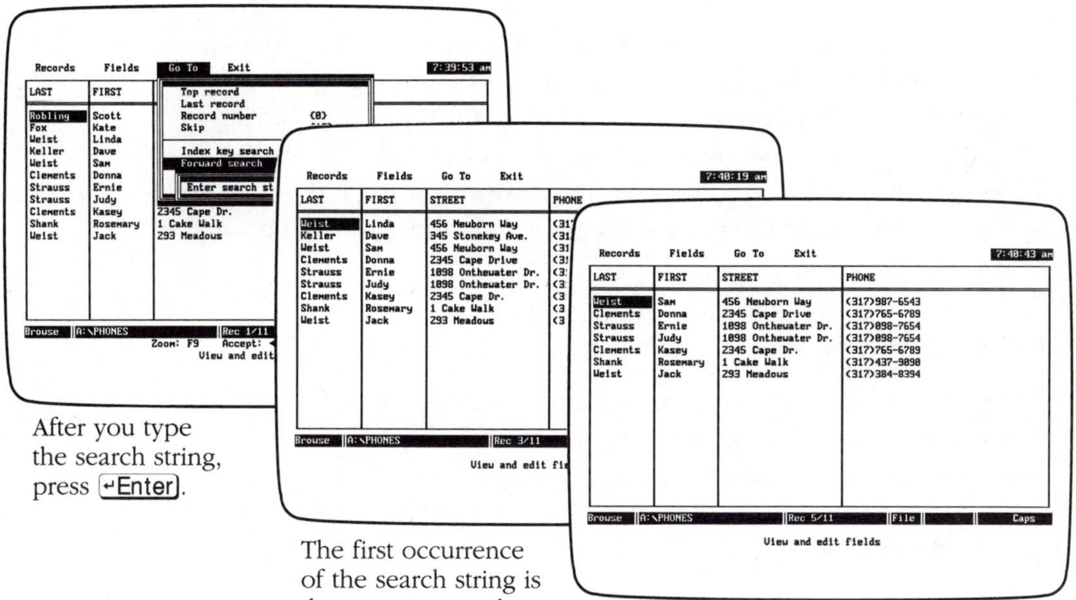

After you type the search string, press ↵Enter.

The first occurrence of the search string is the current record.

Press ⇧Shift F4 to find the next occurrence of the search string.

Finding the Previous Occurrence of a String

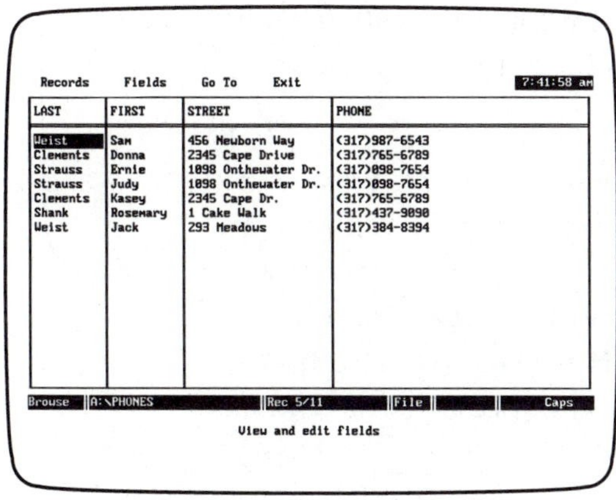

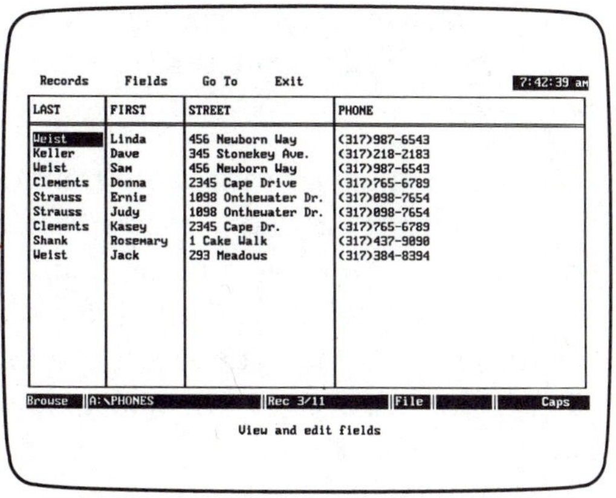

You also can find the previous occurrence of your search string.

Press ⇧Shift F3 to find the previous occurrence.

You can see that **Forward search** and **Backward search** are more precise tools for finding data than the cursor-control keys and menu options that simply position the current record pointer. Still, having to enter the exact search string is limiting. If you use two dBASE IV features—wild cards and **Match capitalization** (set to **NO**)—you can avoid having to ensure that the search criterion and the field contents match exactly.

Using Wild Cards

dBASE IV permits two wild cards—symbols that tell dBASE IV to accept a variety of characters—in specifying a search string. The asterisk (*) wild card represents one or more characters; the question mark (?) wild card represents any single character. You can use wild cards to make search criteria more flexible.

For example, if you specify the search string *San** when the cursor rests on the CITY field, a forward or backward search finds any record in which the contents of the city field starts with *San.* You might find records containing San Francisco, San Jose, or Santa Fe. If you can't recall a first name, but think that the one you want starts with a *B* and ends with an *a,* the search string *B*a* can find *Belinda, Brenda,* or *Barbara.*

You can use the wild card at the front of a search string as well as in the middle or at the end. Suppose that you recall only the name of a street address, *Cape,* but not the house number. You can conduct a search of address fields based on the search string **Cape** and find all records in which the address is *Cape Drive.* However, you also find other addresses, such as any house number on Caper Lane or Capella Circle.

If you find more records than you want, try to restrict the scope of the wild card by specifying additional letters. For example, if you know the address you seek is a *Drive*, type the search string **Cape Dr**. By including "Dr" in the search string, you eliminate lanes, circles, roads, and so on. By excluding "ive" at the end of the search criterion, you allow for variations in spellings of *drive* such as *Drive* or *Dr.*

Use the ? wild card to replace single characters in search strings. For example, if you are not sure whether the phone-number field in the record you seek is 123-4567 or 133-4567, specify a search criterion of 1?3-4567. You can mix both wild cards to make the most flexible search criteria. For example, to find all addresses on Cape or Cane Drive, enter the search string **Ca?e Dr**.

Using Match Capitalization

The last option on the Go To menu is **Match capitalization**. The options are **YES** and **NO**. The default setting is **YES**.

When capitalization is set to **YES**, the characters in the search string must match the contents of the record, including capitalization. In the previous example, **Cape Dr**, you may not find all addresses on Cape or Cape Drive if you do not capitalize the street name when adding a few records (if you type *cape*, not *Cape*).

In a **Forward search** or **Backward search**, dBASE IV treats capital letters and lowercase letters differently. The letters *A* and *a* are two different letters to the computer. Yet, for purposes of your search, they are the same.

Select **Match capitalization** on the Go To menu and set it to **NO**. Subsequent searches treat upper- and lowercase characters the same. A dBASE IV search operation now treats *123 Cape Dr* like *123 cape dr*. Set the **Match capitalization** option prior to each search, if necessary.

Alternatives to Exact-Match Searches

Forward search and **Backward search** are improvements over simply positioning the current record pointer. Still, having to enter an exact search string is limiting. Use wild cards and match capitalization as alternatives to exact-match searches and thereby create more powerful searches.

Using Wild Cards

Use wild-card characters to replace portions of search strings.

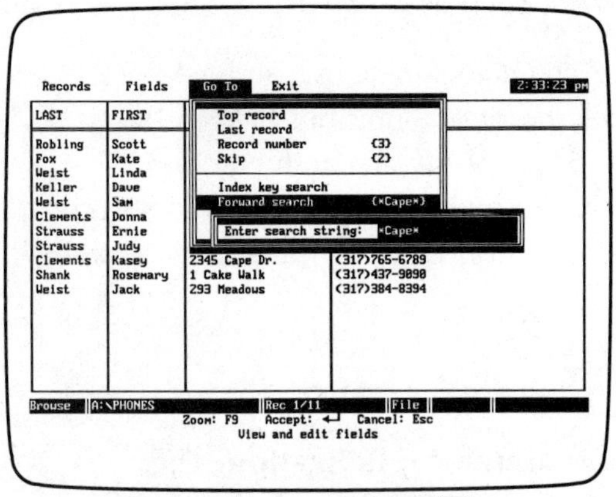

From the Go To menu, press F to select Forward search, and enter the search string *Cape*.

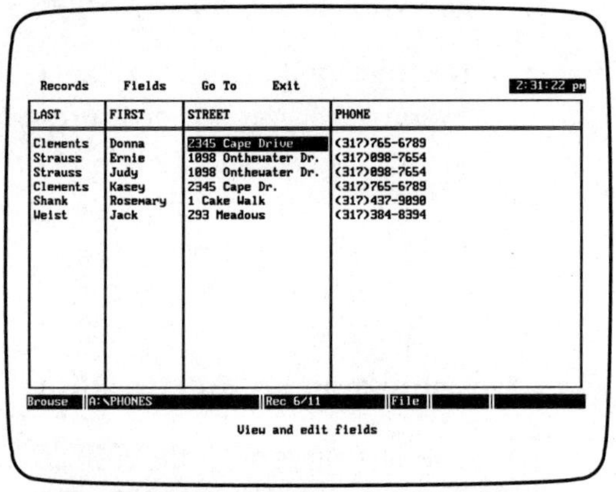

Press ↵Enter. The search finds all addresses on Cape Drive regardless of the spelling of Drive.

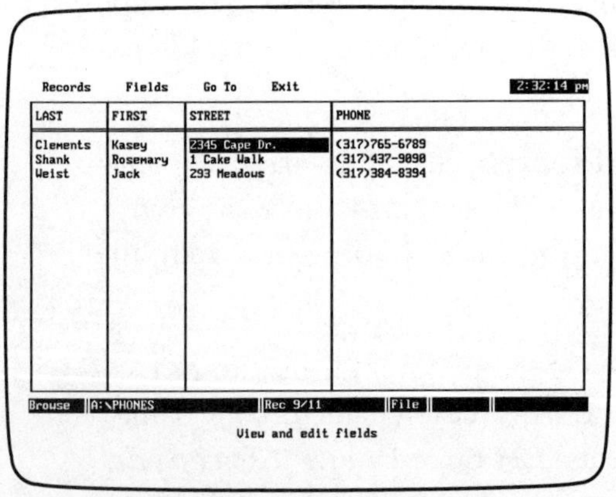

Press ⇧Shift F4 to find the next occurance. An address on Cape Dr. is found as well.

Wild-Card Characters

- * Represents one or more characters
- ? Represents any single character

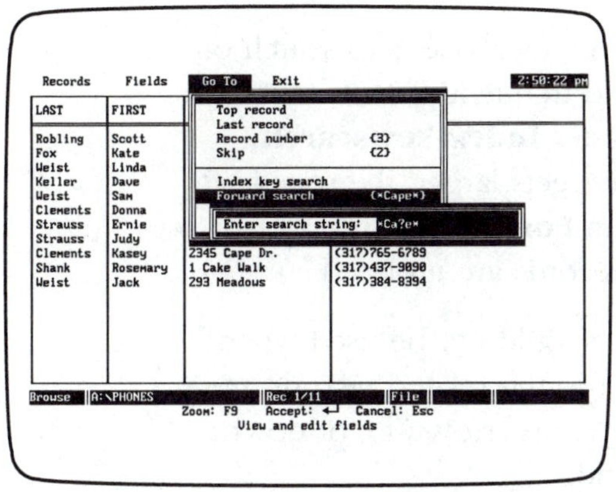

From the Go To menu, press F to select **Forward search** again. Type the search string *Ca?e*.

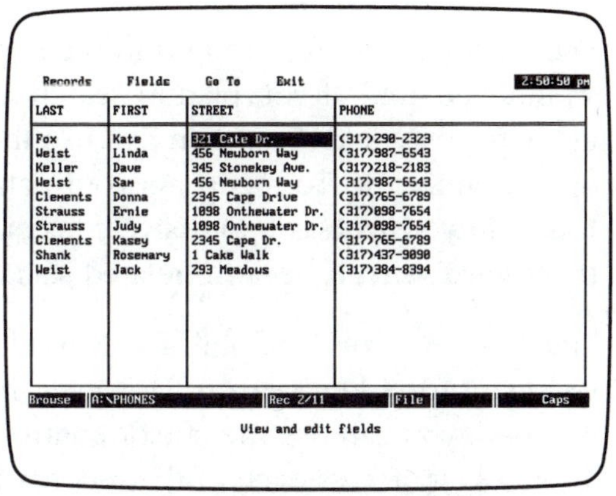

Press ↵Enter. All street addresses on Cape, Cate, and Cake are found.

Using Match Capitalization

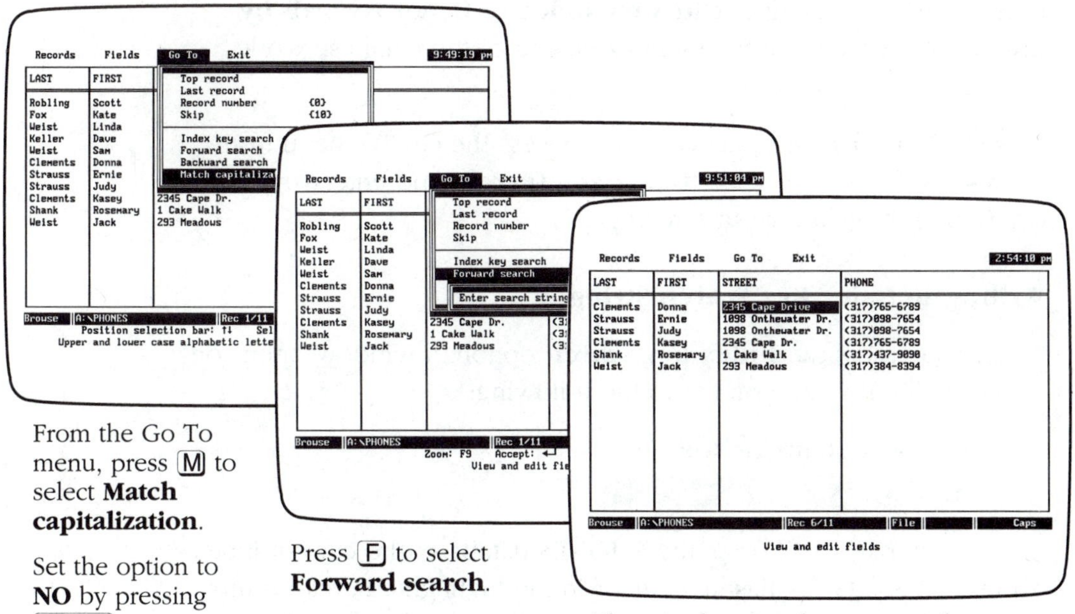

From the Go To menu, press M to select **Match capitalization**.

Set the option to **NO** by pressing ↵Enter.

Press F to select **Forward search**.

Type the search string *CAPE* and press ↵Enter.

The search string does not need to match capitalization exactly because the search is no longer case-sensitive.

Searching on an Indexed Field

The most efficient way to find information in a database is to search on an indexed field. If you plan to search a field frequently, create an index for that field. You then can use the faster **Index key search** option on the Go To menu. As your database gets larger, the speed of **Index key search** is impressively faster than **Forward search** or **Backward search** because related sets of records are grouped.

The Shift-F3 (Prev) and Shift-F4 (Next) keys should not be used when you use **Index key search**. However, because the related records are grouped, you can use the cursor-control keys, up arrow (↑), or down arrow (↓) to access each of the records found.

Accessing the Index Key Search Option

To use the **Index key search** option, activate the appropriate index, or—if the index does not exist—create it. You create an index or activate an index using **Create new index** or **Order records by index**, respectively, on the Organize menu of the database work surface.

To search the current or active index, access the Go To menu from Browse or Edit mode, select **Index key search**, and enter your search criterion in the window on-screen.

Writing an Index Key Search String

When you access the **Index key search** option, a window opens on-screen with a message similar to the following:

Enter search string for
LAST:

In this example, which uses the PHONES database, the current index expression is *LAST.* A flashing cursor in the highlighted area prompts you to enter the search string. Keep the following items in mind as you write the search criterion:

- If the index expression was created with the UPPER() function, the string you search for must be uppercase. The expression UPPER(NAME) requires that you search for MARIANNE, not Marianne.
- You can enter a partial search string representing the first characters in the index. For the expression UPPER(FIRSTNAME), you can search for MAR rather than MARIANNE. Do not, however, be too brief. MAR also can find names like MARK, MARCELLA, and MARCUS.
- **Match capitalization** is not effective in index key searches. Your index should use the UPPER() function, and your search string should be all capital letters.
- Wild-card characters are not available in index key searches.
- An index that combines two fields, such as UPPER(STATE+CITY), does not permit you to find all the cities named PORTLAND because you can enter only a partial search string representing the first characters in the city name. You have to create an index for just the city field in order to search for the city PORTLAND.

In summary, the **Index key search** option is just one of eight options on the Go To menu that you access from Browse or Edit mode. The first four options merely reposition the record pointer so that you can find a record. The other options relate to specifying a *single* search criterion.

You can perform most simple searches through the Data panel of the dBASE IV Control Center, discussed in this chapter. However, you may need to create search criteria that will be used by other Control Center panels, such as the Report or Labels panel. dBASE IV provides extensive search capabilities in the Query panel options presented in the next chapter.

Searching on an Indexed Field

The most efficient way to search a database is to search one of its indexes. If a field will be searched frequently, make that field an indexed field.

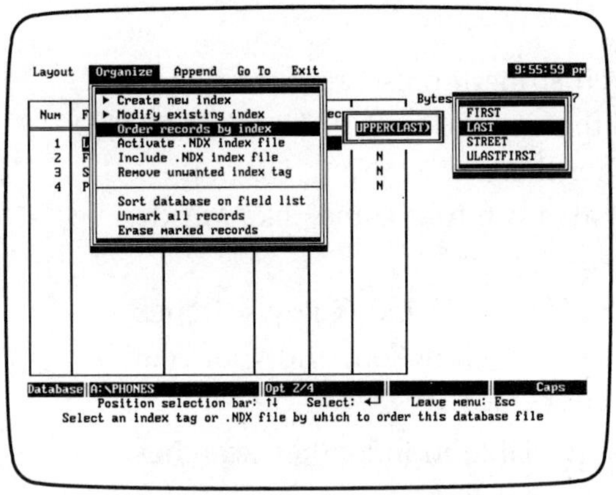

To activate the appropriate index, start from the Control Center and press ⇧Shift F2 to display the data-design screen.

Press Alt O to select the Organize menu.

Press O to select **Order record by index**.

Select the appropriate index.

Press F2 to return to Browse mode.

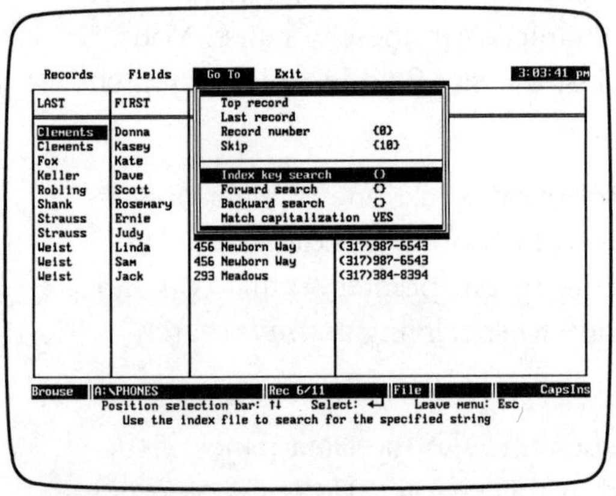

Press Alt G to access the Go To menu.

Press I to select **Index key search**.

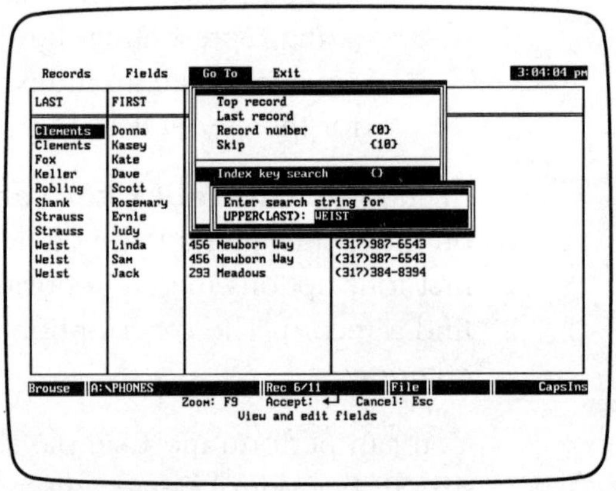

Type the search string and press ↵Enter.

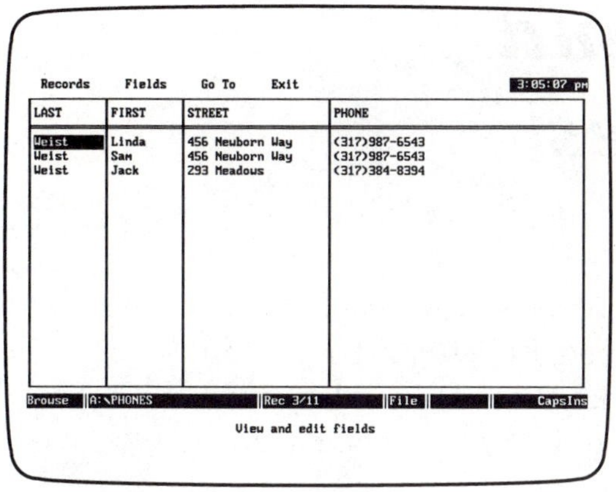

Notice that the records found are related by last name. The records are grouped because the index is controlling the database.

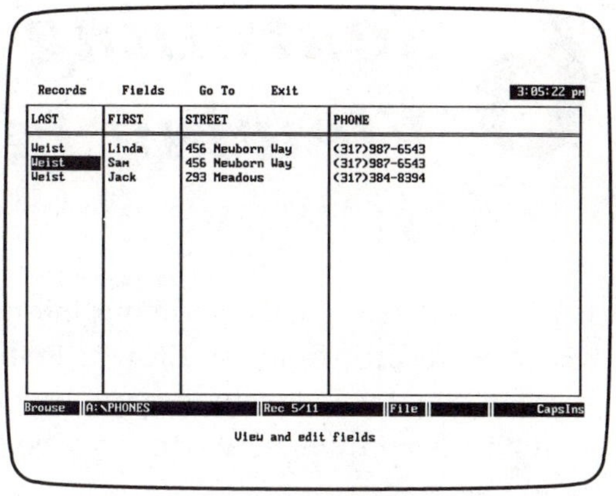

Use ↑ or ↓ to scroll through the records.

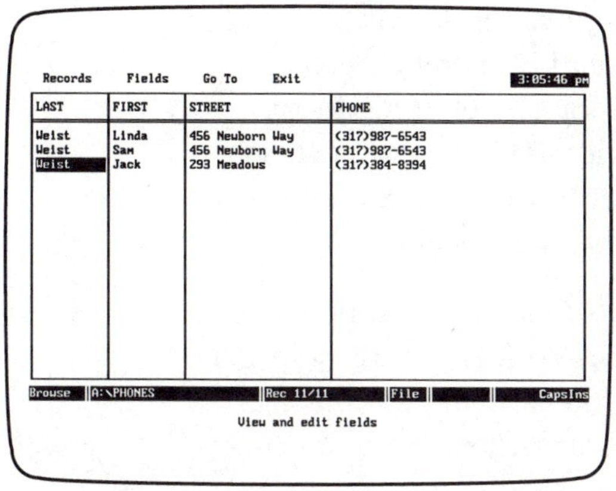

Shift F3 (Prev) and Shift F4 (Next) should not be used with **Index key search**. They are used only with Forward an Backward search.

6 Searching and Viewing Files

If your database is small and your information needs are simple, searching records from the Browse/Edit screen, as described in the last chapter, may be adequate for you. If your database is larger, however, searching from the Query panel on the Control Center can be much more effective.

As databases increase in size—in both number of fields (data items) and number of records—search criteria can become complex, increasing search time dramatically. For example, in a medical-center database of several thousand patients, each record may contain 50 fields (name fields, complete-address fields, physical-description fields, prior-medical-history fields, and so on). Instead of merely seeking records by a single string (such as the name of the referring doctor), you might want to find the names and phone numbers of all patients over 45 years of age, with a family history of heart disease, and who have not had an electrocardiogram within the last 2 years.

Setting up searches from the Control Center's Query panel offers many advantages over simple searches from the Go To menu in Browse/Edit mode. For example, using a query search, you can limit the Browse/ Edit screen display to selected records (such as patients experiencing heart disease) and only specific fields within records (each patient's number, sex, age, and medication).

With a query search, you can rearrange the order of fields on the Browse/Edit screen, and you also can determine which fields and records are made available to Browse edit, Quick report, Reports, and Labels. You can access data from more than one database or save a query to disk for later use. A query's search string can be quite complex, including calculations and multiple search conditions.

What Is Covered in This Chapter?

In this chapter, you learn about

- Organizing the query-design work surface
- Using options on the query Menu bar
- Setting up a file skeleton and a view skeleton
- Locating character, numeric, and logical data, as well as dates, based on one or more search conditions
- Using operators in search strings

Key Words Used in This Chapter

Calculated fields	The middle portion of the query-design work surface skeleton where the user defines fields that are not part of the database
File skeleton	The top portion of the query-design work surface where the user specifies the field contents used to select records in a query operation.
Filter	The Query process for hiding database records that do not match specified search condition.
Operator	A symbol used in a query to select a record based on a variety of data matches or numeric conditions. An operator shows the relationship between data and search criteria.
View skeleton	The bottom portion of the query-design work surface where the user specifies the fields to display (on-screen or to the printer) from the records selected.

If your database is small and your information needs are simple, searching records from the Browse/Edit screen may be adequate for you.

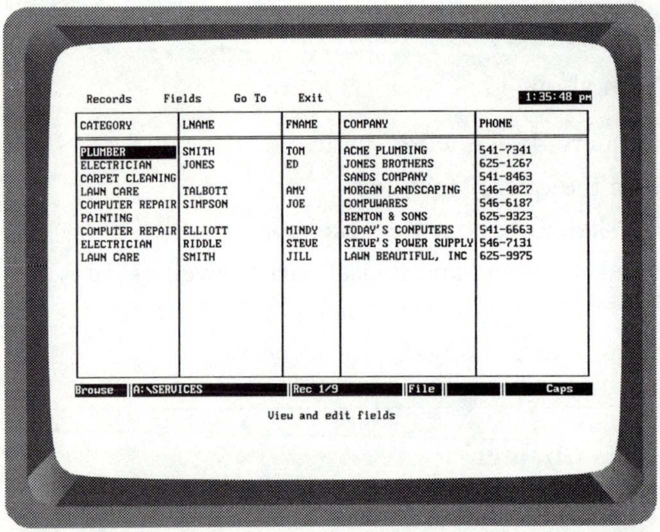

Your office phone book of maintenance services, vendors, and other support services is a simple database.

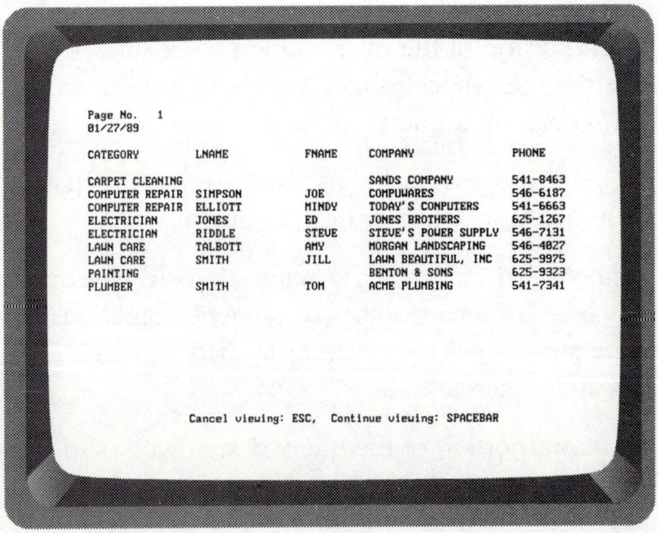

Your output needs may be satisfied with listings from Quick Report.

As your databases increase in size, search criteria can become complex. In a hospital setting, a patient medication system can easily become two databases working together with 150 fields in each.

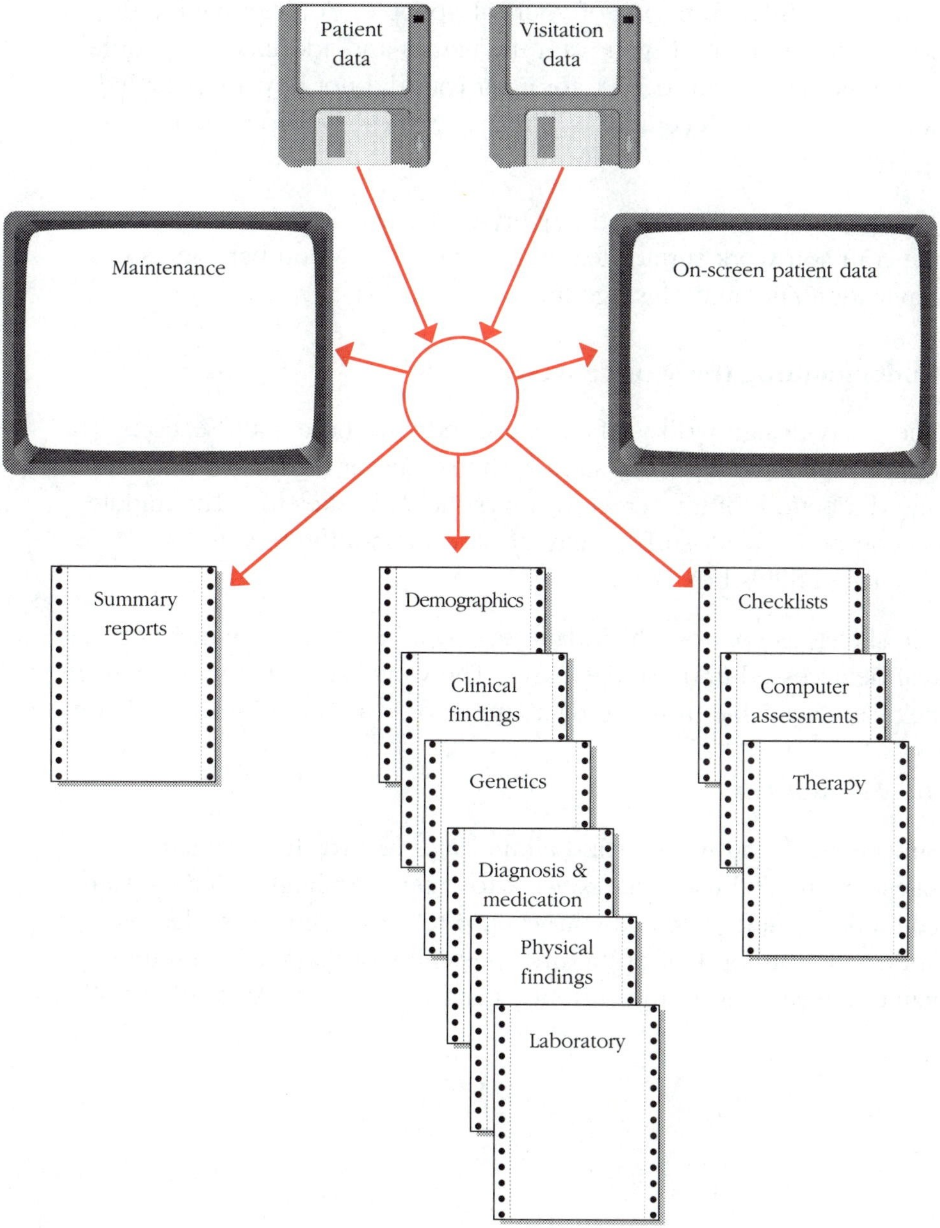

You access the query screen from the Query panel in the Control Center. The query screen gives you a comprehensive tool for accessing your database. Suppose that you want to know all the customers who bought a vehicle from one of your salespeople. You can handle this with a simple query. If you want the names and addresses of people who paid more than $15,000 for a car (but did not buy an extended warranty) during December or January, you can set up a more complex query.

The query screen includes the query-design work surface as well as all the common work-surface features, such as the Menu bar, Status bar, Navigation line, and Message line.

Understanding the Work Surface

The query-design work surface is divided into three main sections. The upper portion of the work surface shows one or more file skeletons and the bottom of the screen displays the view skeleton. The middle section of the work surface may display a condition box and a Calculated fields box.

File skeletons control which databases will be used and which records will be accessed in those databases. The view skeleton controls which fields are available from the database records selected by file skeletons.

The File Skeleton

Suppose that you want to find all the sales records for a certain salesperson. You use a *file skeleton* to enter the search criteria—data common to all the records you want to retrieve. The file skeleton appears in the top half of the query-design work surface, with the name of each field in the current database displayed. An arrow indicates that additional field names are off the screen to the left or right. You type your search criteria under the appropriate field name. For example, if you want to find records of car sales in which the sales representative's initials are RS, you type *RS* under the SALES_REP field name.

dBASE IV allows you to use up to eight file skeletons on the query-design work surface at one time. You can link the files together to operate as one file.

The View Skeleton

Perhaps you want to see only the vehicle-identification number and the date of delivery from the records you searched for sales representative RS. You can use the *view skeleton*, which appears in the bottom half of the query-design work surface, to enter your specifications. After retrieving files with the file skeleton, you can use the view skeleton to indicate fields to display or print from records that meet your search criteria. You can have one view skeleton per query; the skeleton contains selected fields from all file skeletons and calculated fields skeletons.

The Calculated Fields Skeleton

If you decide to compute a one percent bonus for the sales representative RS, you use the *calculated fields skeleton*. This skeleton appears below the file skeleton on the query-design work surface. Use the calculated fields skeleton to define fields that are not part of the database. Calculated fields are not actually part of the database, but are created by using data in a record. In the example, you can create a calculated field BONUS by multiplying the CAR_PRICE database field contents by 1 percent.

The Condition Box

If you want to see all the deleted records in your database (something you cannot specify in the file skeleton) before you erase them from the database, you use a *condition box*. This box appears at the lower right of the area between the file skeleton at the top of the screen and the view skeleton at the bottom of the screen. The condition box lets you set a *filter* to control the data you retrieve from the database. Usually the conditions are not associated with data fields, because you can enter criteria based on field contents in the file skeleton.

Using the Status Bar

The Status bar at the bottom of the screen provides information about the query-design work surface. Five segments appear across the Status bar; the first three concern query mode. The word **Query** appears in the first segment to remind you that you are using the query-design work surface. The second segment displays the drive, path, and file name of the current database.

The third segment displays either **File 1/1** or **Field 1/1**, depending on the location of the cursor. If the cursor rests at the far left side of the screen, the **File** message is displayed; otherwise the **Field** message is displayed. The indicator **1/1** displays the file or field position out of the total files or fields. The indicator changes according to the location of the cursor, the number of fields in the database structure, and the number of open files.

Using the Navigation and Message Lines

You can use the following keys to move around the query screen and enter criteria. Watch the Navigation line; it displays many of the available keys for specific procedures.

F3/F4	Moves the highlighter between the file skeleton, the calculated fields skeleton, the condition box, and the view skeleton. F3 moves to the previous skeleton, and F4 moves to the next skeleton.
←/→	Moves the cursor within a field (column)
Tab/Shift-Tab	Moves the highlighter left or right, respectively, one column
End/Home	Moves the highlighter to the first or last field, respectively
↑/↓	Moves the highlighter up or down a row, respectively, within a skeleton field
F5	Moves a field between the file and view skeletons
F6/F7	Within the view skeleton, F6 selects a field to move, and F7 moves the field.

Also watch the Message line for instructions about how to use the work surface. Messages also appear if you attempt to use a dBASE IV feature in an incorrect manner. You also see instructions about the features you select from a menu.

Using the Query Screen

The query screen has a work surface that acts as a comprehensive tool for accessing your database. From this work surface, you can create simple or complex queries.

Understanding the Work Surface

The query work surface is divided into three main sections: the file skeleton and calculated fields skeleton are in the upper portion of the screen; the view skeleton is at the bottom; and a condition box may be in the middle.

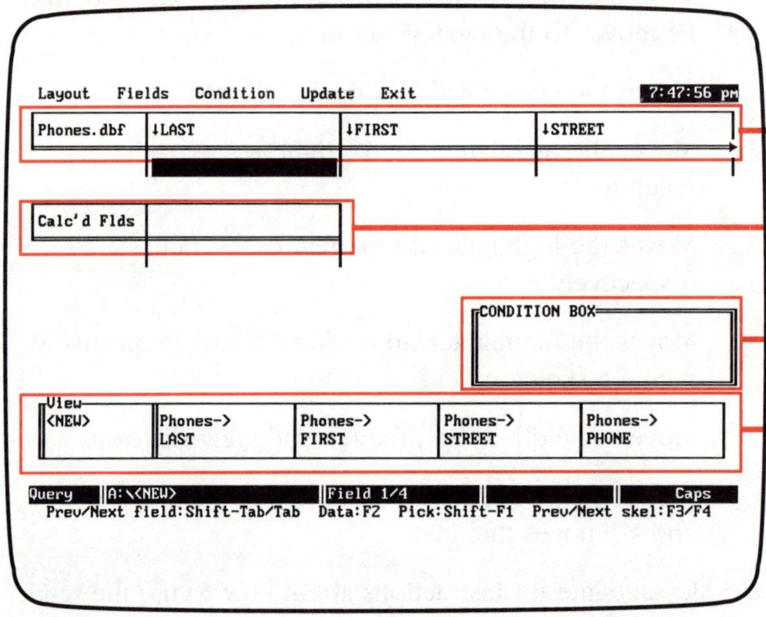

File skeletons control which databases will be used and which records will be accessed in those databases.

The view skeleton controls which fields are available from the database records selected by file skeletons.

File skeleton	(Required) A graphic display of the database design. The leftmost segment contains the file name. Field names follow the file names. Search and sort criteria are written in columns beneath the appropriate field names. Up to eight file skeletons may be open at one time.

Calculated fields skeleton	(Optional) When you create a calculated fields skeleton, you are creating new information. The new information is part data taken from a file and part literal information. For example, a calculated field might be the unit price from the file skeleton times 0.1—a sale discount applied to every record.

Condition box	(Optional) Enter conditions that apply to the entire file. Use this box to specify complex conditions involving several fields or conditions *not associated* with fields—such as the DELETED() function.

View skeleton	(Required) The view skeleton is a graphic layout of those fields from the file skeletons and the calculated fields skeleton that will be used as output. There is only one view skeleton per query.

Using the Query Screen

Using the Status Bar

The Status bar at the bottom of the screen provides information about the query work surface. Five segments appear across the Status bar.

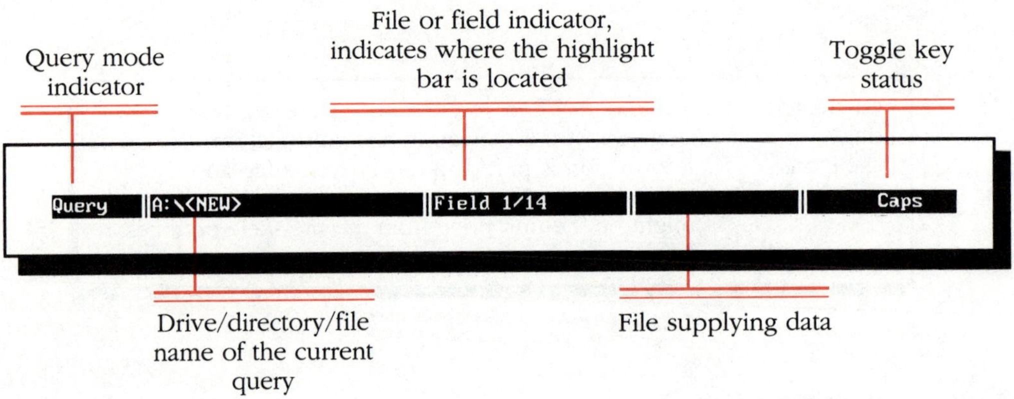

Using the Navigation and Message Lines

Use the keys listed on the Navigation line to move around the work surface. Refer to the Navigation line frequently because not all keys are active at the same time.

Press F5 to move a field between a file skeleton and the view skeleton

Press F3 or F4 to move the highlight bar between skeletons

```
Remove from view:F5  Select:F6  Move:F7  Prev/Next skeleton:F3/F4
```

Press F6 to select a field to be moved within the view skeleton. Extend the selection to adjacent fields by pressing Tab or Shift Tab.

Press F7 to move a field within the view skeleton. Press ← or → to move the selected field. Press Enter to park the field.

Watch the Message line for important instructions and prompts when moving around the work surface.

Additional keys for moving around the work surface are also available.

Home/End	Moves the highlighter to the first or last field, respectively, in the current skeleton
←/→	Moves the cursor left or right, respectively, within the highlight bar where specifications are typed
↑/↓	Moves the highlight bar up or down a line, respectively, in the field column
Tab/ Shift Tab	Moves the highlighter right or left, respectively, one field in the current skeleton

Setting Up File and View Skeletons

To set up the file and view skeletons on the query-design work surface, you first select the database(s) to use in the search. You automatically open a file skeleton for each selected database. For example, if you activate a membership database, you might see the following field names across the *top* of the screen:

BILL_LNAME	(last name of person to bill)
BILL_FNAME	(first name of person to bill)
MEM_DATE	(membership date)
TYPE	(membership type—single, family, corporate),
DUES	(amount of annual dues)
DUES_DUE	(month dues are due)
SIG	(special interest group)
NEWS	(Newsletter? Yes or No)

Within each file skeleton area, you enter the current query specifications in the columns under the applicable headings (field names). For example, if you want to find all members who list genealogy as a special interest, you type *Genealogy* as the query specification in the column under the SIG heading.

dBASE IV also requires that you create for each query a view skeleton—a list of fields across the bottom of the screen that determines the fields used in any query outputs to the screen or printer. Without a view skeleton, you cannot return to, or go to, one of the other work modes such as Browse/Edit, Forms, Reports, or Labels.

To understand how to use a view skeleton, suppose that you are interested in the names and type of membership of only those members indicating a special interest in genealogy. You can limit the view skeleton to just the three fields BILL_LNAME, BILL_FNAME, and TYPE. Any output to the screen or printer is now limited to only those records where the special interest is genealogy (as specified in the file skeleton) and only those fields within each record that provide name and type of membership data (as specified in the view skeleton).

Creating a File Skeleton

A query requires at least one database to be active. In query jargon, the fields in the database you want to search form the file's "skeleton." Recall that a *file skeleton* is just a listing across the top of the screen of all field names in the database. When you create a new query, begin by highlighting one of the databases listed in the Control Center Data panel, press Enter and select **Use file**. Next move to the Query panel, select **<create>** and press Enter.

The first screen you see is the query-design work surface. At the top of the screen, the file skeleton appears automatically, displaying the file names of the newly opened database in sequence, left to right across the screen.

If you access a query without first opening a database, you see a blank query-design work surface. At the top of the screen, you see the Menu bar on which the Layout menu is highlighted. Select **Add file to query**. A list of database names appears on the screen; select a database by highlighting your choice and pressing Enter.

You can access the query-design work surface from any other work mode. Other work modes include Browse/Edit, Forms, Labels, and Reports. The file skeleton automatically contains the fields of the database in use just before you accessed query from another work mode. Use the Layout menu to add or remove databases from the query, and then proceed to create the new query. When you exit the search operation, you see an option to return to the calling work surface.

Removing a File Skeleton

You can have one or more databases specified in the file skeleton, which controls the records to be included in the current search (query) operation. If you need to remove a database from the query, highlight the database name at the left of the file skeleton. Access the Layout menu, and select **Remove file from query**.

Creating a View Skeleton

Once you determine the records you want to search, you must specify which fields within the records you want to display on-screen or print. You cannot exit query mode back to the calling-work mode, or exit to the data mode (F2 [Data]) without setting up a view skeleton.

You can create a view in either of two different ways, both of which transfer field names from the file skeleton to the view skeleton. You can transfer all file skeleton field names to the view skeleton in one operation, or you can transfer field names one at a time.

First, you can place all file skeleton field names into the view skeleton. Do this by moving the highlighter *under the database name* at the extreme left side of the file skeleton and pressing F5 (Fields). The F5 key is a toggle: press it once to copy all file skeleton field names to the view skeleton; press it again to remove all field names from the view skeleton.

Generally, you won't need or want to include all fields in the view skeleton; you probably won't want all the fields to be displayed or printed. The more fields in a database, the more likely you need only selected items for each separate query. For example, if you want to call all society members who do not currently subscribe to your newsletter, you need only a list of names and phone numbers—not the contents of other fields, such as the month that dues are due and the date of membership.

To transfer one field name at a time to or from the view skeleton, move the highlighter to the desired field name in the file skeleton and press the F5 (Fields) toggle key. The field name appears to float across the screen. Repeat the sequence until the view structure across the bottom of the screen shows *in order* the field contents you want to be displayed or printed from the search.

Removing Fields from the View Skeleton

dBASE IV makes removing a field name set up in the view skeleton easy. Suppose that you include the field NEWSLTR (as a logical field—**Newsletter? Yes or No**) in a view skeleton, but the file skeleton contains a search criterion to limit records to those in which N appears in the NEWSLTR field (that is, those members who do not subscribe to the newsletter). You do not have to include information in your screen display or printout that is used as a search condition. To remove a field name from the view skeleton, position the highlighter on the unwanted field and press F5 (Fields).

Moving Fields within a View Skeleton

You can easily move a field *within* the view skeleton on-screen. Use F3 (Prev) and F4 (Next) to move the highlighter between the file and view skeletons. (The Navigation line indicates what keys are available.) Move the highlighter to the view skeleton. Highlight the field you want to move somewhere else within the view skeleton by pressing F6 (Select). To include more than one field in the move—the fields must be next to one another—use Tab and Shift-Tab. Press Enter to end the selection process, press F7 (Move), use Tab and Shift-Tab to move the highlighted fields, and press Enter to park the fields.

You now know the basic procedure for setting up a query—open a file skeleton (*all* field names appear in the selected database) and specify one or more field names in a view skeleton. If you generate a query at this point, you see *all* records, but only those field names in the view skeleton. For example, you might want to list *all* membership records, but limit the output to only names and membership dates. To generate output of only records meeting the specified criteria, you must provide additional information in the file skeleton.

Setting Up File and View Skeletons

The query-design work surface uses a query-by-example technique to help you find information in your databases. You fill out a form telling dBASE IV what information you want from your databases. The query-design work surface is that form. It is a graphic representation of your database.

Creating a File Skeleton

First, you must specify what database to use. Do this by adding a file skeleton to the work surface.

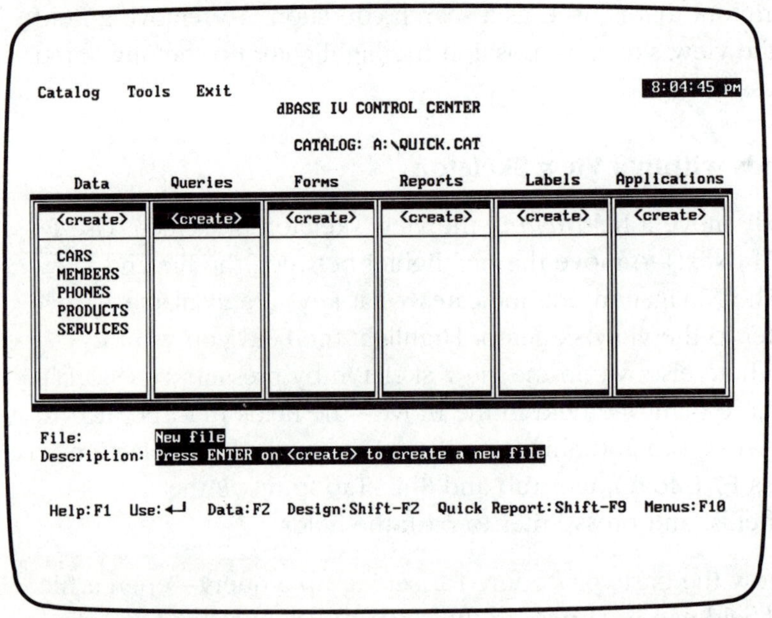

At the Control Center, select **<create>** from the Queries panel.

No database is in use.

Because no database is in use, the query work surface appears with **Layout** selected automatically.

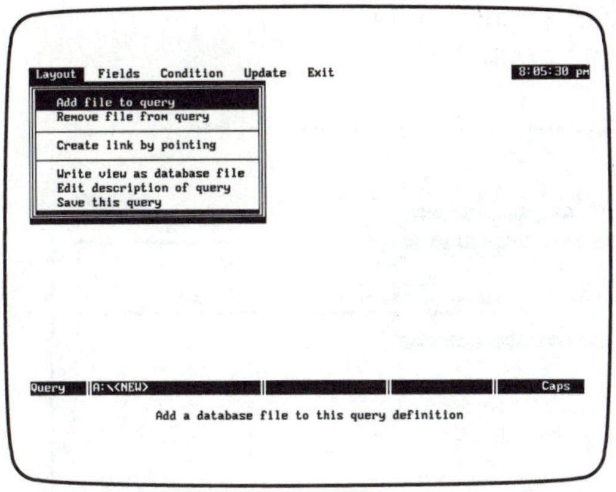

Press ↵Enter to select **Add file to query**.

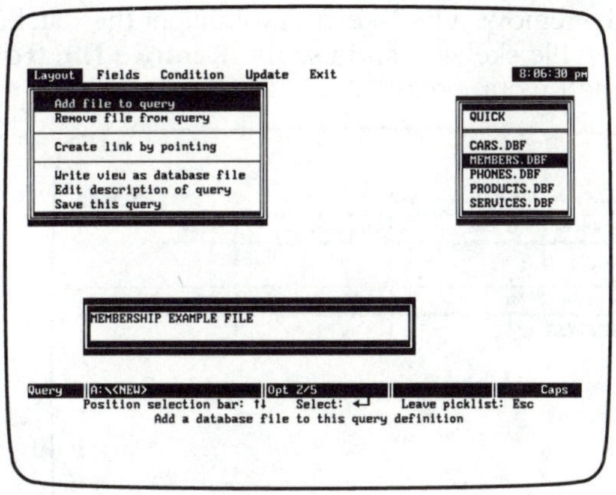

Select the desired database.

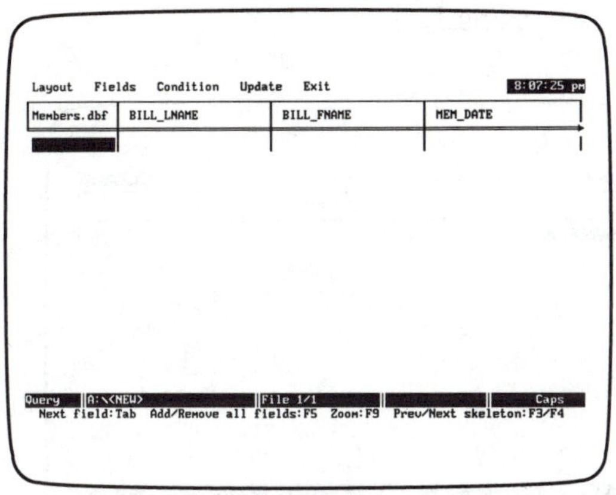

Check that the file skeleton for the database selected appears across the screen below the Menu bar. If a database is already in use, you see this screen immediately.

You also can enter the query-design work surface from work surfaces other than the Control Center.

Removing a File Skeleton

To remove a file skeleton, highlight the database name at the left of the file skeleton and use the **Remove file from query** option on the Layout menu.

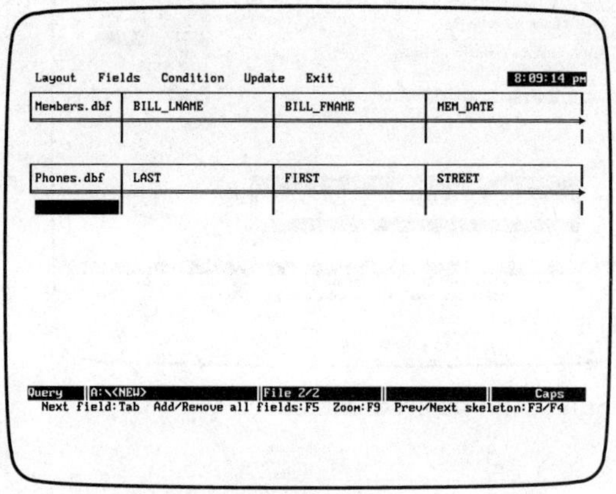

Using the F3/F4 (Prev/Next) keys, highlight the database name to be removed.

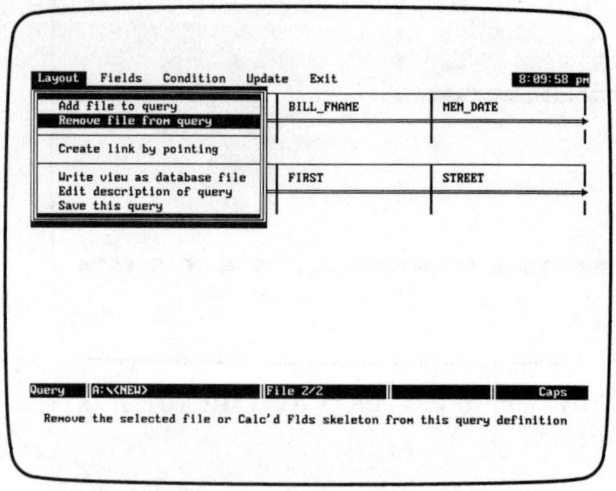

Press Alt L to select the Layout menu, highlight **Remove file from query**, and press ↵Enter.

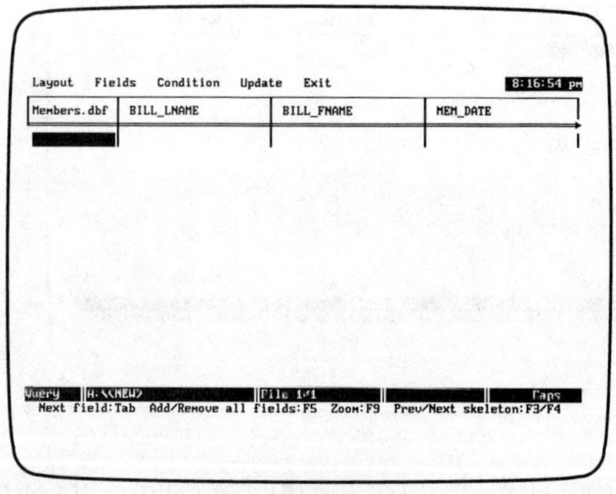

Check that the file skeleton has been removed. If you remove the only file skeleton, you automatically see the Layout menu so that you can add a file to the work surface.

Creating a View Skeleton

Every query must have a view, and you can have only one view per query. The view skeleton tells dBASE IV what data fields you want to see and how they should be arranged across the screen.

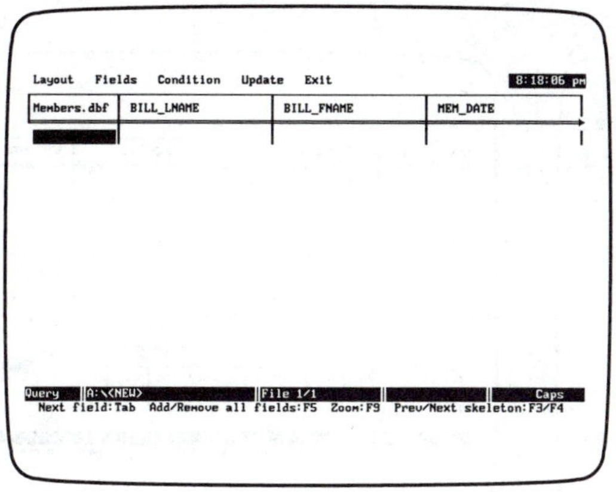

To transfer all fields to the view skeleton, use Tab or Shift Tab to position the highlighter under the database name.

Press F5, the Fields key, to create the view skeleton.

All fields are transferred from the file skeleton to the view skeleton.

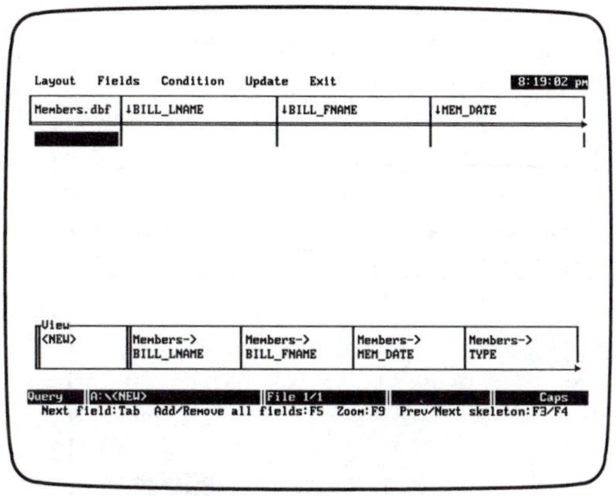

To transfer a single field to the view skeleton, highlight the field name in the file skeleton and press F5. The F5 key acts as a toggle switch for adding or removing a single field.

Removing Fields from the View Skeleton

To remove a field from the view skeleton, highlight the unwanted field in the view skeleton and press [F5], Fields.

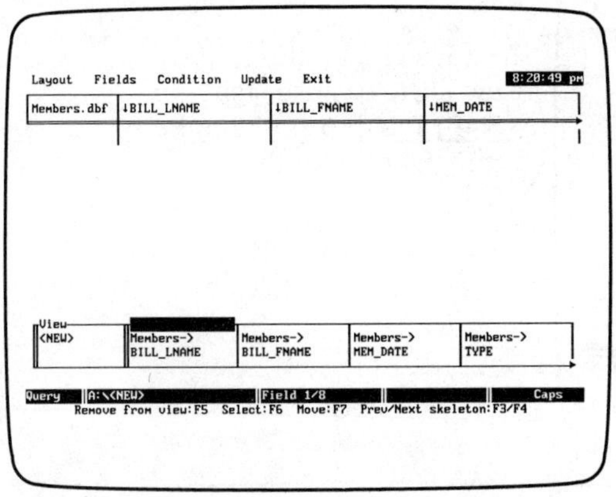

Press [F4], the Next key, until the highlighter is on the view file.

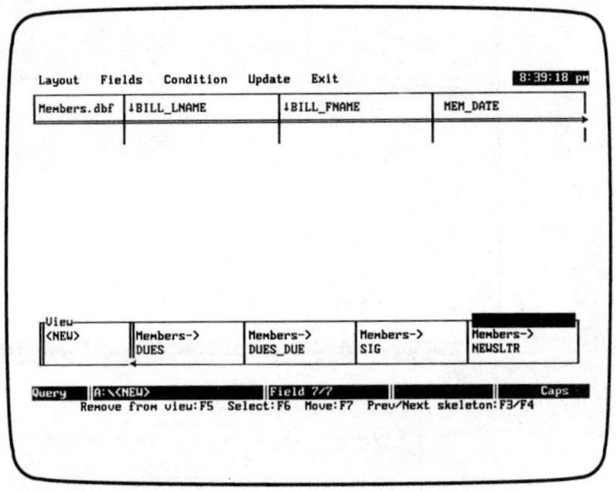

Using [Tab] or [Shift][Tab], position the cursor on the unwanted field.

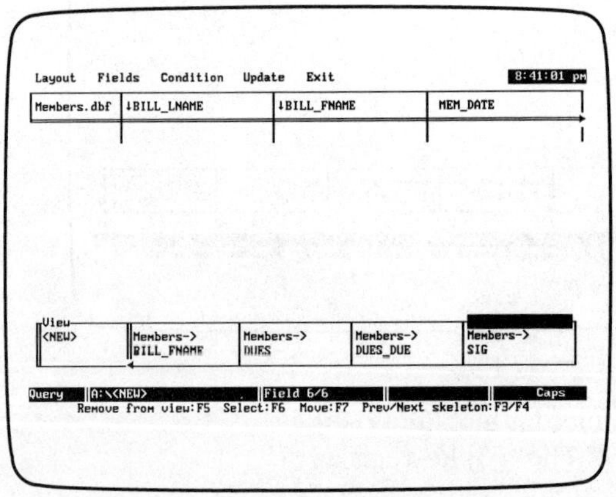

Press [F5] to remove the field.

Moving Fields within a View Skeleton

After the fields are in the view, you can rearrange them easily.

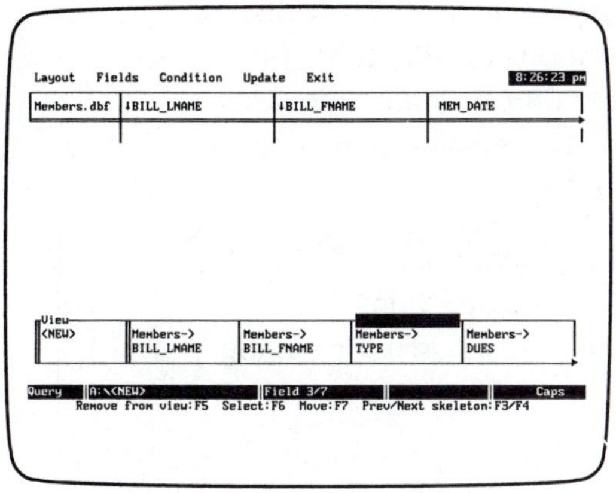

Using Tab or Shift Tab, position the highlighter on the field to be moved.

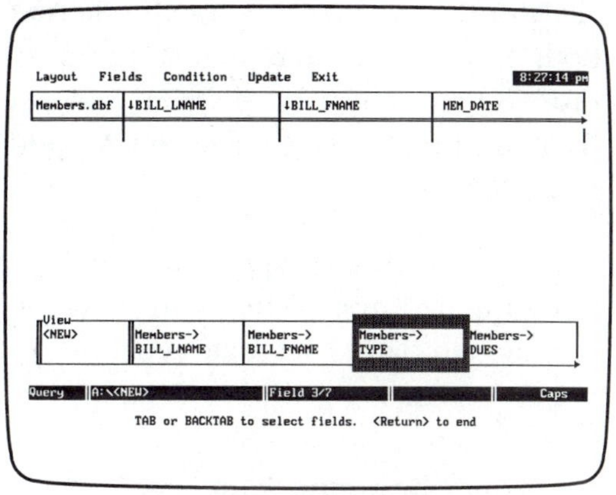

Press F6 to select the field to be moved, and then press Enter to confirm the selection.

Press F7 to select the move operation.

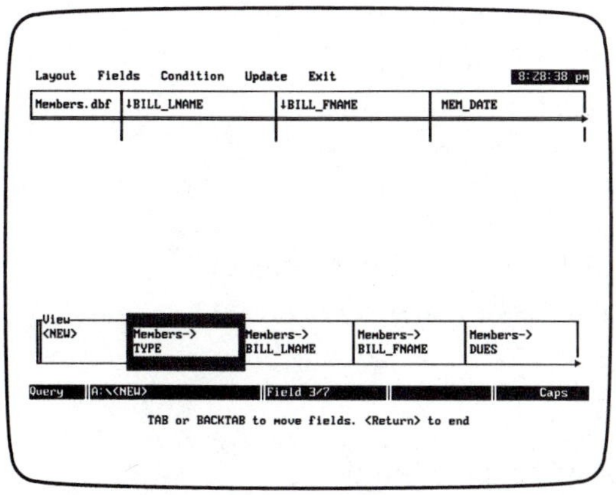

Use Tab or Shift Tab to reposition the highlight bar where the selected field is to be moved. Press Enter to complete the move.

The selected field appears after the field containing the highlight bar. Now you can use Tab or Shift Tab to move the selected field one position at a time. Press Enter when the field is in the appropriate position.

> To select two or more adjacent fields, press F6 to select the first field, use the Tab and Shift Tab keys to include adjacent fields, and then press Enter to confirm the selection.

Making Simple Queries

The simplest query involves searching for records based on the content of a single field. Once you create the appropriate file and view skeletons, and enter the search criterion in the file skeleton, you can both execute the query and store the specifications for the query on disk so they can be used again. For example, you can search the CARS database for all records whose CAR_PRICE field is greater than or equal to 10,000.

You can search any type of data field including memo fields. Field types queried more often than others include character, numeric, logical, and date. Each data type has a few rules of its own for writing search criteria.

Locating Character Data

To perform a query on a character field, move the highlighter bar—using Tab or Shift-Tab—to the character field name in the query-design work surface's file skeleton. You then must type the search specifications within quotation marks. (Remember that all *character* expressions must be enclosed in quotation marks.) For example, to search a car-sales database for all records for LASTNAME fields containing the name "Fox," you type *"Fox"*. Or to produce a list of all cars sold to buyers in ZIP code 46321, you enter *"46321"* under the ZIP field in the file skeleton.

After you create a view skeleton, you can quickly look at the results of your query if you press the F2 (Data) key to access Browse/Edit mode.

Locating Numeric Data

To find car-sales records for cars priced at $17,500, position the highlighter under the numeric field CAR_PRICE in the file skeleton. Type *17500* and press Enter. (dBASE IV does not align the number to the right like most numeric fields, but the search still works.) Notice that numeric data is typed without quotation marks.

To query a numeric field for a specific number, type the number in the appropriate column. You do not need other symbols or braces. Add a period, however, to show decimal places or a minus sign (–) to indicate a negative number. Do not use other punctuation, such as dollar signs or commas.

Locating Logical Data

To query a logical field for its true/false (or yes/no) condition, move the highlighter to the appropriate field. Then type, within periods, the logical condition to be searched. Enter *.T.*, *.t.*, *.Y.*, or *.y.* to represent a true condition. Or enter *.F.*, *.f.*, *.N.*, or *.n.* to represent a false condition.

For example, to locate in a car-sales database all car buyers who did not buy the extended warranty, move the highlighter under the file skeleton column that contains the logical field (such as WARRANTY). Type *.F.* or *.f.* or *.N.* or *.n.* as the search criterion.

Locating a Date

When entering search criteria based on date fields, type the date within curly braces ({}). The curly braces indicate that a date is enclosed. For example, to search for the record of a buyer whose car was delivered on January 24, 1989, first position the highlighter under the DATE_DEL field name in the file skeleton. Then type *{01/24/89}* and press Enter.

These simple query examples demonstrate searches limited to a single parameter (condition). The examples show the differences between writing search specifications for character, numeric, or logical data types, or for a date. dBASE IV, however, can handle such complex search conditions as searching for a series of entries or a range of numbers.

Making Simple Queries

The simplest query involves searching for records based on the content of a single field. The way you enter the search criterion varies depending on what type of data the field contains: character data, numeric data, logical data, or a date.

Using the automobile customer database, for example, you can make many useful inquiries.

First, set up the query.

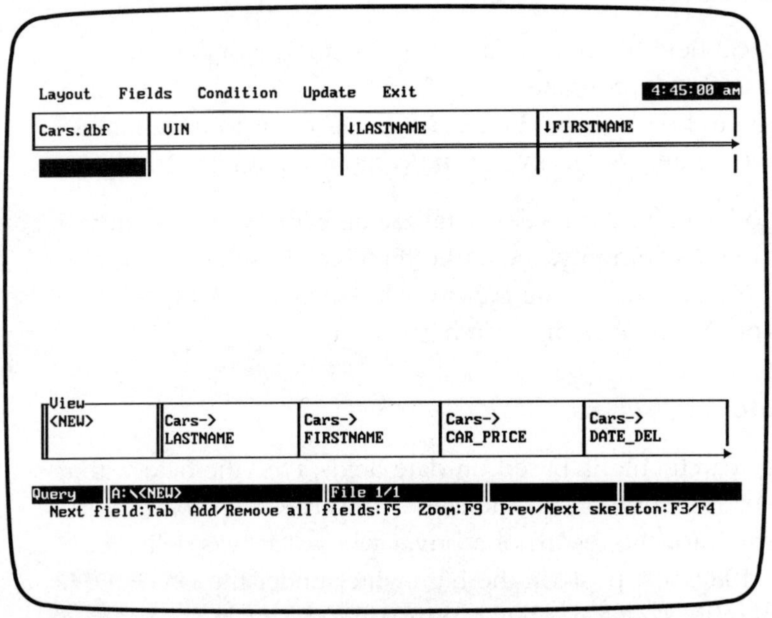

Create a query, and add the file and view skeletons.

Notice that the view skeleton has been limited to selected fields. This is so that you can view your queries easier in Browse mode. You want to structure your views to focus on specific information.

Locating Character Data

Query a character field, such as LASTNAME, for all customers named “Fox”.

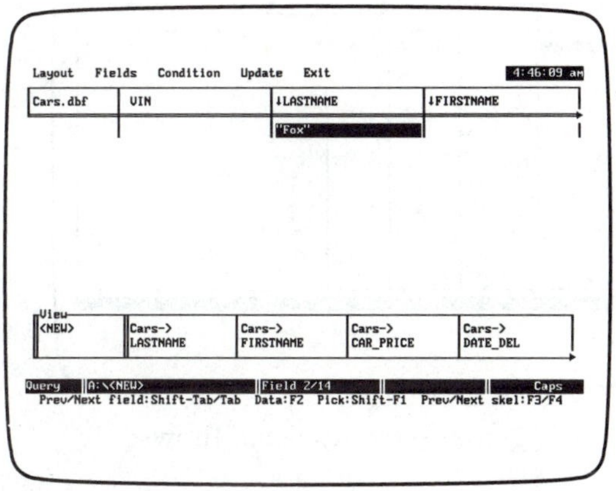

Move the cursor to the appropriate field and type the name you want to locate in quotation marks. Use correct capitalization.

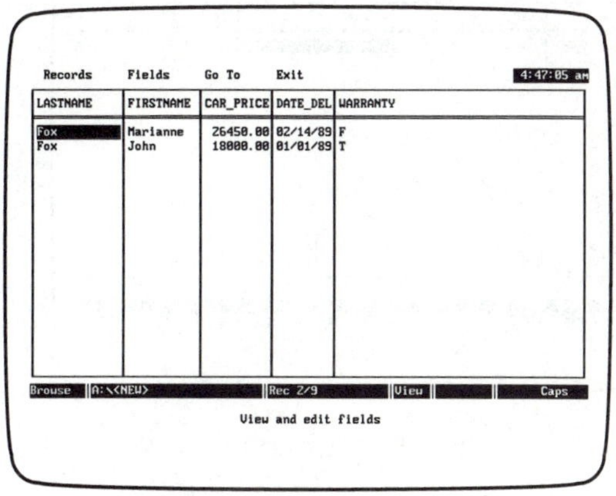

Press F2, the Data key, to see the results in Browse mode.

If the Edit screen appears, press F2 again.

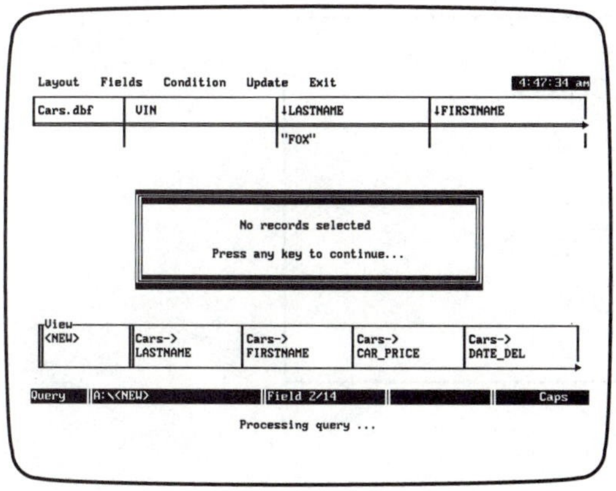

If no records are found, you see this screen. The records you are searching for may not be in the database. (Be sure to double check your criteria for spelling and capitalization.)

Making Simple Queries

Locating Numeric Data

Query a numeric field, such as CAR_PRICE, for any sale of exactly $12,500.

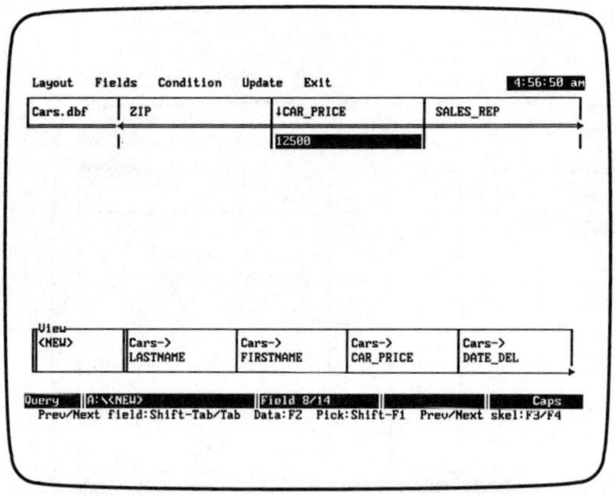

Enter the amount in the appropriate field.

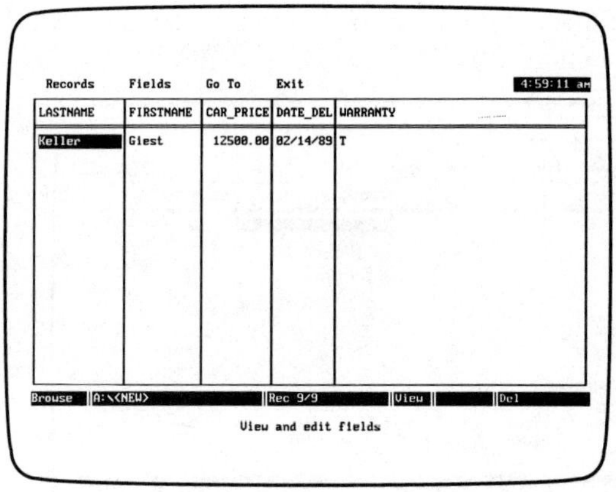

Press F2 to see the results in Browse mode.

Numeric fields contain only numbers, a decimal place, and a minus (–) sign, if necessary. Do not use quotation marks, commas, or dollar signs.

Sample Numeric Criteria

Valid	*Invalid*
100	$100
42563.27	42,567.00
–250	"2000"

Locating Logical Data

Query a logical field, such as warranty purchased, for all customers who did not buy a warranty.

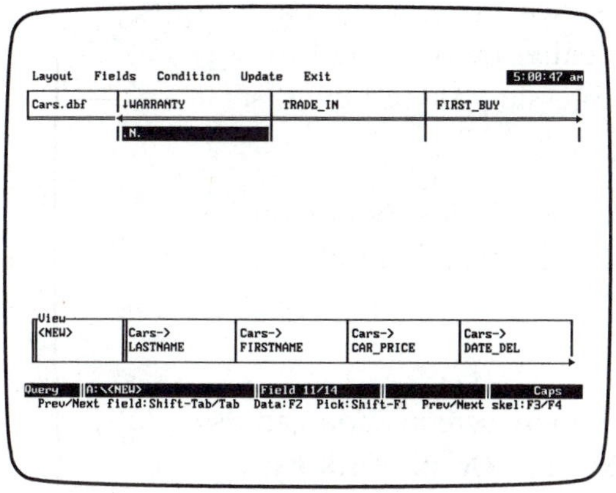

Enter .N. in the appropriate field.

Remember, logical fields can contain

TRUE .T./.t./.Y./.y.

FALSE . F./.f./.N./.n.

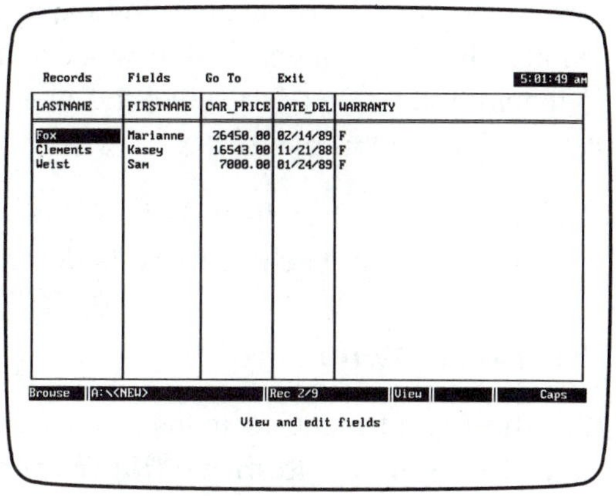

Press F2, the Data key, to see the results in Browse mode.

Locating a Date

Query a date field, such as the date a vehicle was delivered, for all sales delivered on a certain date.

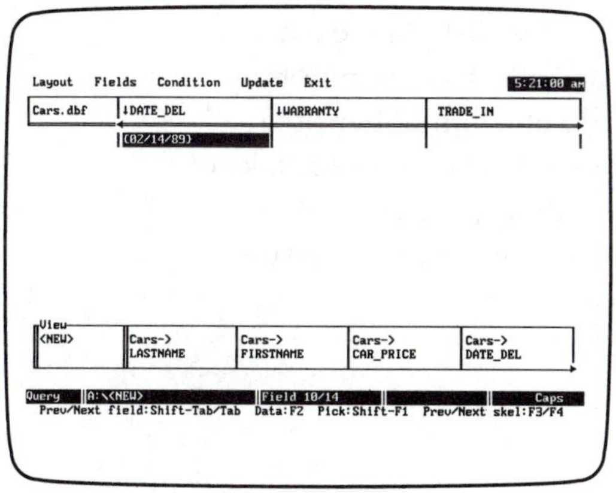

Enter the desired date, enclosed in curly braces {}, in the appropriate field.

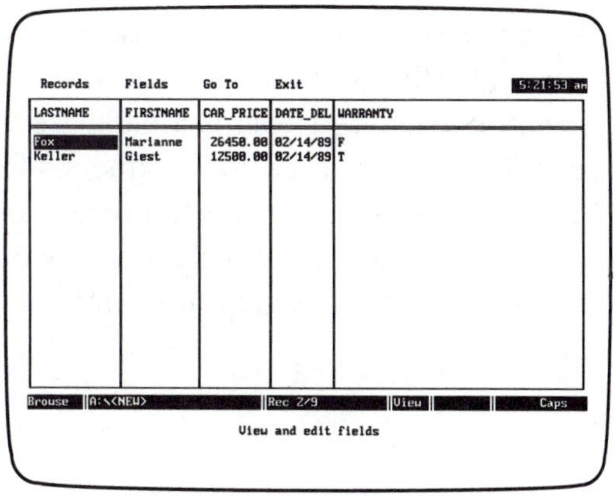

Press F2, the Data key, to see the results in Browse mode.

Using the Query Menu Bar

The Menu bar on the query-design work surface contains the names of five menus that activate querying capabilities. Access the Menu bar choices from the query-design work surface either by pressing F10 (Menus) and → or ← to select the menu or pressing Alt and the first letter of the menu name.

The query Menu bar displays five choices: Layout, Fields, Condition, Update, and Exit. Each of these is described in the text that follows.

The Layout Menu

Use the Layout menu to manage files on the query screen. You can use **Add file to query**, **Remove file from query**, and **Create link by pointing** to manage files in the file skeleton. The **Create link by pointing** option causes the records in two or more files to be linked together by one common field. Related records from different databases are available to dBASE IV to use as if they were one big record. Select **Save this query** to save the query specifications (not the data) to disk without exiting.

You can choose **Write view as database file** to create a new database limited to the records selected by the query and the fields selected by the view. You might use this option to create a test data file, exchange data with other software products, or select specific accounting or inventory data. Test data is a database with a minimal number of records. They are used to test queries for known results. If the results of your query produces expected results on a small test database, then you have confidence that the query would work on a large database where you cannot verify the results.

Keep in mind that creating a new database uses valuable disk space quickly. You may be able to access the data just as efficiently by working with the original database and creating the necessary views and queries.

The Fields Menu

Use the Fields menu to manage the fields in the view skeleton. You can select **Add field to view** and **Remove field from view** to move fields between the view skeleton and the file skeletons.

Use **Edit field name** to change a field name in the view skeleton. Remember, view skeleton field names come from the file skeleton and become column headings in Browse/Edit and Quick Report. You also can use **Edit field name** to refer to calculated fields in the view skeleton and condition box.

Use **Create calculated field** to create or access an existing calculated fields skeleton. You then can enter a valid dBASE IV expression. The Shift-F1 (Pick) expression builder is now available. Delete calculated skeletons using **Remove files** on the Layout menu.

Use **Sort on this field** and **Include indexes** to arrange the record sequence in the view output. If you choose the sort feature, you can specify one of the four sort collating types—Ascending, Ascending dictionary, Descending, Descending dictionary. Use **Include indexes** to include indexes in sorting data. With **Include index** toggled on, all indexes for the current database appear as fields to the right of the file skeleton. Index expressions become the field names, and a pound sign (#) appears next to each name designated as an index.

The Condition Menu

Use the Condition menu to control condition boxes on the work surface. You can select **Add condition box** or **Delete condition box** for the query design. Conditions affect the entire query. Use Shift-F1 (Pick) to use the expression builder. F9 (Zoom) allows you to see any expression that is too large to fit in the condition box. The **Show condition box** option is a toggle; when set to NO, the option will hide the box to conserve space on the screen.

You often use a condition box when you want to see deleted records. Suppose that you want to print a list of deleted records prior to erasing them permanently from the database. To create a filter so that dBASE IV acts only on deleted records, create a condition box and enter the DELETED() function.

The Update Menu

You can use the query-design work surface to make changes at one time to every record in the database or to groups of records. A query acts as an update query when you place one of the four update operators (**REPLACE**, **APPEND**, **MARK**, and **UNMARK**) in the far left column of the query-design work surface, containing the database name.

Update queries operate on a single database. Although you can have several databases defined in one query, only one database can have an update operator under it. An update query appears on the Center Control panel with an asterisk (*) next to its name.

The **REPLACE** operator causes the contents of one or more data fields to be replaced according to instructions placed in that field's column. Begin instructions with the word *with*. For example, to cause the LASTNAME field in the Cars database to be changed to all uppercase letters in each record in the database, type *REPLACE* under the database name, then type *with UPPER(LASTNAME)* under the field name LASTNAME.

The **APPEND** operator lets you add (append) records from one database to a target database. The source database contains the records to be appended to the end of the target database. Instructions in the field columns control the movement of data between the databases.

Use **Mark** and **Unmark** to designate groups of records for deletion or remove the marks as necessary. Selection criteria entered in field columns determine which records are marked or unmarked. Records marked for deletion remain in the file until they are removed from the database. Remove marked records using the **Erase marked records** option on the Organize menu found on the data-design work surface.

Use the **Perform the update** option to activate the update. At the end of the update, you see a message indicating the number of records changed. If you want to see how a replace operation worked, remove the "replace" operator and "with" instructions by moving the cursor to that column and deleting or spacing over the contents. Now you can invoke the query with only the criteria applying to the records that need replacement, and you can confirm their replacement.

The Exit Menu

Use the Exit menu to leave the query session. You can **Save changes and exit** to leave the query session and save the query design for use later. Or you can **Abandon changes and exit** to leave the session without saving your query design. If you entered the query session from the forms, labels, or report work surfaces, you see an option to return to that work surface.

Using the Query Menu Bar

The Menu bar on the query-design work surface contains the names of five menus that activate querying capabilities.

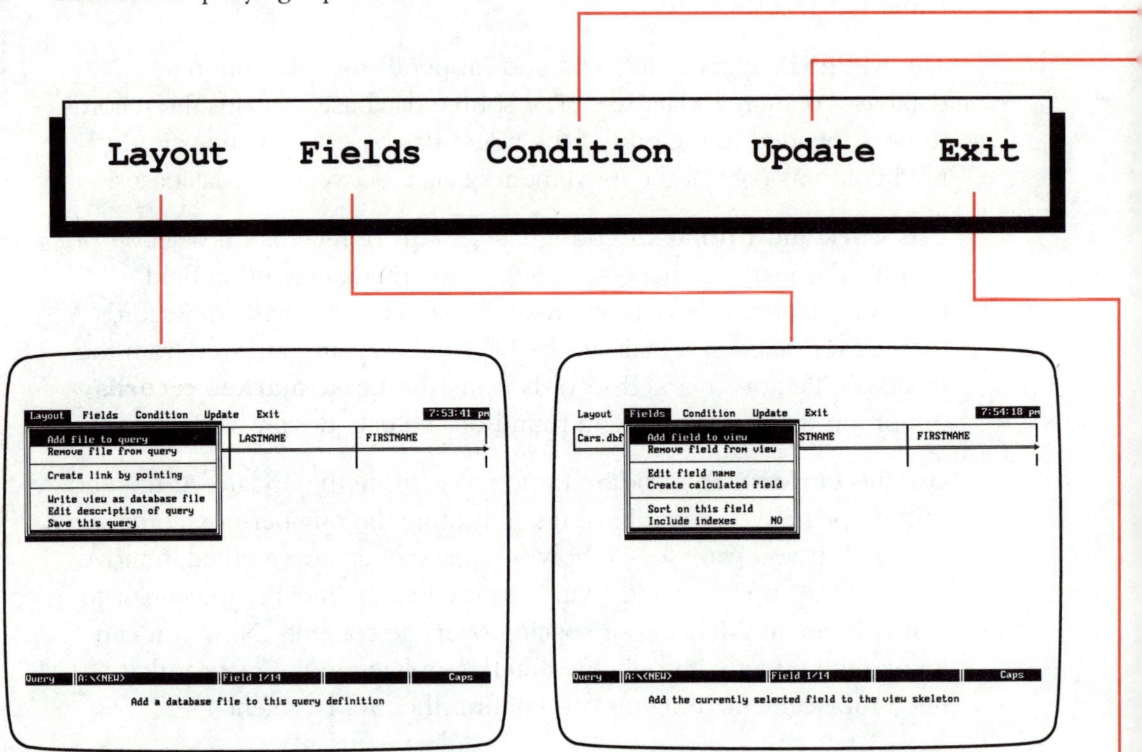

Use **Layout** to manage file skeletons. You can add or remove a file from a file skeleton, link files, and save a query without exiting. You can use **Write view as database file** to create a new database limited to the records and fields specified by the query.

Use **Fields** to manage the fields in the view skeleton. You can use **Add field to view** or **Remove field from view** to move fields between the view skeleton and file skeletons. Use **Create calculated field** to create or access an existing calculated fields skeleton.

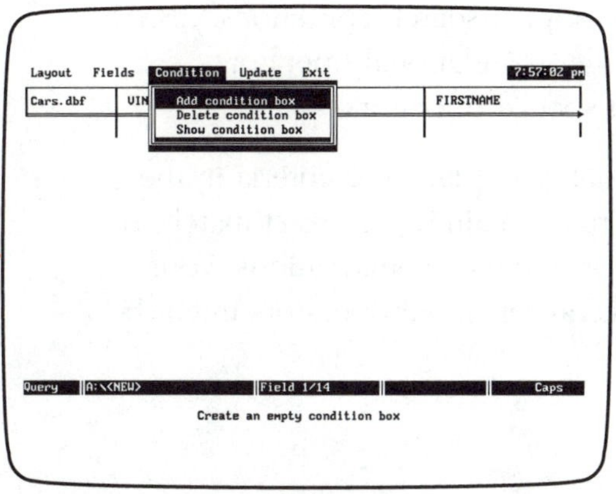

Use **Condition** to add or delete condition boxes. You often use a condition box to list deleted records before you erase them permanently.

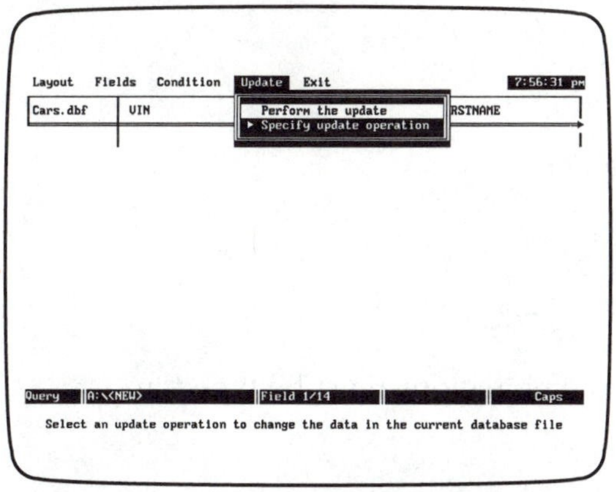

Use **Update** to update groups of records at one time, making uniform changes to every record in a database. Update operations you can perform include replacing fields, appending records, and marking and unmarking records.

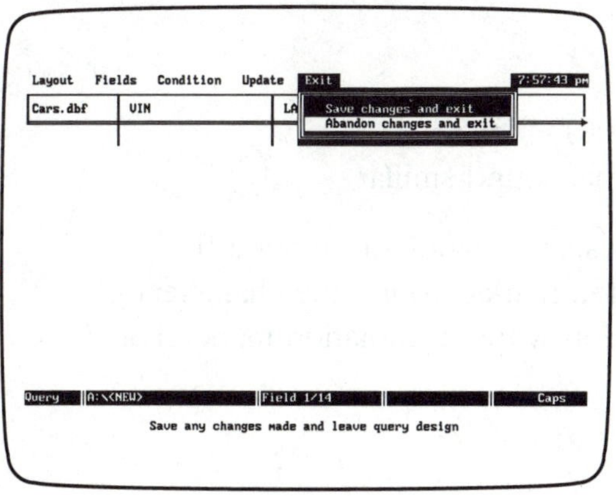

Use **Exit** to leave the work surface, saving or abandoning the changes just made.

Using Operators

Using operators, you can state more complex search conditions. dBASE IV offers you three basic types of operators: relational operators, relational operator combinations, and special operators.

You are not limited to searches in which you place the criteria in the file skeleton and find only those records containing an exact match. By using one of the relational operators or operator combinations, your searches can prove more flexible. Several relational operators might be familiar to you.

Basic relational operators include:

=	Equal to
>	Greater than
<	Less than

Relational operator combinations include:

>=	Greater than or equal to
<=	Less than or equal to
<> or #	Not equal to

Caution: The preceding operator combinations must be typed in the sequence shown.

Special operators include:

$	Field Contains
Like	Wild-card search for patterns
Sounds Like	Search for words that sound similar

You can enter a character or numeric search condition under a file skeleton field name by typing quotation marks around the character condition or typing the number criterion without quotation marks. For example, type *"Fox"* as the search condition if you need to find all car sales records in which the buyer's last name is "Fox." By typing exactly what you want to find, you are requesting an Equal to (=) search.

Using Basic Relational Operators

As you can see, you can accomplish the same results in two ways. For example, you can type *="Fox"* as the search condition. Using operators, you can be more flexible about typing expressions. For example, a search condition can work with blanks preceding the expression { ="Fox"} or blanks between the equals (=) operator and the literal criteria "Fox" as in {= "Fox"}. The characters between the quotation marks, however, must appear exactly as the data in the records appears.

Use the Greater than (>) operator to find all records where the field content exceeds the stated amount. For example, to create a search criterion in a customer database that finds all customers who paid more than $15,000 dollars for a car, position the highlighter under the car-price field name in the file skeleton and type *>15000*. On the other hand, you can find all persons who paid less than $15,000, by using the Less than (<) operator and typing *<15000*.

You also can use the > or < operators to locate character-field contents that fall *after* (>) or *before* (<) a certain letter or letter combination in the collating sequence. For example, to find the records of all car buyers whose last names start with M or a subsequent letter of the alphabet, type *>"L"* as the search condition.

Imagine applying basic operators to dates! If you type the search condition *<{01/15/89}*, for example, you can find all records dated before January 15, 1989.

Using Operators

Relational Operators extend your ability to search for data by helping you ask more complex questions. Earlier you learned that specifying exact criteria, such as $24,000 or {01/20/89}, produced very narrow results. By including one of the following operators, operator combinations, or special operators in your search criteria, your searches become more flexible.

Basic Operators		
	=	Equal to
	>	Greater than
	<	Less than
Operator Combinations		
	>=	Greater than or equal to
	<=	Less than or equal to
	<> or #	Not equal to
Special Operators		
	$	Field Contains
	Like	Wild-card search for patterns
	Sounds Like	Search for words that sound like

Using Basic Relational Operators

Using the Equal to (=) operator has the same effect as using no operator. "Fox" and ="Fox" produce the same result.

Use Greater than (>) to find all records for cars sold after 01/15/89.

Enter the Greater than condition in the appropriate field.

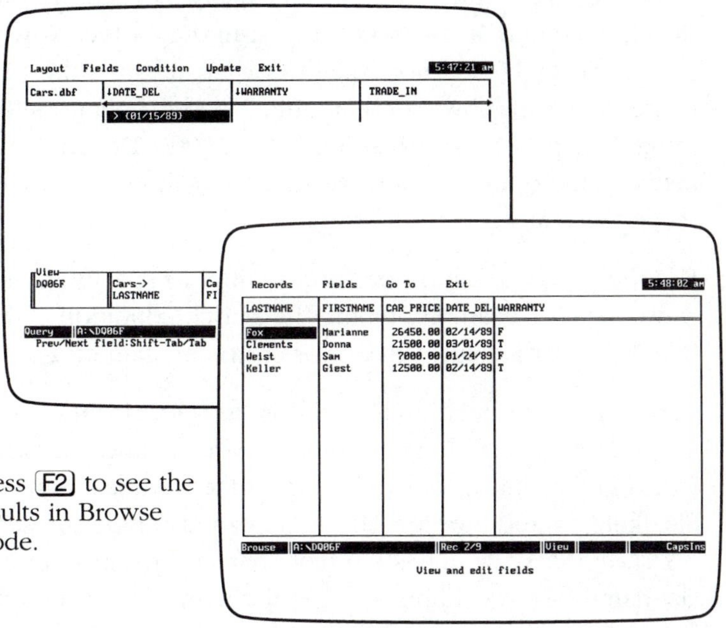

Press F2 to see the results in Browse mode.

Other Examples

>"F"	Find all records whose field contents begin with G through Z.
<{01/15/89}	Find all records whose date field is before 01/15/89.
<{01/16/89}	Find all dates before 01/16/89.
>24000	Find all records whose field is greater than 24000.

Using Relational Operator Combinations

Combining operators adds more flexibility to your search criteria. Suppose, for example, that you want all records in which the car price is $15,000 or higher. If you state your search condition as *>15000,* you miss records in which the price is exactly $15,000. If you state your search condition as *>14999* you risk finding a record where the price is $14,999.50—which is not equal to or greater than the $15,000 search figure. You can, however, combine > and = operators for the correct result. The proper search string is >= *15000.* Do not leave any blanks between the operators, and be sure to include the equal sign (=) as the second operator.

Use the <> combination or the # symbol to specify the Not Equal condition. For example, typing the search condition *# "Fox"* or *<>"Fox"* finds all records except those for customers named Fox.

You can use the relational operators to select from character fields. For example, to select all the records with last names starting with the letters M through Z, move the highlighter to a last-name column in the file skeleton and type >= *"M".* (You can also type the search string *>"L".*) dBASE IV searches the first character position in each record's last-name field, deciding whether the name in the record starts with the letter M or a subsequent letter in the alphabet.

Using Special Operators

Three special operators—Contains ($), Like, and Sounds Like—make your searches even more flexible and versatile. Many searches go beyond merely determining a relationship. You may need to find a set of characters embedded in a larger character string, locate every address on a particular street, or find a name that sounds like, but is not spelled like, another word.

Using Contains ($)

Use the Contains ($) operator to find a set of embedded characters in a larger string of characters. Suppose that you keep a furniture store's inventory records, and you need to generate a list of all lamps in stock. Assume that the word *lamp* could appear anywhere within the description field (beginning, middle, or end). If you type a search criterion with the Contains operator ($), such as *$"lamp"*, dBASE IV finds *Floor lamp*, *brass lamp*, *hanging lamp*, and *lamp table.*

Consider another example. Assume that you maintain an inventory of computer-related products. To find each type of double-sided, double-density disk (DS/DD) you carry in stock, regardless of size (such as 5.25 inches or 3.5 inches), use the $ operator in the search criterion. Because the phrase could be anywhere in the description, move the highlighter to the appropriate column in the file skeleton and type *$ "DS/DD".* This search criterion finds all records containing *DS/DD* but not those containing *ds/dd.* Recall that the search criterion—in this case "DS/DD" must be written exactly as it appears in the data field. If data could appear in the data field in upper- or lowercase, use one of dBASE IV's features called a *function* to find the data you want.

Perhaps, however, you want to find both upper- and lowercase listings. One way to perform non-case-sensitive searches involves setting up a calculated field. To set up a calculated field to search for *DS/DD* regardless of case, first select the Fields menu from the Menu bar and choose **Create calculated fields**. Next position the highlighter in the empty field-name box on the calculated fields skeleton; and type *UPPER(fieldname)*, replacing *fieldname* with the name of the field to search. Finally, position the highlighter in the column below the field name and type *"DS/DD".*

Recall that you can perform non-case-sensitive searches in the Data panel **Index key search** by creating indexes using the UPPER() function to make all index contents uppercased. You accomplish the same non-case-sensitive search with the **Create calculated fields** option in query. One purpose, therefore, of calculated fields is to manipulate data with dBASE IV's functions.

You also can use the Contains $ operator to search the content of memo fields. For example, you might have a prospective-customers database that includes a memo field for recording buyer preferences and other comments. To find all records in which a prospective car buyer has stated a preference for the color blue, move the highlighter under the appropriate memo field in the file skeleton and type *$ "blue"*.

Using the Like Operator for Wild-Card Searches

You can create wild-card searches without going into the Query panel. After you select the Go To menu in the Browse/Edit screen, choose **Search Forward** or **Search Backward** and specify a search condition containing the appropriate wild card. For example, you can type the search string **Cape Drive* to find records in your phone-number database containing Cape Drive and any house number.

Wild cards work in query as they work in searches initiated solely from Browse/Edit mode. In both cases, dBASE IV searches all records for your search condition. A primary advantage of a query-initiated search is that you can limit or control the records in the database that are available for the reports and label features to use.

You can use * to replace any group of characters and ? to replace any single character. You must, however, type the operator *Like* first. For example, to find all the addresses on Cape Drive in your phone-number database, type *Like* "**Cape Drive*". The search criterion tells dBASE IV to look for Cape Drive and accept any characters that precede the words Cape Drive. If you do not know if Cape is a Drive or a Street, change the search condition to *Like* "**Cape**".

You can combine wild cards if you are unsure of the spelling. For example, if a street name might be Cape or Cate, type *Like* "**Ca?e*". The stated search string can find records in which the street name is Cape or Cane, as well as those in which the street name is Cake or Camel.

To set up a calculated field to search for *Like* "**Ca?e**" regardless of case, first select the Fields menu from the Menu bar on the query-design work surface and choose **Create calculated fields**. Next, position the highlight in the empty-field name box on the Calc'd flds line and type *UPPER(fieldname)*, replacing *fieldname* with the name of the field to search—in this case *STREET*. Finally, position the highlight in the column below the field name and type *Like* "*Ca?e*"*.

Using the Sounds Like Operator

In setting up most of your query search conditions, you know how to spell at least part of the desired field contents. However, one of dBASE IV's new features, Soundex, lets you find field contents based on a "sounds like" search condition. In other words, you can use a version of the Like operator, Sounds Like, to guess at the spelling in a field and possibly get results.

For example, suppose you have a first-name field in your database, and the entry you are searching for is "Kasey." You have already tried a search condition *Like "Casey"* without finding the correct record, and you can't think of an alternate spelling. Try using the Sounds Like operator by moving the highlight under the appropriate field-name column in the file skeleton and typing the search condition *Sounds Like "KC"*.

Using Sounds Like requires some trial and error. For example, if you type the search condition *Sounds Like "Casey"* or *Sounds Like "Casee"*, dBASE IV does not find a record containing "Kasey." If, however, you type the search condition *Sounds Like "KC"* or *Sounds Like "Ksee"*, dBASE IV can find a record containing "Kasey."

Using Operators

Using Relational Operator Combinations

Combine query operators to extend your search power. When relational operators are combined, you can ask more flexible questions using Less than or equal to, Greater than or equal to, or Not equal to.

You can ask for information that *includes* selected records.

Enter <={01/15/89} to select all records whose date field is on or before January 15, 1989.

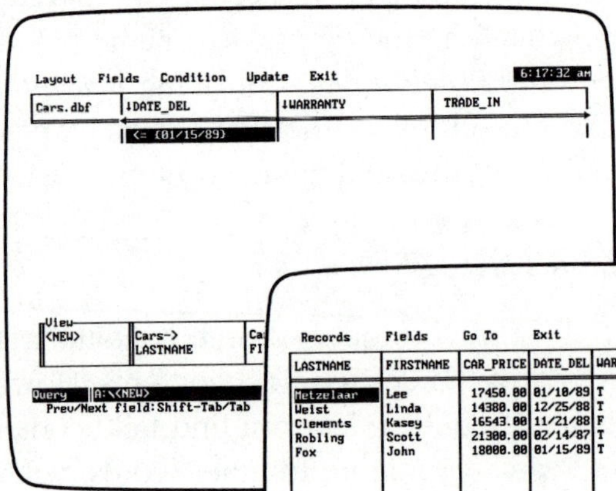

Press F2 to see the results in Browse mode. Notice that John Fox's record has a date equal to January 15, 1989, while all other records are before that date.

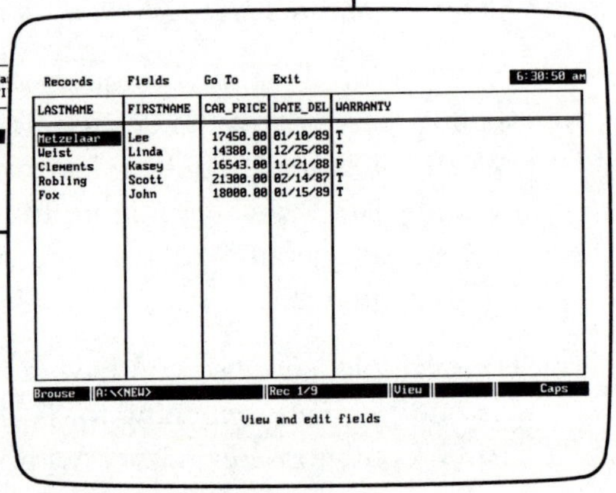

Without combining operators, you had to write <{01/16/89} to see all records on or before 01/15/89. Now you can write <={01/15/89}, which is easier to read and understand at a glance.

You can ask for information that *excludes* selected records.

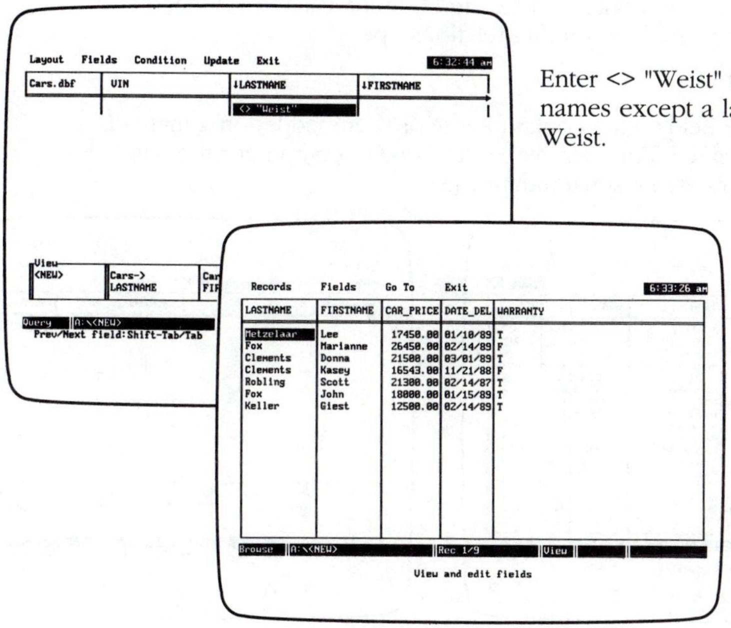

Enter <> "Weist" to select all names except a last name of Weist.

Press F2 to see the results in Browse mode. Notice that the query was successful.

The criteria could also be written as # "Weist"

Other Examples

>={01/15/89}	Select all records whose date field is on or after 01/15/89.
<="G"	Select all records whose character field begins with A through G.
#.12	Select all records except those whose numeric field is .12.

Using Special Operators

Three special operators—Contains, Like, and Sounds Like—provide search powers that go beyond finding relationships.

Using Contains ($)

Product descriptive fields often contain key words embedded in a manner that is difficult to search. For example, a database of computer products might contain several items concerning disks.

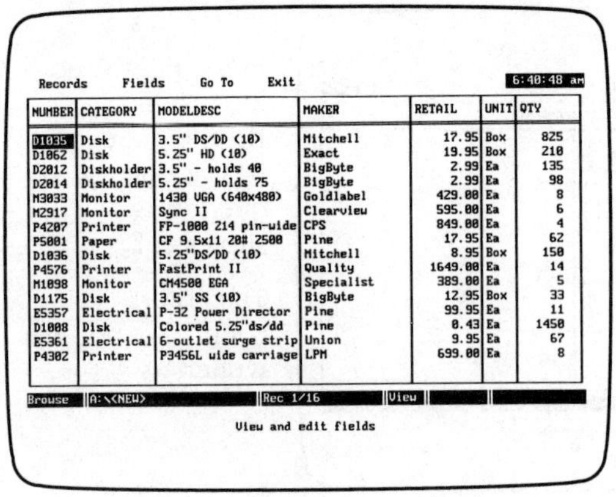

Use Contains to locate records about double-sided/double-density disk (DS/DD) products.

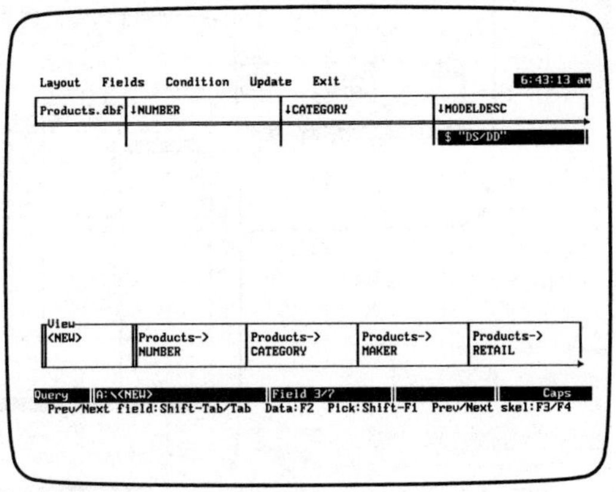

Enter the criteria $ "DS/DD" in the appropriate column.

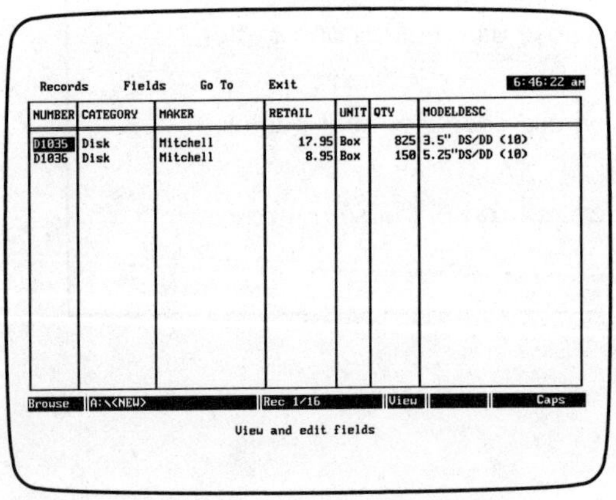

Press F2 to see the results in Browse mode.

Notice that the search was case sensitive and missed records with ds/dd (lowercase).

To write non-case-sensitive search criteria, create a calculated fields skeleton that uses the UPPER() function, and then search for DS/DD products.

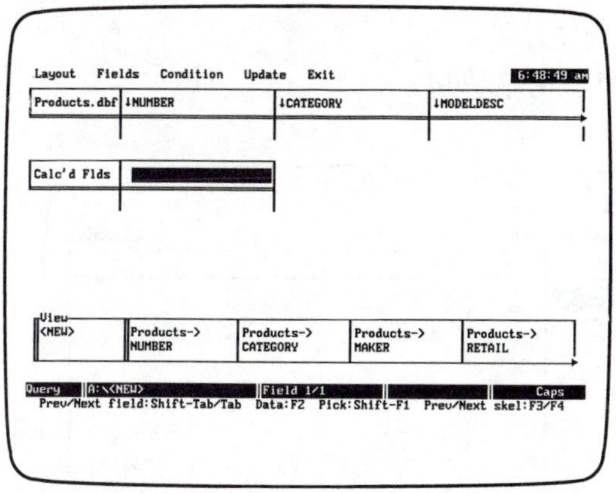

Press Alt F to select the Fields menu, and then press C to select **Create calculated field**.

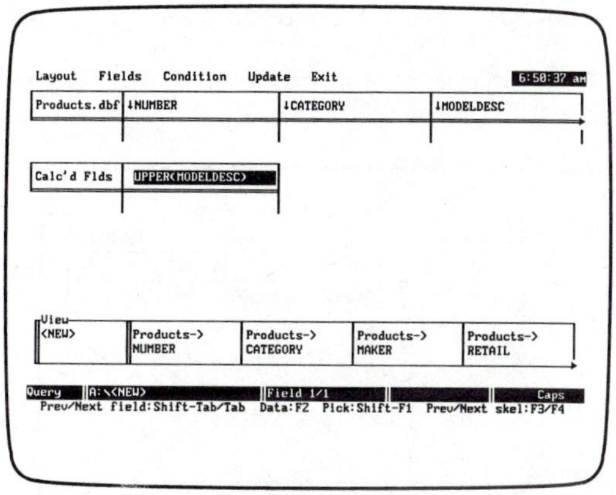

In the calculated fields box, enter the function UPPER(MODELDESC).

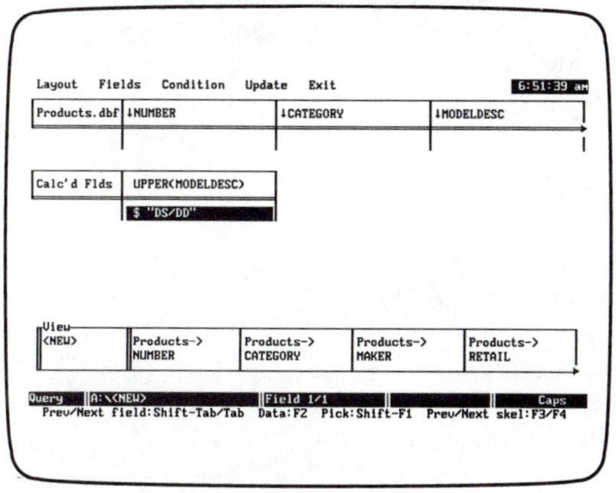

In the calculated fields column, enter the search criteria $ "DS/DD"

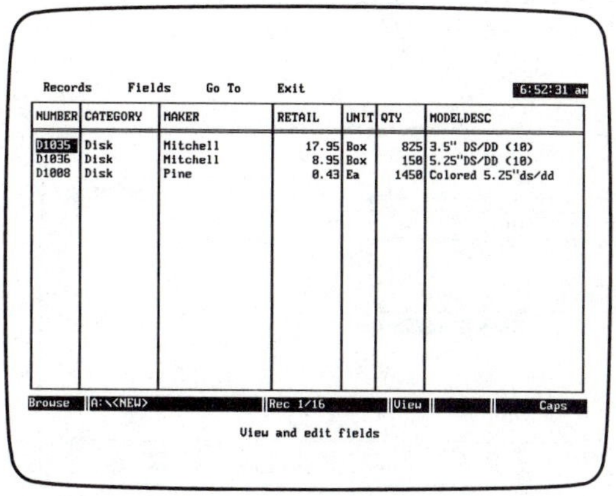

Press F2 to see the results in Browse mode.

Using the Like Operator

Wild cards work in the Query panel the same way they work in the Data panel. The * replaces a group of characters in a search criteria string, and the ? replaces a single character.

Locate records of all customers who live on streets named Cape, Cate, or Cake.

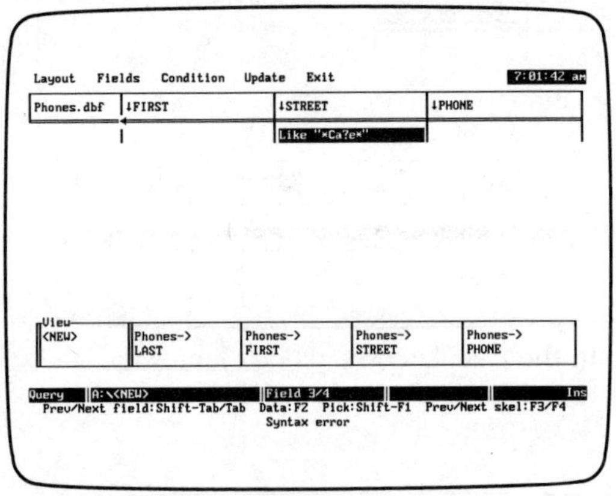

Enter Like "*Ca?e*" in the appropriate column.

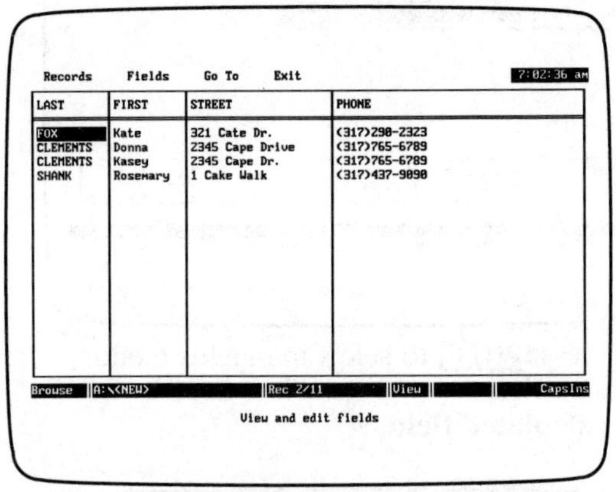

Press F2 to see the results in Browse mode.

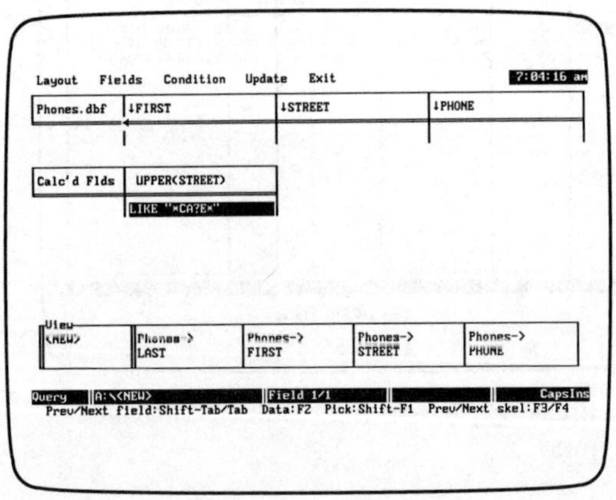

To perform a non-case-sensitive search, instead use the calculated fields skeleton and the UPPER() function.

Using the Sounds Like Operator

If you ever have been in the situation where you remember a name vaguely but not the spelling, you can appreciate the Sounds Like operator.

Suppose that you have a customer named *Kasey*, but you cannot remember the spelling. Use a phonetic or abbreviated spelling.

Enter the search criteria preceded by the operator Sounds Like—in this case, Sounds Like "KC"

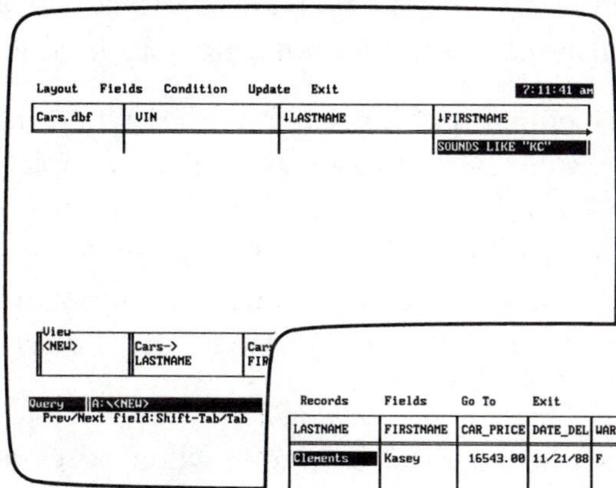

Press F2 to see the results in Browse mode.

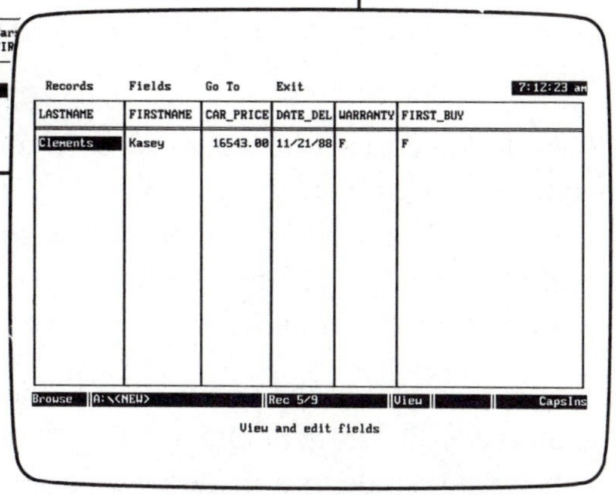

> Sounds Like is the least precise operator. You must experiment with your search criteria. For example, specifying *Casey* and *Casee* with Sounds Like does not find any records.

Expanding Query Power

Using relational operators (variations of =, >, <) and special operators ($ Contains, Like, and Sounds Like) in a search condition helps you search a file when you are unsure of an exact match criterion. Much information you search for, however, is more complex than merely looking for information in a single field. Query search conditions can be quite complex, spanning several fields (AND logic) and containing several specifications within a single field (OR logic). You can also apply some calculations to query results and sort the query output.

Use AND logic in setting up your search criteria when *all* conditions must be met for dBASE IV to find a record. For example, salesman Roger Stone wants a follow-up contact list of all his customers who bought a car more than two years ago. To compile the list, he can find all records in a car-sales database in which the salesman is Roger Stone (initials RS in the SALES_REP field) *and* the date of delivery is less than two years ago.

Use OR logic to set up your search criteria when *only one* search condition must be met for dBASE IV to find a record. Imagine that you maintain a furniture inventory. If a customer offers two color preferences when asking whether an item is available, you can produce a list of couches in either color—for example, red OR blue.

You can combine AND and OR conditions within a single query. For example, you can generate a listing of all couches in stock that are either red or blue and made by a specific manufacturer.

Querying your database for information is not just limited to locating records. Several arithmetic operators summarize data in query mode and you can see the results in the data mode. Summary operators include:

Operator	Use on Data Types	Explanation
AVERAGE or AVG	Float/Numeric	Averages the contents of the specified column
COUNT or CNT	Character/Date/Float/ Numeric/Logical	Counts the number of records that meet the query criteria. If no search criteria are specified, then all records are counted.
MAX	Character/Date/Float/ Numeric	Finds the highest or maximum value of a group of records
MIN	Character/Date/Float/ Numeric	Finds the lowest or minimum value of a group of records
SUM	Float/Numeric	Totals the contents of the specified field for a group of records

To include an arithmetic operator in your current query, simply type the operator under the applicable field name in the file skeleton. For example, type *SUM* under the CAR_PRICE field name to total all car sales. You do not see individual records when you view the data in Browse/Edit mode, but summary figures appear in their respective columns. You can create more than one summary figure in a single query and in a field column of that query. For example, you can both SUM and AVERAGE new car prices in a car-sales database.

You can also enhance your query by sorting the output. If you cause the output to sort through instructions within the query, the file is Read Only. A message, **Read only**, appears in the Status bar indicating that while in Browse/Edit you cannot change records. The query sort is particularly useful for sending output to Report or Label mode.

Using AND Conditions

And relationships can exist between data fields. Suppose you maintain a membership database that includes a type-of-membership field (family, single, corporate, and so on) as well as a major-interest-area category (such as genealogy or history). You might want to see and edit all records of corporate members whose special interest is history.

Once you open the membership database and access the Query panel, enter each search condition under the associated field name in the file skeleton that appears across the top of the screen. For example, type *="C"* beneath the TYPE field name, and then type *"History"* beneath the SIG (special-interest group) field name. You must enter the two criteria *on the same line* in their respective columns in order for dBASE IV to know you are expressing an AND condition. That is, all conditions on the same line must be met in order for a record to be selected.

Remember to set up the fields you want to see in the view skeleton across the bottom of the screen. You can then press F2 (Data) to view the results of your query in Browse/Edit mode.

You can also create AND relationships within a single field (column). This capability helps you locate all records in a range. For example, suppose you want to see all records for members whose dues are to be paid in the second quarter. If the field indicating the month dues are due is called DUES_DUE, and the field contains a number (1 through 12) indicating payment month, you can enter the specification *>=4, <=6* beneath the field name DUES_DUE in the file skeleton. dBASE IV locates all records whose DUES_DUE dates are Greater than or equal to 4 (**"4"** represents April) *and* Less than or equal to 6 (**"6"** represents June).

Recall that specifications for character fields are typed differently from numeric specifications. To locate all the names that begin with F through R in the LASTNAME field, type *>="F",<="R"* in the LASTNAME field.

Using OR Conditions

Often you ask to see data that meets one condition OR another. Most OR conditions relate to the contents of a single field. For example, you might want to see all records in a membership database where the member type is Single (S) or Family (F). Enter each OR condition one below the other under the associated field name in the file skeleton. Referring to the membership example, you type *"S"* (remember to include the quotation marks) on the first line below TYPE in the file skeleton, then type *"F"* on the second line below TYPE.

You now know how to enter both AND and OR relationships associated with a single field (column). An AND relationship is specified on one line separated by commas. On the other hand, an OR relationship is specified on two lines within the single column on the file skeleton.

Once in awhile you might want to set up a query based on contents of one field *or* contents of a separate field. For example, suppose you want to find the records for which the TYPE membership is F (Family) *or* for which SIG (special interest group) is Genealogy. You must enter the search conditions on separate lines or else dBASE IV assumes an AND condition. Referring to the membership example, type *"F"* on the first line below TYPE in the file skeleton, and then type *"Genealogy"* on the second line below SIG.

A word of caution. Writing AND and OR queries can be far more complex than the examples in this book. As you learn to use more complex queries, follow one golden rule. Test your query before you use it on the actual database. Make a small test database—you can extract the records from the larger database. Do not include more records in the test database than you can reasonably look at to verify manually the results of your queries. Before you run a query, identify all records that should be acted upon by the query in the test database. If the query finds every record you are looking for—and no extra records—then you can run your query on the real database with confidence.

Expanding Query Power

As your data grows more complex, so do the queries you make. Four additional operators and techniques expand your query power: AND conditions, OR conditions, summary operators, and sorting query results.

Using AND Conditions

AND conditions are two (or more) criteria that must be true before the record is selected. AND relationships can be found between different fields and within the same field. One AND relationship you search for frequently is the range. You can use various techniques for writing AND conditions in queries.

You can use an AND relationship *between* fields.

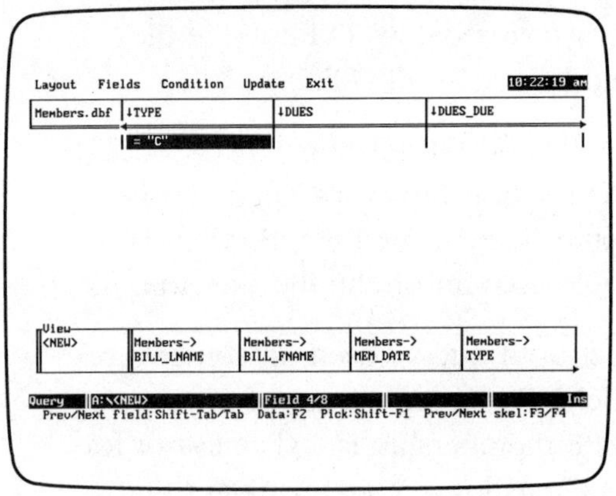

First, enter a search condition in one field. For example, in the TYPE field, enter = "C"

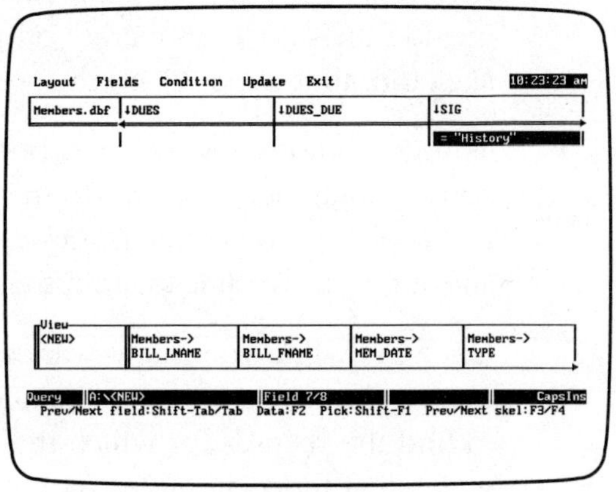

Next, move the highlight bar to another field, such as SIG. Enter the condition = "History"

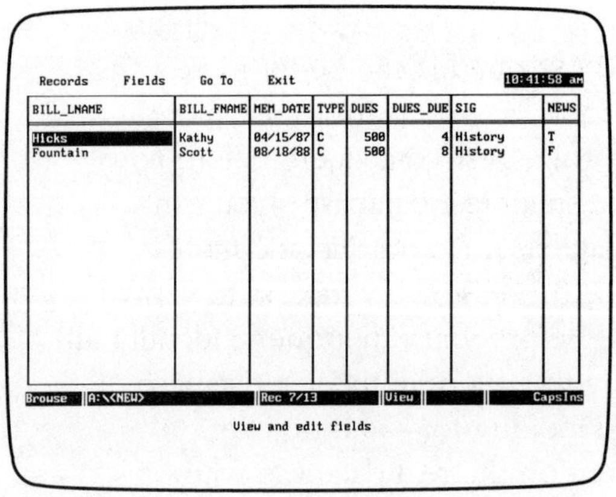

Press F2 to see the results in Browse mode.

The search criteria were written on the same line in their respective columns. dBASE IV treats these fields as an AND relationship and selects records only if both criteria are true.

You can use an AND relationship *within* a field. In addition, you can limit the search to a range of data.

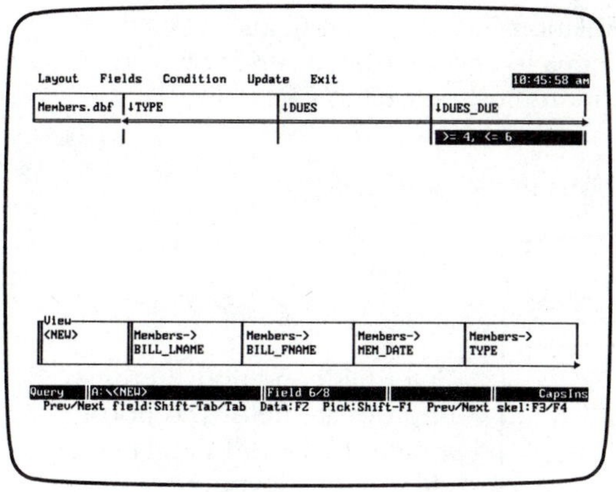

Enter the search criteria in the appropriate column. For example, type >= 4, <= 6 in the field DUES_DUE.

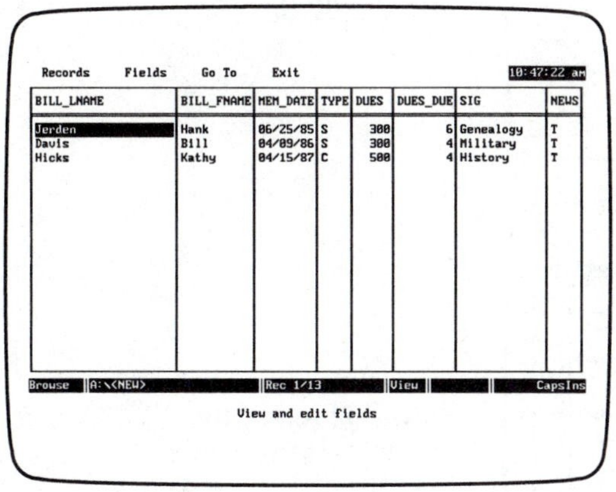

Press F2 to see the results in Browse mode.

The two criteria in the DUES_DUE field are treated as an AND relationship, and only records in the range 4 through 6 are selected.

Using OR Conditions

OR conditions, like AND, can have relationships between fields as well as within a field. Use OR conditions to choose from a series of conditions. However, only one condition must be true to cause the record to be selected.

You can use a number of OR conditions in the same field.

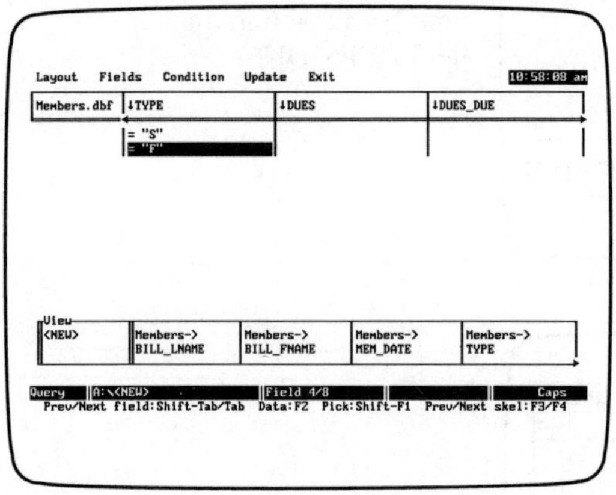

Enter OR conditions in the appropriate field. To choose a record whose TYPE is either S or F, type ="S", press ↓, type ="F", and press ↵Enter.

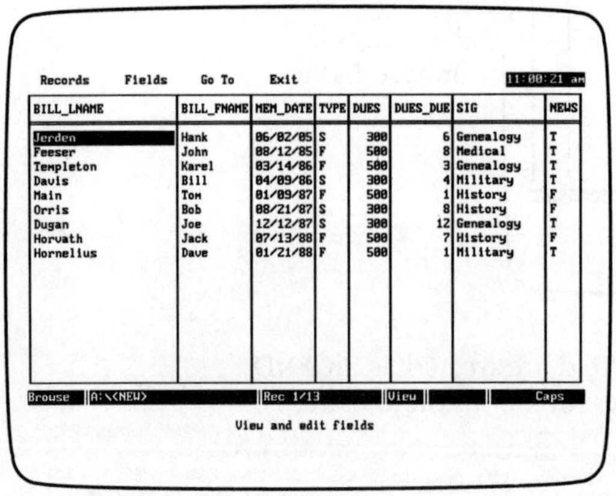

Press F2 to see the results in Browse mode.

Notice that each OR condition is entered in the same field but on different lines. Entering conditions on different lines tells dBASE IV that the conditions are in an OR relationship. All members of a TYPE S or F are selected.

You can use OR conditions in separate fields. Enter OR conditions for separate fields in nearly the same manner as you did in the same field.

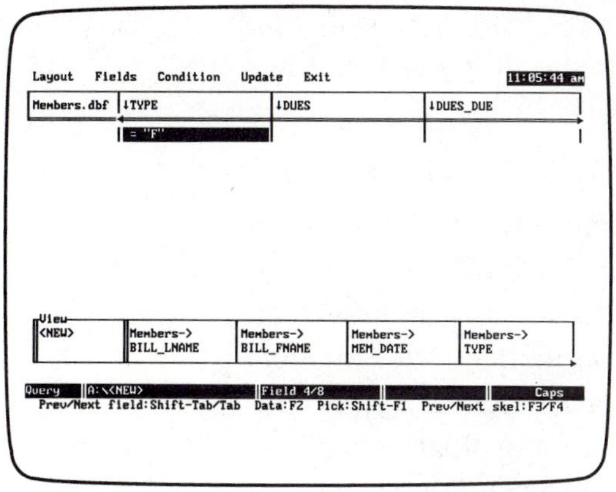

To choose a record whose type is F or whose SIG is genealogy, first type ="F" and press ↓.

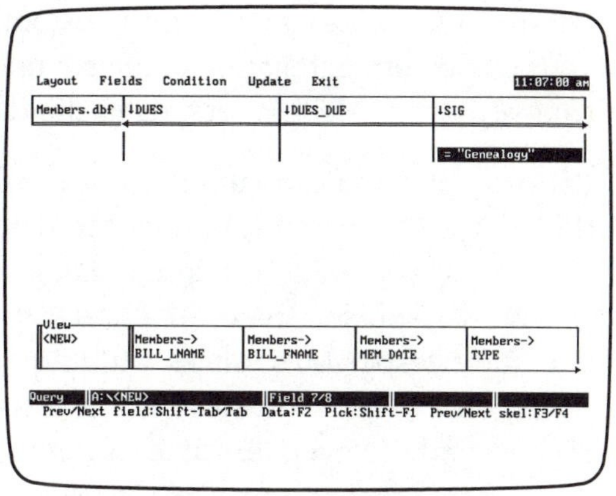

Using Tab or Shift Tab, move the highlighter to the SIG column, enter ="Genealogy" on the second line, and press Enter.

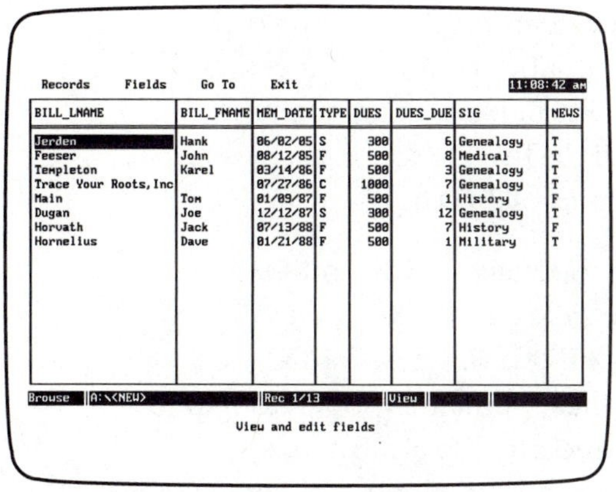

Press F2 to see the results in Browse mode.

Notice that these OR conditions were entered in different columns and on different lines.

WARNING

When mixing AND and OR relationships, test your query carefully before making queries with actual data.

Using Summary Operators

dBASE IV lets you summarize the values in some fields—thus creating information—without setting up custom reports. You need only apply your choice of aggregate (summary) operators to all records in the database or to selected records in the database.

For example, you can sum the values of all cars sold by typing *SUM* (lowercase is acceptable) under the field name CAR_PRICE in the file skeleton. If you want to add the values of only the cars sold by a specific salesperson, type *SUM* under the field name CAR_PRICE; and type the salesperson's initials within quotation marks under the field name SALES_REP. You can substitute AVG or AVERAGE in place of SUM to find the average value of a numeric field or float field. To see the sum or average, press F2 (Data) and the Browse/Edit screen appears with the values under the associated field names. The records themselves do not appear.

Suppose you would like to know how many new car sales are made to buyers living in the ZIP code area of the dealership. dBASE IV provides the aggregate operator COUNT to total the number of records meeting specified search conditions. Referring to the dealership example, type *"46032", COUNT* beneath the field name ZIP in the file skeleton. To see the record count under the ZIP code field, press F2 (Data).

dBASE IV provides two additional summary operators: MIN and MAX. Apply these operators to character and date fields as well as numeric and float fields in order to find the lowest (MIN) or highest (MAX) value. Like other operators, you can apply these remaining operators to all records in the database or to only those records limited by search conditions. For example, to find the most recent date when a buyer took delivery on a new car, type MAX under the field name DATE_DEL in the file skeleton. You can have only one aggregate operator in a column (field) at a time. You can, however, have aggregate operators in more than one column at a time.

Sorting Query Results

You can sort the results of a query by entering a sort operator in the appropriate fields. When you sort from a query, the query results are designated as "read only," which means you cannot update the records. The message **Read Only** appears in the fourth segment of the Status bar.

Normally, you sort the results of a query when the results are used by the Report or Label panels. To see and *edit* your records in an organized manner, access the Organize menu in Browse/Edit mode and use the indexing or sorting options.

Suppose you want to see on-screen your car-sales records sorted in ascending sequence by last name. Move the highlight to the file-skeleton column containing the last-name field name. Press Alt-F to access the Fields menu, then select **Sort on this field**. From the next menu with four sorting sequences, choose **Ascending ASCII** and the operator **Asc1** appears in the column. Now, in Browse mode, your data appears sorted on last name. Note that **Read Only** appears in the Status bar. In other words, you can scroll through the database viewing records; but you cannot change the contents of records displayed by a query.

Be sure to exit from any query by selecting **Exit** from the query Menu bar. You can then select **Save changes and exit** to leave the query and save the query design for later use. Or, you can select **Abandon changes and exit** to leave the session without saving your query design. If you entered the query from the Forms, Labels, or Report work surfaces, you have an option of returning to the same work surface.

Up to this point in the book, the chapters deal with the first two panels of the dBASE IV Control Center: Data and Query. The remaining four chapters discuss, in order, the other Control Center panels—Forms, Reports, Labels, and Applications.

Expanding Query Power

The query features you have learned so far help you find records in your database. Summary operators help you summarize facts about your data. Sort operators provide the ability to sort the data selected during a search.

Using Summary Operators

The following summary operators are available in the query work surface:

Operator	Description
AVERAGE or AVG	Averages the content of the specified numeric field
COUNT or CNT	Counts the number of records selected
MAX	Finds the highest value in the specified field
MIN	Finds the lowest or minimum value in the specified field
SUM	Totals the values in the specified field

Only one summary operator can appear in a field at a time. However, several operators may appear in a skeleton.

Generate some summary information about the car sales database.

Until you are comfortable using AND and OR, generate each summary separately.

Enter the AVERAGE operator in the CAR_PRICE column and press F2.

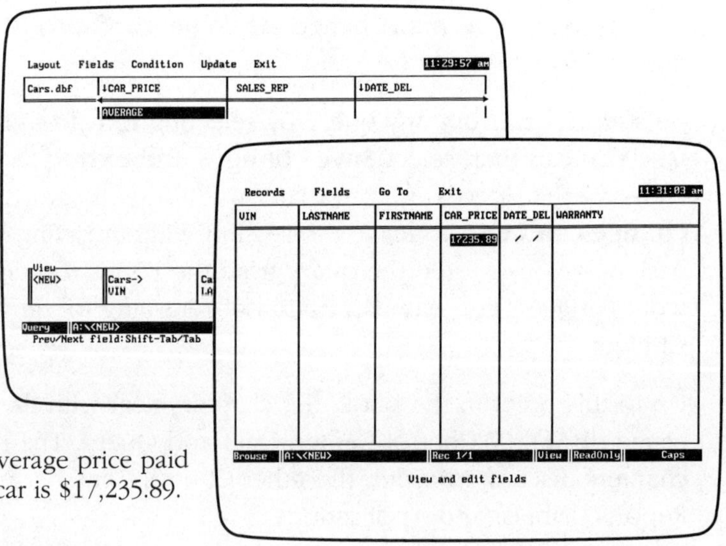

The average price paid for a car is $17,235.89.

To count how many customers do not have warranties, enter the search criteria, .F., and the COUNT operator in the WARRANTY column.

Press F2 to search.

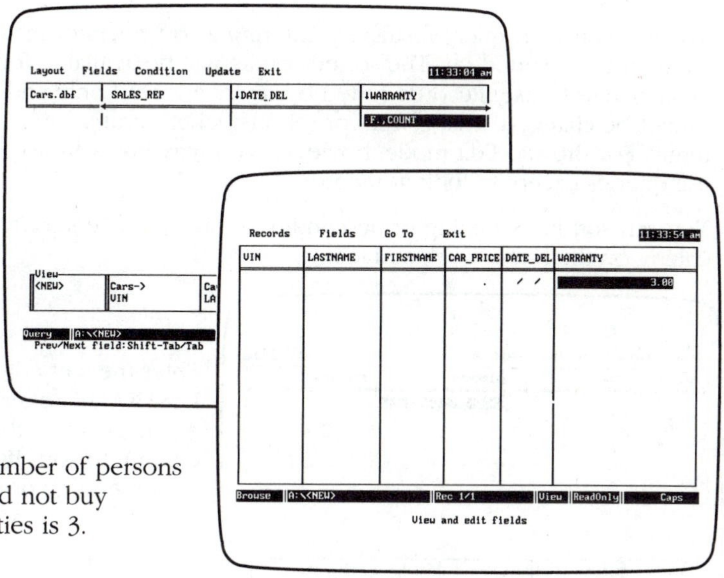

The number of persons who did not buy warranties is 3.

To see when the last car was delivered, enter the MAX operator in the DATE_DEL column.

The last date a car was delivered is March 1, 1989.

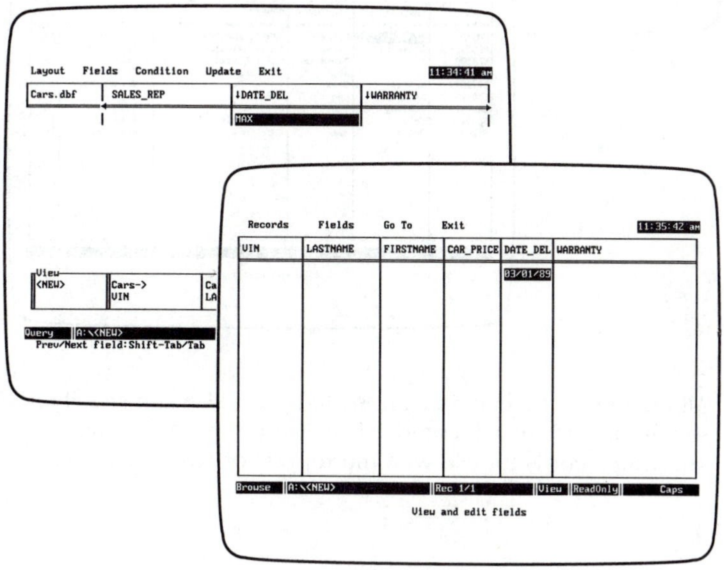

Sorting Query Results

You can sort your query results by entering a sort operator in the field to be sorted on. The sorted results will be available for other panels to use. Records sorted by query are read only and cannot be changed. This is fine for reports, labels, and some forms. For Browse/Edit mode, however, you may not want to use queries except to look at records.

You can sort in ascending or descending sequence by entering criteria on the query work surface.

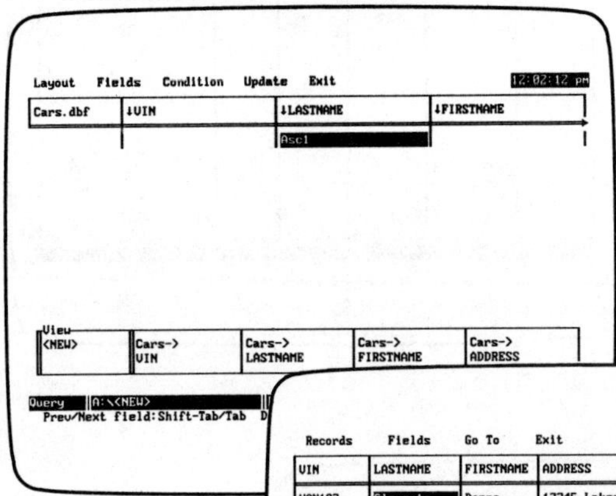

Enter the sort criteria Asc1 in the LASTNAME column. The 1 after Asc means that this is the 1st column to sort. If you are sorting in descending order, enter Dsc1.

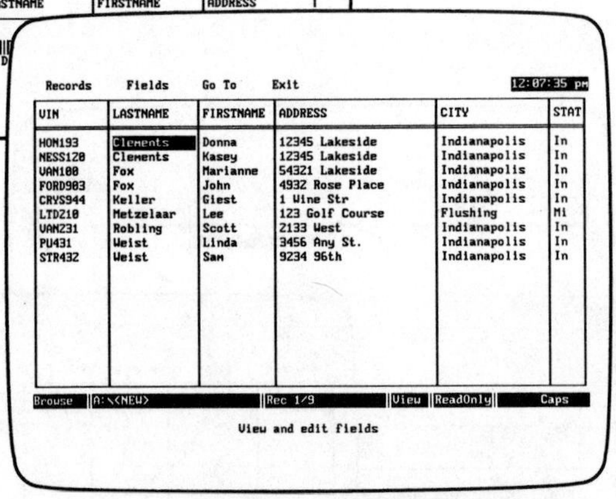

Press F2 to see the results in Browse mode.

All records in the database are sorted. You also can specify a sort along with search criteria. This is often necessary when selecting records for use with the reports or labels features.

You can sort in ascending or descending sequence by entering criteria through the menus.

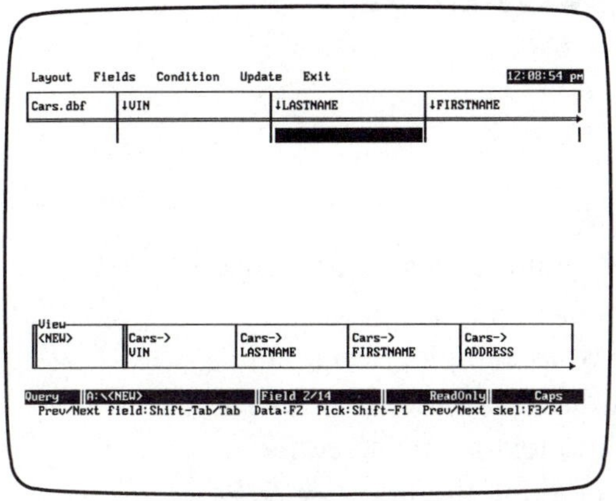

Position the highlighter on the column to be sorted.

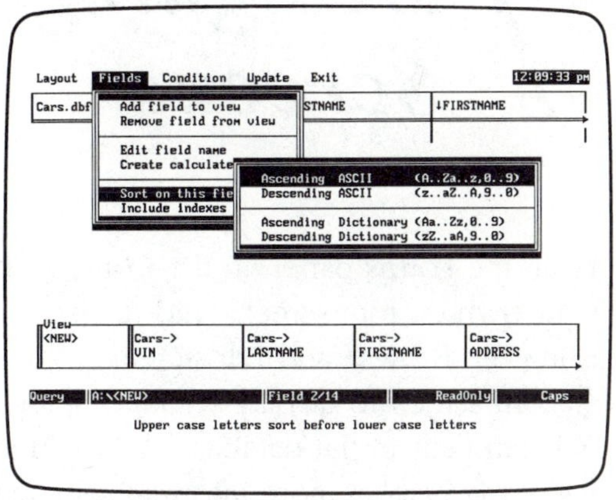

Press Alt F to pull down the Fields menu. Then press S to select the **Sort on this field** option. Notice the four sorting options.

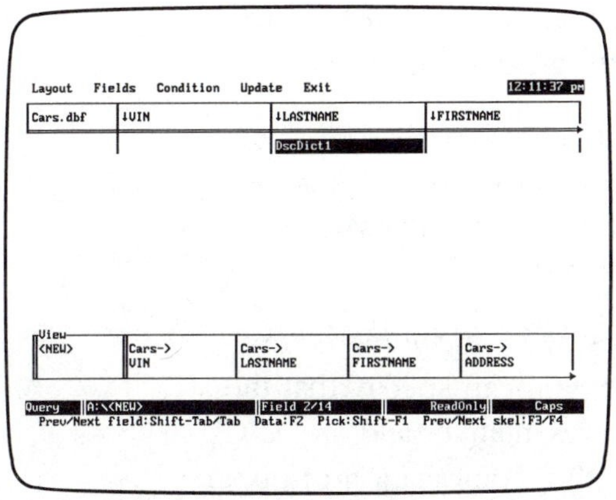

Select **Descending dictionary**.

Notice that the code for this option, DscDict1, ends with a 1. You can sort on a second field, such as FIRSTNAME (within the LASTNAME column). If you sort on a second field, its sort operator ends in 2.

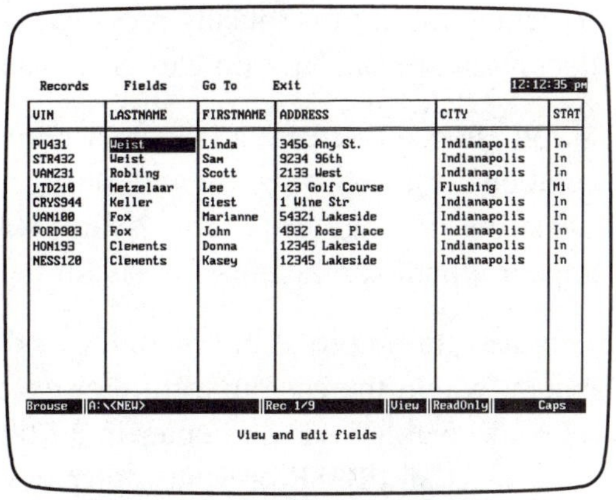

Press F2 to see the results in Browse mode.

The results are sorted backward from Z to A (descending sequence).

7 Designing Custom Screens

From the Forms panel on the Control Center, you can design and create your own custom screens and realize a number of advantages over using the Browse and Edit screens. You can, for example, design a custom screen to display selected fields in a different order than the fields appear in the database. You can also add text to the screen to make the display more informative, such as entering the title *Car Sales Database.*

Perhaps the most common use of the Forms panel involves creating data-entry screens that look like the paper forms (source documents) on which the data is initially recorded. When the screen and a source document are similar, you can enter data with greater speed.

If you choose to create a custom screen, you can establish your own contents for the Navigation and Message lines. For example, you can cause the message **Enter the 2-digit state code in uppercase** to appear whenever the cursor rests on the state field.

You also can improve the accuracy of data entry by including editing criteria within the custom form. For example, you can specify that the only acceptable initials to enter in a sales representative field are ABC, XYZ, or LCM. dBASE prevents entry of any other combination of upper- or lowercase letters.

The Forms panel provides access to improving your screen display of data. You can also customize printed output in the form of custom reports and custom labels.

What Is Covered in This Chapter?

In this chapter, you learn about

- Designing custom screens
- Creating a custom form
- Controlling data entries and displays
- Editing data entries
- Using custom forms

Key Words Used in This Chapter

Custom form	A screen you design for data entry or information display, as compared to the standard dBASE Browse or Edit screens
Edit options	Features that can be used with any field on a custom form to control and edit data entries
Editor	The limited dBASE IV word-processor. You can use it in a variety of settings, including creating a custom screen or entering narrative in a memo field
Layout mode	The Editor's mode when you access the Forms panel to design custom forms
Picture function	An editing feature similar to a *template* except that *picture function* applies to an entire field, making it, for example, all uppercase
Template	A pattern of editing characters that control what data can be entered in a field

Introduction

Using the Forms panel on the Control Center, you can design your own custom screens (forms) as alternatives to the Browse and Edit screens.

A custom screen created from the car sales database

Custom forms can

1. *Reduce data entry time, if the custom forms look like your paper forms*
2. *Prevent entry of data that does not meet specified criteria or that is not within a specified range.*
3. *Provide on-screen help to data-entry personnel by furnishing custom prompts and screen messages.*
4. *Allow data entry only in certain fields.*

Using the Forms-Design Screen

As you learn dBASE IV's many features, you can see some similarities between various screens. The top of the forms screen, for instance, displays a Menu bar like the data and query screens. (You will read about this Menu bar in detail shortly.) Most of the forms screen displays the work surface, with the Status bar, Navigation line, and Message line below the work surface.

Understanding the Work Surface

The data-design work surfaces—such as those for creating a file structure or entering data in Browse or Edit mode—follow a standard format. When you create a file structure, for example, you must complete name, type, width, and decimal information for each field as prompted on the screen. The work surface for adding or editing records is also clearly defined: one record on each screen in Edit mode, and records in row-and-column format in Browse mode. The query work surface is also structured to control how it is used, with the file skeleton across the top and the view skeleton at the bottom.

The forms work surface is less structured than that of either data or query. You create a form on this work surface much as you might take a clean piece of paper and start drawing a design. Think of the work surface (also called the *Editor*) as your paper. Your tools are the options in the Menu bar, the information items in the Status bar, and the keyboard combinations and instructions described in the Navigation and Message lines.

You already are familiar with the Editor—the work surface is the same one you use to write the contents of memo fields. The Editor has two modes, *word wrap* and *layout*, depending on which dBASE IV feature you are using. When you enter comments in a memo field after accessing the Data panel, you use the Editor in word-wrap mode. Word-wrap mode works like a word processor and is ideally suited for entering continuous text.

When you access the Forms panel, the Editor is in *layout* mode. Layout mode, appearing as a blank screen or a "blackboard," is ideally suited for designing forms. You can type anywhere on the blackboard, which appears as a large highlighted square between the Menu bar and the Status bar. The blackboard holds the form you are creating, such as a standard form to enter all data concerning a car sale.

Design a form on the work surface as you would on paper. You can enter text, such as titles, general instructions, and field names, anywhere on the blackboard. For example, move the cursor to the top of the form and type a title, such as *Monthly Sales Recap.* Next, move the cursor to the location where the first field should appear. If the first field is the customer's name, type *CUSTOMER NAME.* Position the cursor where the contents of the customer name field should appear—usually a few spaces to the right of the field name.

Then, using the Menu bar, select the option to add a field to the screen; and tell dBASE IV to display the contents of the customer name field. You also can tell dBASE IV how the data should appear, associate editing criteria with that field, and even have a message appear on the Message line when the user moves the cursor to the data field.

By using the **Line** or **Box** options, you can draw lines on the work surface or lines to box portions of the screen. You also can add fields to your form, and move or copy text and fields. As you use more complex databases, your forms may become too large to fit on one screen. Making multiple screen forms is easy. When you exceed one screen, the Editor creates a second screen like the second page of a two-page form.

Using the Status Bar

The Status bar contains the standard five segments for displaying information about the current editing session. The first segment displays **Form** to show that you are using the Forms panel.

The second segment displays the disk drive, path, and name of the form file on which you are working. If you are creating a new form, you see the current disk drive, path, and the word **<NEW>**. For example,

A:\<NEW> shows that you are creating a new file on disk drive A in the root directory (\).

The third segment displays the row number and column number of the current cursor position on the work surface—for example **Row:9 Col:14**. The cursor marks where you can begin adding text, a line, or a field. A standard screen displays 25 lines by 80 columns. (A *column* in this context means a single-character position.) The forms work surface (the Editor) itself—the large highlighted area—is only 20 lines by 80 columns.

Note: In computer terms, the count of rows and columns begins with 0. In the Status bar, you see row numbers starting with 0 and column numbers 0 through 79.

The fourth segment shows the database in use—for example, **File:Cars**. You can update only one database at a time. If you think about it, a form design is meaningful only if it references data from a specific database. When you activate your new form, the associated database opens automatically.

The fifth segment displays whether toggle keys are on, the same function reserved for the last segment of the Status bar in other work surfaces. Recall that the toggle keys include Num Lock, Caps Lock, and Ins; the presence of **Num**, **Caps**, and **Ins** indicates that the keys are active.

Ins indicates that the screen is in *insert* mode rather than *typeover* mode. The cursor shape also indicates which mode you are in. In insert mode, the cursor is a small square (■). However, in typeover mode, the cursor shape changes to an underscore (_).

Using the Navigation and Message Lines

The Navigation line shows which function keys you currently can use on the forms work surface. The Message line immediately below the

Navigation line periodically displays messages as you work on the surface.

Five key combinations appear in the Navigation line. Use the F5 (Fields) key to insert the specifications that link a field from the current database to the work surface. When you press F5, a window appears on-screen, containing a list of fields that are part of the current database. To transfer a field to the work surface, simply highlight the field name and press Enter.

The F6 (Select), F7 (Move), and F8 (Copy) keys work together to help you arrange text and fields on the screen. Use the F6 (Select) key to highlight the rectangular portion of the screen you want to manipulate.

After you highlight (select) the data area to manipulate, decide the action you want to take. Press F7 (Move) to move the selected text to a different location, or press F8 (Copy) to reproduce the text at a new location on the work surface. The process is much like moving fields in the view skeleton of the query work surface.

Use Shift-F7 (Size) to change the size of a window, box, or field. A window displays memo contents on-screen; a box focuses attention on the data within. You can expand or shrink a window or box on-screen. You determine the size (width) of a field at the time you create the field in the database structure. If you modify a database structure by enlarging or narrowing a field used in a form, use Shift-F7 (Size) to make a corresponding change to the field in the form.

One message on the Message line describes the field where the cursor is currently positioned. Recall that the work surface is made up of text and fields. When you position the cursor on one of the fields, the Message line indicates the field structure (field name, type, width, and decimal places). Each name contains both the file name and the field name. For example, the display **CARS->VIN** tells you that the **VIN** field is part of the **CARS** database.

Using the Forms-Design Screen

You will see similarities between the forms-design screen and other design screens, but the forms-design work surface is less structured than the data and query work surfaces. You will use the same Editor you used to enter Memo fields.

Understanding the Work Surface

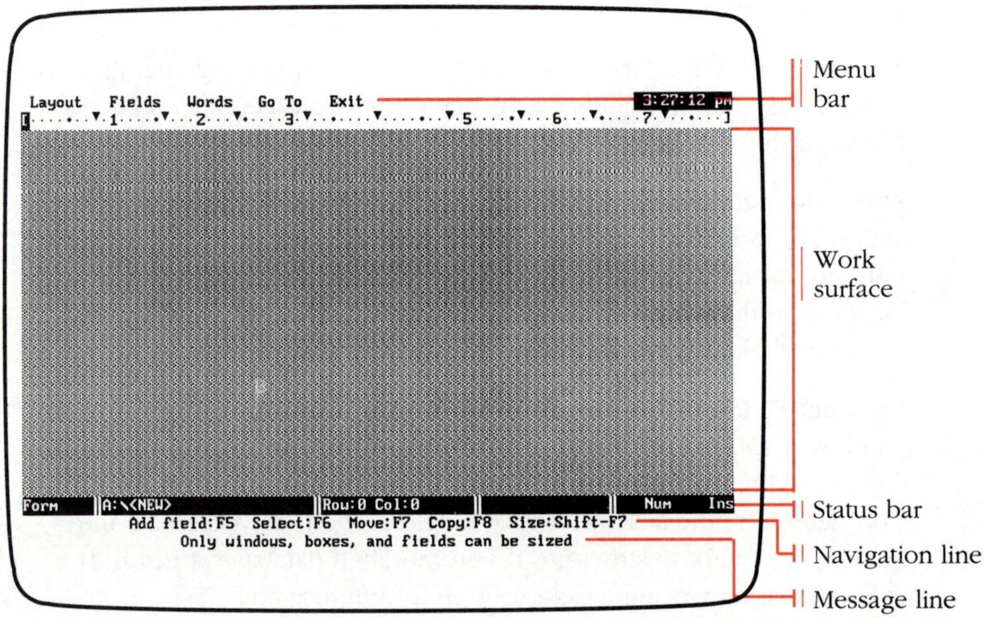

On the forms work surface, the Editor operates in layout editing mode. Each line is separate from others—text does not wrap. You can type text on this surface, add data fields, draw boxes and lines, and move or copy portions of the screen.

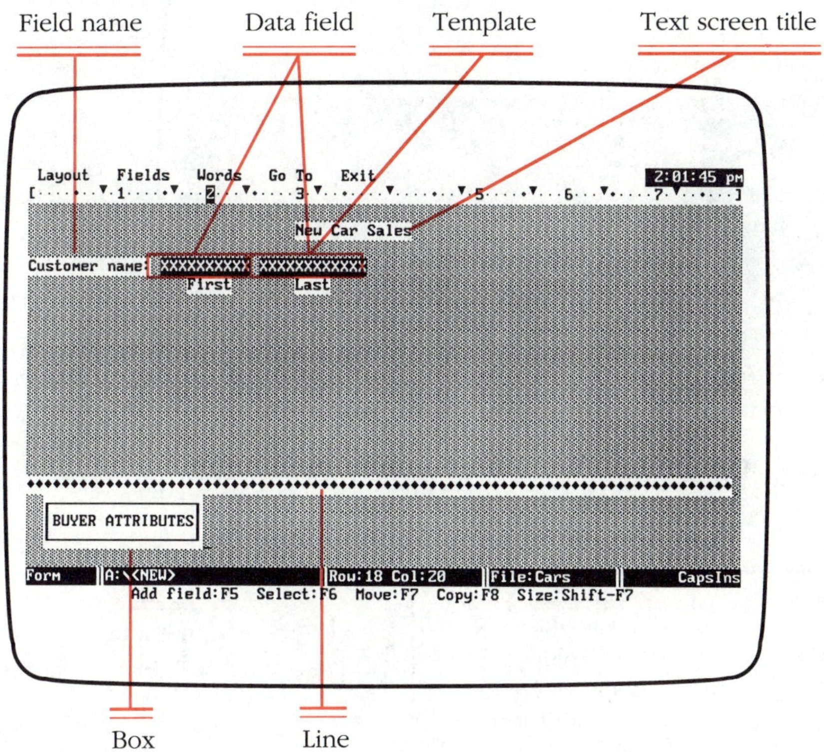

Using the Status Bar

The Status bar is divided into five sections. Each section displays information designed to keep you informed of the status of the current form.

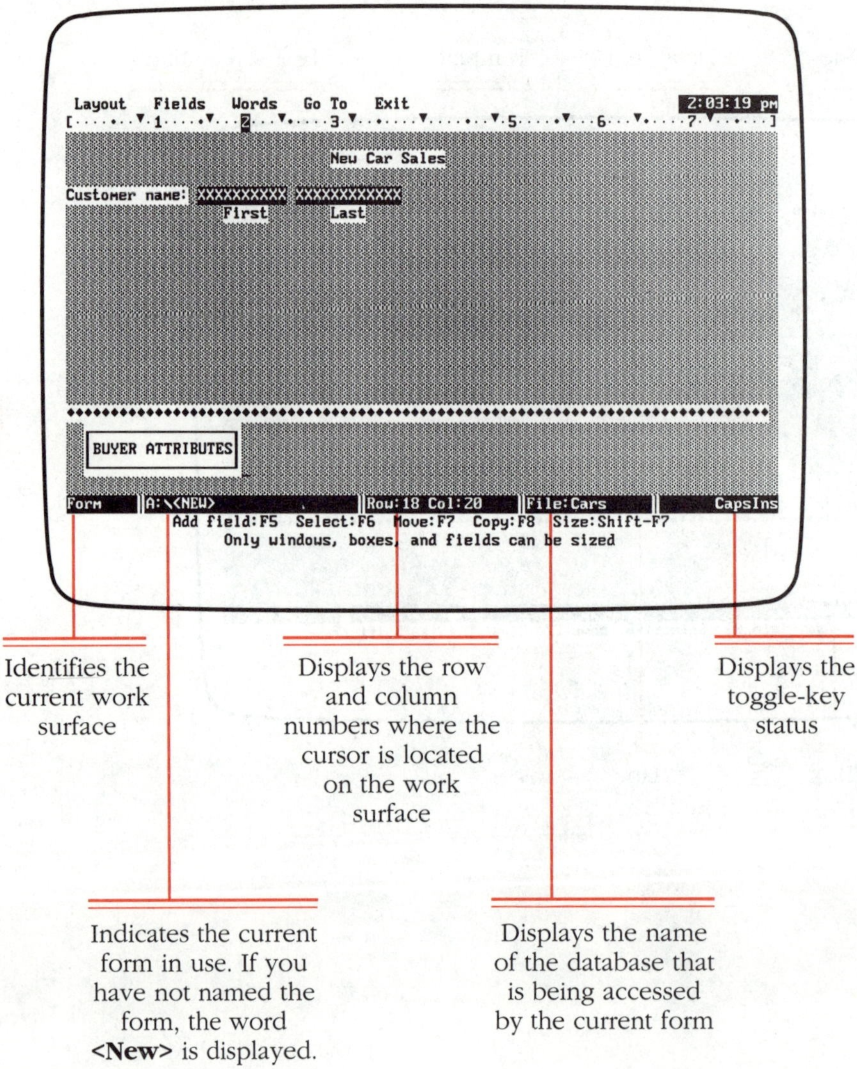

Using the Navigation and Message Lines

Use the Navigation line to stay informed about what keys are active at the moment. These keys change while you are copying and moving items on the work surface.

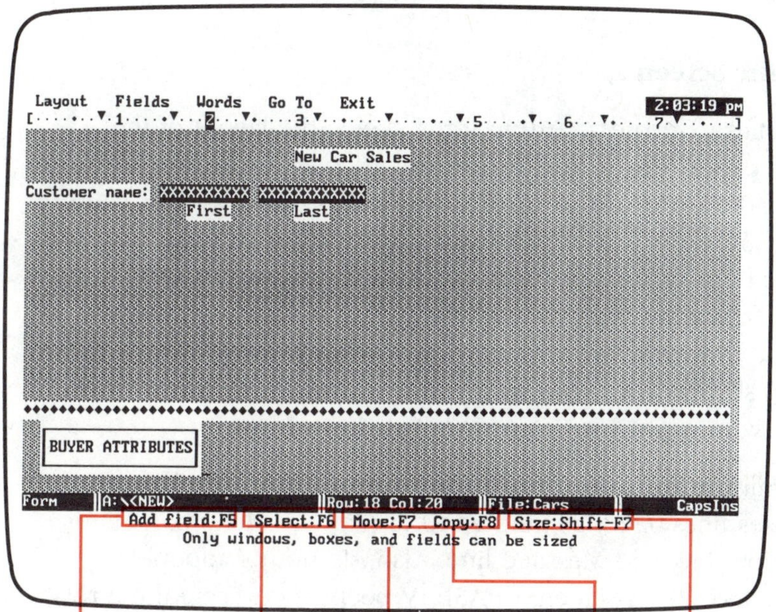

Press F5 to see a list of fields, and then select a field to transfer to the work surface.

Watch the Message line for important instructions when moving, copying, or sizing items on the work surface.

Press Shift F7 to increase or decrease the size of a window box or template.

Press F6 to highlight a rectangle on the work surface. This rectangle can be deleted, moved, or copied.

Press F7 to move the highlighted rectangle to another location on the work surface. Press F8 to copy the highlighted rectangle.

Creating a Custom Form

Now that you know about the forms work surface, you can begin creating a custom screen. The work surface's keys and menus comprise your tools for creating forms and make easy work of selecting or rearranging fields and entering text. You, however, first must decide what you want your custom form to look like.

Designing the Screen

Before you start to create a custom form, sketch the layout of the screen(s) on paper. The dimensions of your screen should be no longer than 80 characters wide by 21 lines long. Even rough drawings can help you organize the layout before you start. Although you can move fields and text around on the forms work surface, you can save time by entering the finished design. You might speed preliminary design work by laying out your tentative screen(s) on a word processor. After you create rough sketches of your fields and text, check your ideas with anyone else who might use or approve the custom form.

When designing a form, use only lines 1 through 21 on each screen. dBASE IV uses lines 0, 22, 23, and 24 to display the Menu bar, Status bar, Navigation line, and Message line. Also, do not use double quotations marks (") on-screen; dBASE IV beeps to indicate the error, but does not specify the nature of it.

As you develop a custom form, periodically check your work by pressing the F2 (Data) key to see what the screen looks like as a data-entry form. The F2 key activates Browse/Edit mode. Return to the design work surface using the Shift-F2 (Design) key.

Use the **Quick Layout** option on the Layout menu if you want all or most of the database fields to display on your custom screen in the order in which they appear in the database structure. You then can delete or rearrange fields following instructions in the Navigation and Message lines, and add your own text to the screen. If you want only selected fields from your database, creating a custom form without using **Quick Layout** is easier. That is, start from a blank screen.

Using Quick Layout

Use **Quick Layout** on the Layout menu to transfer at one time all fields to the forms-design work surface. The resulting display looks similar to the Edit screen because one field appears on each line and each field appears in the order created. The fields you transfer display the field name and field template.

A *template* is a pattern of editing characters which controls the type of data that can be entered in the field. The template itself appears on the work surface screen in the data field. Suppose, for example, that the first of the transferred fields is LASTNAME, defined in the file structure as containing character data and having a maximum width of 15. On the forms-design work surface, you see **LASTNAME !XXXXXXXXXXXXXX**. LASTNAME is the name of the field, and the remaining portion forms the template. You can interpret the parts of the template as follows:

! Determines that a letter appears in uppercase—in this example, the character in the first position

X Indicates that you can enter a letter, number, or special character in the position

Each data type has its own template on a forms-design work surface. Templates are discussed in detail later in the chapter.

Accessing a Blank Forms-Design Work Surface

To access a blank forms-design work surface, start from the Control Panel and select **<create>** on the Forms panel. If you already have a database in use, you see a blank work surface. If the database in use is not the one you want, press Alt-L, then select **Use different database file or view** and specify your database choice. On the blank work surface, press F5 (Fields) to select one field at a time to add to the form design.

Creating a Custom Form

Designing the Screen

Begin creating your new form by sketching a rough draft of the finished form.

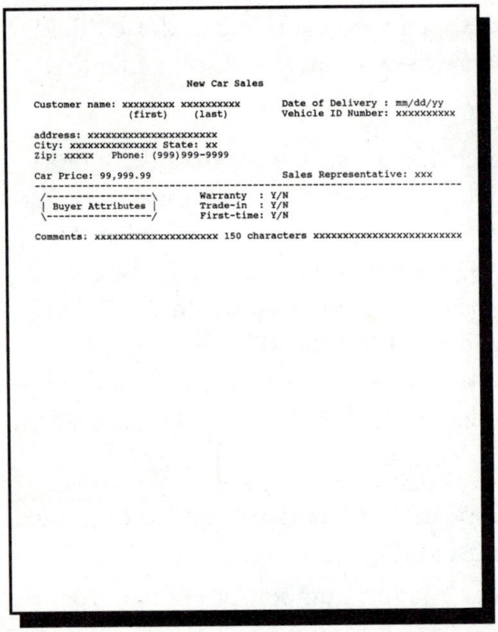

```
                         New Car Sales

Customer name: xxxxxxxxx xxxxxxxxxx      Date of Delivery : mm/dd/yy
                (first)    (last)        Vehicle ID Number: xxxxxxxxxx

address: xxxxxxxxxxxxxxxxxxxxxx
City: xxxxxxxxxxxxxxx State: xx
Zip: xxxxx   Phone: (999)999-9999

Car Price: 99,999.99                     Sales Representative: xxx
----------------------------------------------------------------------
 /-----------------\        Warranty  : Y/N
 | Buyer Attributes |       Trade-in  : Y/N
 \-----------------/        First-time: Y/N

Comments: xxxxxxxxxxxxxxxxxxxx 150 characters xxxxxxxxxxxxxxxxxxxxxxxx
```

The proposed layout is designed very close to scale. It reflects field sizes from the database structure, but uses different field names than those in the database structure.

Remember: The dimensions of your form are columns 0 to 79 and rows 0 to 24. Because dBASE IV uses rows 0, 22, 23, and 24, limit your design to rows 1 through 21.

You do not have to use all your database's fields in your custom screen.

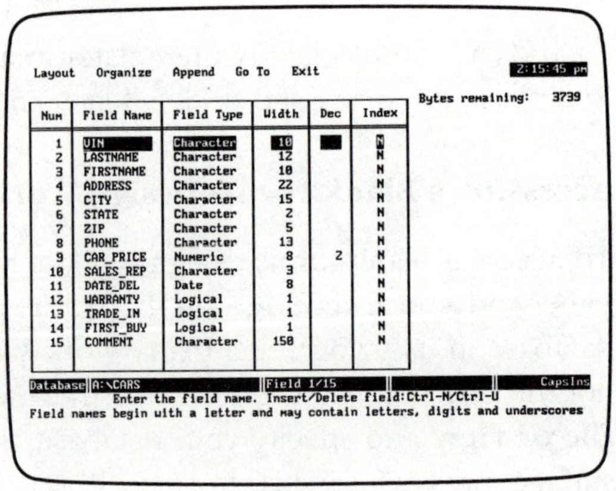

Layout Organize Append Go To Exit 2:15:45 pm

Bytes remaining: 3739

Num	Field Name	Field Type	Width	Dec	Index
1	VIN	Character	10		N
2	LASTNAME	Character	12		N
3	FIRSTNAME	Character	10		N
4	ADDRESS	Character	22		N
5	CITY	Character	15		N
6	STATE	Character	2		N
7	ZIP	Character	5		N
8	PHONE	Character	13		N
9	CAR_PRICE	Numeric	8	2	N
10	SALES_REP	Character	3		N
11	DATE_DEL	Date	8		N
12	WARRANTY	Logical	1		N
13	TRADE_IN	Logical	1		N
14	FIRST_BUY	Logical	1		N
15	COMMENT	Character	150		N

Database A:\CARS Field 1/15 CapsIns

Enter the field name. Insert/Delete field:Ctrl-N/Ctrl-U

Field names begin with a letter and may contain letters, digits and underscores

Using Quick Layout

Quick Layout transfers all fields in the database to the work surface in a few keystrokes.

Press Alt L to access the Layout menu.

Press Q to access **Quick Layout**.

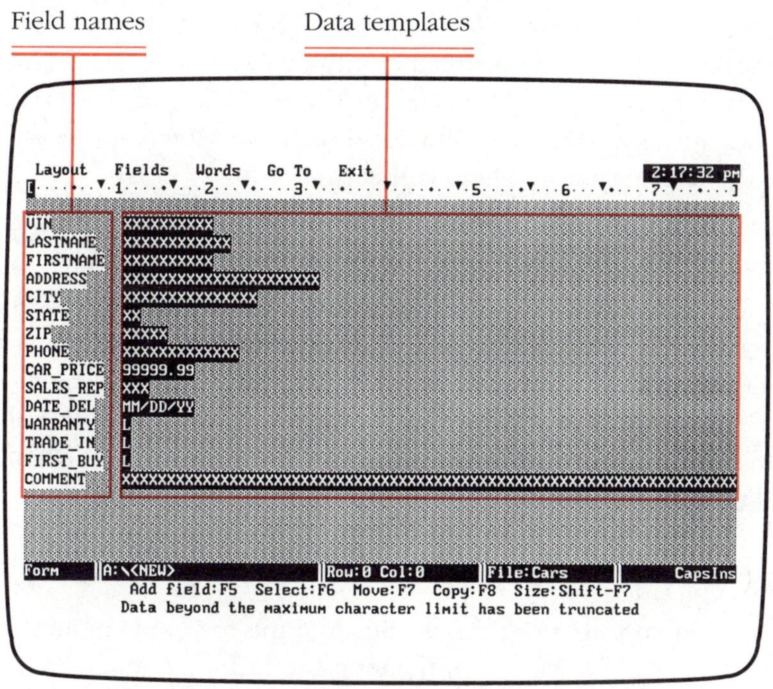

Quick Layout is similar to the Edit screen in Browse/Edit mode. Field names are taken from the database structure. Templates are based on the field type, width, and decimal positions.

Creating a Custom Form

Whether you use **Quick Layout** or create a custom form from a blank screen, you can add text, rearrange fields, create boxes and lines, and include editing criteria with each field.

Adding Text

Each form you design contains text as well as fields. The text can include a title at the top of the form and names for each field. You can use the field names from the database structure. dBASE IV's 10-character limit, however, may make interpreting some field names difficult. For example, if you have VIN as a field, enter the text *Vehicle Identification Number* to help the user understand the field contents to follow.

You may prefer to enter all the form text first, leaving space for each field template. (Each template occupies as much space as the field width specified in the file structure.) Use the arrow keys to position the cursor, and then type your text, editing with Backspace and Del. Remember that word wrap is not active. Refer to your rough sketches of the screen layout to make sure that you have included all your fields. Periodically, press the F2 (Data) key to see what the actual form looks like. When you are satisfied with the design, you can add the field templates.

Adding Fields

To add a field template, position the cursor at the row and column on the work surface where you want the template to start. (Generally, place the cursor to the right of the field name.) Press F5 (Fields) to open a window with two columns. The first column contains a list of names from the database structure. The second column contains a list of calculated fields.

After you select the name of the field template to be transferred to the work surface, another window appears. The upper portion of the window displays the field name, type, width, and number of decimal positions. You can enter editing instructions, discussed later, in the bottom portion of the window.

To transfer the field template to the work surface, press Ctrl-End. To cancel the transfer, press Esc. When you make the transfer, the field template appears on the work surface at the location of the cursor. These notations appear on the Navigation line. Continue selecting fields, entering editing specifications, and transferring the templates until all fields you want to display are on the work surface.

Moving and Copying Fields

You can move or copy any rectangular area of the work surface to another position on the work surface. *Moving* removes the rectangle from one area of the work surface and places it in another location. *Copying* leaves the rectangle in the original area and duplicates the block in another location. The steps to move or copy are nearly identical. Moving and copying can include text and fields. You cannot move or copy part of a field.

To *move* a rectangle on the work surface, position the cursor at the upper left corner of the rectangle and press F6 (Select). Then mark the rectangle to be moved by highlighting the area with the right-, down-, up-, and left-arrow keys. After the area of the "from" range is highlighted, press Enter.

Next, press F7 (Move) and position the cursor where you want the rectangle to appear. As you position the cursor, you can watch the highlighted background of the rectangle move. When you press Enter again to mark the start of the "to" range, the rectangle disappears from the original location and moves to the new location.

To *copy* a rectangle on the work surface, repeat the steps to highlight the area you want to duplicate. Position the cursor at the upper left corner of the rectangle, press F6 (Select), press the arrows keys to mark the rectangle, and then press Enter to complete marking. Press F8 (Copy), place the cursor where you want the duplicate area to appear, and press Enter.

Creating a Custom Form

Accessing a Blank Forms-Design Work Surface

If you want only selected fields from your database, create a custom form without using **Quick Layout**. Start from a blank screen.

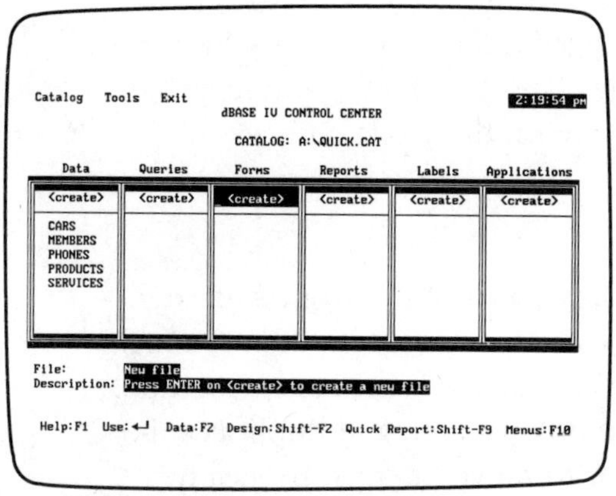

From the Control Center, select **<create>** on the Forms panel.

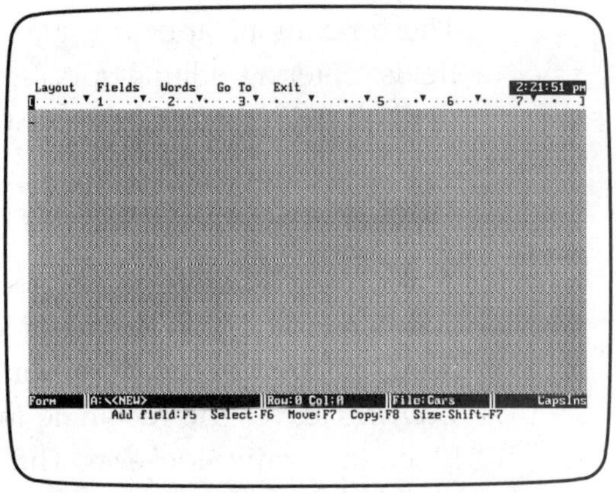

If you already have a database in use, you see a blank work surface.

If the database in use is not the one you want, press Alt L and press U to select **Use different database file or view**. Then specify your database choice.

Use ↑ or ↓ to highlight the database name and press ←Enter.

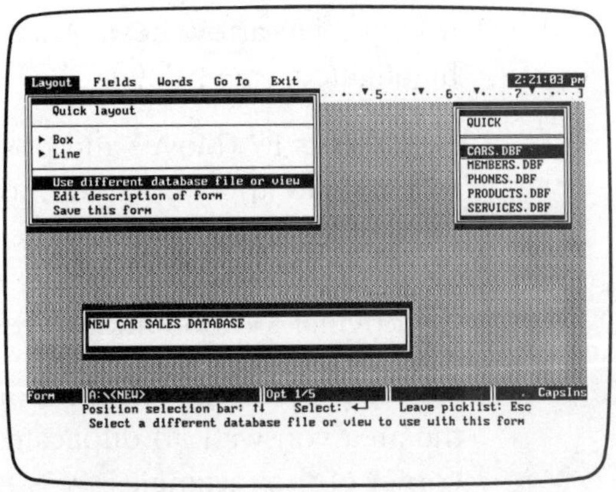

You can add text and add, move, copy, or remove fields whether you create a custom form from a blank screen or use the **Quick Layout** option.

Adding Text

Enter all the form text first, leaving space for each field template.

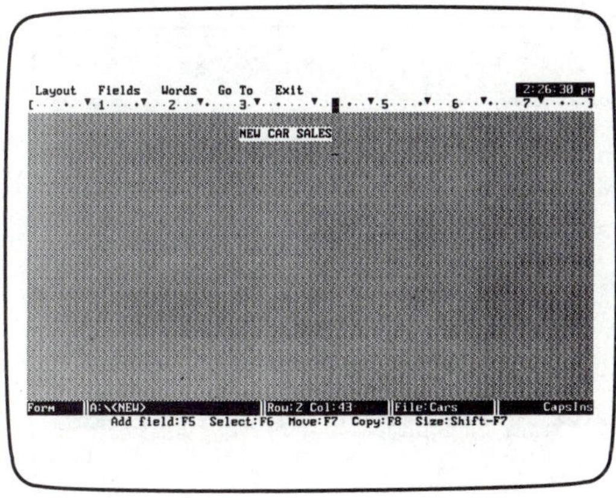

To add text, position the cursor and type. Begin by adding the form title.

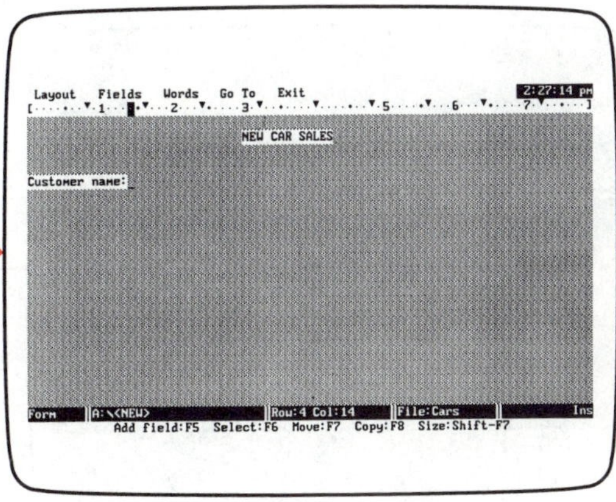

Next, begin adding field names. Remember that you are typing only names. The actual field templates are added later.

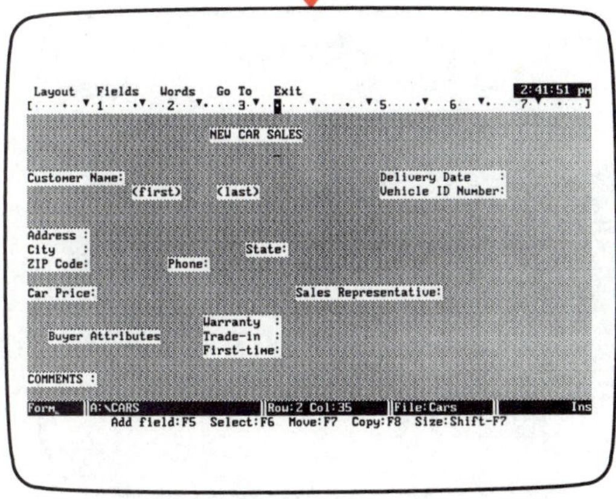

Continue adding text field names and other text information.

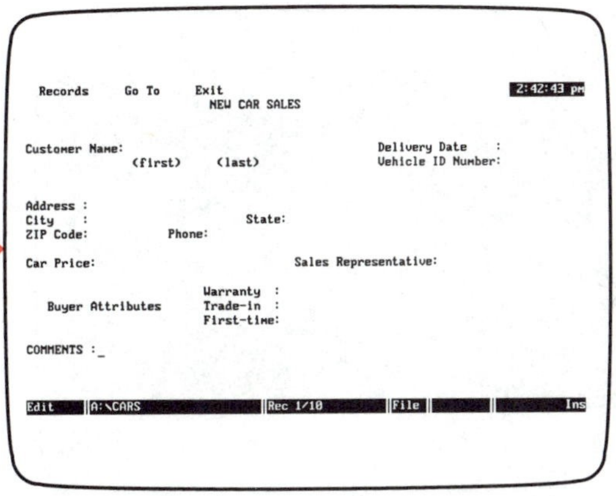

Press F2 to preview how your form is progressing. It will take a few seconds for dBASE IV to generate the form.

Press Shift F2 to return to the forms-design work surface.

Creating a Custom Form

Adding Fields

The next step is to transfer fields from the database to the work surface.

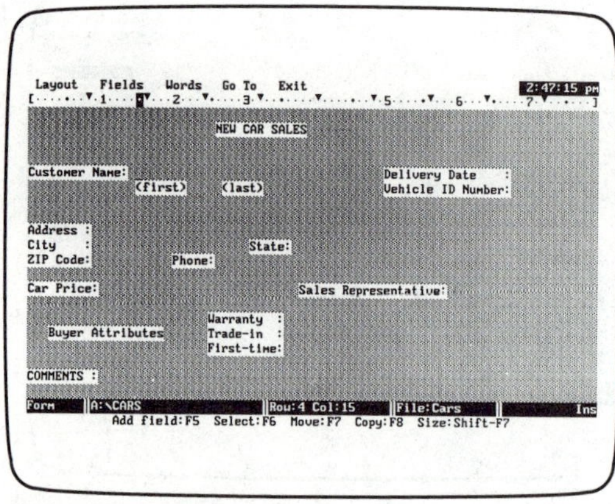

Position the cursor where the field is to be placed.

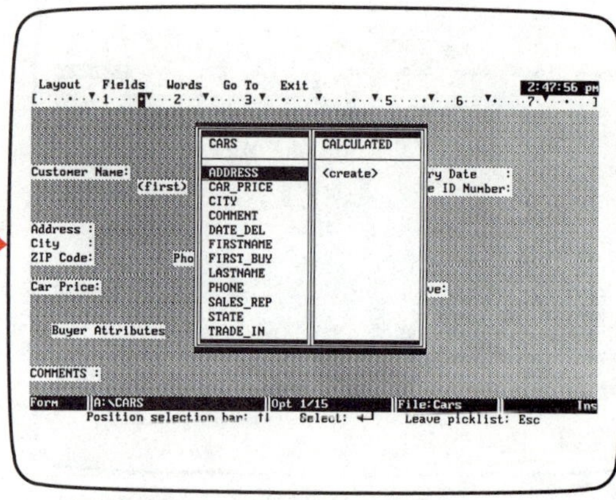

Press F5 to add a field. A list of fields is displayed on the screen.

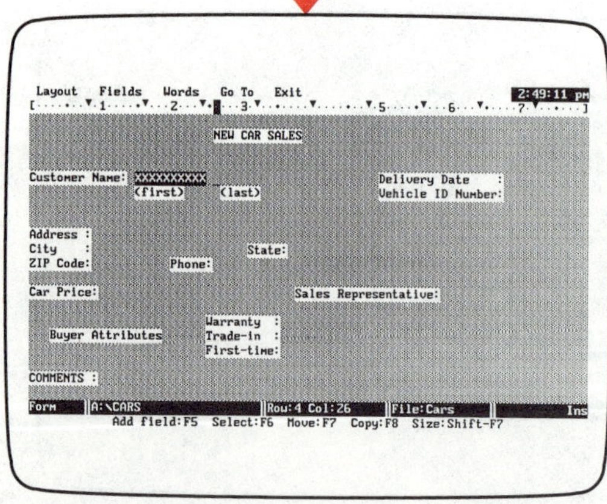

Select the field to be added and press ↵Enter.

Press Ctrl End to accept the default template.

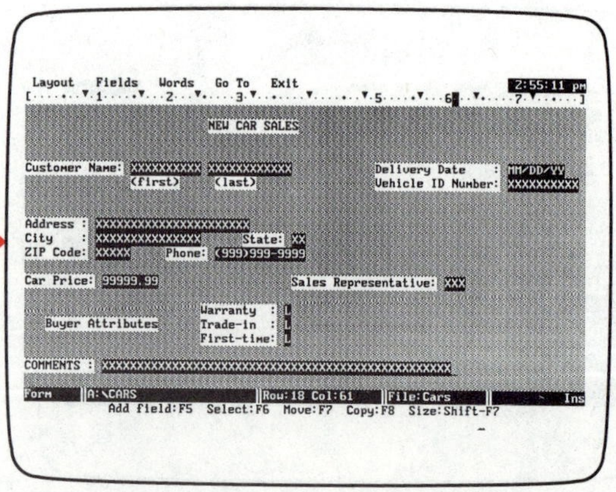

Finish adding fields to your form.

Don't worry that things may need slight rearranging. The Move and Copy features let you adjust the final screens.

Moving and Copying Fields

Next, make final adjustments to the form. The process for moving or copying a portion of your work surface is nearly the same. **Move** duplicates a selected area on the work surface and erases the original area. **Copy** duplicates the area but does not erase the original.

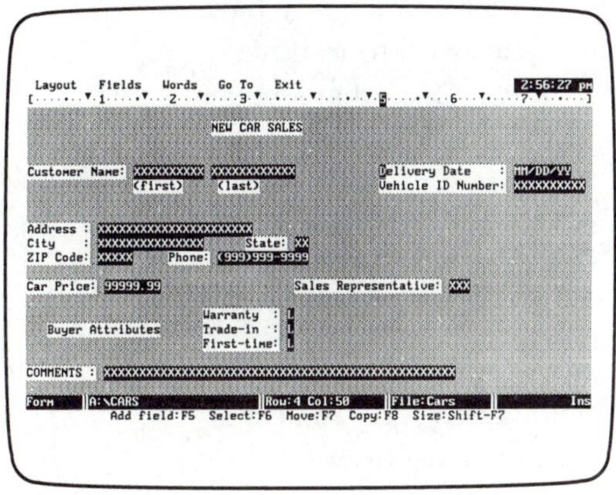

Position the cursor at the upper left corner of the rectangle to be moved.

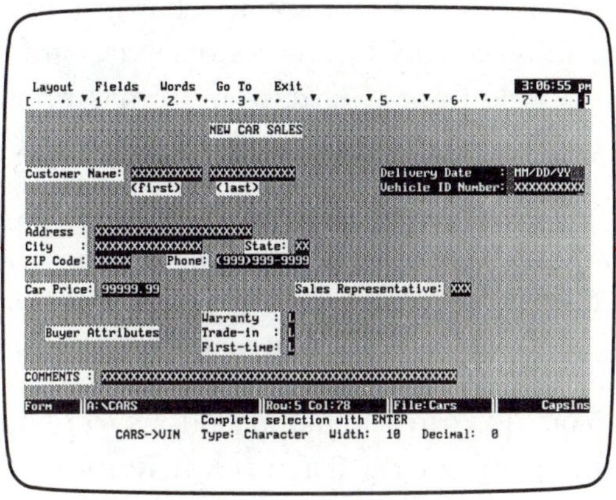

Press F6 to select the area to be moved. Then use ← and → to highlight the area to be moved and press ↵Enter.

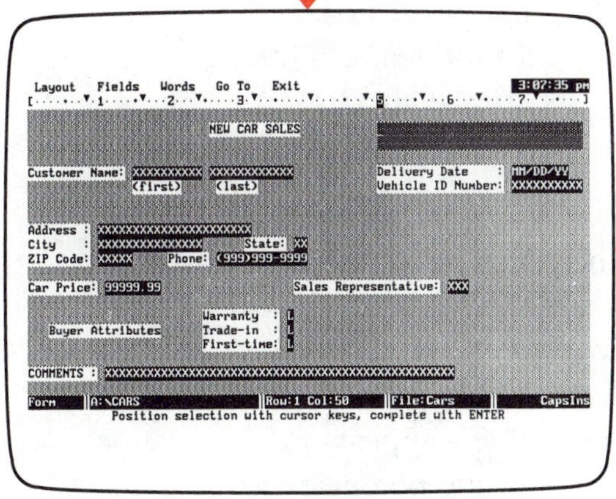

Press F7 to activate **Move**. Move the cursor to the location where the item should be moved.

To **Copy**, press F8 instead of F7.

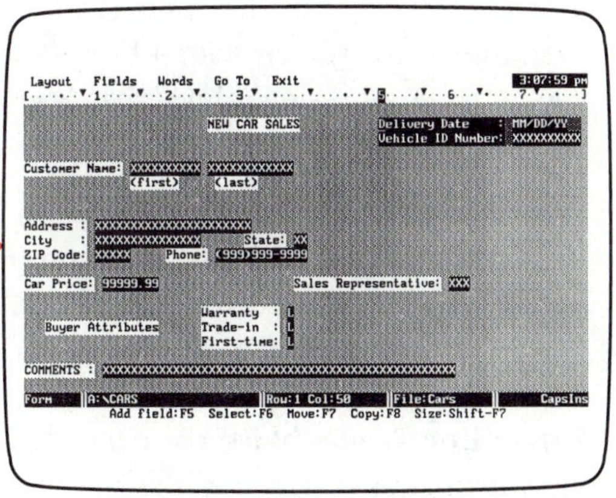

Press ↵Enter to complete the move.

Removing Fields

As you work with forms, you may decide to remove a data field from a forms-design work surface. For instance, suppose that you already have removed a field from the database structure and you need to remove the field from your custom forms, reports, and labels. Or perhaps you transferred the wrong field to the work surface.

You can remove a field two different ways. If you position the cursor on the field template you want to remove and press the Del key, the template disappears from the screen. Do not forget to remove the text field name and any other related text using Backspace and Del.

You also can use menu options to remove a field. Press Alt-F to access the Fields menu. Then select **Remove field** to open a window containing a list of the database fields. Select the field name you want to remove, and all occurrences of that field name disappear from the form.

Using Box and Line Draw

If you want, you can surround groups of fields, text instructions, or even the whole screen with a box. Both **Box** and **Line** features offer you a choice of a single line, a double line, or a special character symbol (256 choices).

You can box a portion of your custom form with only a few steps. Press Alt-L to select the Layout menu from the forms-design work surface. After you choose the **Box** option, a window appears with three choices: **Single line**, **Double line**, and **Using specified character** (using a keyboard character as a border). Suppose that you choose **Single line**. Your choice of characters—a single line—appears inside the cursor square. Position the cursor anywhere on the perimeter of the box you intend to draw and press Enter. Use the arrow keys to expand the size of the box to fit over the area you want to fill. Complete the box by pressing Enter.

To draw using the **Line** feature, follow the steps for creating a box, with one exception: select **Line** from the Layout menu instead of **Box**. Choose **Single line**, **Double line**, or **Using specified character**. Press Enter after positioning the cursor where you want the line to start, and begin drawing. After you use the arrow keys to draw lines, press Enter to finish drawing.

To remove a box, position the cursor anywhere on the box line. Press the Del key, and the box disappears. To remove a line, use your choice of Backspace, Del, or the space bar. As an alternative, you can select **Line** from the Layout menu, choose **Using specified character**, and select ASCII code 32, which is a space (from the list of 255 characters that can appear on-screen). Now position the cursor on the line and draw it again. You are drawing with a blank, which has the effect of erasing the line. As usual, press Enter to complete the process.

Saving the Custom Form

You can spend a lot of time creating and testing each custom form. Do not wait until the custom form is completely finished before you store it to disk. Saving your work at regular intervals is a good idea while you are in the creating process in order to minimize loss of data in case of a power interruption. Choose **Save this form** from the Layout menu to store the current form without exiting the forms-design work surface. You must supply up to an eight-character file name when you save a custom form for the first time.

Use the Exit menu to leave the forms work surface. Your choices are to **Save changes and exit** or **Abandon changes and exit.** If you are saving the form for the first time, you must supply the name of the form. If you are modifying a previously saved form, the form is automatically saved under its original name.

Creating a Custom Form

Removing Fields

If a field is no longer needed on the form, remove it by using the Delete key or the Fields menu.

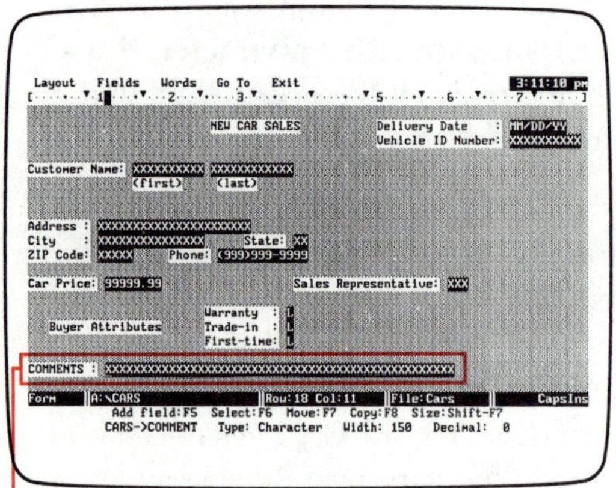

Position the cursor on the unwanted field template.

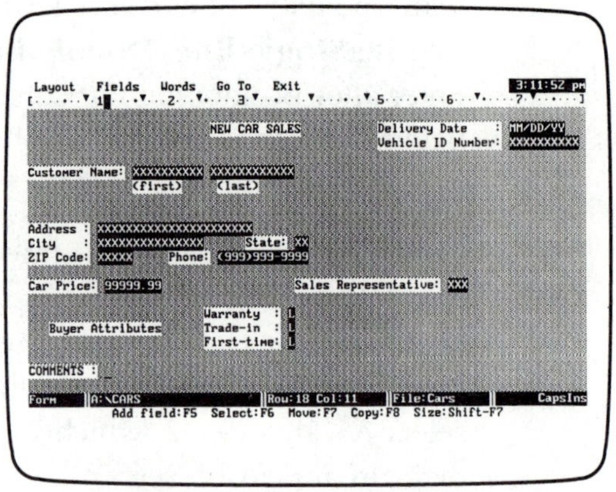

Press [Del] to remove the template. Be sure to erase the field name as well.

If the field exists in one or more places on the screen, you can use the Fields menu to remove all occurrences of the field.

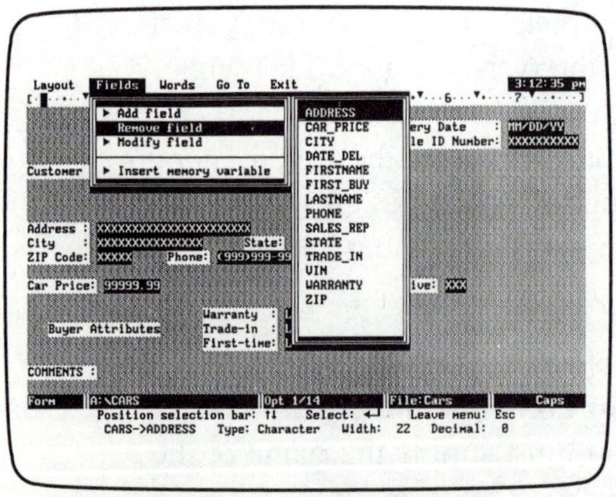

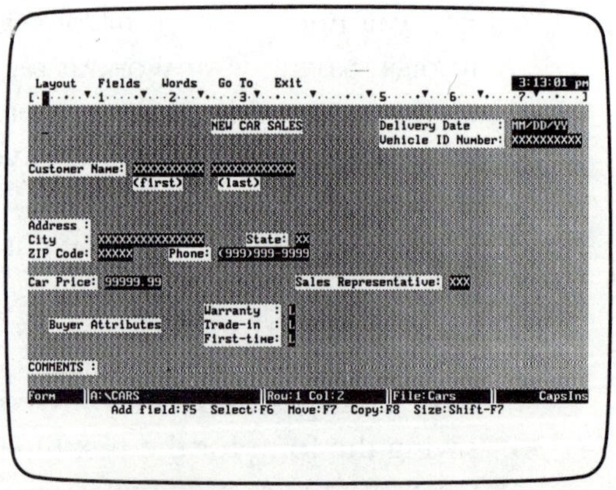

Press [Alt][F] to access the Fields menu.

Press [R] to select the **Remove field** option, and then select the field name to be removed.

Press [↵Enter] to remove all occurrences of the field.

Using Box and Line Draw

To draw attention to a particular portion of your form, put a box around the area. The process is similar to highlighting an area to be moved.

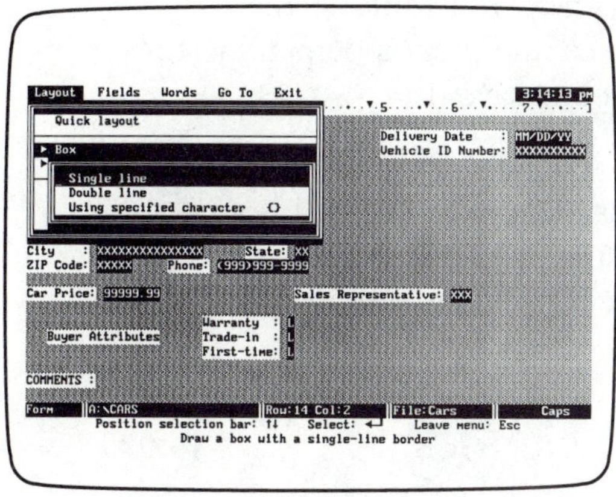

Press Alt L to access the Layout menu.

Press B to select **Box**.

Select the type of box border, such as **Single line**.

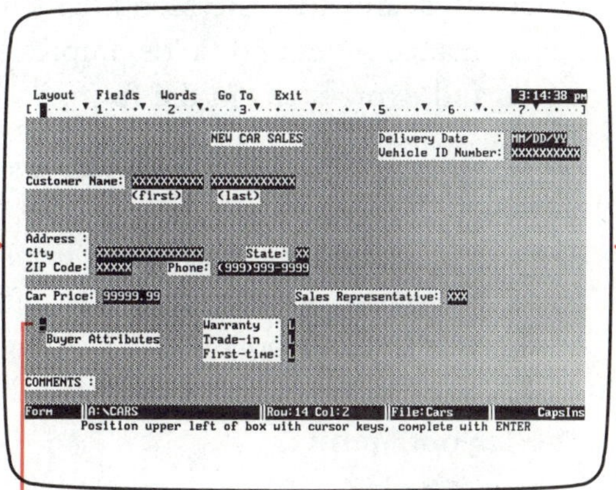

Position the box symbol in the upper left corner of the area you want to enclose.

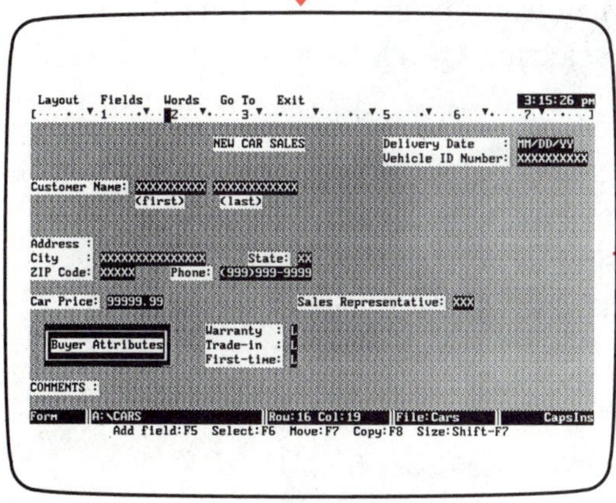

Press ↵Enter to anchor the box.

Use ↑, ↓, ←, and → to draw the lines that form the box.

Press ↵Enter to complete the box.

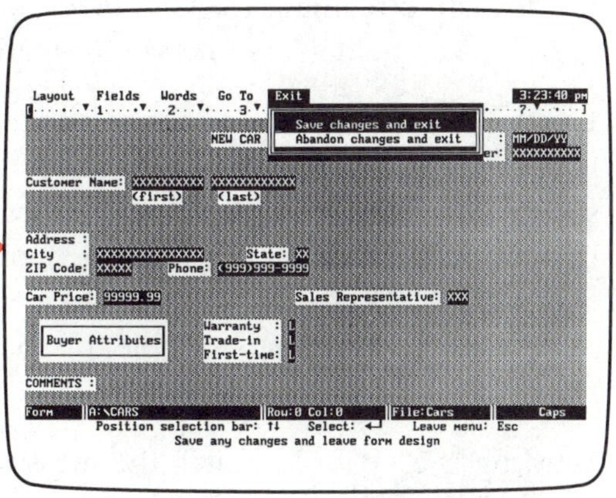

To exit from the work surface, press Alt E.

Press S to save the form.

If you are creating a new form, you are asked to enter a form name.

Using the Forms-Design Menu Bar

dBASE IV offers menu options to help you use the forms-design work surface (blackboard). The Menu bar's menus help you work with the Editor, manage files and fields, improve screen and printed output, locate words and expressions in the form, and exit and save data.

Four of the menus—Layout, Fields, Go To, and Exit—appear in the data and query Menu bars as well as in the forms Menu bar. Although some of the Forms options are different from the Data and query options, the general purposes are the same. The fifth menu—Words—offers options to improve screen display.

The Layout Menu

Use the Layout menu options to transfer all fields to the forms-design work surface, draw boxes and lines on the work surface, and perform general file-management tasks.

Quick Layout transfers *all* fields from the current file to the work surface. The fields appear one field per line, just as they do in Edit mode. If you plan to rearrange several fields, you may want to use F5 (Fields) to transfer each field as you need it instead of selecting **Quick Layout**.

Use the **Box** and **Line** options to enhance the appearance of the form you are designing. Either option offers a choice of single, double, or special-character lines. Use **Box** to draw a line around a designated area on the form—such as dollar signs ($) enclosing a car price or a single line around all customer-address data. Select **Line** from the Layout menu to draw any other single, double, or special-character lines of your choice.

Drawing is easy if you watch the messages on the Navigation and Message lines. For example, if you select **Line** and then **Single line**, you see the message **Position start of line with cursor keys, complete with ENTER** on the Navigation line.

If you want to change databases, use the Layout menu option **Use different database file or view**. If you access the forms work surface when no database is in use, the Layout menu appears with **Use different database file or view** highlighted. The custom form that you design, like a Browse or Edit form, is used to enter and display data in a database. Before you design or use a custom form, you first must put a database in use.

Select **Edit description of form** to change the form description in the catalog. Choose **Save this form** to store the current form without exiting the forms-design work surface. If you are modifying a form, save the revised version under a different name, in case you want to restore the original design.

The Fields Menu

The Fields menu offers options to manage fields on the forms-design work surface. Use **Add field** to add a field to the design form. You can select the field name you want from the list that appears in a window on-screen. dBASE then allows you to restrict the chosen field's content by using the picture-function window that appears on-screen. For example, you can specify that the only valid entries for the SALES_REP field are RS, TW, JM, and SF (the initials of four sales representatives).

You also can add a calculated field to the form by selecting **Add field**. For example, you can calculate a BONUS field by multiplying the contents of a CAR_PRICE field by the bonus percentage. Select **Add field** and choose the appropriate field from the Calculated fields column. If a calculated field does not exist, you can create it by selecting **<create>** in the Calculated fields column and following the instructions on the Message line.

To eliminate a field from the form you are designing, position the cursor on the field and select **Remove field**. The highlighted data field disappears. You then must remove any text describing the field, using the Del, Backspace, or space bar keys.

An advantage of using a custom form is that each field within the form can have editing criteria attached. To change the criteria for a field—for example, to add a new salesperson's initials to the list of allowable entries in the SALES_REP field—position the cursor on the field and select **Modify field**. When the picture function menu appears, select the appropriate edit function. You can use picture functions to cause the data field to convert input to all uppercase, accept only alphabetic characters, store a default value in a field, prompt the user with a message, and so on.

Use **Insert memory variable** to include in the computer's memory special fields that are not part of any database. You often use this option with dBASE IV's Structured Query Language (SQL) feature. Refer to Que's *dBASE IV Programming Techniques* for more information about memory variables and SQL.

The Words Menu

The Words menu provides options to assist the Editor in enhancing printer and screen displays. Select **Display** to change screen output. You can change a monochrome monitor's display by changing intensity, underlining, reversing video, or causing an item to blink. With a color monitor, you can create impressive screens using 1 to 8 or 1 to 16 colors, depending on your monitor. Note that **Style** is not applicable to the forms work surface.

Choose the **Position** option to align text between margins. You can justify text on the left or right margin, or center text.

Select **Add line** and **Remove line** to adjust lines on a form. You also can remove a text line by pressing F6 (Select), highlighting the line you want to remove, and pressing Del.

Use **Write/read text file** to exchange portions of the design surface with other files on disk. As you create a form on the work surface, you can select a portion of the form, using the F6 (Select) key, and *write* it to a disk file, without saving the entire form. Similarly, as you design a form, you can *read* a text file stored on disk into the screen you are designing.

The Go To Menu

The Go To menu options position the cursor and locate data on the forms work surface, like the Browse or Edit options of the Data panel. (The options **Top record**, **Last record**, **Record number**, and **Skip** are not included on this menu because fields and text comprise the forms work surface, not records.)

Choose **Go to line number** to position the cursor on a specific line of the work surface. Select **Forward search** and **Backward search** to position the cursor on an item you are searching for. If **Match capitalization** is set to **YES**, be sure that you type the search criteria exactly as it appears in the database record—including capitalization—or you won't find the text. Remember to press Enter to toggle **Match capitalization** between **YES** and **NO**.

Use **Replace** to substitute a word or phrase for another word or phrase. For example, suppose that a company name appears in several places on a multiple-page form, but the company is now under new ownership. You can substitute the new company name for the old company name—electing to skip an occurrence of the old name, to replace each occurrence of the old name, or to replace all occurrences of the old name at once. The content of the old field entry is replaced completely with the new entry.

The Exit Menu

Use the Exit menu to leave the forms work surface. Your choices are to **Save changes and exit** or **Abandon changes and exit.** If you are creating a new form and you **Save changes and exit,** you must supply the name of the form. If you are modifying an existing form, the form is automatically saved under its original name.

Caution: If you want to save the form under a different name and keep both the modified version and the original version, save the form under a different name, using the Layout menu's **Save this form** option. Then you can exit using the **Abandon changes and exit** option.

Using the Forms-Design Menu Bar

Several of the menus on the forms-design Menu bar will be familiar. You already have used Layout, Fields, Go To, and Exit. There are, however, a few new options among the forms-design menus.

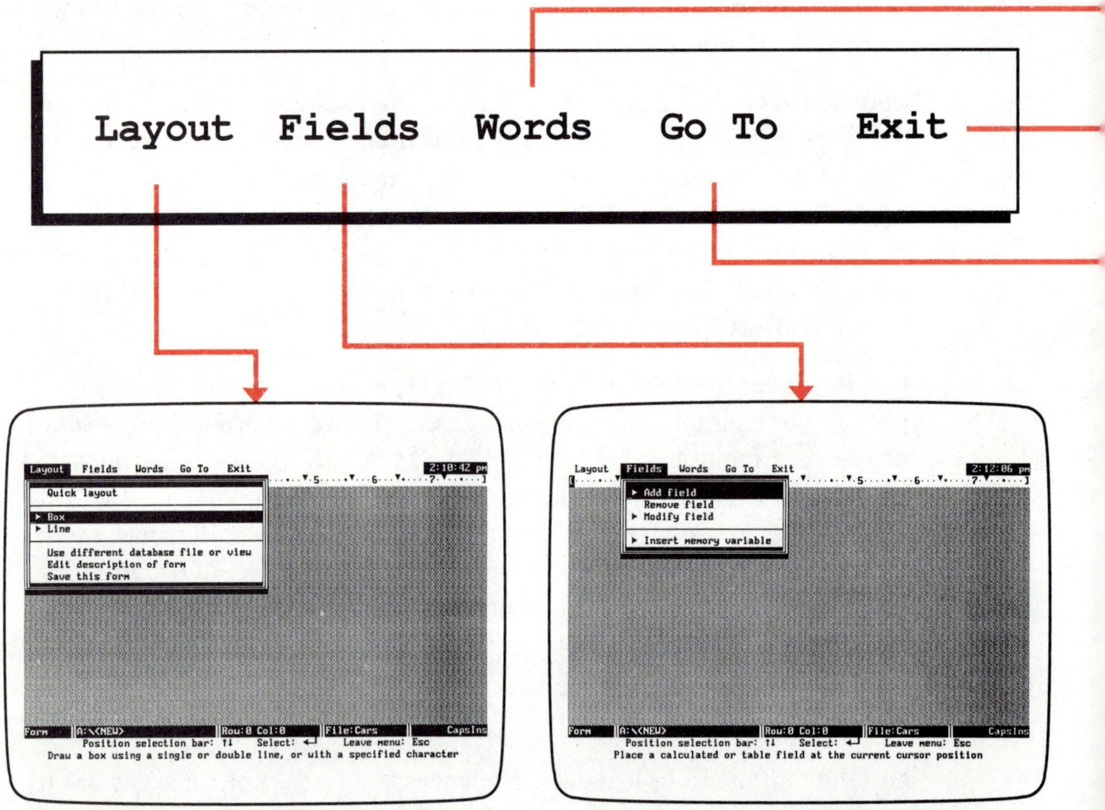

Use **Layout** to create a Quick Layout form, draw boxes and lines, select a new database, edit the form description in the catalog, or save the form without exiting the work surface.

Use **Fields** to add, modify, or delete fields on the forms work surface. The **Add field** and **Remove field** options produce a window displaying the names of the fields from which you can select. **Modify field** uses a series of windows you can use to add powerful editing criteria to each field.

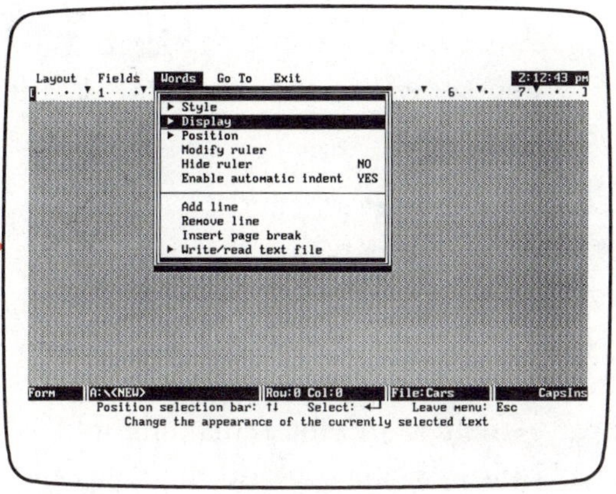

Use **Words** to enhance the form and work surface. The **Display** option lets you change your screen output by adjusting the intensity on a monochrome monitor or adjusting the colors on a color monitor. On the work surface, you can add and remove lines, adjust the print ruler, and read and write external files.

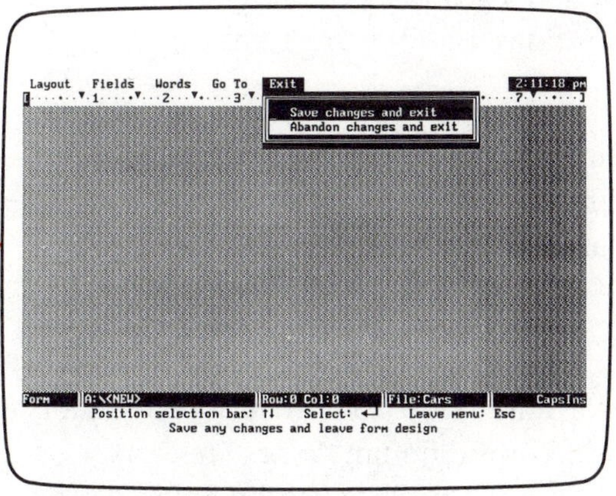

Use **Exit** to leave the work surface, saving or abandoning the changes you've made.

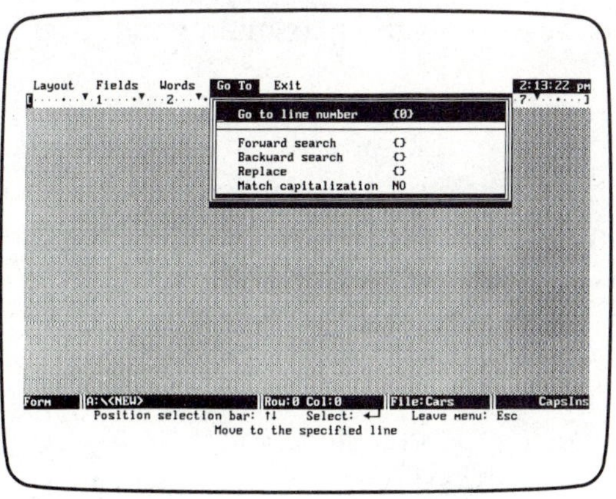

Use **Go To** to locate and replace work surface items or position the cursor on the work surface.

Using Templates and Picture Functions

When you design your own custom forms, you probably expect to use the forms to enter or display data. Whenever you enter or display data in dBASE IV, editing instructions control the data.

The instructions that control data are called *templates* and *picture functions*. Templates control individual positions within the data field. For example, suppose that you create a character field for an inventory part number, and you specify a width of 8. Further assume that the first character position is always a letter, the next two positions are always numeric, the fourth position is always a letter, and the remaining four positions are always numeric (**A12X2456**). When you add the data field to the custom form, you also can add a template to the field. This template allows only letters in positions 1 and 4. Positions 2, 3, 5, 6, 7, and 8 accept only numbers.

Picture functions control the entire field. For example, the function symbol ! forces all characters within the field to be uppercase. Templates and picture functions can work at the same time.

Using Templates

When you enter data in Browse or Edit mode, each field where data is to be entered appears in inverse video or a different color. The cursor appears in the first field on the screen where data can be entered. The width of the highlighted data area represents the maximum width of the data field in the database.

When you add a data field to the forms work surface, a highlighted area representing the size of the data field appears at the cursor. On the work surface, the characters you see in the highlighted area form the template.

Templates offer a way of editing data as it is entered in a field. For example, suppose that you define CITY in a database structure as a character-type field having a width of 15. If you transfer the CITY field to the forms-design work surface, you see the default template **XXXXXXXXXXXXXXX**. Each X tells dBASE IV to accept any character in the associated position.

Change the template to **AAAAAAAAAAAAAAA** so that dBASE IV accepts only letters. The template **!AAAAAAAAAAAAAA** tells dBASE IV to convert the first letter to uppercase (!) and accept only letters in the remainder of the field. Study the following template symbols:

Symbol	*Action*
A	Accepts only letters (A–Z, a–z)
L	Accepts only logical characters (Yy, Nn, Tt, Ff)
N	Accepts only a letter or digit
X	Accepts any character
Y	Accepts only logical characters Y or N
9	Accepts only a digit or a sign (+ or –)
#	Accepts only a digit, a blank, or a sign (+ or –)
*	Displays leading zeros as *
$	Displays leading zeros as $
!	Converts a letter to uppercase
.	Positions a decimal point
,	Uses commas for large numbers

You can edit the default template that appears when you transfer a field to the forms-design work surface. To edit the template after the field is added to the screen, position the cursor on the data field and press Alt-F to access the Fields menu. Then choose **Modify field**.

When you add or modify a field, an edit window appears. The upper portion displays general information about the field. The lower portion lets you access **Template**, **Picture functions**, **Edit options**, and **Border lines**.

If you select **Template**, the cursor appears in the existing template, marking the position for you to begin editing. Another window opens to display the list of available template symbols. Change the template symbols as necessary, press Enter to accept, and exit the modify-field window. The new template controls data entry when the form you have designed is in use.

Using Templates and Picture Functions

Templates and picture functions control the data that is entered in a field or the data seen when a field is displayed on the screen. A template controls individual character positions; a picture function controls the entire field.

Understanding Default Templates

Quick Layout places all field names and their associated default templates on the forms-design work surface. If you create your own custom form from a blank forms-design work surface, you see the default templates for each field you place on the form.

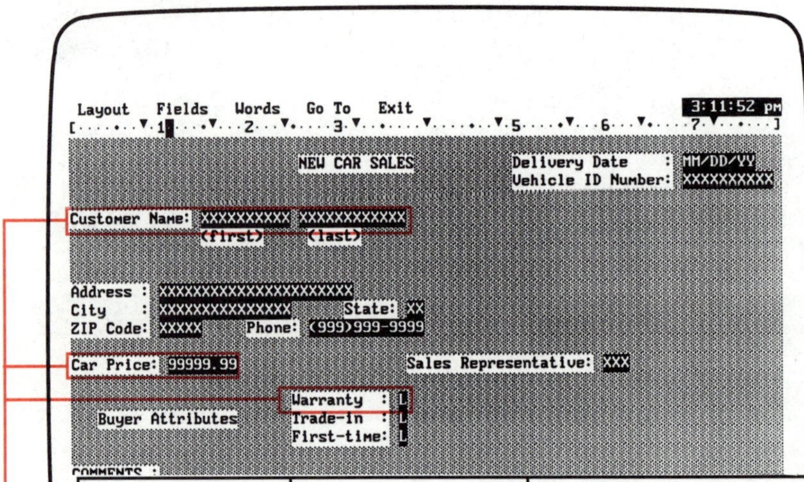

Field	Template	Code that controls data entry or screen display
Customer Name	XXXXXXXXXXXX	X Accepts any character
Car Price	99999.99	9 Accepts only a digit or a sign (+ or –)
Warranty	L	L Accepts only a logical character (Yy, Nn, Tt, Ff)

Modifying Templates

Use the **Modify field** option on the Fields menu to change a template. Some of your choices include limiting entry to alphabetic characters or forcing alphabetic characters to become uppercase.

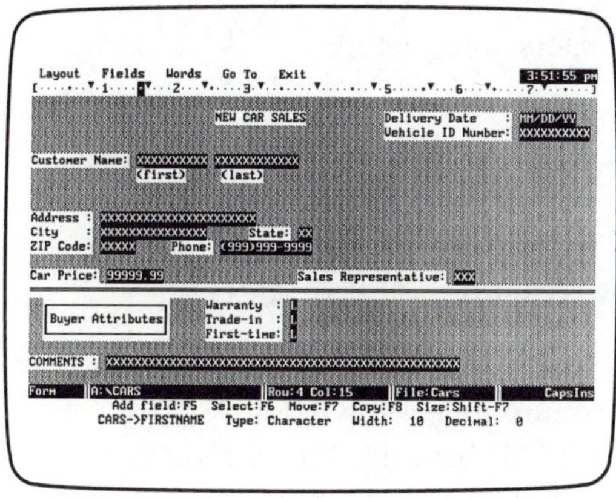

Position the cursor on the field to be modified.

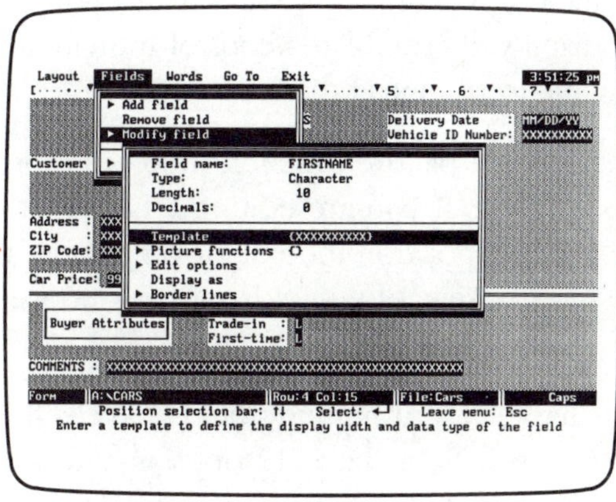

Press Alt F to access the Fields menu.

Press M to select **Modify field**.

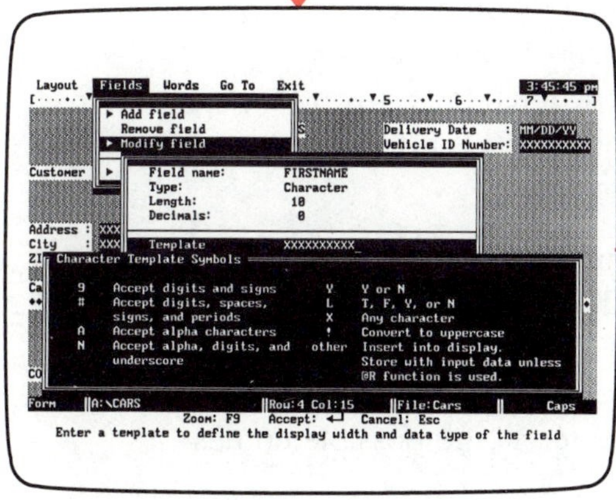

Press T to select **Template**. The cursor appears at the end of the template, and a list of symbols is displayed.

Note, for example, that an exclamation point (!) converts a character to uppercase.

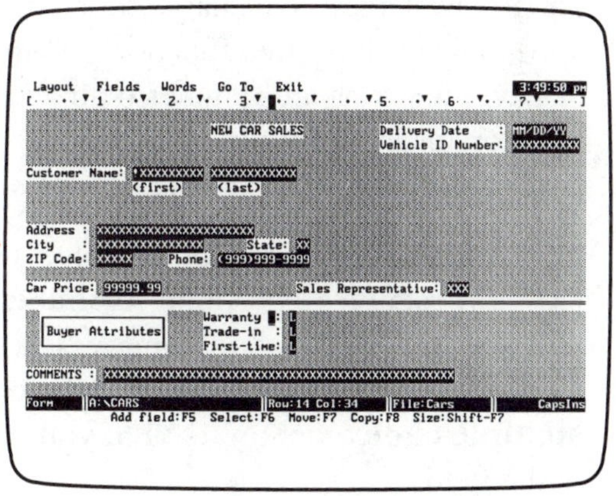

Edit the template to substitute your choice of symbols.

Press ↵Enter to accept the new template.

Press Ctrl End to accept the modifications and return to the work surface.

Using Picture Functions

Picture functions, like templates, control data as it is entered or displayed. Templates control individual characters, and picture functions control the entire field.

Editing a picture function involves a process similar to that of editing a template. If you are editing a field that is on the forms-design work surface, position the cursor on the field you want to modify and press Alt-F to select the Fields menu. Choose **Modify fields**, and then select **Picture functions**.

Character and numeric fields have different picture-function windows. Numeric fields have 12 options, and character fields have 11. When you select an option, you see an explanation on the Message line. If you require more information, press F1 (Help).

Some picture functions may not be applicable, and therefore are not available, at certain times. The cursor does not stop on functions that are not available. Unavailable functions have a different screen appearance from active functions. With a monochrome monitor, inactive functions are dimmer than active functions (unless you have the monitor intensity turned too high). Color monitors use colors instead of dimming to distinguish inactive options.

Most of the picture functions involve switching the option to **YES** or **NO**. For example, the option **Alphabetic characters only** on the character picture-function window is a **YES** or **NO** field. A few options ask that you enter more information. For example, if you set the **Multiple choice** option to **YES**, you must enter all the possible entries in the field.

To better understand the concept of a picture function, take a look at one of the character picture-function options that is particularly useful with custom screens—the **Multiple choice** option. You can use this feature to associate multiple choices with a field. Users can scroll through the list of choices by pressing the space bar and then pressing Enter when the appropriate choice appears.

Suppose, for example, that a SALES_REP field in a car sales database is defined as a character field with a width of 3—for the salesperson's initials. Further assume that the current sales force consists of three individuals: John Paul Tiller, Nancy Ann Jerden, and Scott David Morgan. You can create a multiple-choice picture function that limits the entire field contents to JPT, NAJ, or SDM—the initials of the current sales staff—thereby eliminating any other data entry.

To activate the feature, access the Fields menu on the forms-design Menu bar, choose **Picture functions**, and select **Multiple choice**. In the window that appears, type the choices consecutively, separating each with a comma. For example, type *JPT,JAJ,SDM*. Press Ctrl-End to accept the multiple-choice options.

The **Scroll within display width** picture function lets you reduce the size of a field display on-screen. The data field size remains the same in the file structure; but when you look at the smaller display on-screen, you must scroll with the right-arrow or left-arrow keys.

Suppose that you have a field that is 150 characters in length. The screen is only 80 characters wide. Instead of displaying only part of the field or using 2 lines, display only 80 characters and instruct users to scroll the contents of the field if they want to read it all.

To activate the feature, select **Scroll within display width** from the picture-functions window. Enter the field size you want to display in the window that appears. Choose the appropriate response from the instructions in the Navigation line: **Accept: Ctrl-End** or **Cancel: Esc**.

Using Picture Functions

Picture functions control the entry or display of data for the entire field. Templates control only individual character positions, and you see templates on the forms-design work surface. You do not see similar codes for picture functions on the forms-design work surface. The two features can work together to control the entry and view of data, or you can use one or the other. Consider some examples.

Case 1: Both a template and a picture function

Field: FIRSTNAME

Template: !XXXXXXXXX

Picture function: Alphabetic characters only

Data entry	Result
marianne	Marianne
Mar8anne	BEEP! Picture functions won't allow entry of a number

Case 2: Picture function only

Field: SALES_REP

Picture function: Multiple choice (with allowable entries for salespersons with the initials JPT, NAJ, and SDM)

When you move the cursor to the SALES_REP field, you see	JPT
Press the space bar and you see	NAJ
Press the space bar and you see	SDM

You do not type the field contents; you press the space bar until the desired entry appears, and then press Enter.

Accessing the Picture Functions Options

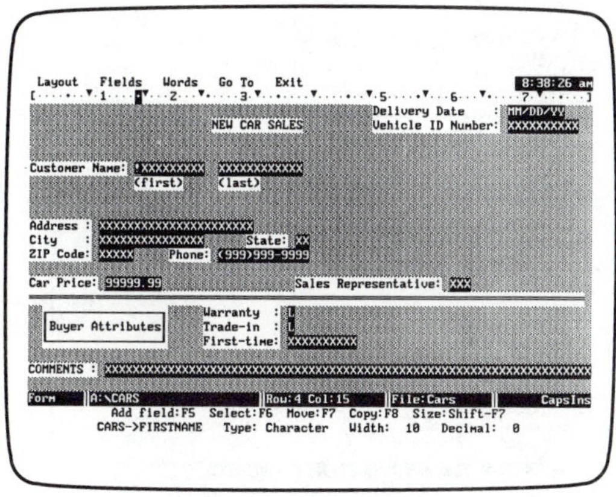

Position the cursor on the field for which you want to establish a picture function and press Alt F to access the Fields menu.

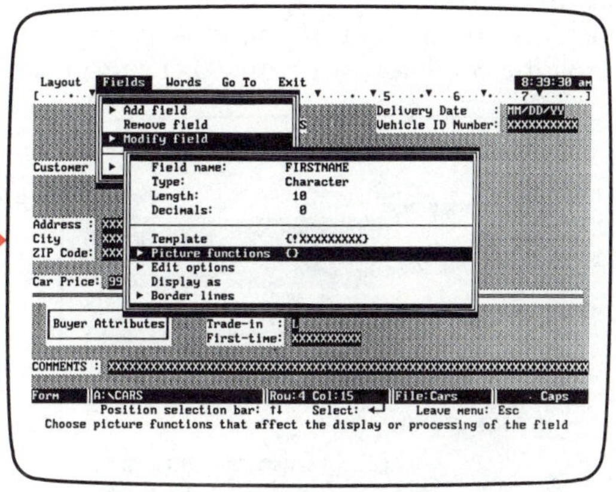

Press M to select **Modify field**.

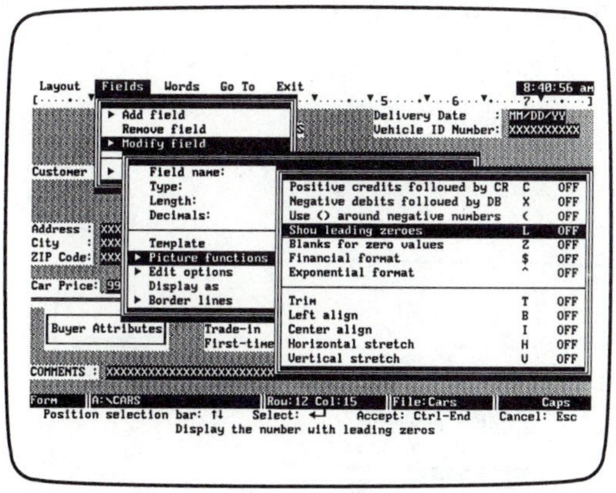

Press P to access the **Picture functions** options.

These are the options you see if the field is *numeric*.

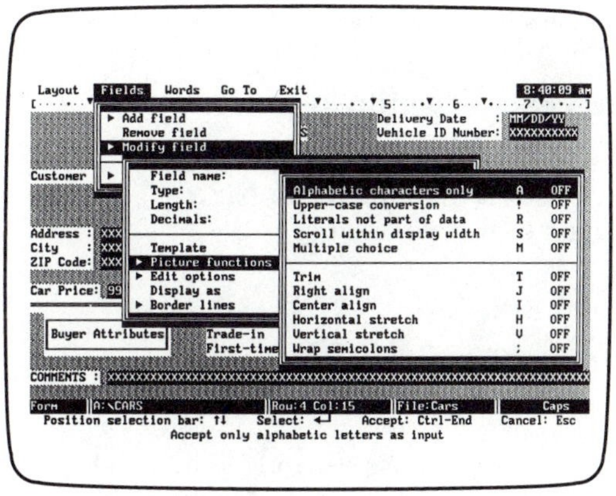

These are the options you see if the field is *character*.

Using Scroll within display width

Suppose, for example, that you have in your database a field 150 characters long. To see this field on the screen, you can use the **Scroll within display width** option and specify a screen display width of 50 characters. When the cursor is on this field, all 150 characters can be seen by using → or ← to scroll the contents within the 50-character screen display.

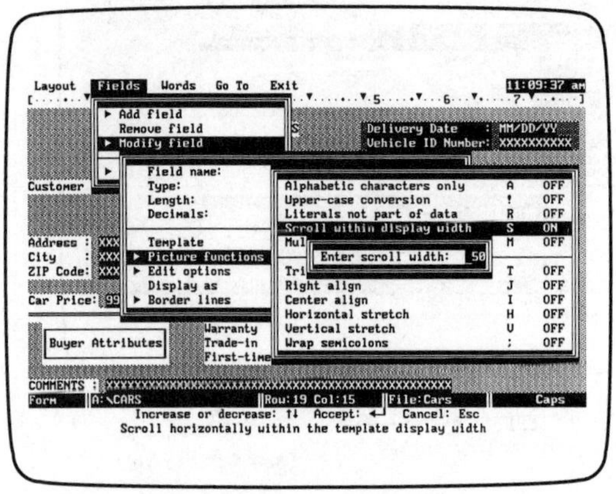

Position the cursor on the field—in this case, the character field COMMENTS—and access the **Picture functions** options.

Select **Scroll within display width** and enter **50**.

Select **Exit** from the Menu bar to return to the work surface.

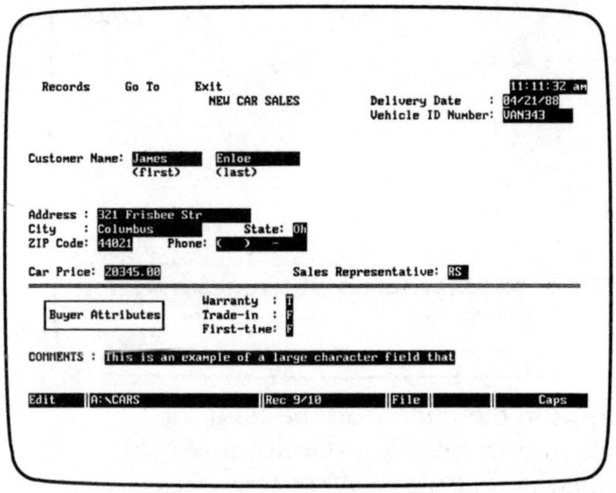

Press F2 to display the custom form and notice the 50-character length of the COMMENTS field.

Use ← and → to scroll the data inside the field narrowed for the screen display.

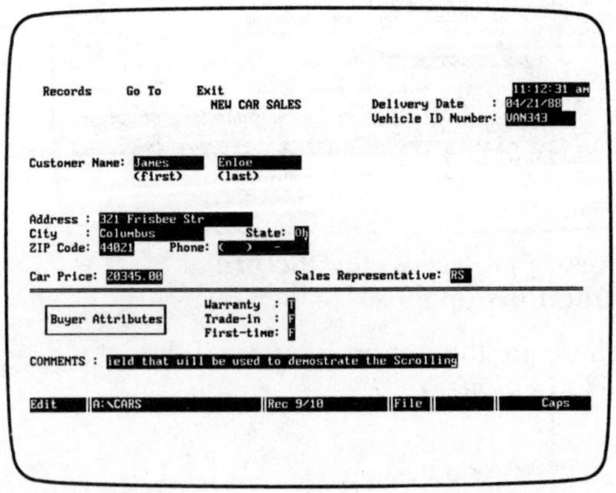

Using Multiple choice

While creating a database structure, you can press the space bar to see the options in a field when the cursor is on a field. You can create this same type of menu using multiple-choice picture functions.

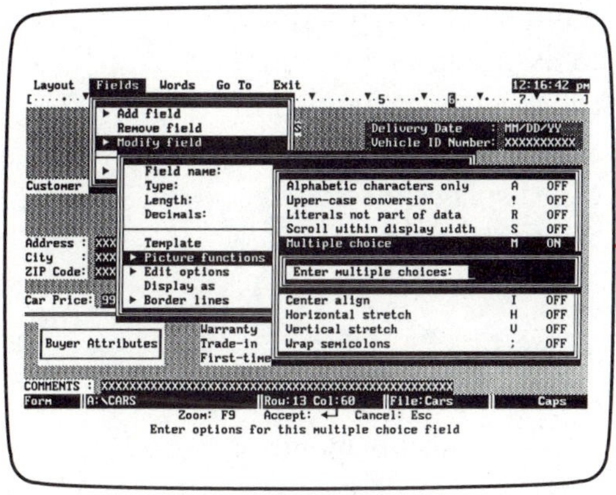

Position the cursor on the field—in this case, the character field SALES_REP—and access the **Picture functions** options.

Select **Multiple choice** from the Picture functions menu.

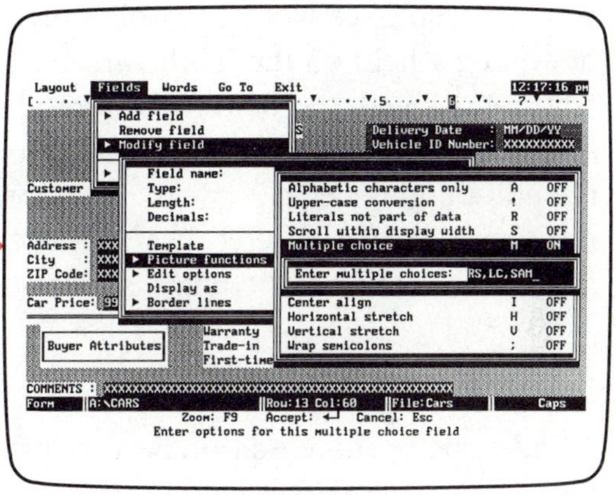

Type the multiple choices in the window that appears.

Separate each entry with a comma. You can arrange the entries in any sequence.

Select **Exit** from the Menu bar to return to the work surface.

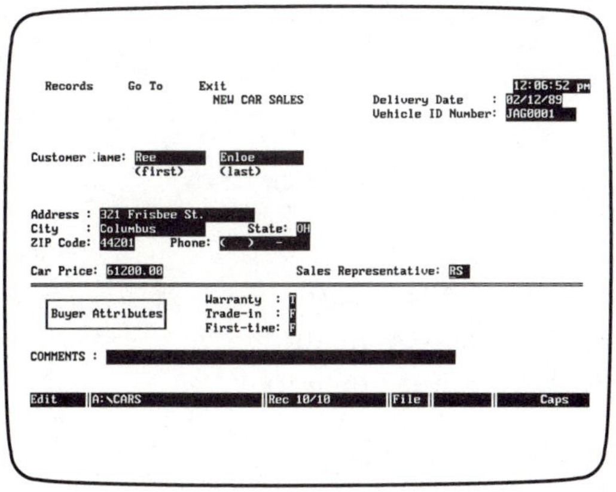

Press F2 to display the custom form and notice that your first multiple-choice options for salesperson's initials are displayed in the field.

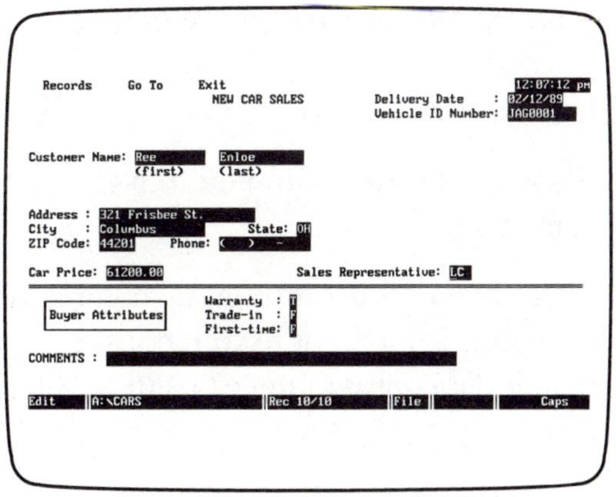

Press the space bar to see the next multiple-choice option. Continue pressing the space bar until the correct entry appears.

Press ↵Enter to accept the choice.

dBASE IV offers nine editing options that give you considerable control over how the user types data. In earlier versions of dBASE, these editing techniques were available only to programmers. When adding or editing a field on the work surface, you can associate one or more edit options with the field by using the numeric or character function screens discussed earlier. When the user places the cursor on the field, the edit options begin to work. The options can display on-screen messages to the user, edit data as it is entered into the field, and take appropriate action if the entry is incorrect.

Accessing and Exiting Edit Options

To add one or more edit options to a field, access the Fields menu on the forms-design Menu bar and select **Modify field** to display an edit window. The upper portion displays general information about the field; the lower portion lists the options **Template**, **Picture functions**, **Edit options**, and **Border lines**. Select **Edit options**, choose the desired option, such as **Editing allowed** or **Message**, supply any information asked for on the screen, and press Enter. You may use one or more options on the same field. Every field on the screen can use these options. To accept the edit options you select, press Ctrl-End.

Using Edit Options

If you set **Editing allowed** to **NO**, a user can view, but not change, the contents of the field.

Select **Permit edit if** to allow editing of a field *only if* the stated condition is met. For example, using the cars database, you might permit data entry in the COMMENTS field if CAR_PRICE is equal to zero.

Use **Message** to display a message at the bottom of the screen whenever the cursor is placed on the field. The feature lets you give a user instructions about how to use the field.

The **Carry forward** option causes data from the field in the previous record to be carried forward to the next record. You might want to use this feature when you add a batch of records to a database, and all the entries for a particular field are the same. Suppose, for example, that the contents of a ZIP code field are the same throughout many of the records you are entering. Using this option on the ZIP code field carries forward the ZIP code from the preceding record so that you don't need to retype it. You can edit automatically entered data, if necessary.

Use **Default value** to place a predetermined entry in the field each time you add a record. For example, if all your records concern customers living in one state, specify the name of the state as the default value. You can edit the value, if necessary.

Establish a **Smallest allowed value** and **Largest allowed value** to specify a range where the field contents must fall. For example, in the cars database, if the price of a car sold cannot be greater than $45,000, then set the **Smallest allowed value** to zero and the **Largest allowed value** to 45000. Although this method does not ensure total accuracy, it does prevent gross errors.

Use the **Accept Value when** option to specify when the user can type data in the field. You can use any valid dBASE IV expression, such as CAR_PRICE<>0, as the condition. The option does not edit the data; it merely determines when an entry is allowed. For example, you might allow an entry into the warranty purchased field only if the car price field is not zero.

Through the **Unaccepted message** option, you can set up a custom message to display if the entry to a field is unacceptable. When data being entered in a field is rejected because it does not meet the criteria set in one of the edit options, you want to provide the user with as much information as possible about the problem. For example, if you enter a value of 50000 in the CAR_PRICE field, it is rejected because the value is greater than the **Largest allowed value**. You might create the following **Unaccepted message**: *Car price must be between 0 and 45000.*

The **Edit options** menu allows you to attach as many as nine powerful editing criteria to any field.

Accessing Edit Options

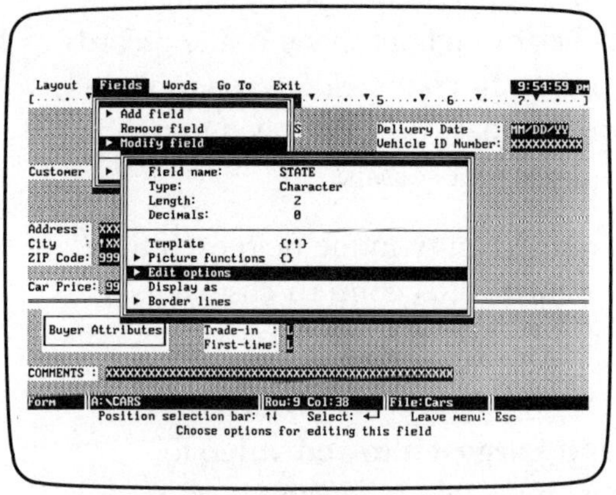

On the forms-design work surface, position the cursor on the field to which you want to attach editing criteria.

Press Alt F to access the Fields menu, and then press M to select **Modify field**.

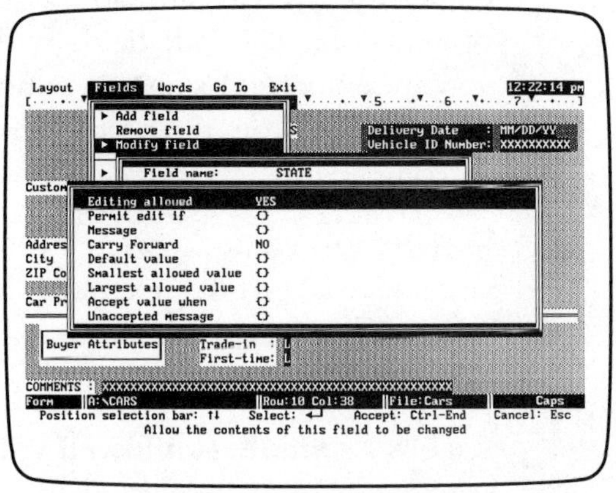

Press E to select **Edit options**.

Nine editing options appear.

You can press F1, the Help key, to access help screens that explain the options. Watch the Navigation and Message lines for additional information.

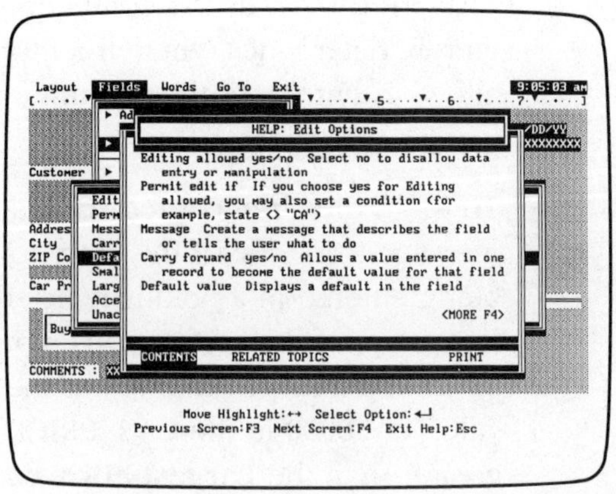

Using Edit Options

You can understand how the edit options work if you look at one option, such as **Default value**. If the contents of a field rarely change, such as IN for the contents of a STATE field, you can cause the contents to appear automatically in the field and avoid typing the data unless a different state is required.

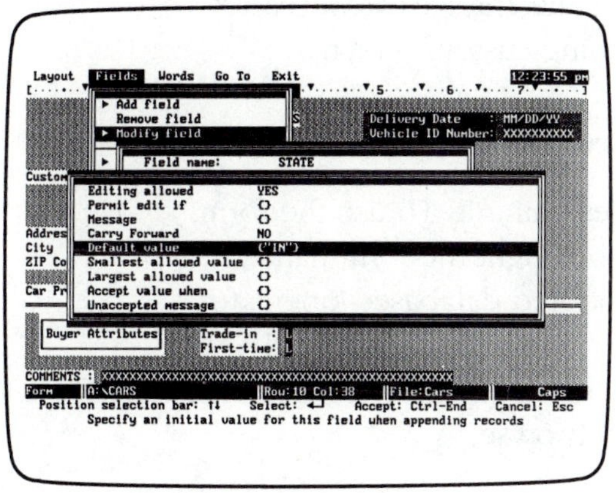

Select **Default value** and type the contents you want to appear automatically in the field. If the data is character data, enclose it in quotation marks (").

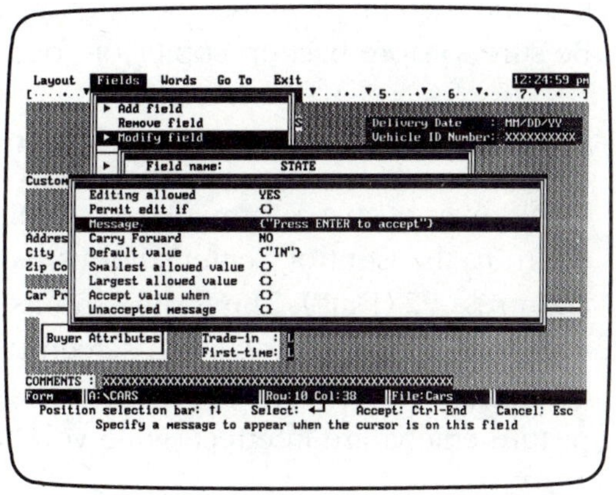

Enter a message to appear whenever the state field is accessed. Select **Message** and type the message enclosed in quotation marks.

Enter other edit options.

Press Ctrl End to accept the edit options.

When you add a record, the default value appears automatically.

Combine any or all of the nine edit options to ensure that the most accurate information possible is entered in the database.

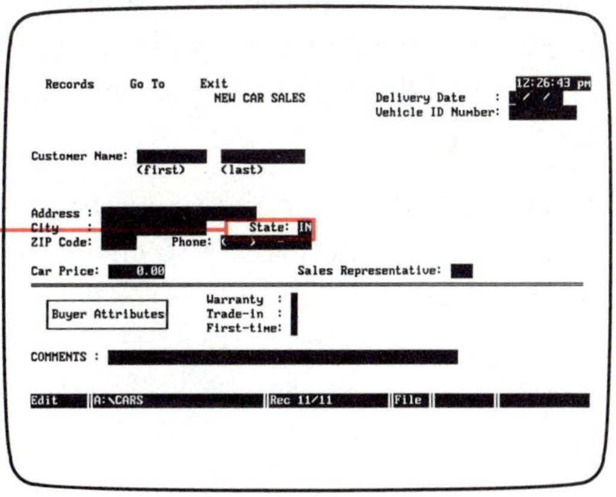

Using the Custom Form

All the time you spend creating a custom screen pays off when you see how your work improves the screen display for data entry or viewing data. Quickly you realize how using the editing features, such as templates, picture functions, and edit options, makes data entry pleasant and more accurate. Take the time to try out your creation, test its built-in editing features thoroughly, and make changes as necessary. Be sure to store backup copies of your working custom screens.

Selecting a Custom Form from the Control Center

Remember to save a form after you finish designing it. To use the form, return to the Control Center's Forms panel, highlight the form name, and press F2 (Data). The form—and its associated database—opens for use, and you see your custom screen displaying the current record. Pressing F2 (Data) again switches you to Browse mode. Your edit-picture criteria are in effect while you are in Browse.

Testing the Form

Before you begin extensive data entry using your new custom form, test the form. Enter a number of practice records. Make intentional errors that cause your edit options to work. For example, try to enter a set of three initials in a SALES_REP field that is not one of the multiple-choice options available for that field. Or try to enter a value that is higher than the maximum value you established for the field. Determine whether or not your messages say what you want them to say.

Inventory all fields on the screen to make sure that you have not forgotten essential fields. Also check that two fields and field names are not reversed.

Consider having someone that does not know dBASE test your data-entry form. Novice users usually encounter any problems that exist in the operation of a custom screen and often can suggest improvements in on-screen messages.

Modifying a Custom Form

After the testing process, or as time passes, your custom form may need changing. Perhaps you discover an error in the design. Or as you periodically validate your database contents, you may find erroneous data. Decide whether you can make changes to the edit options in order to prevent errors.

You may need to add or delete fields in your database or change the width of a field. Whenever you change your database structure, be aware that you may have custom forms, reports, or labels to change as well.

To change a custom form, return to the Control Center work surface. Highlight the form name you want to change, press Enter, and select **Modify layout**. The current forms-design work surface appears. At this point, you should feel comfortable changing text on the work surface, accessing and modifying a field, moving items around the work surface, or deleting items.

Much of this chapter's contents are about creating custom data-entry screens. Keep in mind, however, that you also can create custom forms to display data, whether you allow that data to be edited or not.

Many of the features you use to produce a custom form—such as the Editor work surface and the picture functions—also can be used to create custom reports and custom labels—the topics discussed in the next two chapters.

Using the Custom Form

You can use your completed custom form as a substitute display for Edit mode. Even if you prefer to enter or view data in Browse mode, the templates, picture functions, and edit options set up in the custom form still operate.

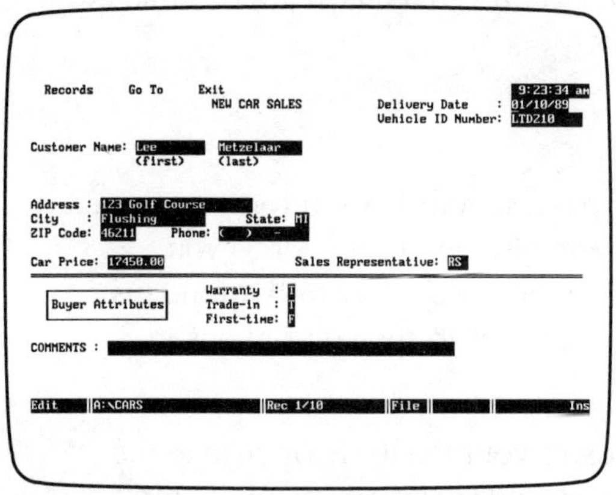

From the forms-design work surface, press F2 to access Browse/Edit mode and display the custom data-entry screen.

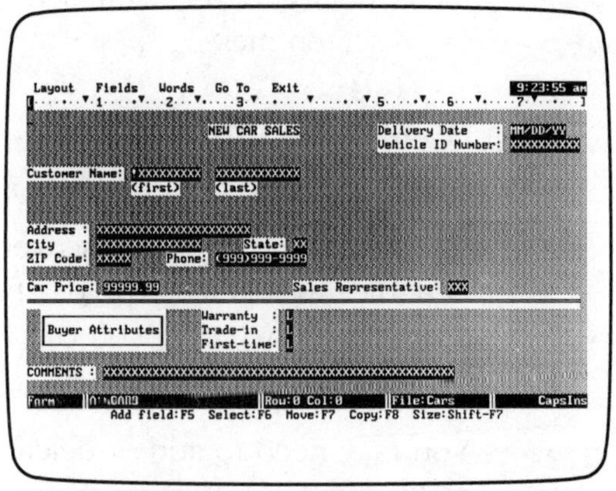

Press Shift F2 to return to the forms-design work surface that creates the custom form.

Selecting a Custom Form from the Control Center

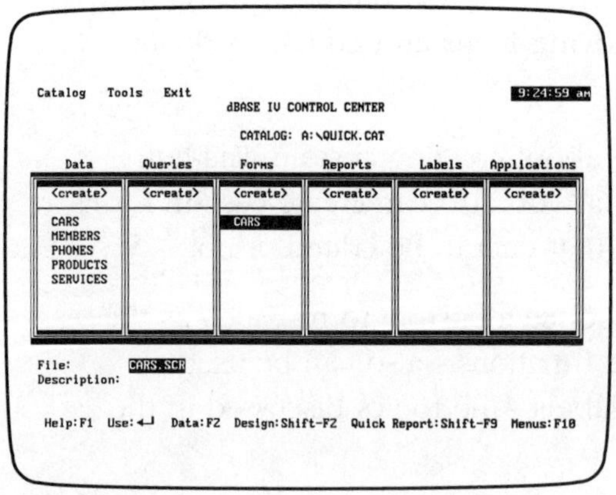

Highlight the custom form name in the Forms panel of the Control Center and press F2.

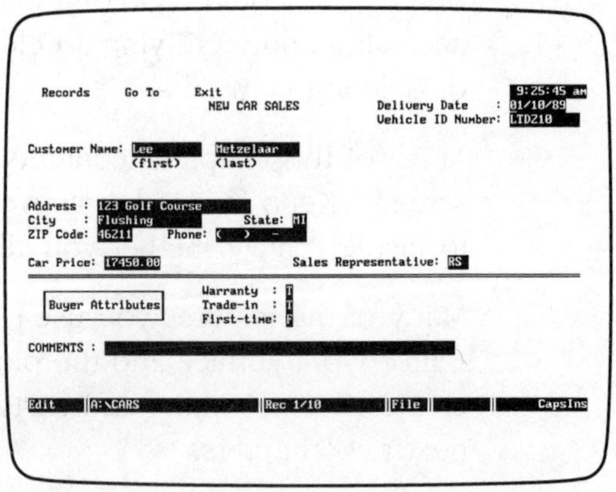

The custom form appears. You can add new records or edit existing ones. If you prefer, you can press F2 to access Browse mode.

Testing the Form

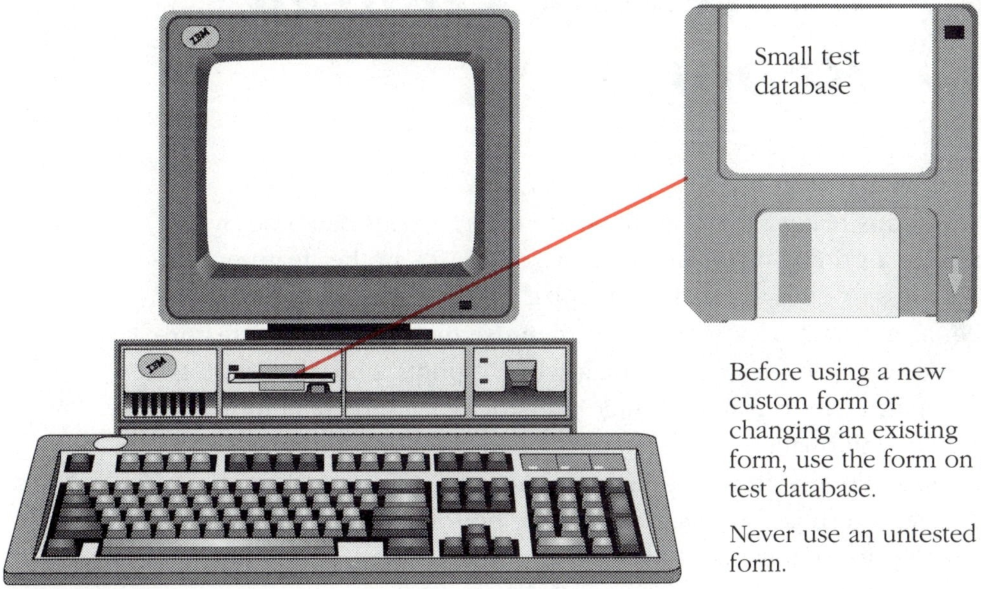

Before using a new custom form or changing an existing form, use the form on a test database.

Never use an untested form.

Modifying a Custom Form

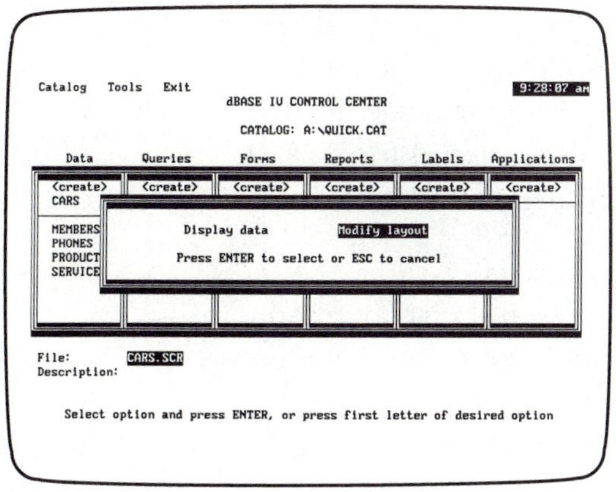

On the Control Center panel, highlight the form name and press ↵Enter.

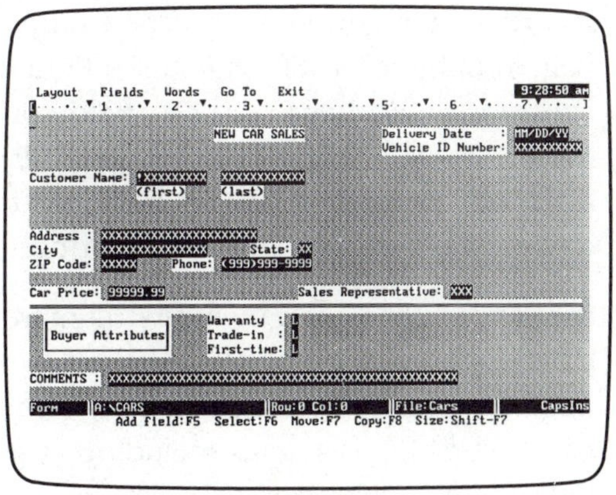

Select **Modify layout** to access the work surface and make necessary changes.

8 Designing Custom Reports

The Reports feature lets you make the most of your database by generating printed information. Using dBASE IV's other features, you can access or query and then organize selected records before printing them as a custom report. You can then use the report-design feature to make calculations, using your data while it prints, and print subtotals and totals, count records, average numeric data, and create other summary information. For example, if you wanted a list of the cars you have sold along with total sales, you can create a report that lists each database record and prints a total at the bottom. You easily can add the average price of a car sold to the end of the report. The Reports feature is a powerful tool for accessing your data.

Pressing Shift-F9 (Quick Report) from the Control Center produces a listing of all fields and records in a database, or selected fields and records in the current view. The output isn't fancy; it places a date and page number on each page, uses field names created in the file structure as headings, and lists field contents. If you manage a car dealership, you might find the quick report output useful for documentation purposes, such as a listing of sales at the end of each day, which you then can check for accuracy.

Simple searches and quick reports merely access and display existing database contents. Suppose that you also would like to see a multiple-page custom report—such as a report that begins with the name of a car dealership, lists items including customer name, car price, and delivery, and subtotals the sales according to the salesperson. Or suppose that you would like to generate a customized mass mailing on the computer, such as a follow-up letter to new car buyers. As a manager of data, you benefit much more from custom output than from a mere listing of database contents.

The dBASE IV Reports panel allows you to create sophisticated custom reports and customized letters. After you design a report layout that you like, you can save it and reuse that layout as many times as you want.

What Is Covered in This Chapter?

In this chapter you learn about

- The elements of a custom report
- The layout of the reports-design screen
- Creating reports using a "quick layout" menu
- Viewing a report on-screen
- Printing a report
- Using the reports-design Menu bar options

Key Words Used in This Chapter

Band	An area on the reports-design work surface related to one of the standard parts of a report. For example, the Page Footer Band specifies items that appear at the bottom of every page.
Column layout	A Quick layouts option in which field information appears side-by-side in column format across each printed line of a report.
Form layout	A Quick layouts option in which field information appears one field per line.
Mailmerge layout	A Quick layouts option for integrating data and calculated fields into a custom form letter.

After you study the organization and features of the reports-design screen, you will find that it makes creating custom reports simple. The screen is organized like all the other Control Center panels. From top to bottom, it includes the Menu bar, work surface, Status bar, Navigation line, and Message line.

Understanding the Work Surface

As you begin to work with the reports-design work surface, think about five standard parts of a report. dBASE IV provides five *bands* (small work surfaces) within the reports-design work surface on which to create your report: Page Header Band, Report Intro Band, Detail Band, Report Summary Band, and Page Footer Band. Each band is related to one of the standard parts of a report. Each band tells dBASE IV what to print on the report.

Think of each band as a mini work surface. If the cursor is positioned in a band, the border of the band is highlighted. As you move the cursor and enter text or fields on the band's surface, the band gets larger.

Page Header

A report can include information repeated at the top of every page. The first line title of a report might be "New Car Sales Report," the second line title "As of: 02/02/89," and the column headings "Customer Name," "Car Price," and "Delivery Date."

Use the *Page Header Band* to specify your choice of items that are repeated every time you print the report, regardless of how the data changes. Aside from titles and column headings, for example, you might include in the Page Header Band the current date, a short description of the report's contents (First Quarter Sales Summary), the name of the report's author, or a page number.

Report Intro Band

A report generally includes *introductory text* near the top of the first page or on a separate cover page, such as the title and author of the report. The introductory text appears only once. Use the *Report Intro Band* to place report headings on the first page of the report.

Detail Band

Use the *Detail Band*, part of the body of the report, to display information from the database records (a listing of each customer's name, the price of the car, and the delivery date). If you want your data to appear in some order, first create a view file using the Query panel. For example, if you are creating a sales report using the New Car Sales database, you might sort your records on last name, then first name. If the report should summarize sales by sales representative, then sort the data by sales representative first, then by customer last name.

Report Summary Band

Use the *Report Summary Band*, part of the body of the report, to display grand totals at the end of the report—for example, total car sales. You can produce subtotals within a report by using optional bands called *group bands*, such as total sales for each salesperson. A *Group Intro Band* appears between the Report Intro Band and the Detail Band. A corresponding *Group Summary Band* appears between the Detail Band and the Report Summary Band.

Page Footer Band

A report also can include optional information repeated at the bottom of every page, such as a page number. Use the *Page Footer Band* to specify your choice of repeating items. Aside from including a page number, you can use this Band to annotate your report with a department name or security-related comments such as "Confidential."

Understanding the Reports-Design Screen

As you begin to work with the reports-design work surface, think about five standard parts of a report, each of which relates to a band on the work surface.

Elements of a Report

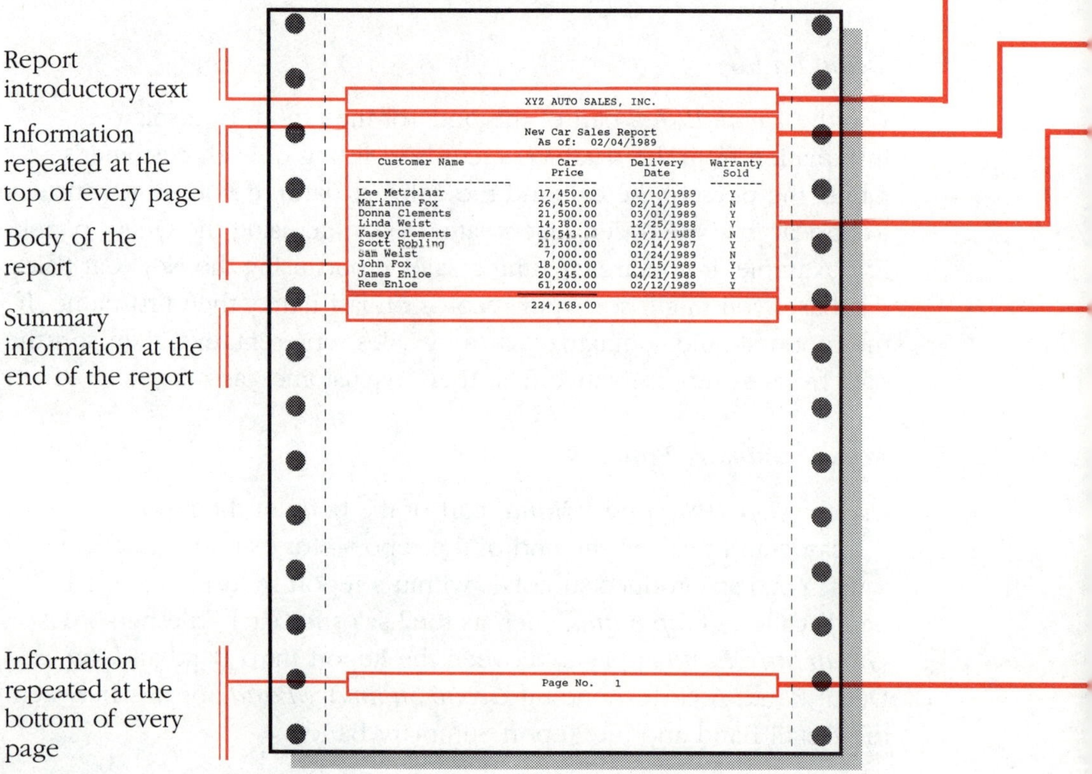

The Reports-Design Work Surface

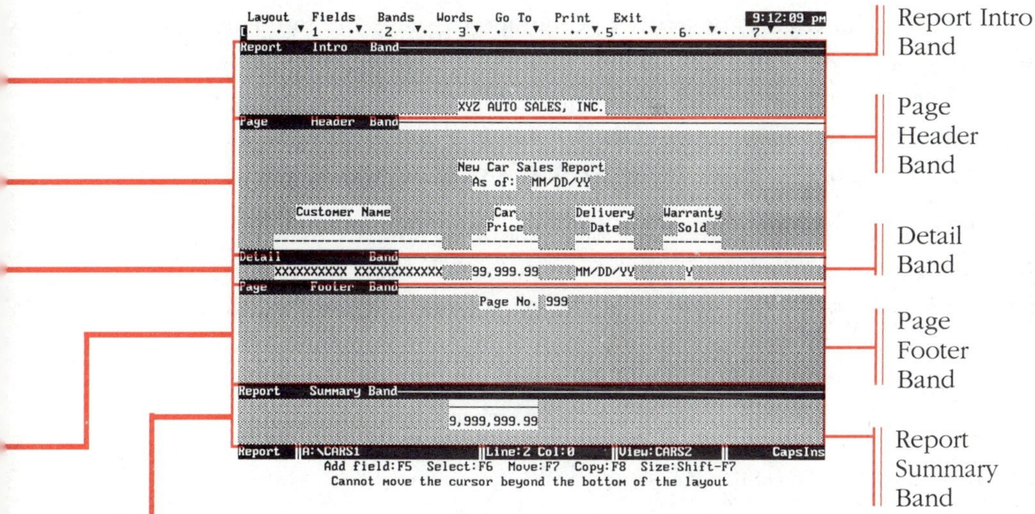

The reports-design work surface is divided into bands—mini work surfaces.

Note: When you first access the work surface, the bands appear in a different order than shown in this example.

Using the Status Bar

The Status bar on the reports-design work surface displays the familiar five segments. The first segment displays **Report** to indicate the Control Center panel you are currently using. Segment two displays the storage location (disk drive and path) as well as the name of the current report form. If you are creating a new form, **<NEW>** appears in this segment.

Segment three indicates the current cursor position. If the cursor rests on a line that names a band, such as the initial Page Header Band, you see **Band 1/5** (the first of five bands). If the cursor rests inside a band (below the band name), you see the line and column information such as **Line:0 Col:0**. Lines and columns begin with zero in each band.

Segment four displays the name of the current database or view file. Segment five displays the status of toggle keys.

Using the Navigation and Message Lines

Although the key options that appear on the Navigation line are the same in both the reports and forms work surfaces, the results of pressing those keys are slightly different. In both work surfaces, you use F5 (Field) to display a list of fields, and then select from that list a field to be copied to the work surface. When you press F5 (Field) from the reports work surface, a window with *four* columns appears. When you press F5 from the forms work surface, however, only *two* columns appear.

The Navigation line displays function keys other than F5 (Field). You can use F6 (Select) to mark an item or area on the reports work surface, just as you did on the query or forms work surfaces. The highlighted area then can be removed using the Del key, moved using the F7 (Move) key, or copied using the F8 (Copy) key. Use the Shift-F7 key to size fields and boxes.

Watch the Message line for instructions about how to use the work surface. Messages appear if you attempt to use a dBASE IV feature in an incorrect manner. You also see instructions about the features you select from a menu. For example, when you add a field to the reports work surface, each of the edit options are explained on the Message line. When selecting, moving, or copying an item, the Message line prompts the action to take next.

Understanding the Reports-Design Screen

Using the Status Bar

The Status bar uses the same general organization and format as other Status bars. Some of the information is unique to the reports work surface.

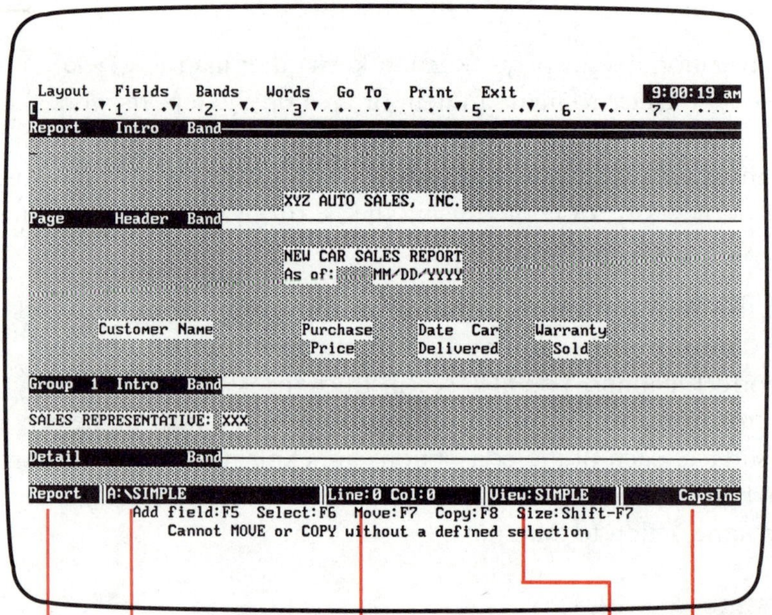

Identifies the current work surface

Indicates the disk drive, directory, and file name of the current report form.

When the cursor is on a band border, you see **Band 1/5** (1=the current band, 5=the total bands in use). When the cursor is on a bands work surface, you see **Line: 0 Col: 0**, depending on where the cursor is positioned.

Indicates the current database or view file

Indicates the status of the toggle keys

Using the Navigation and Message Lines

Use the Navigation line to stay informed about what keys are active at the moment. These keys change while you are copying and moving items on the work surface.

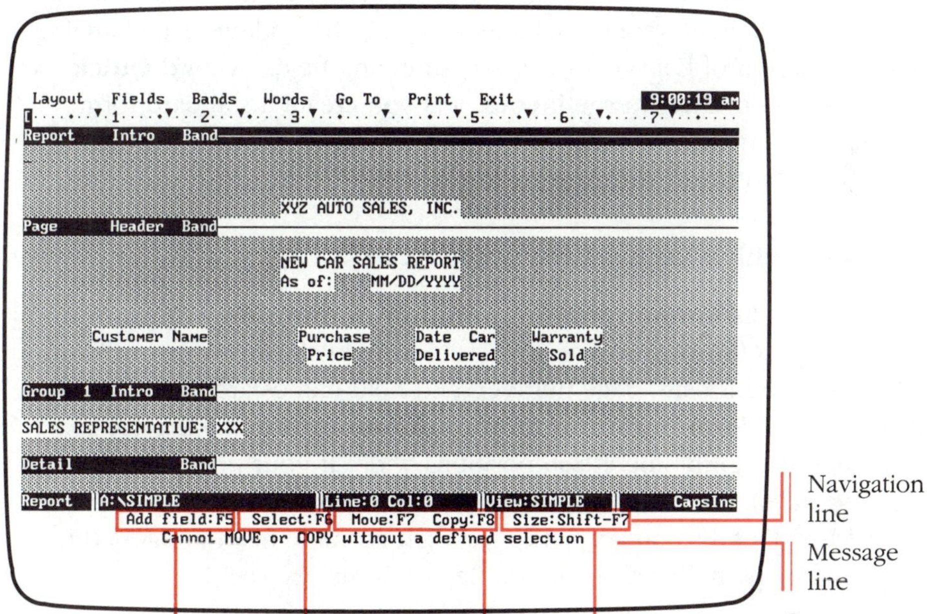

Use F5 to see a list of fields and select a field to be copied to the work surface.

Use Shift F7 to increase or decrease the size of a field or box displayed on the screen.

Use F6 to highlight a rectangle on the work surface. This rectangle can then be deleted, moved, or copied.

Use F7 to move the selected field to another location on the work surface. Use F8 to copy the selected item.

Watch the Message line for important instructions and prompts when moving, copying, or sizing items on the work surface.

Creating Quick Reports

The **Quick layouts** option on the Layout menu helps you build a report design with little effort. Two of the quick layout options, **Column layout** and **Form layout**, copy all fields in the database or view to the reports-design work surface. The fields appear in the order they were created in the database or described in a view. You then can modify the standard quick layout as you want by adding text, changing the description of field names, and rearranging fields. A third **Quick layouts** option, **Mailmerge layout**, lets you create a standard form letter and then merge specific data from records (such as name and address) to automate the preparation of mass mailings.

Deciding Which Report Layout You Need

If you select **Column layout**, fields appear side-by-side in column format across the printed line, similar to the Quick Report layout (Shift-F9). The current date, page number, and field names are automatically placed in the Page Header Band; the field names become the column headings. The print line is 255 positions wide. If your print line exceeds 255 characters, the excess positions are cut off. Fields are added to the Detail Band; and summary fields, for each numeric field, are added to the corresponding locations in the Report Summary Band.

If you select **Form layout**, fields appear one field per line, just as they do in Edit mode. If you select **Mailmerge layout**, the **Detail Band** opens in word-wrap mode. Use this form to create standard letters that integrate data fields from the database into the body of the letter.

For example, if you want to add headings, a dollar total of sales, and the average price of a car to a list of all cars sold, use Quick **Column layout**. If you want a list of cars sold, but want to print one car per page so that you can distribute them to sales people, use the Quick **Form layout**. If you want a letter personalized with individual customer information, use the **Mailmerge layout** feature. These three Quick layouts are available to assist you in making simple reports.

Selecting a Report Layout

You can work from either a database or view file to create a report. If you use a database file, its fields are all included in your report. If you use a view file, you can choose a limited number of fields to include in your report.

You set up a view through the Query panel. You limit the fields you want to see, determine the order of the fields chosen, and even set up calculated fields, as necessary. If you do not want to use every field in the database or do not want fields or records displayed in the actual database order, sort the database and set up a view before you select either of the first two **Quick layouts** options.

To create a report from the Control Center, open the appropriate database or view file, move the cursor to the **<create>** option in the Reports panel, and press Enter. (If a database or view file is not opened, you hear a beep and see a message telling you to place a database in use.) Select **Quick layouts**, and choose **Column layout**, **Form layout**, or **Mailmerge Layout**.

To create a report from the reports-design work surface, save the report design currently in use if you have made changes to the report. Press Alt-L to select the Layout menu. If appropriate, choose **Save this report** to save the current report and remain on the Reports work surface. Select **Use different database file or view** if the new report uses a database or view other than the current one. Finally, select **Quick layouts**, and choose **Column layout**, **Form layout**, or **Mailmerge Layout**.

Modifying a Report Layout

You do not have to accept a quick-layout report as the final report design. You can edit the column headings. You also can add report titles to the Report Intro Band and add other text throughout the report. Use the options on the Navigation line to rearrange fields.

Creating Quick Reports

The **Quick layouts** option on the Layout menu helps you build a report design with little effort. From the Control Center, open the database or view file, move the cursor to the **<create>** option on the Reports panel, and press ↵Enter.

Press Q to select **Quick layouts** and display the three quick layout options.

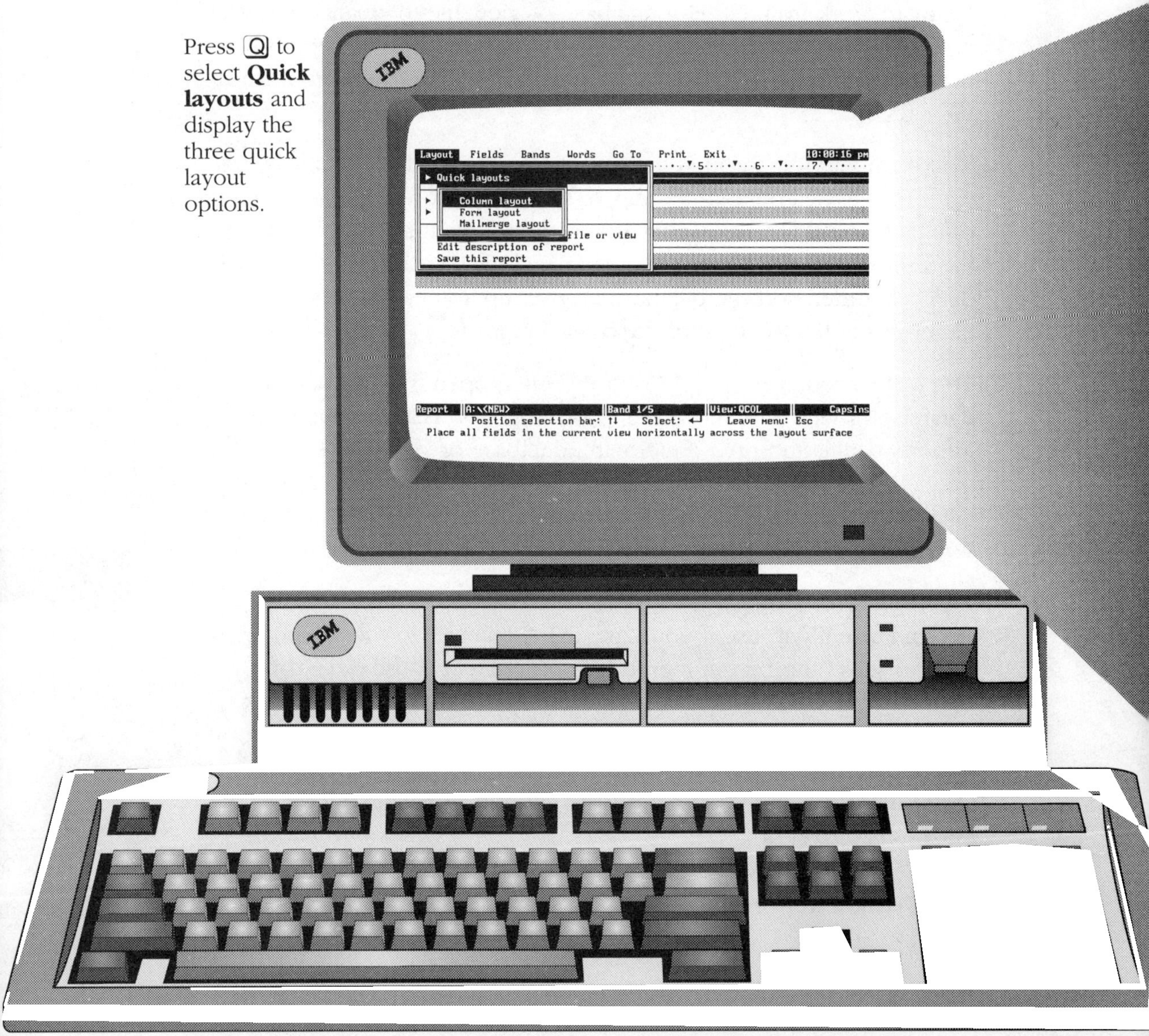

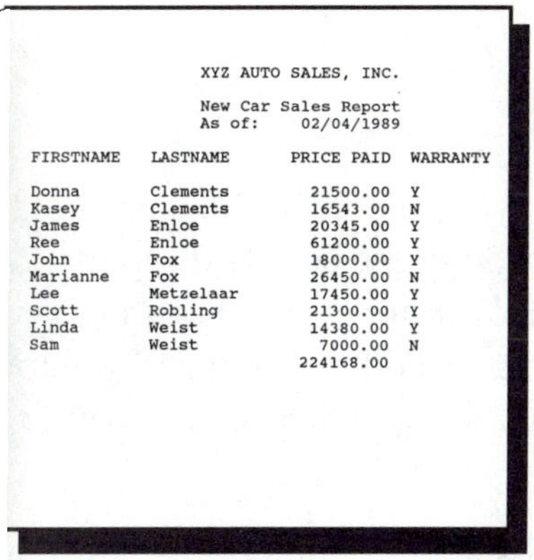

```
                    XYZ AUTO SALES, INC.

                    New Car Sales Report
                    As of:     02/04/1989

FIRSTNAME    LASTNAME       PRICE PAID   WARRANTY

Donna        Clements         21500.00   Y
Kasey        Clements         16543.00   N
James        Enloe            20345.00   Y
Ree          Enloe            61200.00   Y
John         Fox              18000.00   Y
Marianne     Fox              26450.00   N
Lee          Metzelaar        17450.00   Y
Scott        Robling          21300.00   Y
Linda        Weist            14380.00   Y
Sam          Weist             7000.00   N
                             224168.00
```

Column Layout

Field information appears side-by-side in column format across each printed line of the report.

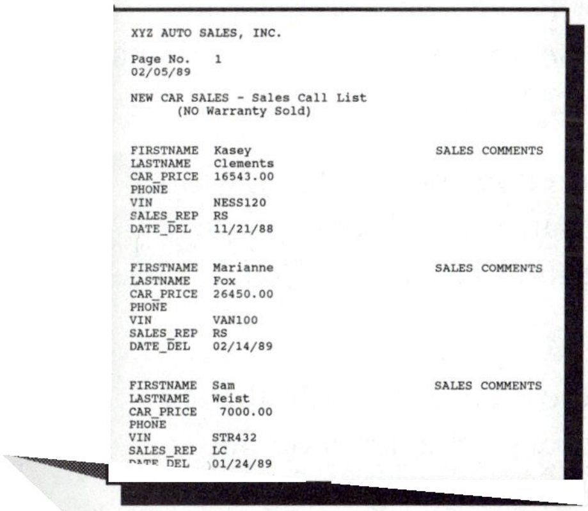

```
XYZ AUTO SALES, INC.

Page No.    1
02/05/89

NEW CAR SALES - Sales Call List
      (NO Warranty Sold)

FIRSTNAME  Kasey                              SALES COMMENTS
LASTNAME   Clements
CAR_PRICE  16543.00
PHONE
VIN        NESS120
SALES_REP  RS
DATE_DEL   11/21/88

FIRSTNAME  Marianne                           SALES COMMENTS
LASTNAME   Fox
CAR_PRICE  26450.00
PHONE
VIN        VAN100
SALES_REP  RS
DATE_DEL   02/14/89

FIRSTNAME  Sam                                SALES COMMENTS
LASTNAME   Weist
CAR_PRICE   7000.00
PHONE
VIN        STR432
SALES_REP  LC
DATE_DEL   01/24/89
```

Form Layout

Field information appears one field per line.

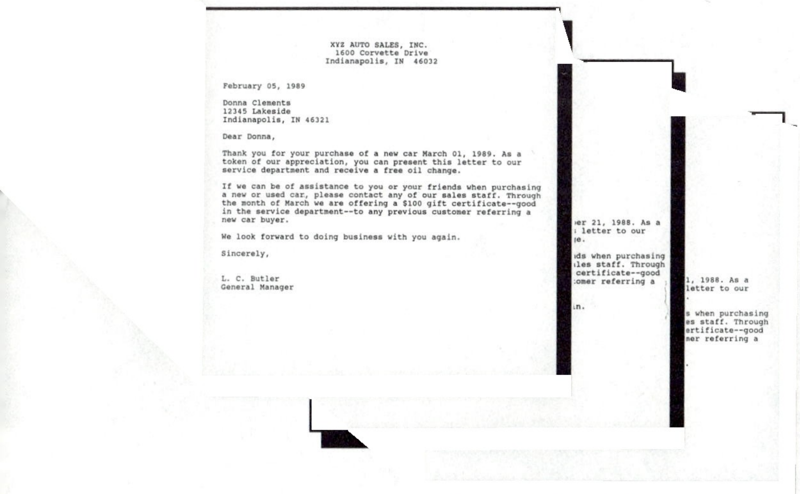

```
                    XYZ AUTO SALES, INC.
                     1600 Corvette Drive
                   Indianapolis, IN  46032

February 05, 1989

Donna Clements
12345 Lakeside
Indianapolis, IN 46321

Dear Donna,

Thank you for your purchase of a new car March 01, 1989. As a
token of our appreciation, you can present this letter to our
service department and receive a free oil change.

If we can be of assistance to you or your friends when purchasing
a new or used car, please contact any of our sales staff. Through
the month of March we are offering a $100 gift certificate--good
in the service department--to any previous customer referring a
new car buyer.

We look forward to doing business with you again.

Sincerely,


L. C. Butler
General Manager
```

Mailmerge Layout

Data and calculated fields are integrated into a custom form letter.

Using Quick Layouts Column Design

If you simply want to produce a column layout report of the current database or view, and you don't want to modify the standard report, press Shift-F9 (Quick Report) in any Control Center panel. You can, however, rearrange the data fields, add text, or add heading and group subtotals by selecting **Column layout** from the Quick layouts menu in the Reports panel.

The standard column layout report includes a page number, the current date, and column titles in the Page Header Band. The data fields are distributed across the Detail Band. A total field for numeric or float data fields appears in the Report Summary Band.

You can customize the report by adding a report title. If you place the title in the Page Header Band, the title repeats on each page of the report. If you place the title on the Report Intro band, the title appears once on the report's first page.

To delete text or fields in a band, use F6 (Select) to highlight the area for deletion and press the Del key. To rearrange the items on the reports-design work surface, highlight the area needing change and press F7 (Move) or F8 (Copy).

When the report is complete, save it to disk using **Save changes and exit** from the **Exit** menu on the reports Menu bar or the **Save the report** option on the Layout menu. To print the report from the work surface, select **Begin printing** on the Print Menu bar. If you exit and save the report design, you also can print the report from the Control Center. Highlight the name of the report on the Reports panel and press Enter. A window appears displaying three choices: **Print report**, **Modify layout**, and **Display data**. Select **Print report**.

Using Quick Layouts Form Design

By selecting the **Form layout** option on the Quick layouts menu, you create a report that looks like the Edit work surface. The page number, date, and column titles appear in the Page Header Band. To create, customize, and print the new report, follow the same procedures used with **Column layout**.

Creating Quick Reports

Using Quick Layouts Column Design

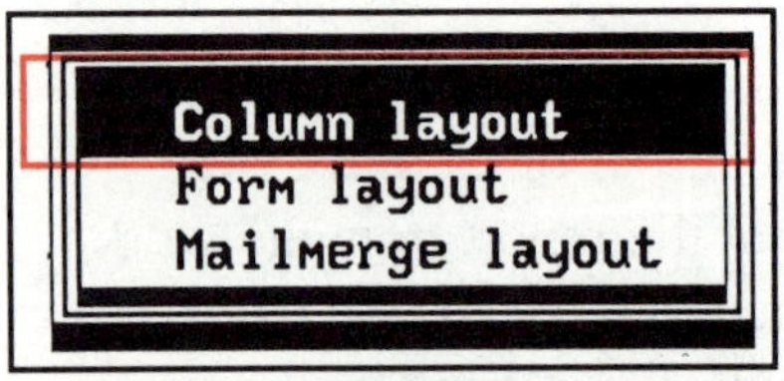

To access the **Quick layouts** option press [Alt][L] to pull down the Layout menu, then press [Q] to see the Quick layouts menu.

To create a report with a column layout, press [C] to select the **Column layout** option from the Quick layouts menu.

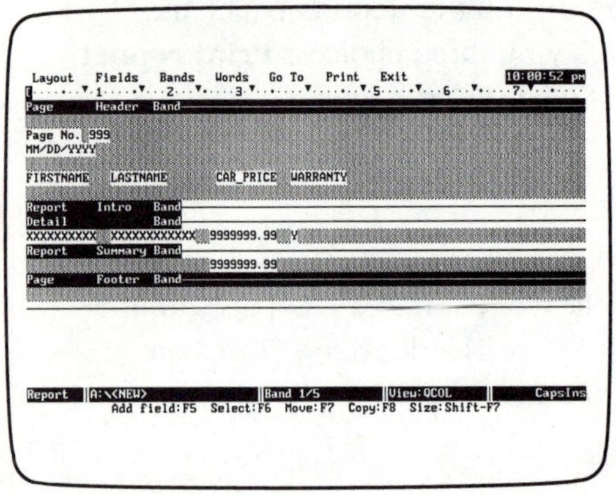

You now see the Quick column layout for the **CARS** database. Notice the Status bar refers to the **QCOL** view file. That view file limited the fields in the **CARS** database to the four fields you see on the screen.

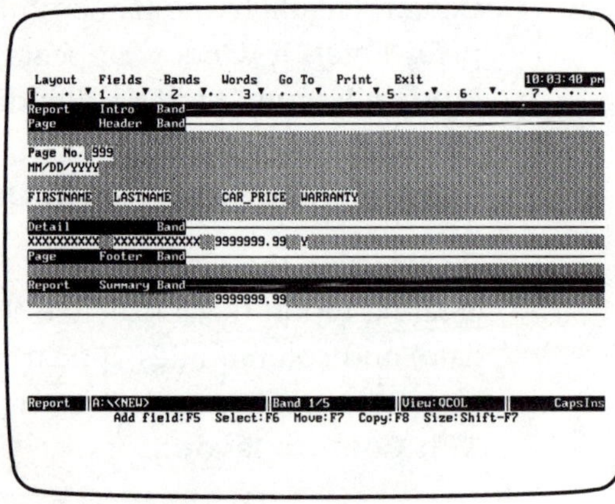

Press [Alt][B], [P] to separate page headers from the Report Intro Band. The Page Headers Band and Report Intro Bands have changed places on the screen. Also, the Page Footer Band and Reports Summary Band have reversed positions. This is OK; these bands will print where they are supposed to.

Position the cursor on the Report Intro Band work surface. Then enter a report heading. Center the heading appropriately.

This heading appears once at the top of the first page of the report.

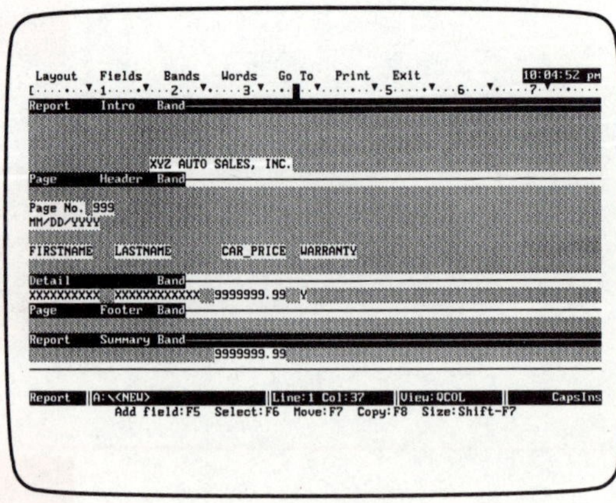

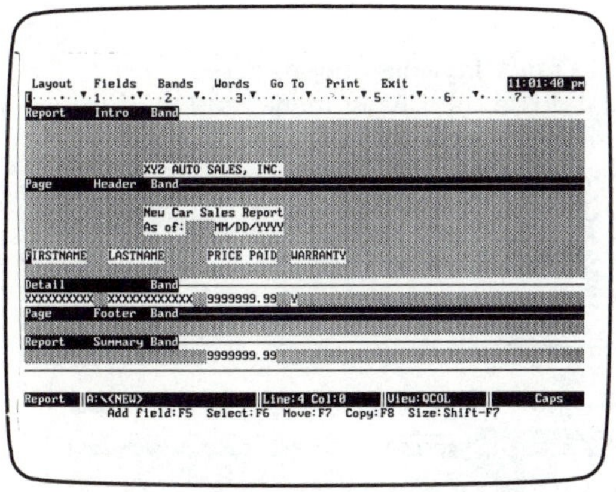

Position the cursor on the Page Header Band work surface. Then enter a page heading and center it appropriately. In this example, the date is created by pressing F5 and selecting the predefined field DATE. Change any column headings to be more readable.

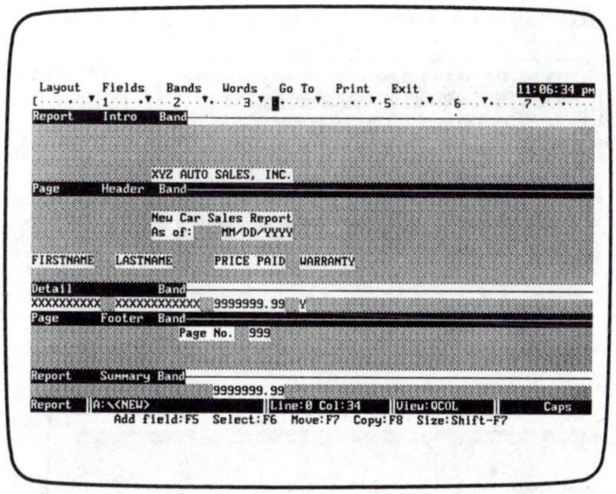

Position the cursor in the Page Footer Band and enter the text *Page No.* Press F5 and select the predefined field PAGENO to add the page number.

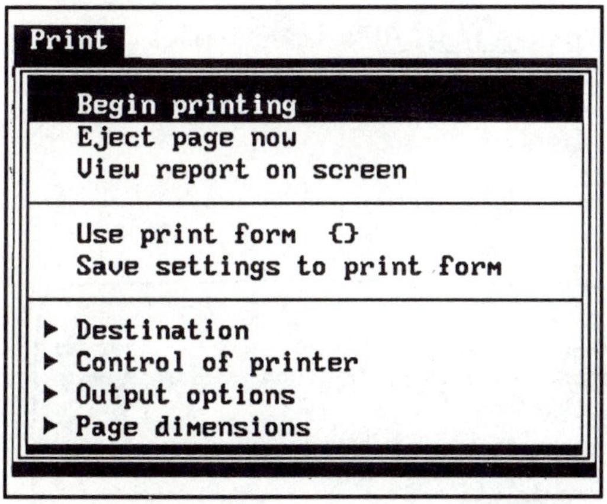

Press Alt P to select the Print menu. Then press V to view the report on-screen or B to begin printing.

You experience a one- to two-minute delay, depending on the speed of your computer, while dBASE IV assembles the report design and prepares to print.

Your changes

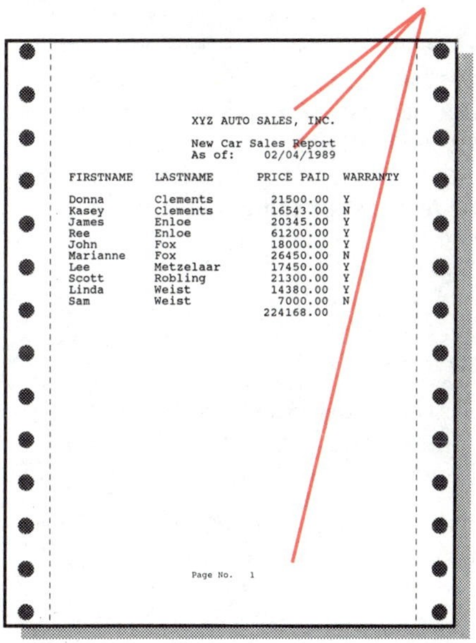

The final report reflects the Quick layouts column design and your changes.

Creating Quick Reports

Using Quick Layouts Form Design

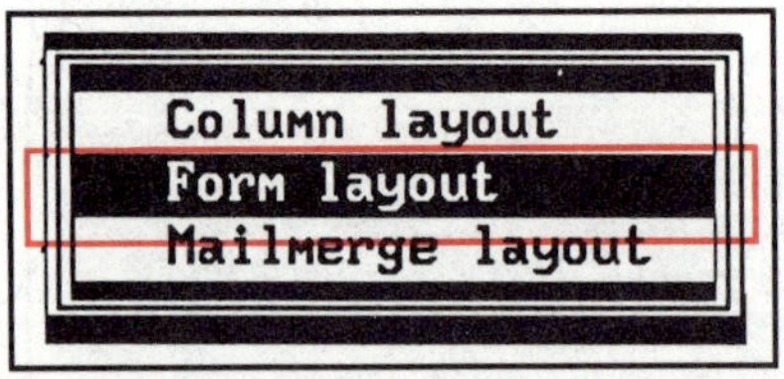

To access the **Quick layouts** option, press Alt L to pull down the Layout menu, and then press Q to see the Quick layouts menu.

To create a report with a form layout, press F to select the **Form layout** option from the Quick layouts menu.

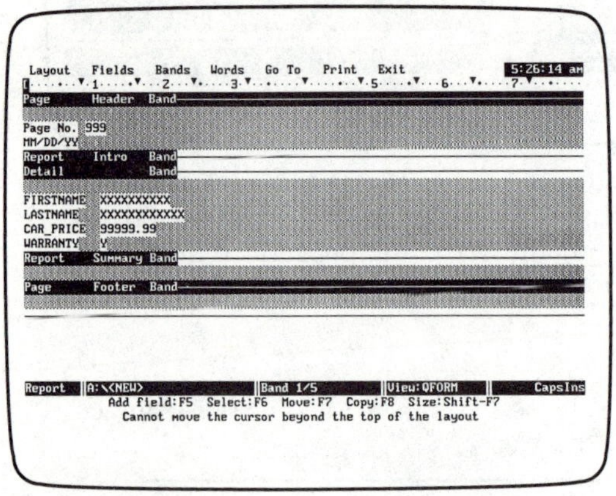

You now see the Quick form layout for the **CARS** database. Notice the status bar refers to **QFORM** view file. That view limited the fields to the **CARS** database to the four fields you see on the screen.

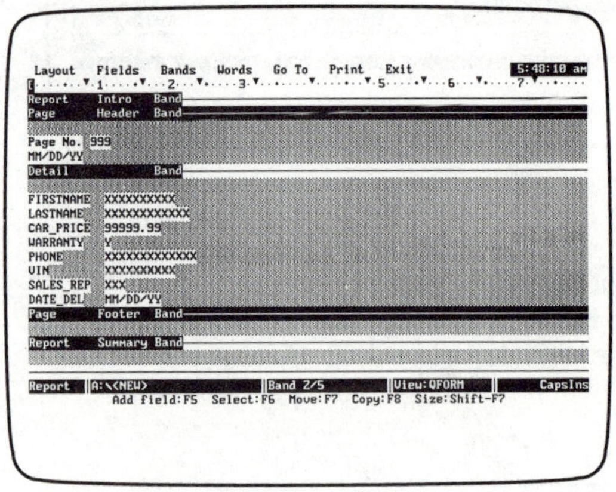

Press Alt B, P to separate page headers from the Report Intro Band. Notice that several bands have changed positions.

Position the cursor on the Report Intro Band work surface. Then enter a report heading.

This heading appears once at the top of the first page of the report.

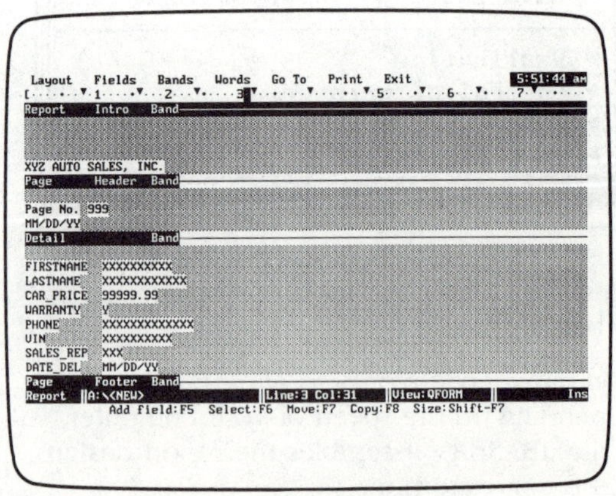

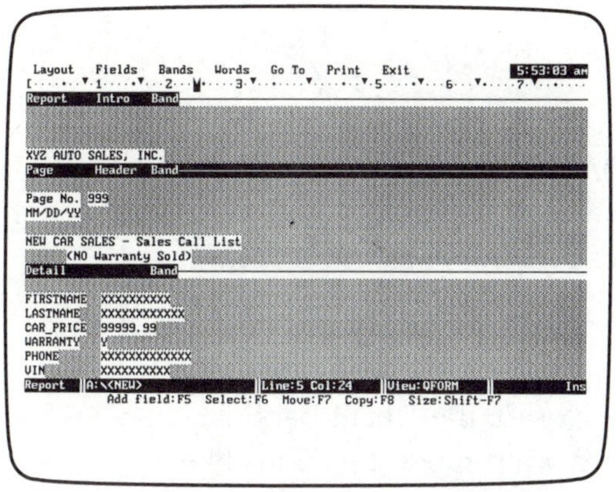

Position the cursor in the Page Header Band and add predefined fields for the page number and date. Also, add two lines of repeating titles.

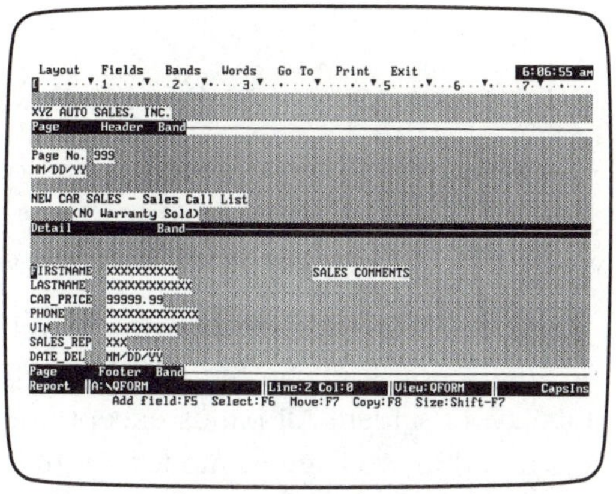

Position the cursor in the Detail Band. Add a place for comments and remove the warranty field.

You also may want to rearrange the detail area or indent portions for easier viewing.

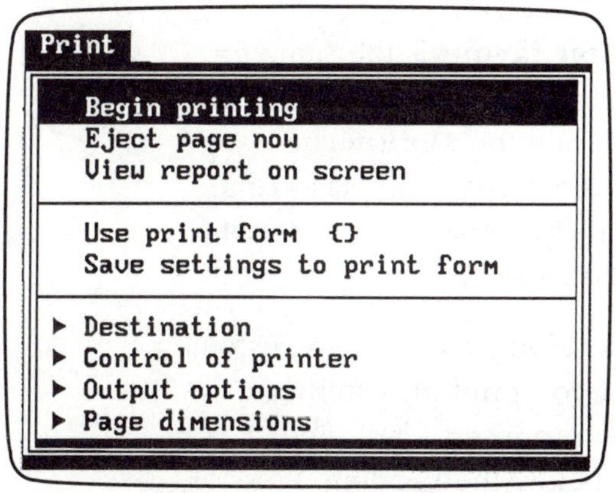

Press Alt P to select the Print menu. Then press V to view the report on-screen or B to begin printing.

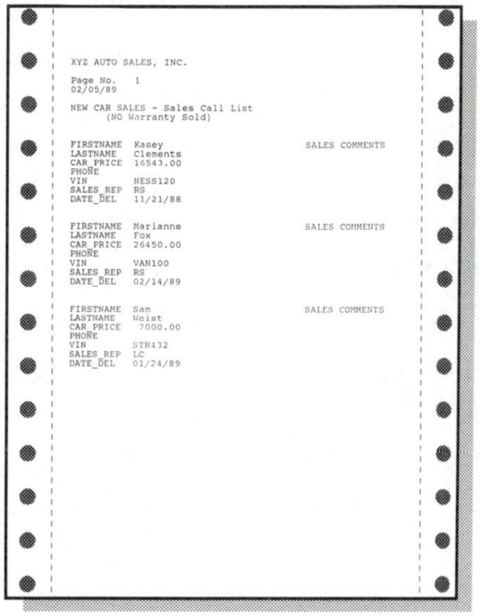

The final report reflects the Quick layout form design and your changes.

Using Quick Layouts Mailmerge Design

The **Mailmerge layout** option is one of dBASE IV's major new features. You can produce custom letters to clients, members, and customers that integrate data from the corresponding database records.

When you select **Quick layouts** and choose **Mailmerge layout**, you see the report form on the screen. No text or fields have been added to this layout screen. All bands except one are closed; the Detail Band is open and in word wrap mode. Because word wrap mode functions like a word processor, you can create your custom letter on the Detail Band.

Suppose, for example, that you want to send a personal letter to each customer listed in a new car sales database. The letter might congratulate the customer on a recent purchase of a new car and include an offer for a free oil change.

The standard letter you create with **Mailmerge layout** is the same for each recipient. You can add several fields of data, however, from each person's record, to personalize each letter. Using the **Mailmerge layout** option, you can enter the field names for first name, last name, street address, city, state, and ZIP code, and let dBASE pull the specific names and addresses for each letter from the database.

Use the following example as a guide for developing your own custom letters. First type your company heading. (If you print on letterhead, leave space for the heading by pressing Enter to insert blank lines. Next, add the current date field a few lines below the heading. Press F5 (Field) to access the menu of fields.

You can select the predefined field called DATE. As an alternative to the usual MM/DD/YY format, you can create a new field that displays a date in a traditional format, such as February 14, 1989. Select **<create>** in the Calculated column. When the Edit window appears, give the new field a name and enter a description. Next type the expression *MDY(DATE())*. The MDY() function presents the contents of a date field in the long form. The DATE() function retrieves the current computer date. The two functions combined tell dBASE IV to print the current computer date in the long form.

Now add the fields for the customer's name and address. Arrange the address to conform to your correspondence style. Next move the cursor to the greeting line and enter the standard *Dear firstname* greeting. Type the word *Dear*, add the field that contains the customer first name, and finish the greeting with a comma.

As you type the body of the letter, feel free to add data from the customer record by using the F5 (Field) key. Pieces of information that are unique to each customer make the letter more personal. For example, you might include the date the customer bought the car. You can press F5 (Field) to display a list of data fields from which you can choose.

Complete the letter and save the form using the Layout menu. To preview the custom letters, follow the procedures to print from the work surface. When the Print menu appears, select **View report on screen**. Continue viewing your custom letters, then making necessary changes to the Report form until you are satisfied with the design. Be sure to resave your design every time you make changes.

Using Quick Layouts Mailmerge Design

To access the **Quick layouts** option, press Alt L to pull down the Layout menu, and then press Q to see the Quick layouts menu.

To create a report with a mailmerge layout, press M to select the **Mailmerge layout** option from the Quick layouts menu.

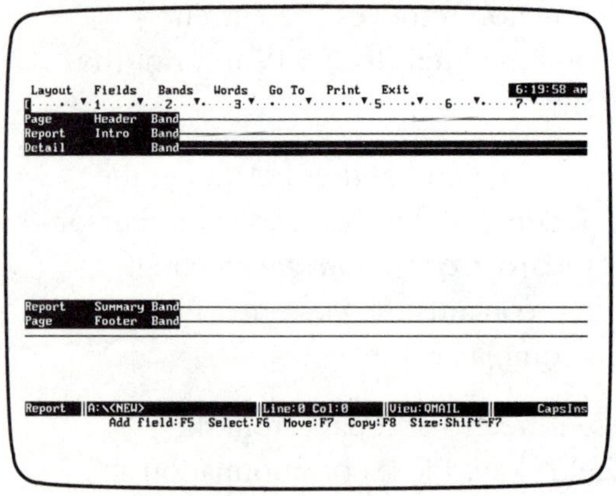

Notice that no text or fields have been added to this layout. The cursor is positioned in the Detail Band, and all other bands are closed.

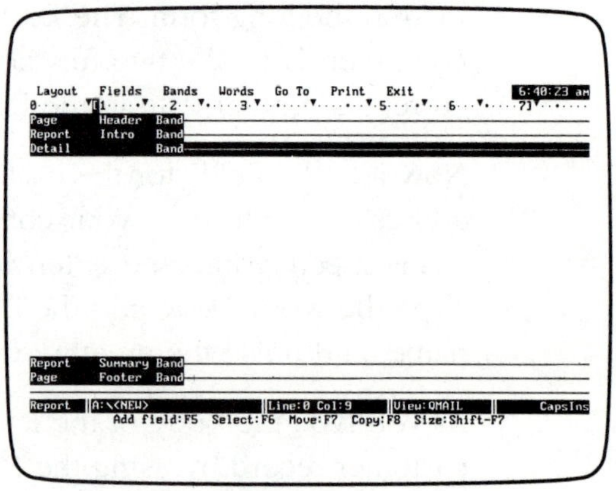

Press Alt W, M to modify the ruler. Use → or ← to position the cursor. At position 10, press [, and at position 70, press] to set the margins at 10 and 70.

Type the letterhead text. If you use letterhead paper, instead leave blank lines for the top margin and letterhead text. Pressing ↵Enter inserts blank lines.

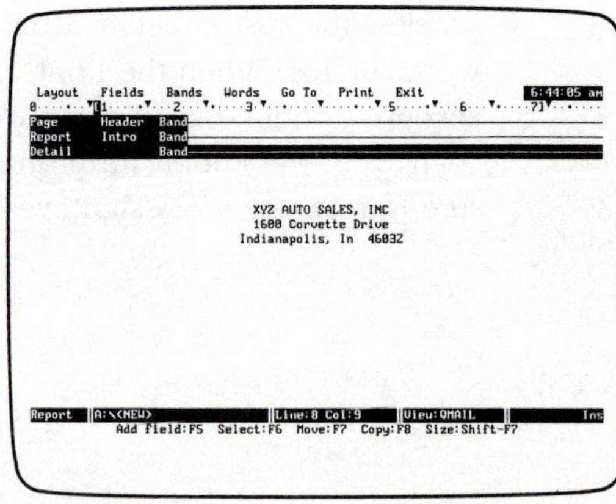

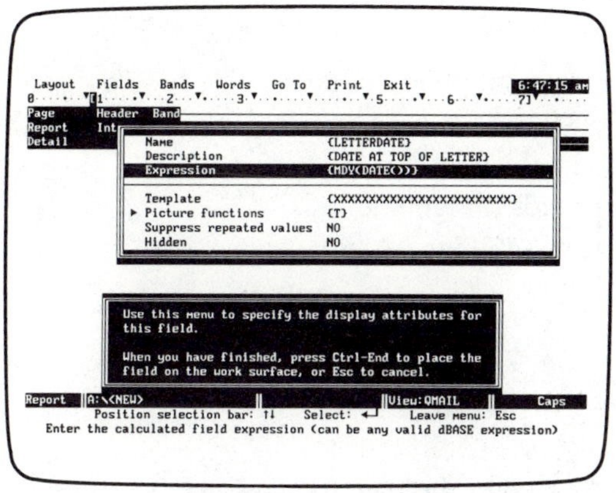

Position the cursor and add the current date. To make the date appear in long form (for example, February 14, 1989), press F5 and create a calculated field with the expression MDY(DATE()).

To cause the year to appear as four digits in your dates, you must turn on the **Century** feature. Before printing, return to the Control Center and pull down the Tools menu. Select **Settings**, and then select **Century**. Press the ↵Enter key or the space bar to toggle **Century** on and off. Exit to the Control Center. All printing and displays now show the year in four digits. The default is **Century OFF**.

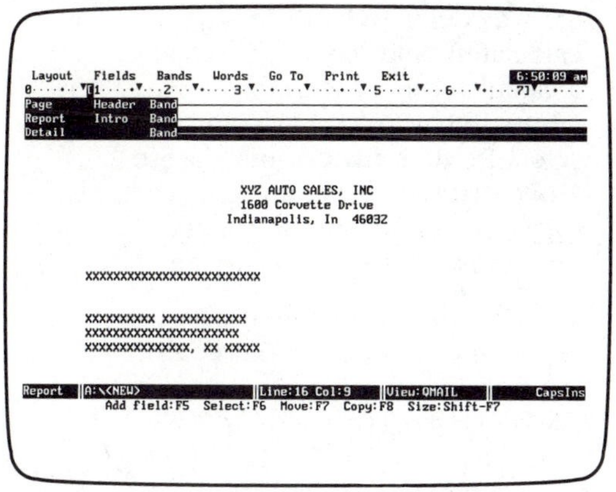

Add the customer address block. Use F5 to add each field. Include the proper spacing and punctuation as you add fields.

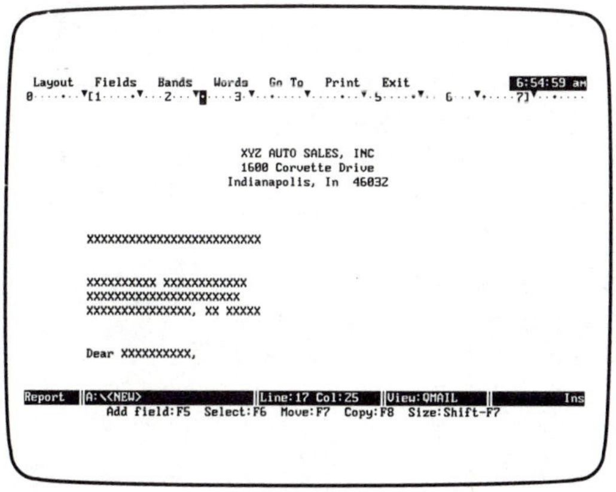

Position the cursor and add the greeting line. Type *Dear,* press the space bar once, press F5, add the customer's first-name field, and type a comma.

Creating Quick Reports

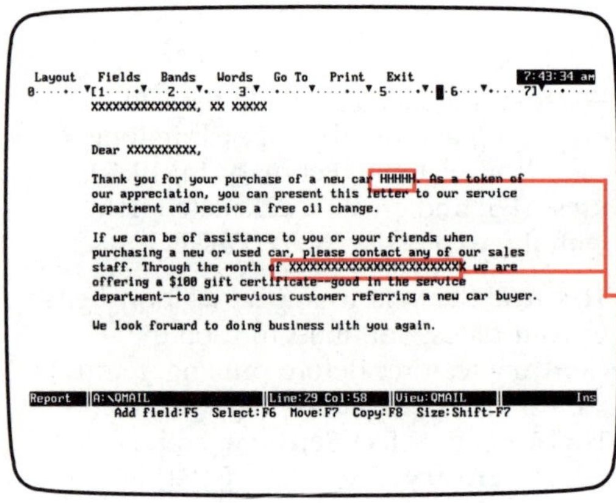

Type the body of the letter.

Include any merge fields that might be necessary.

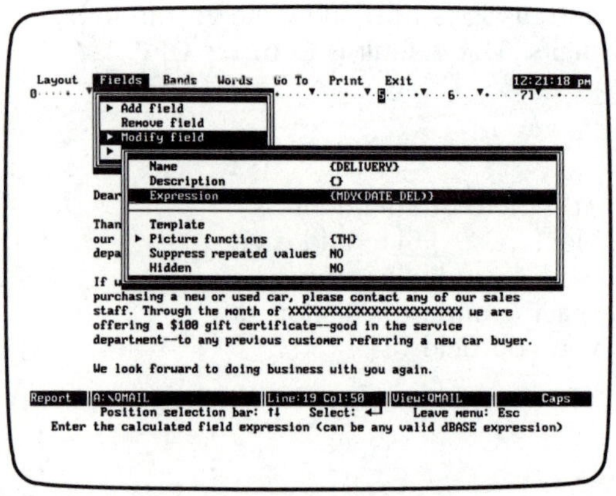

To enter the date the customer's car was delivered, create a calculated field. Press F5, create a calculated field with the expression MDY(DATE_DEL), select **Picture functions**, choose **Horizontal stretch**, and press Ctrl End to accept the changes and return to the work surface.

To enter the promotional date, repeat this procedure, but enter the expression CMONTH(DATE( )+45).

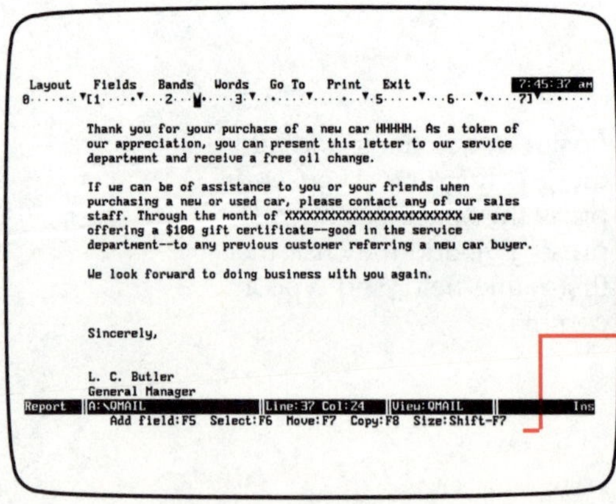

Enter the signature block.

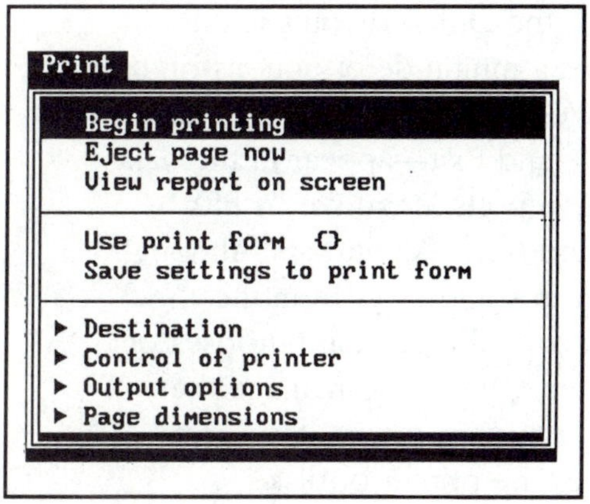

Press Alt P to select the Print menu. Then press V to view the report on-screen or B to begin printing.

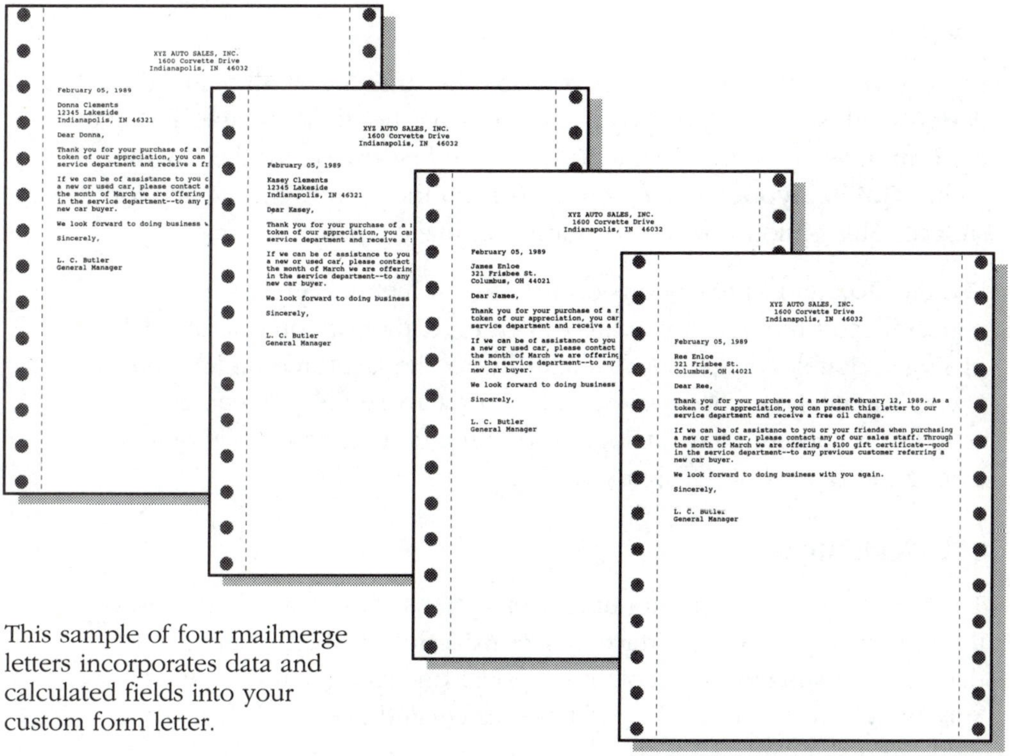

This sample of four mailmerge letters incorporates data and calculated fields into your custom form letter.

Using the Reports-Design Menu Bar

You can further enhance your reports with the Quick Layouts feature in many ways. The reports Menu bar includes a multitude of options on the following menus: Layout, Fields, Bands, Words, Go To, Print, and Exit. Four of the menus—Layout, Fields, Go To, and Exit—appear in the data, query, and forms Menu bars as well as the reports Menu bar. A fifth menu, Words, also appears in the query and forms Menu bars. Although the options on the reports Menu bar differ in some ways from the options of the same name on other Menu bars, the general purposes of those options are the same. Use a sixth menu, Bands, to manage the design work surface on which you create a custom report. A seventh menu, Print, controls print files you send to the printer or disk.

The Layout Menu

Use choices on the Layout menu to copy the structure of all fields to the design work surface, draw boxes and lines on the work surface, and perform general file management tasks. The first option on the Layout menu, **Quick layouts**, copies *all* fields from the current file to the work surface. This option is discussed earlier in this chapter.

Use the **Box** and **Line** options on the Layout menu to enhance the appearance of the report you are designing. Either option offers a choice of single, double, or special character lines. The last three options on the Layout menu allow you to use a different database file or view, edit the report description in the catalog, or save the current report without exiting the reports-design work surface.

The Fields Menu

The Fields menu provides a number of options for managing fields on the reports-design work surface. Select **Add field** to add a field to the design work surface. Four columns appear on-screen that enable you to specify field names from the database, calculated fields, predefined fields, and summary fields.

You can select the field name you want—such as SALES_REP—from a list of field names that appears in the first column. You also can add a calculated field to the report by choosing the appropriate field from the second column, the calculated fields column. If a calculated field does not exist, you can create it.

Access the third column to select one of four predefined fields. You can add the current **Date**, **Time**, or **Pageno** to a header or footer in your report. (The date and time are automatically generated according to the date and time you specify when starting your computer.) Select the **Recno** (record number) option if you want to include the number for each record reported in the detail section.

The fourth column appears in two parts. The upper portion contains seven summary functions that you can apply to all appropriate fields: Average, Count, Max (the maximum value), Min (the minimum value), Sum, Std (Standard Deviation), and Var (Variance). The lower portion contains a list of summary fields that you define. Place your choice of the summary fields in the Report Summary Band.

You can do more than add fields to your design work surface. To eliminate a single field from the form you are designing, position the cursor on the field and select **Remove field**. The highlighted data field disappears. To eliminate all occurrences of a single field, position the cursor in the text area off of any field and select **Remove field**. A window appears displaying field names from the database. Select the name of the field you want to remove. You then must remove associated text describing the deleted field by using the Del, Backspace, or space bar keys.

Select **Modify field** to change a field's established editing criteria. For example, to add another ZIP code to a ZIP code list, position the cursor on the field name ZIP and select **Modify field**. When you create or modify a calculated or summary field—such as a calculated field in an inventory database used to multiply units on-hand by unit price—you can select an edit option to hide the calculated field from view. Use **Change hidden field** to make hidden calculated and summary fields visible again.

The Bands Menu

Most of the options on the Bands menu fall into one of two categories: options that relate to adding group bands and options that change the attributes (characteristics) of existing bands. Use group bands to display subtotals in the detail section of a report. The group bands can be stacked one inside another to produce nested subtotals. For example, group bands within a report on sales receipts can generate subtotals for each salesperson, cash register, or department.

To add a group band, move the cursor to a position just above the Detail Band and select **Add a group band** from the Bands menu. You then must select the **Field value**, **Expression**, or **Record count** option to establish the condition that produces the subtotal. For example, you can specify the field value SALES_REP to produce a report subtotaled by salesperson. You can also specify **Record count** and enter the number of records you wish to process in each group of records. **Record count** works with other options such as **Field value**. For example, you can subtotal by car sales, by groups of five records, and by sales representative. Each sales person would see individual sales in groups of five records. Express value, the least-used option, permits you to create a valid dBASE expression—by typing or using Shift-F1 (Pick)—to control subtotaling.

To remove a group band, move the cursor to the group band and select **Remove group** from the Bands menu. Use the **Modify Group** option from that menu to change the type of value that controls the group, and set **Group intro on each page** to **YES** if you want an associated group heading to appear on each page of multiple pages dealing with one group.

A number of options on the Bands menu allow you to set characteristics of the current bands. For example, use **Open all bands** to ensure that each band prints. Set **Begin band on new page** to **YES** if you want each group to begin on a new page. The **Word wrap band** option switches the Editor mode between layout and word wrap.

Other options on the Bands menu change the pitch (characters per inch), change the print quality between letter quality and draft print, and control the line spacing with a band. The last option, **Page headings in report intro**, causes page header and page footer information to print in the Report Intro Band. When you create a cover letter for a report, set this option to **NO**.

The Words Menu

The Words menu provides a variety of options to alter printed output, change screen display, and manipulate text within a report. The **Display** option is not available on the reports work surface and therefore appears dim.

Select **Style** to access fonts (print styles) such as bold, underline, italic, superscript, and subscript. (Your printer may not support all these fonts.) Use the other options on this menu to align text between margins, add or remove lines, or exchange portions of the design surface with other surfaces or files.

The Go To Menu

The Go To menu options position the cursor and locate data on the reports work surface. Use the **Go to line number**, **Forward search**, **Backward Search**, **Match capitalization**, and **Replace** options to locate or replace a word or phrase.

The Exit Menu

Use the Exit menu to leave the Reports work surface. Your choices are to **Save changes and exit** or **Abandon changes and exit.** If you are creating a new report and you **Save changes and exit,** you must supply the report name. If you are modifying an existing report, the report is automatically saved under its original name.

Using the Reports-Design Menu Bar

Four of the menus on the reports-design Menu bar—Layouts, Fields, Go To, and Exit—appear also in the data, query, and forms Menu bars. The Words menu also appears in the query and forms Menu bars.

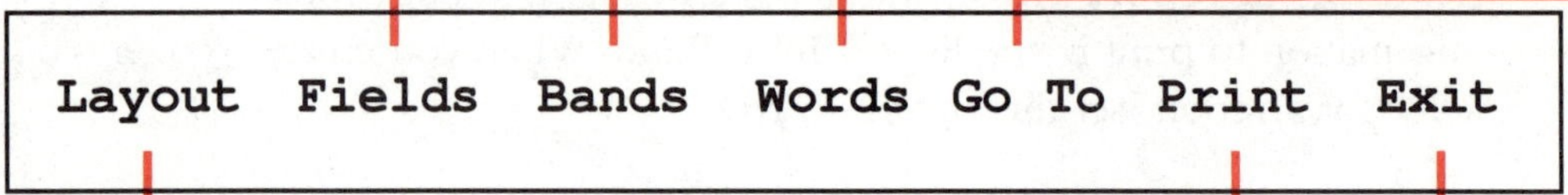

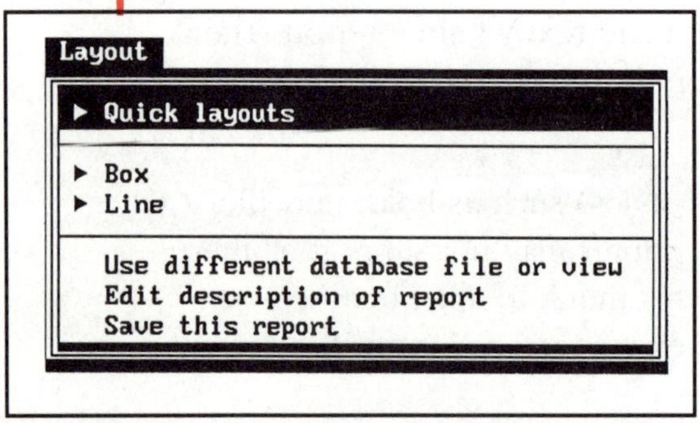

Use **Layout** to create **Quick layouts** of column, form, and mailmerge reports; draw boxes and lines; change databases and views; and save your forms.

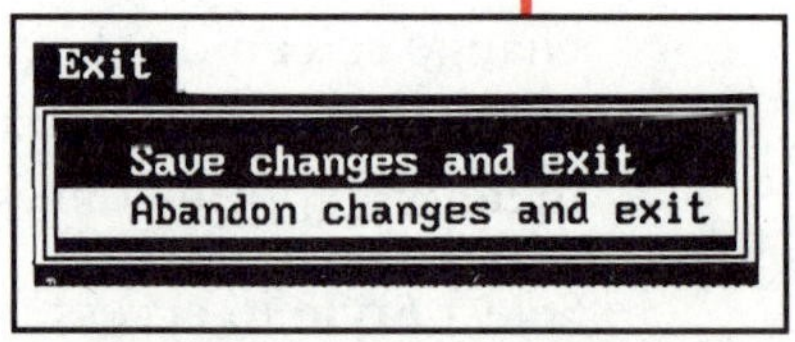

Use **Exit** to leave the work surface, saving or abandoning the changes just made.

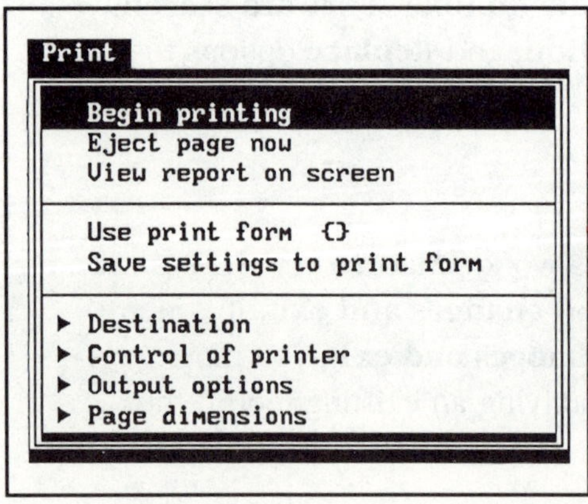

Use **Print** to print the report to an attached printer or to a disk for later printing. Control your printer from this menu.

```
Fields
 ► Add field
   Remove field
 ► Modify field
 ► Change hidden field
```

Use **Fields** to add fields to the work surface or remove them. **Add field** and **Remove field** produce a window with a list of field names you can choose from. **Modify fields** uses a series of windows you can use to add powerful editing criteria to each field.

```
Bands
 ► Add a group band
   Remove group
 ► Modify group
   Group intro on each page        NO

   Open all bands
   Begin band on new page          NO
   Word wrap band                  NO
   Text pitch for band             DEFAULT
   Quality print for band          DEFAULT
   Spacing of lines for band       DEFAULT

   Page heading in report intro    YES
```

Use **Bands** to add and remove bands on the work surface. Also, control how bands and band work surfaces operate.

```
Words
 ► Style
 ► Display
 ► Position
   Modify ruler
   Hide ruler                  NO
   Enable automatic indent     YES

   Add line
   Remove line
   Insert page break
 ► Write/read text file
```

Use **Words** to enhance the printed output. **Style** offers bold, underline, italic, subscript, and superscript print fonts. While using the Editor, you can add and remove lines, adjust the print ruler, and read and write external files.

```
Go To
   Go to line number       {0}

   Forward search          {}
   Backward search         {}
   Replace                 {}
   Match capitalization    NO
```

Use **Go To** to locate, or locate and replace, work surface items, or position the cursor on the work surface.

9 *Designing Custom Labels*

Think of the word *label*, and what comes to mind? You probably envision a small mailing label attached to an envelope—a label containing name, street address, city, state, and ZIP code information. But did you ever consider that a Rolodex® card or an envelope is really a label? While a Rolodex card and an envelope are larger than most mailing labels, they both contain name and address information.

With dBASE IV, you can treat any standard area, up to 255 lines high and up to 255 characters wide, as a label. In addition, you are not restricted to name-and-address kinds of data. You can include any field from a database in a label design. For example, you can create labels with department names to attach to paper folders or labels that note the locations and contents of inventory storage bins.

Use the labels feature to produce name tags or badges displaying data such as the name and title from an employee database. Create sheets on which to record the physical count of inventory items, each sheet displaying the part number and part description of an item in an inventory database. Design labels to mark samples in laboratory research projects, each label containing the sample number and the sample date recorded in the research database. Let your imagination be your guide!

The sort and search features you use in queries and reports apply as well to labels. You can, for example, print your mailing labels in ZIP code order to take advantage of lower presorted mailing rates. Or you can quickly limit the production of mailing labels to only those records in a membership database for which a member indicates an interest in genealogy. You often can reduce mailing costs by eliminating duplicate records in the database before you generate mailing labels.

What Is Covered in This Chapter?

In this chapter, you learn about

- The layout of the labels-design screen
- Designing labels
- Saving label designs
- Printing labels
- Using the labels-design Menu bar options

Key Words Used in This Chapter

Dimensions	A menu option, which appears only on the labels-design Menu bar, that provides options for controlling the size of the label and the placement of the label on the page.
Labels work surface	An area on which you place text and fields to form a standard label.
Predefined field	One of four fields—other than fields in the database structure and calculated fields—that you can add to a label. For example, DATE is a predefined field.
Predefined size	One of nine standard label sizes already established by dBASE IV. The nine sizes include five mailing labels, two envelopes, and two Rolodex cards.

Introduction

When you hear the word *label*, you probably visualize a small mailing label attached to the outside of a mass mailing envelope.

By using the dBASE IV labels feature, you will find dozens of uses for labels, including Rolodex cards, file folder markers, postcards, name tags, and more.

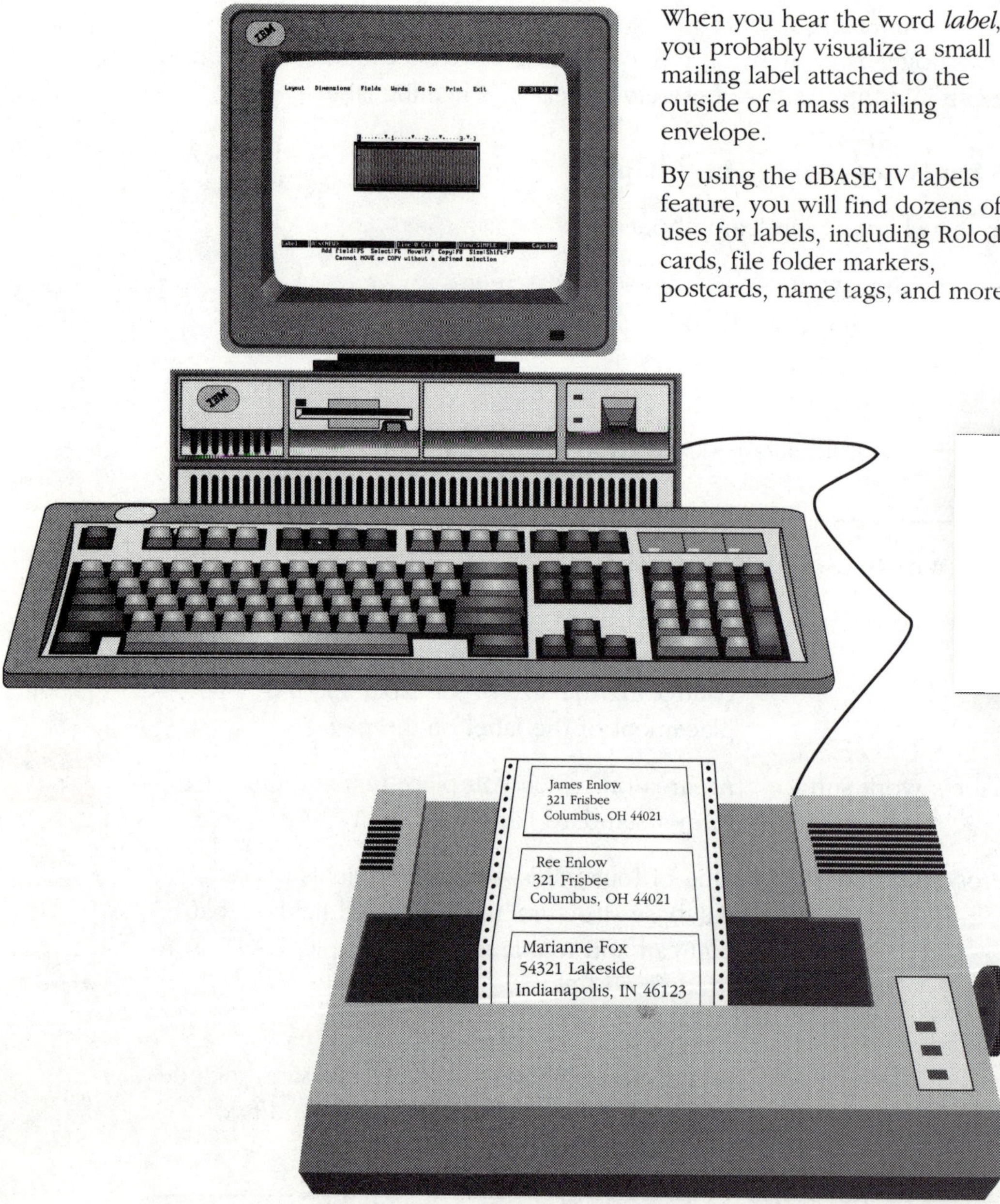

Disk labels

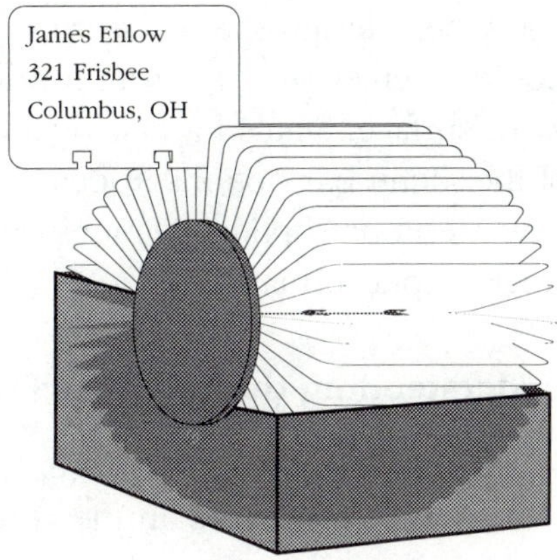

Rolodex files

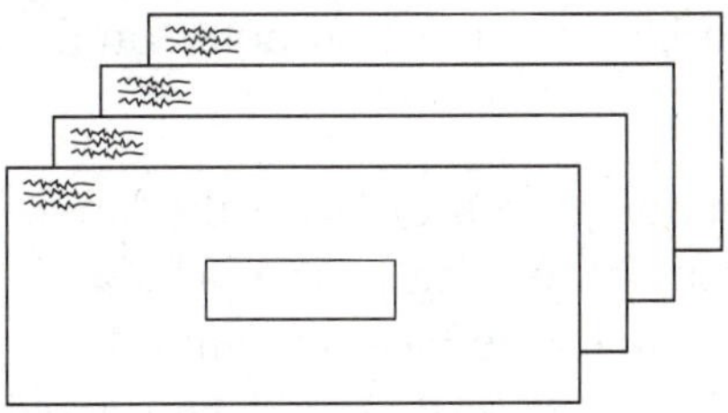

Custom mailings

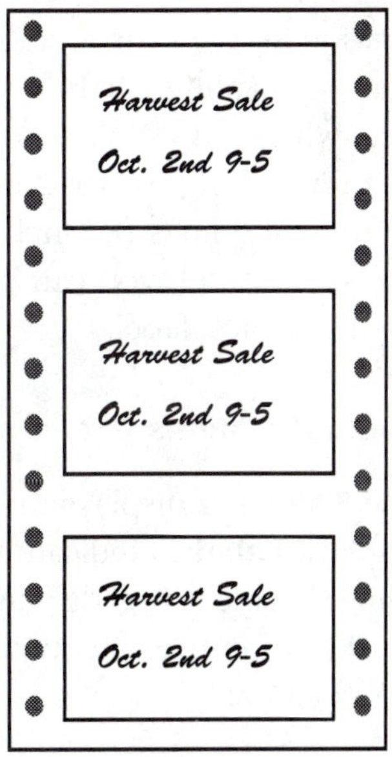

Reminder postcards

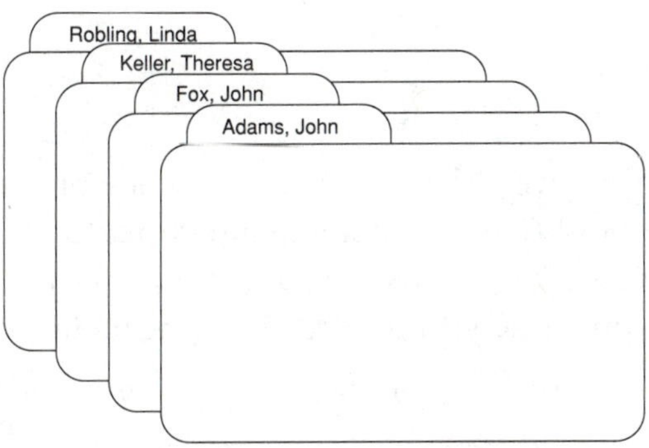

File folder labels

Understanding the Labels-Design Screen

The labels-design screen is organized in the same manner as the other Control Center panels. From top to bottom, it includes the Menu bar, work surface, Status bar, Navigation line, and Message line. All but one of the Menu bar options appear on other dBASE IV Menu bars. Use the new Menu bar option, Dimensions, for entering specifications about the label output format.

Understanding the Work Surface

The labels-design work surface, located between the Menu bar and the Status bar, is a window in the center of the screen. Because the Editor is operating in layout mode, text does not wrap. You can attach fields and text to the labels work surface much like you position notes on a message board.

The size of the work surface varies, depending on the size of the label. dBASE IV permits you to create labels that are as long as 255 lines and as wide as 255 characters. dBASE IV predefines the most common label sizes for mailing labels, envelopes, and Rolodex cards. The default label size, which dBASE IV uses unless you specify a different size, is 15/16 of an inch long by 3 1/2 inches wide. If you use the standard print settings of 6 lines per inch down the label and 10 characters per inch across the label, you can place 5 lines by 35 characters of information on the default label.

Using the Status Bar

The Status bar displays the standard five segments. The first segment displays **Label** to indicate the Control Center panel you are currently using. Segment two displays the disk drive, directory, and name of the label form in use. If you are creating a new form, **<NEW>** appears in this segment.

The third segment indicates the current cursor position according to lines and columns. If the cursor is in the upper left corner of the labels work surface, you see **Line:0 Col:0**. The lines and columns are counted beginning with zero.

Segment four displays the name of the current database or view file being used. The fifth segment displays the status of the toggle keys.

Using the Navigation and Message Lines

The Navigation line contains descriptions of the function keys that are active while you use the labels-design work surface. You see the same function keys when you create labels as you see when you create forms and reports. Press F5 (Fields) to add a field to the work surface. A window with three columns appears. Column one contains a list of fields from the current database or view file. Column two displays the **<create>** option for creating calculated fields along with any calculated fields that you previously set up in a query.

The third column contains several predefined fields. You can select from the options **Date** (the current date), **Time** (the current time), **Recno** (record number), and **Pageno** (page number). While you are not likely to choose any of the predefined options for mailing labels (the most common use of the labels feature), you might incorporate the options in other applications. If you create a standard label design for printing Rolodex cards, for example, you might include the current date to document the day of the most recent update.

You can select a field from column one, column two, or column three by highlighting your choice and pressing Enter. Repeat the process to place additional fields on the labels-design work surface.

You can use F6 (Select) to highlight an item or area on the work surface. After an area is marked, you can delete the area using the Del key, move the area using the F7 (Move) key, or copy the area using the F8 (Copy) key. Watch the Message line for instructions about how to use the labels-design work surface.

Understanding the Labels-Design Screen

The labels-design screen is divided into five basic segments.

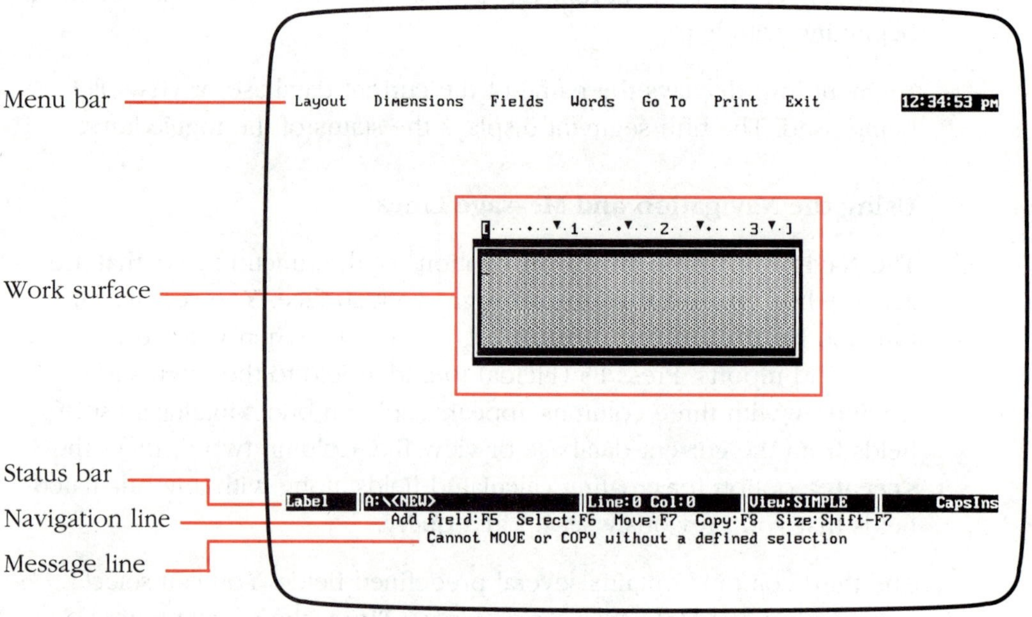

Understanding the Work Surface

The size of the work surface varies with the height and width of the label you are creating. You can select one of nine predefined label sizes or create your own label size. The maximum label is 255 lines high by 255 characters wide.

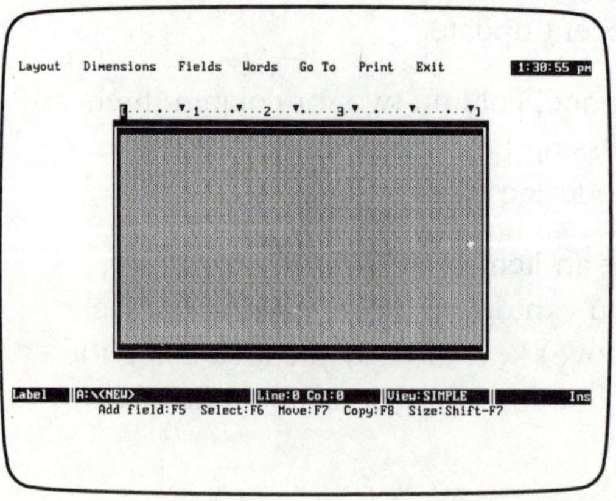

This is your work surface if you select the predefined label size Rolodex (3" × 5").

Using the Status Bar

The Status bar follows the same general organization and format as other Status bars. Notice that some of the information is unique to the labels work surface.

Identifies the current work surface

Displays the current cursor position

Indicates the status of the toggle keys

```
Label  |A:\<NEW>              |Line:0 Col:0  |View:SIMPLE  |      CapsIns
          Add field:F5  Select:F6  Move:F7  Copy:F8  Size:Shift-F7
              Cannot MOVE or COPY without a defined selection
```

Identifies the disk drive, directory, and file name of the current labels form

Specifies the current database or view file

Using the Navigation and Message Lines

Press F5 to display a list of fields from which you can select a field to be copied to the work surface.

Press F7 to move the highlighted portion to another location on the work surface. Press F8 to copy the highlighted portion.

Press F6 to highlight a rectangular portion of the work surface. This rectangle then can be deleted, moved, or copied.

Press ⇧Shift F7 to increase or decrease the size of a window box or template.

```
 Add field:F5 | Select:F6 | Move:F7  Copy:F8 | Size:Shift-F7
    Cannot MOVE or COPY without a defined selection
```

Watch the message line for important instructions when moving, copying, or sizing items on the work surface.

Designing and Creating a Label

When you create a label design, plan the label layout, duplicate the layout on the labels-design work surface, print sample labels, and store the tested label design for later use. Planning the layout for labels is a two-part process: you must determine the layout of the labels within the area of the page and arrange the contents within each label area. You create the layout for labels using function keys and menu choices. Print sample labels to check the layout, and then save the completed design.

Understanding Label Layout on the Page

Determining the text and data to include in a label is only part of the label design process. You must tell dBASE IV how to print the labels down and across the page. First, you must tell dBASE IV the size (height and width) of the label—specified in inches—on which you will be printing. In addition, you must tell dBASE IV exactly where to place each label on the page.

The printhead is said to be in its *home position* when it is at the far left side of the paper. Labels may be *indented* (or *offset*) from the left side of the page. You must specify the indentation in number of characters.

Because labels print consecutively down the page, you must decide how many *lines between labels* should be skipped. If you are off a line in your decision, the printing begins to creep up or down off the edge of the label, and the labels are not usable. When you decide how many lines to leave between labels, take into consideration how many lines per inch your printer prints (six lines per inch is common). Getting the labels set up just right on the page may require some trial and error.

dBASE IV lets you print from 1 to 15 labels across the page. You must specify only the number of labels (columns) and the number of *spaces between columns.*

You provide these specifications through the Dimensions menu. The Dimensions menu is explained later in this chapter.

Designing the Label

Labels generally include only a few fields out of all the fields in a database. Plan your label on paper. If you are designing your label on plain stock, first draw the outline of the label, carefully measuring the height and width. Sketch your label design on an actual label if you have one.

On your paper layout, pencil in the area for each field. If you have a ruler that measures 10ths, 12ths, and 16ths, you can easily mark off the area for each field. Keep modifying the layout arrangement until all the fields you want to include fit on the label.

You may need to change print pitch from 10 to 12 or 16 characters per inch in order to fit everything on the label. Just be sure that your printer supports the alternate pitch. After you create this model on paper, you can use the layout to create the label in dBASE IV.

Accessing the Labels-Design Work Surface

To access the labels-design work surface, open a database or view file from the Control Center. Move the cursor to the Labels panel and select **<create>**. If you select **<create>** without first opening a database or view file, you hear a beep. A help box appears on the screen advising you that a database or view file must be opened before you can create a label using fields from the database. If you are modifying a label design you already created, select the label name from the Labels panel.

Designing and Creating a Label

Designing labels is a two-part process. First, you must decide how the labels will print on the page.

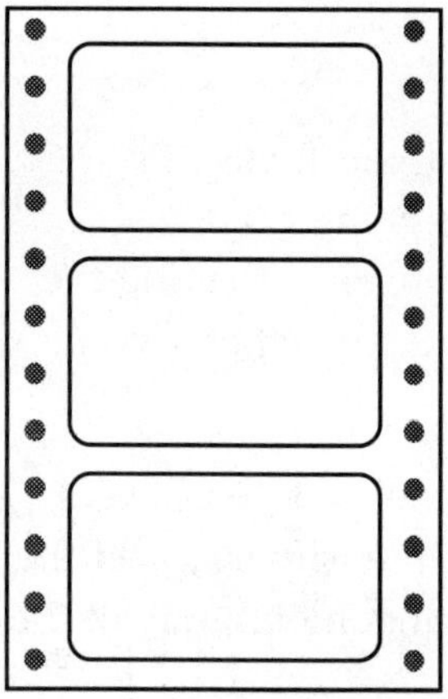

1-up

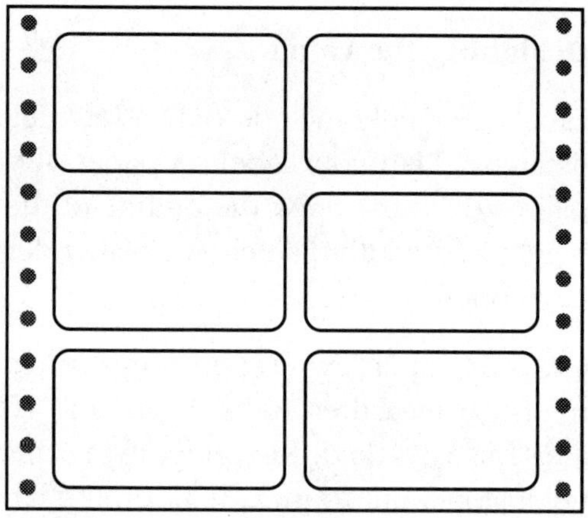

2-up

You can print labels in 1 to 15 columns across the page. The maximum width that a label or group of labels can occupy is 255 characters.

Second, you must decide what information should be printed and how it should be arranged.

```
329 Oak Street, Indiana
Tom 46032 Indianapolis
Jones (317) 123-4567
```

This label is not organized in a logical or useful format!

Understanding Label Layout on the Page

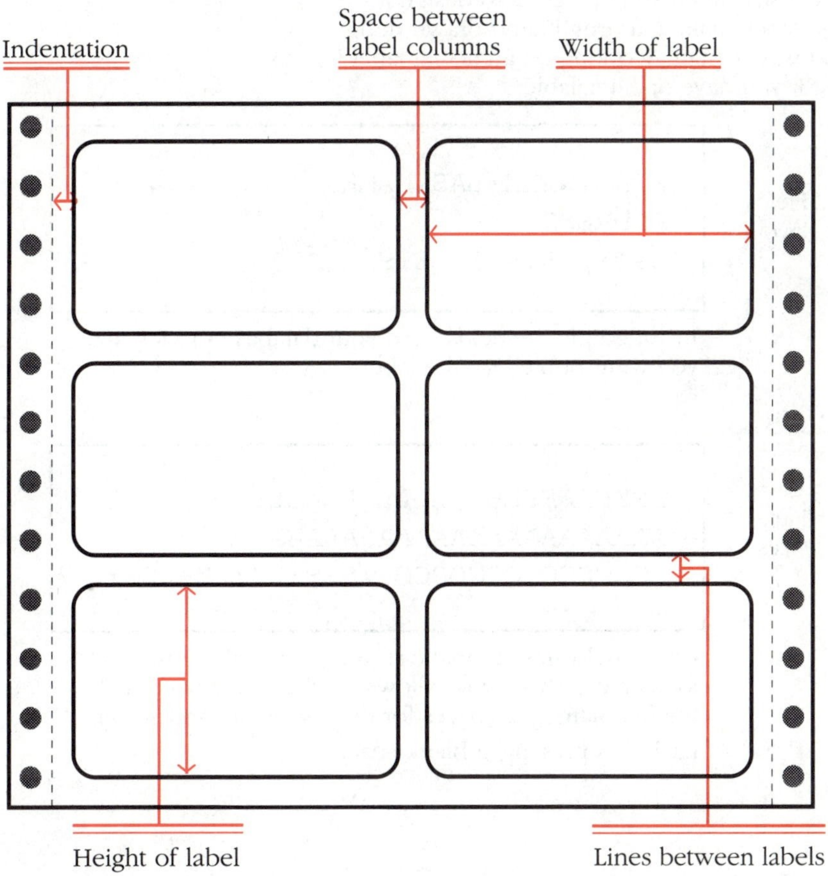

When you begin to create your labels, you must provide dBASE IV with these five specifications. You enter them by using the Dimensions menu.

Designing and Creating a Label

Designing the Label

The next step in creating labels is to design a sample label. Making a rough hand-drawn design is a good way to start. Working on an actual label is easiest if you have one available.

Fields layout

```
FIRSTNAME·LASTNAME
ADDRESS
CITY,·STATE··ZIP
```

Include only the fields from your database or view that you want printed on the label.

Field sizes

```
FFFFFFFFFF·LLLLLLLLLLLL
AAAAAAAAAAAAAAAAAAAAAA
CCCCCCCCCCCCCCC,·SS··ZZZZZ-ZZZZ
```

Check field sizes to make sure that everything fits—and looks nice. This layout allows 10 character spaces for the first name, 12 spaces for the last name, and so on. Each · represents a blank space.

Accessing the Labels-Design Work Surface

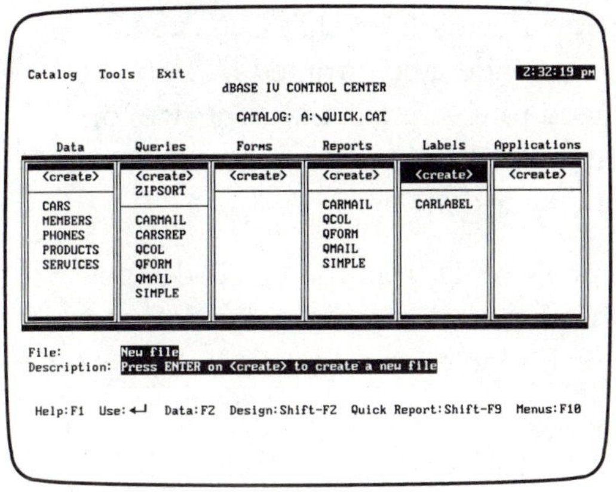

Select the database or view file. Then select **<create>** on the Labels panel.

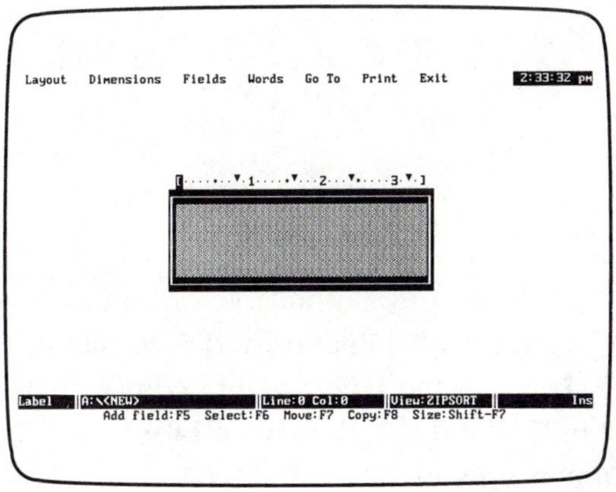

The work surface Editor is in layout mode. The work surface ruler is visible, but not active. You can change the size of the label only by accessing the Dimensions menu.

Setting Up the Work Surface

On the initial work surface, you see a default label that is a standard 15/16 of an inch high by 3 1/2 inches wide label, printed in 1 column across the page. If the label you need to create is a different size, or you want to print more than 1 column of labels on a page, you need to change the specifications with the Dimensions menu.

To access the Dimensions menu, press Alt-D from the labels-design work surface. To change the size of the label, select the **Predefined Size** option. A submenu appears with nine optional label sizes:

15/16 × 3 1/2 by 1
15/16 × 3 1/2 by 2
15/16 × 3 1/2 by 3
11/12 × 3 1/2 by 3 (Cheshire)
1 7/16 × 5 by 1
3 5/8 × 6 1/2 envelope (#7)
4 1/8 × 9 7/8 envelope (#10)
Rolodex (3 × 5)
Rolodex (2 1/4 × 4)

If the label size you need is on the list, select the applicable option. If you do not see the label size you need, exit the **Predefined Size** menu by pressing Esc. Referring to your sketch of the label design, complete the **Width of label** in characters (1–255) and the **Height of label** in number of lines (1–255) on the Dimensions menu.

Use the **Indentation** option on the Dimensions menu to specify the number of characters between the left margin of the label paper and the left edge of the label itself in column 1. Use a ruler to measure the distance between the leftmost printhead position on the printer and the leftmost character position of the initial continuous-form label. Indentation is initially set at zero. You can select the option **Lines between labels** to determine proper spacing down a page. The initial setting is 1 line between labels.

If you print more than one label across a page, enter the specifications for **Spaces between label columns** (initially set at zero) and **Columns of labels** (initially set at one) on the Dimensions menu.

Adding Fields and Text

You add fields to the labels-design work surface just as you add fields to the forms and reports work surfaces—by pressing the F5 (Fields) key and selecting from options in the windows. If there is any text to print on the label, enter it before adding fields. For example, if the label is an envelope, you might enter the company name and address in the upper left corner, thereby automating the return-address information.

Make final adjustments to the surface arrangement using the F6 (Select), F7 (Move), and F8 (Copy) keys. You can remove fields using the Del key or the **Remove fields** option on the Fields menu. You also can remove selected rectangular areas of the work surface using the F6 (Select) and Del keys.

Saving, Testing, and Printing

You can save your label design and continue to work on the label work surface by selecting the **Save this label design** option from the Layout menu. Or, you can choose **Exit** to leave the work surface and save or abandon your design.

When you finish your label design (and periodically while you are creating it), you can select the **View labels on screen** option from the Print menu to display your label design on-screen. You can compare the screen image to your rough sketch of the label. To test the label design, load some continuous-form label paper into the printer, and then select the **Generate sample labels** option from the Print menu. This option produces a printout of XXXX's that represent the maximum number of lines and characters per line. To print the labels, choose **Begin printing**.

Setting Up the Work Surface

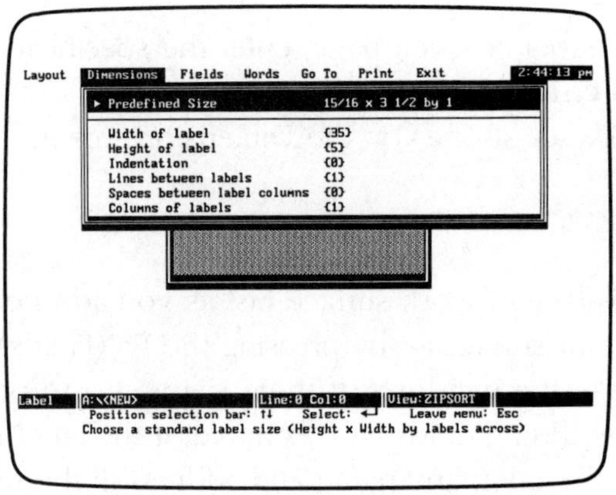

From the labels-design work surface, press Alt D to select the Dimensions menu.

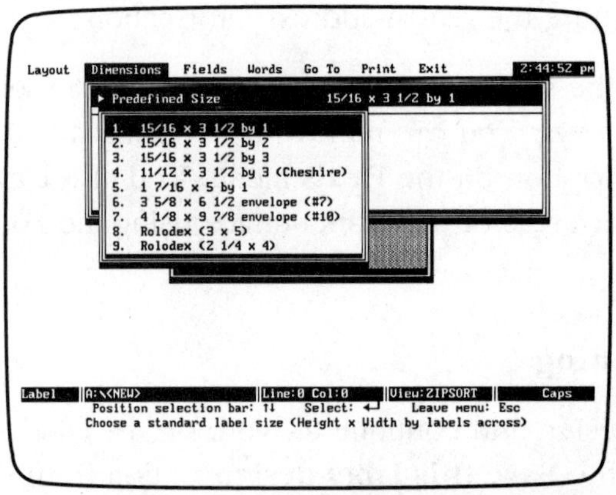

Press P to select the **Predefined Size** menu. If you are using one of the common label sizes, select that option from the menu.

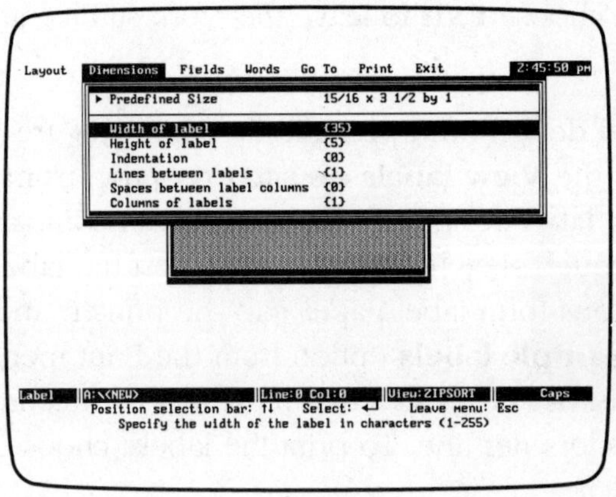

If you are not using one of the common label sizes, complete each of the label specifications on the Dimensions menu.

Adding Fields and Text

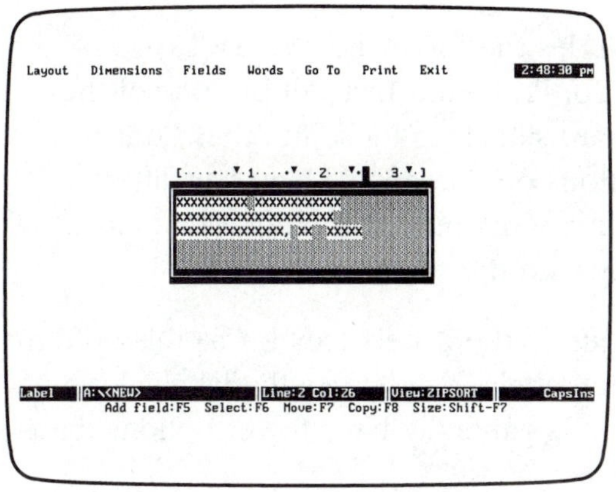

Use the F5 key to place label fields on the work surface. Add any needed text and rearrange the fields and text as needed until the label is how you want it.

Saving, Testing, and Printing

To save your label design and continue working on the label surface, press Alt L, then S, and provide a name for the label.

To view your label design on-screen, press Alt P and then V.

To print a sample of your labels, press Alt P and then G.

To print all the labels, press Alt P and then B.

Using the Labels-Design Menu Bar

The labels-design Menu bar includes the following menus: Layout, Dimensions, Fields, Words, Go To, Print, and Exit. All but one of the labels-design Menu bar options are similar to those in other Control Center panels. Although the options on the labels Menu bar differ in some ways from the options of the same name on other Menu bars, the general purposes of those options are the same.

The **Dimensions** option is unique to the Labels panel. Use this option to define the format of the output labels. As you use the labels-design work surface, notice that the menus generally have fewer options than similar menus on other Menu bars.

The Layout Menu

Use choices on the Layout menu to select database and view files and save your labels-design form. Options for creating quick layouts and line and box drawing are not available on the labels work surface.

The Layout menu option **Use different database file or view** allows you to change the database in use. If you access the labels work surface when no database is in use, the Layout menu appears and the highlighter rests on **Use different database file or view**. You must open the database associated with the label you intend to design.

Select **Edit description of label design** to change the label description in the catalog. Choose **Save this label design** to store the current label without exiting the labels-design work surface. If you are modifying a label, you might want to save the revised version under a different name, in case you want to restore the original design.

The Dimensions Menu

Use the **Dimensions** menu to enter specifications about the size of the labels you want to create and to indicate the position of the labels you want to print. Use **Predefined Size** to select one of nine standard label sizes: five mailing label sizes, two envelope sizes, and two Rolodex sizes. When you select a predefined label, the specifications change to match your selection. For example, the default predefined size is **15/16 × 3 1/2 by 1**, for which the standard height is 5 lines and the standard width is 35 characters. If you select **Rolodex (3 × 5)**, the height of the label changes to 14 lines and the width of the label changes to 50 characters.

If the label size you want does not appear on the **Predefined Size** list, you must enter the individual specifications for width, height, indentation, lines between labels, spaces between label columns, and number of label columns.

Use **Width of label** to specify the width of the label; the maximum width is 255 characters. Label dimensions usually are given in inches. For example, you might use a standard 15/16" × 3 1/2" label. If you are printing in 10 pitch (10 characters per inch), you can specify a maximum width of 35 characters. (You multiply 3 1/2 by 10 to get 35.) Using 12 pitch, however, you can print 42 characters in the same space. (Multiply 3 1/2 by 12 to get 42.)

Specify **Height of label** as the number of lines to print. Most printers produce 6 lines per inch; many can be set to 8 lines per inch. You can print 5 lines on a 15/16-inch-high label.

Use **Indentation** to leave a margin on the left side of a label. (If you specify **Offset from the left**, the print value adds to the indentation you specify to form a total left-hand margin on the label.) Suppose, for example, that the printhead lines up with the left edge of continuous-form label paper and a four-character space separates the left edge of the label from the left edge of the paper; you need to specify an indentation of 4.

Select **Lines between labels** to set the spacing between labels. Spacing can be 0 to 16 lines. **Spaces between label columns** separates the labels that are printed in 2 or more columns across the page. **Columns of labels** determines how many columns to print across the page. You can print 1 to 15 columns.

The Fields Menu

The Fields menu offers options to add, remove, or modify fields on the labels-design work surface. Use **Add field** to add your choices of three types of fields: fields already defined in the database or view, calculated fields, and the predefined fields **Date**, **Time**, **Recno**, or **Pageno**.

To eliminate a field from the label you are designing, position the cursor on the field and select **Remove field**. To eliminate all occurrences of a field from the label, position the cursor in the text area off of any field, select **Remove field**, and select the name of the field to remove. You then must remove associated text using the Del, Backspace, or space bar keys.

A primary advantage of using a custom label is that each field within the label can have editing criteria attached. To change the criteria for a field—for example, to change the template used to describe ZIPCODE—position the cursor on the field and select **Modify field**.

The Words Menu

The **Words** menu provides options to assist the Editor in enhancing printer and screen displays. The **Display** option, which controls screen display rather than printed output, is not applicable to the labels work surface and therefore appears dim.

Select **Style** to enhance printed output. You can choose from six print enhancements: normal, bold, underlined, italic, raised (superscript), and lowered (subscript). (Your printer may not support all these print enhancements.)

Choose the **Position** option to align text between margins. Text can be justified on the left or right margin, or centered. **Add line** is not active on the labels work surface. To add a line, position the cursor at the beginning of the line below your new line position and press Enter. Use **Remove line** to adjust the lines on the labels form. Use **Write/ read text file** to exchange portions of the design surface with other surfaces or files.

The Go To Menu

The Go To menu options position the cursor and locate data on the labels work surface. Choose **Go to line number** to position the cursor on a specific line of the work surface. Select **Forward search** and **Backward search** to position the cursor on an occurrence of the search condition you specify. Use **Replace** to substitute a word or phrase for an existing word or phrase.

The Print Menu

Use the Print menu to view labels on-screen or to direct printing to the printer or to a disk file for later printing. You can store print specifications and use them again.

Choose **Begin printing** to start printing using currently set specifications. Select **Eject page now** to cause the printer to eject paper and begin printing at the top of the paper. Use **Generate sample labels** to print samples of the label design. Select **View labels on screen** to preview the labels on-screen. Use the next two menu options to store and reuse label designs. The last four options control the type and format of printed output.

The Exit Menu

Use the Exit menu to leave the labels work surface. You can **Save changes and exit** or **Abandon changes and exit.** If you are creating a new label and you select **Save changes and exit**, you must supply the name of the label. If you are modifying an existing label, the label is saved under its original name.

Using the Labels-Design Menu Bar

All but one of the menus—Dimensions—appear on other dBASE IV Menu bars.

```
Layout  Dimensions  Fields  Words  Go To  Print  Exit
```

```
Layout
  Use different database file or view
  Edit description of label design
  Save this label design
```

Use **Layout** to use a different database or view, to edit the description of the label design in the catalog, or to save your label design under its current (or a new) name. There is no quick layout menu option for labels.

```
Exit
  Save changes and exit
  Abandon changes and exit
```

Use **Exit** to leave the work surface while saving or abandoning the changes you've just made.

```
Print
  Begin printing
  Eject page now
  Generate sample labels
  View labels on screen

  Use print form  {}
  Save settings to print form

► Destination
► Control of printer
► Output options
► Page dimensions
```

Use **Print** to view the labels on-screen, to print samples of the label design, to print all the labels, or to save them to a disk file for later printing.

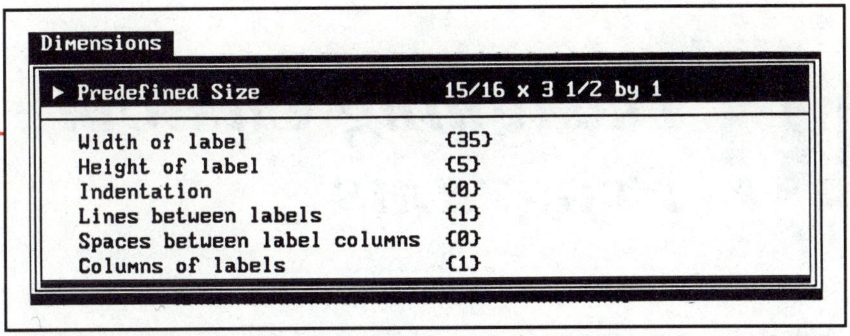

Use **Dimensions** to select one of nine predefined label sizes or to design a custom label size by specifying the lines between labels, the spaces between labels, and the distance between the left edge of the paper and the left edge of the label.

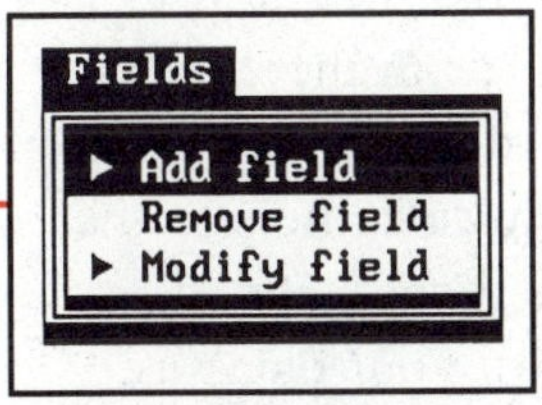

Use **Fields** to add, remove, or modify fields on the labels-design work surface. You can **Add fields** from three windows: fields in the database structure, calculated fields, and predefined fields.

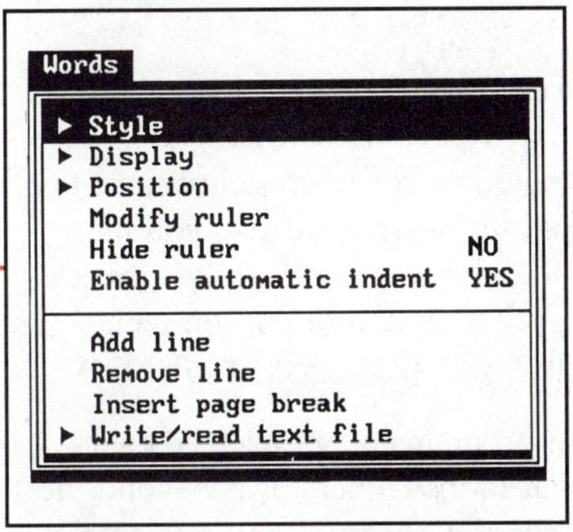

Use **Words** to enhance your printed output. The **Style** option offers normal, bold, underline, italic, subscript, and superscript printing enhancements. While using the Editor, you can add and remove lines, adjust the print ruler, and read or write external files.

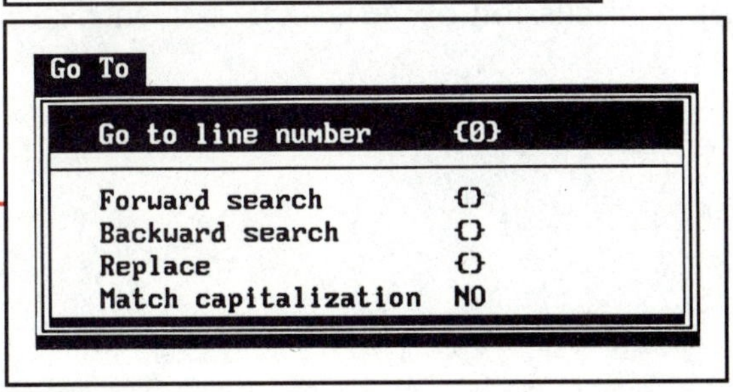

Use **Go To** to position the cursor on a specified line number or to locate or replace work-surface items.

10 *Designing Custom Programs*

The sixth and last panel on the Control Center, Applications, allows you to set up your own system of related menus and programs so that even someone unfamiliar with dBASE IV can enter and edit data and produce reports or labels. You might, for example, create a combination of menu options and screen messages that help a user produce custom letters to all customers who buy a car in the current month and produce mailing labels for envelopes. Another database user might access the elaborate menu system to add new customers to the database or change the information in a customer's record. By developing a complex menu system, you can control your database operations in many different ways.

When you access the Applications panel, you have the options to create your own application from scratch or to use dBASE IV's Applications Generator, which assists you in creating applications. Keep in mind, however, that to create applications from scratch, you must know dBASE programming code. Using the Applications Generator, you can create your own horizontal, pull-down, and pop-up menus. To use either option, you must be familiar with all aspects of dBASE IV.

Showing you how to write your own programs or set up a custom program or application with the Applications Generator is beyond the scope of *dBASE IV QuickStart*. A discussion of the dBASE IV Control

Center, however, is incomplete without a brief overview of the power of the Applications panel. Consult Que's *dBASE IV Programming Techniques* for an in-depth discussion of the Applications panel.

What Is Covered in This Chapter?

This chapter gives you an overview of the following topics:

- The Applications Generator
- Programs and applications
- The dBASE IV Quick Applications feature
- Design your own applications

Key Words Used in This Chapter

Application	One or more programs working together to accomplish an objective
Program	A set of commands (instructions or specifications) written in a programming language. dBASE IV creates a program for you when you set up a custom screen, report, or label. You also can create your own programs.
Quick Application	An option to create a *single* menu application to add, change, or browse data, remove records marked for deletion, print reports or mailing labels, and sort data

Understanding the Applications Generator

With dBASE IV's Applications Generator, you can link related databases and existing programs with a complex menu system. By developing this menu system, you can control your database operations in many different ways.

You access the Applications Generator by selecting **<create>** on the Applications panel. You then can choose either **dBASE program** (the option for creating programs from scratch) or **Applications Generator**.

Before you learn more about the Applications Generator feature, you first need to understand what is meant by both a *program* and an *application.*

What Is a Program?

If you have designed a dBASE IV query, form, report, or label, you have created a program—a set of specifications or instructions. For example, you create a program when you use the Query panel to design views that tell dBASE IV what records and fields to access. If you want to use the view more than once, you can store these instructions on disk to avoid retyping. You also create programs when you develop a custom form to enter your data, design a custom report to display your data, or enter specifications to print custom labels. These specifications stored on disk can be called programs.

Programs, such as views, forms, reports, and labels, are easy to create in dBASE IV because you simply access the appropriate Control Center panel, enter fields, text, or search conditions on-screen, and save the design to disk. Whenever you save your work, dBASE IV creates the lines of code (program instructions) to produce what you have specified. The name you assign each program appears in the appropriate Control Center panel. To reactivate the selected program and execute the specifications from disk storage, you select the program name from the list of names within the Control Center panel.

You are not limited in dBASE IV to creating programs through the Control Center panels. You can create more elaborate instructions or commands that link individual programs by means of a menu system. These related programs, called applications, are discussed in the text that follows.

What Is an Application?

An application is simply a set of related programs. In earlier chapters, you follow the creation of a car sales database and its associated views, a form for data entry, several reports, and a label design. Such related programs form an *application*. You can improve on dBASE IV's Control Center operations by creating a complex menu system from which to access a custom screen for data entry or produce a custom report without ever seeing the Control Center.

Menus are the heart of any dBASE IV application. Working from the Control Center, you access a number of horizontal Menu bars, associated pull-down menus, and free-standing pop-up menus created by dBASE IV. Using the Applications Generator, you can create your own menus.

From the Applications panel of the Control Center, you can access two powerful options for creating sophisticated programs: **dBASE program** and **Applications Generator**.

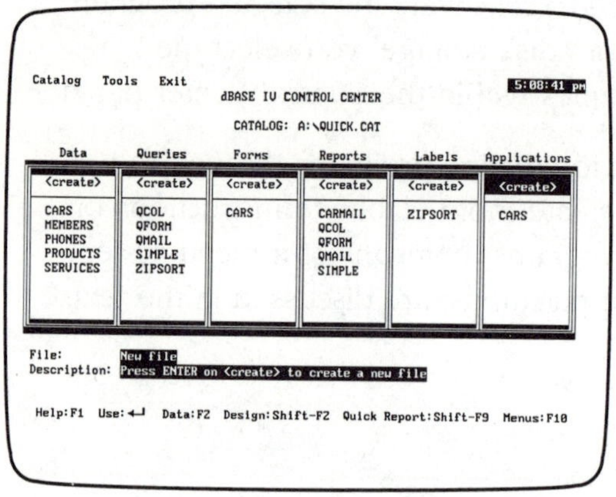

On the Control Center's Applications panel, position the highlighter on **<create>** and press ↵Enter.

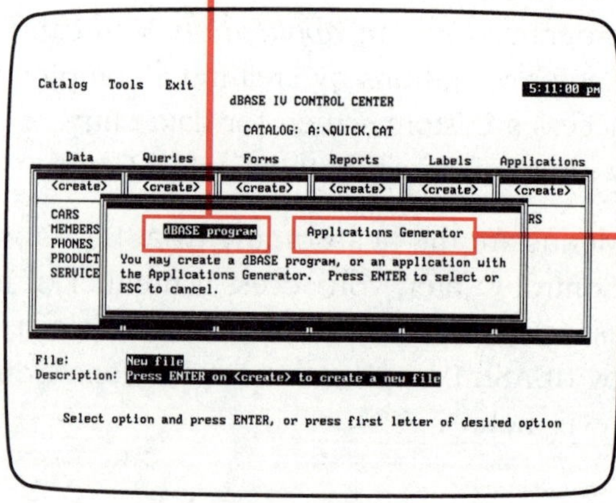

Select either **dBASE program** or **Applications Generator**.

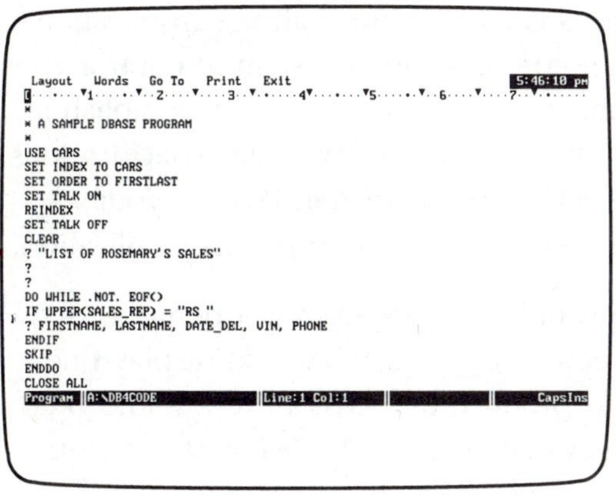

Selecting **dBASE program** causes the Editor to appear in word-wrap mode. You now can write programs using dBASE IV's command language, a programming language that gives you maximum control over your data.

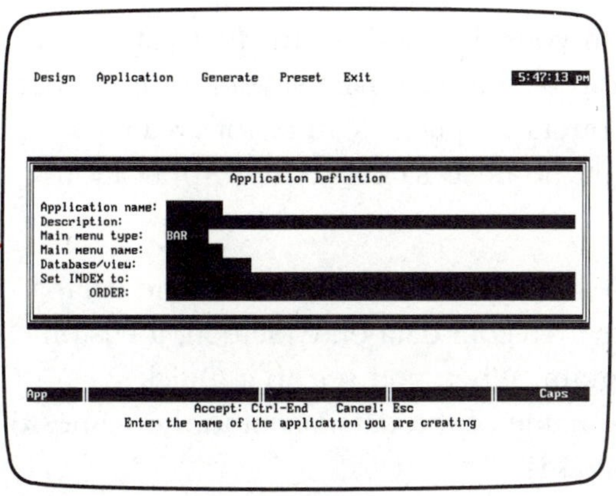

Selecting **Applications Generator** causes the first of several forms and menus to appear. By completing the forms and using the menus, you can instruct dBASE IV to create sophisticated applications without the labor and problems of programming. The Applications Generator creates a series of menus that uses the programs you created in the Queries, Forms, Reports, and Labels panels.

The features available through the Control Center let dBASE IV write most of your programs for you.

Using the Applications Generator

When you access the Applications Generator through the Applications panel, you can begin to design a complex menu system to control your application (one or more programs working together to accomplish an objective). In a manner similar to other panels, you enter specifications on-screen; when you select the **Save** option, dBASE IV uses your specifications to create the menu system that controls your application.

You can let dBASE IV design a simple menu system to open one database, to permit editing of records in the database, to display one custom data-entry screen, and to produce one custom report and one custom label. The simple menu system is called a *Quick Application.* You also can design your own menu system, incorporating multiple custom screens, reports, and labels.

Creating a Quick Application

Getting current information from your database means that you constantly must add, change, and delete data. Like several of the other panels, the Applications panel offers a "quick" feature for creating a maintenance application without the need to master the Application Generator.

To use the Quick Application feature, you first must create the database using the Data panel and create a custom data-entry screen, a custom report, and a custom label program. When you set up a Quick Application, you must enter the name of the database and the names of the form, report, and label programs.

dBASE IV then creates a single menu application with the following options: **Add Information**, **Change Information**, **Browse Information**, **Discard Marked Records**, **Print Report**, **Mailing Labels**, **Reindex Database**, and **Exit from <database name>**. A user who does not know dBASE IV can use this menu to perform minimum database maintenance tasks without accessing the Control Center.

Designing Your Own Application

The limited menu choices generated by a Quick Application may not meet your needs. For example, although you might have six custom reports for one database, a Quick Application limits you to one custom report. In cases like this, you can use the Applications Generator to design and create your own extensive menu system.

If you decide to design your own application, you must work through a basic organizing process, whether you design the application yourself or simply attempt to describe your needs to a database professional who designs the actual application. Design the menu system that supports your application, and then determine the reports, labels, and other files you must create to use your application. Using the car sales database as an example, step through a process for creating an application. First plan a *horizontal menu* to access the major functions the application should perform, such as the following:

Maintenance	Reports	Labels

Now think about adding pull-down menus displaying options to perform specific tasks within those functions, such as the following:

Maintenance	*Reports*	*Labels*
Add records	Monthly Sales	All New Car Owners
Change records	Prospect List	Rolodex Labels
Browse records	Warranty Work List	No Warranty Owners
Delete records	Sales in Process	
Reindex database	Sales Demographics	

Although you don't work through the mechanics of using the Applications Generator in this book, you can see the possibilities for creating applications tailored specifically to your needs. The dBASE IV Control Center is a powerful tool, but keep in mind that you control the number of panels you are comfortable using!

Installing dBASE IV

To install dBASE IV on a hard disk, you must have at least 4M of hard disk storage space. The Developers Edition of dBASE IV requires at least 5.2M of hard disk space. However, because you also need disk space for storing data tables and their related disk files, a minimum of about 6M to 7M of disk space is highly recommended. To determine the amount of free disk space on your hard disk, you can use the DOS command CHKDSK:

C>CHKDSK

Before you type **CHKDSK** at the **C>** prompt, make sure that the DOS file CHKDSK.COM is located on the hard disk. If the file is not in the current directory or in the path given by the latest path specifier, the following error message appears:

Bad command or file name

You must install dBASE IV from a floppy disk, which normally is drive A:. During installation, the installation program interacts with you by issuing prompt messages that tell you what action the installation program is taking and what you need to do next. Because dBASE IV requires a hard disk, you normally install dBASE IV to drive C:. Drive C: is also normally the start-up drive because most users boot from drive C:.

In some cases, users boot from a floppy if they need to start DOS when their hard disk is configured to boot OS/2 or some other operating system. In other cases, users may have their hard disk partitioned into additional logical drives such as D: and E:. If you are booting from DOS-based floppies on an OS/2 system or have logical drives configured beyond C:, you will need to modify the installation steps where your different circumstances become apparent.

To begin installing dBASE IV, have ready all the system disks from the dBASE IV package. Then follow these steps:

1. Start the system with either a cold boot or a warm boot and wait for the DOS system prompt to appear.
2. Insert the dBASE IV Installation Disk into drive A:.

   If you are starting the system from drive C:, you can switch to drive A: by typing **A:** at the **C>** prompt:

   C>A:

   With this step you make floppy disk drive A: the current active drive. Unless specified otherwise, drive A: remains the default disk drive.
3. Type **Install** at the **A>** prompt:

   A>Install
4. Follow the prompts that appear on-screen during the installation process.

Software Registration

The first time you install the dBASE IV program files on the hard disk, you are prompted to enter your name, your company name, and the serial number (which can be found on System Disk #1). After these items are entered, they are saved on a system disk file and are displayed on subsequent use of the program. You must be careful not to make any mistake in entering these items; after your entries are saved, they cannot be altered. If you type the wrong serial number, you will need to start the installation again.

The DBASE Directory

In addition to software registration, a number of important tasks are accomplished during the installation process. First, the installation process creates a directory named DBASE on drive C:, if it has not already been created. The disk space within the directory will be used to stored all the dBASE IV program and configuration files.

System Configuration

After creating the DBASE directory, the installation process copies all the dBASE IV program files onto the hard disk in that directory. In addition, two configuration files are created. The first one, named CONFIG.SYS, is a system configuration file that will be saved on the disk (drive A: or drive C:) from which you start the computer.

dBASE IV is a program that instructs the computer to perform the tasks required for managing a database. The computer program consists of a set of commands that are coded and stored on the dBASE IV system files. Before dBASE IV is loaded into memory, the computer must be informed about the environment in which the program is to be operated. For example, the number of files to be used by the program and the amount of memory to be reserved for data storage must be specified before the program is loaded. The default disk drive for data storage also must be designated so that the disk operating system can locate the data files when they are needed. You provide this information in a procedure called *system configuration.*

System configuration involves specifying necessary parameters, such as the number of files and the size of reserved memory. Booting the computer begins the execution of instructions stored in ROM. The computer is instructed to initialize the input and output devices and to allocate memory space for normal processing. By default, DOS sets at 8 the number of files that can be open at one time; however, 5 files are used by DOS, leaving only 3 for the user's programs. Because dBASE IV can accommodate many more files, the number of files is set to 40 during system configuration.

The processor sets aside a certain amount of computer memory as temporary working space for manipulation of disk data. This temporary working space is reserved in blocks of RAM that are called *buffers.* The more buffers you reserve, the faster processing is achieved. The total number of buffers is restricted by the amount of RAM available on the computer system. Because the dBASE IV program itself and the active data files used in the program compete with buffers for memory space, the number of buffers should not be set too high. Otherwise, you will not have enough memory for storing your database files during processing. With a minimum of 640K RAM in the computer, you can safely designate 15 memory buffers—the number recommended by the dBASE IV developers.

The CONFIG.SYS file, which is created by the installation process, contains at least the following two lines:

FILES=40

BUFFERS=15

If a CONFIG.SYS file is already present on the boot disk, these two lines are added to the current contents of the file during the installation process. To verify the contents of the CONFIG.SYS file, you can enter **TYPE CONFIG.SYS** at the root directory of the boot disk, as in the following examples:

A>TYPE CONFIG.SYS

or

C>TYPE CONFIG.SYS

You also can modify the contents of the CONFIG.SYS file by using a line editor (such as the EDLIN.COM program in the DOS disk) or a text processor.

dBASE IV Configuration

In addition to the system configuration CONFIG.SYS file, a dBASE IV configuration file named CONFIG.DB is created and saved in the \DBASE directory at the root level during the installation process. The CONFIG.DB configuration file contains processing commands that initiate certain operations when the program is first activated.

The CONFIG.DB file later can be used to set up all the parameters and commands for starting dBASE IV when it is invoked. The contents of the

CONFIG.DB file created by the installation process may look like that shown in figure A.1.

```
C:\DBASE>type config.db

*
*        dBASE IV Configuration File
*        Tuesday August 23, 1988
*

COLOR OF NORMAL      = W+/B
COLOR OF HIGHLIGHT   = GR+/BG
COLOR OF MESSAGES    = W/N
COLOR OF TITLES      = W/B
COLOR OF BOX         = GR+/BG
COLOR OF INFORMATION = B/W
COLOR OF FIELDS      = N/BG
COMMAND              = ASSIST
DISPLAY              = EGA25
SQLDATABASE          = SAMPLES
SQLHOME              = C:\DBASE\SQLHOME
STATUS               = ON

C:\DBASE>
```

Fig. A.1. The contents of the CONFIG.DB file.

You can change the contents of the CONFIG.DB file by using a line editor or a text processor.

dBASE IV is designed to be used on a system with a hard disk. During processing, the program assumes that drive C: is the working hard disk. If you want to designate a different hard disk for your storage space, you can specify it in the configuration file by modifying the CONFIG.DB file to include the following command:

DEFAULT=<*default disk drive*>

You enter the drive letter in place of <*default disk drive*>.

Hardware Setup

During the installation process, you also are prompted to specify the hardware configuration for use in dBASE IV. The hardware configuration can include, among other elements, the type of monitor, printer, and printer port. Information on such hardware configuration is stored in an appropriate file in the DBASE directory as well.

You can specify as many as four custom printers with dBASE IV. To set up these printers, you enter the printer port (such as LPT1 or LPT2), the name of the printer, and its driver during the hardware setup process. Figure A.2 shows the setup for the Epson LX-80 and HP® LaserJet™.

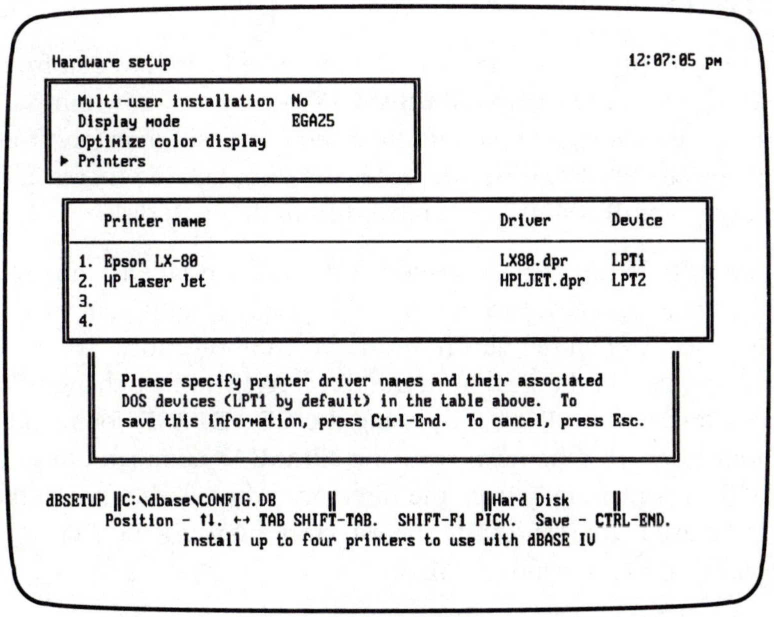

Fig. A.2. The setup for the Epson LX-80 and HP LaserJet.

Uninstalling dBASE IV from the Hard Disk

The process of uninstalling dBASE IV involves removing all the program files that are copied from the program disks during the installation process. To uninstall dBASE IV from your hard disk, you need to specify the disk directory in which the program files are stored. To perform the uninstalling operation, you use a program called DBSETUP.EXE, which normally is saved in the DBASE directory. To execute DBSETUP.EXE, you first change your working directory to the dBASE directory by using the **CD** (Change Directory) command at the **C>** prompt:

```
C>CD \DBASE
```

From the DBASE directory, you can execute the DBSETUP program by typing the program name at the prompt:

```
C>DBSETUP
```

In response to the program name, you are presented with a menu from which you can select the **Uninstall dBASE IV** option, as shown in figure A.3. You then are prompted to enter the drive and directory from which to uninstall the dBASE IV files. After the uninstalling process, all the program files of dBASE IV are removed from the hard disk.

Because dBASE IV is not copy protected and can be installed as many times as you want, you also can uninstall the program from your hard disk simply by erasing all the files from the \DBASE directory. To use this method to erase all the files from the directory, you first change your current directory to \DBASE by using the **CD \DBASE** command. From that directory, you then can issue the **ERASE *.*** command to remove the files permanently from the directory. After all the files in the directory are erased, you can delete the directory by using the **RD** (Remove Directory) command:

```
C>CD \DBASE
C>ERASE *.*
Are you sure (Y/N)?Y
C>CD \
C>RD DBASE
```

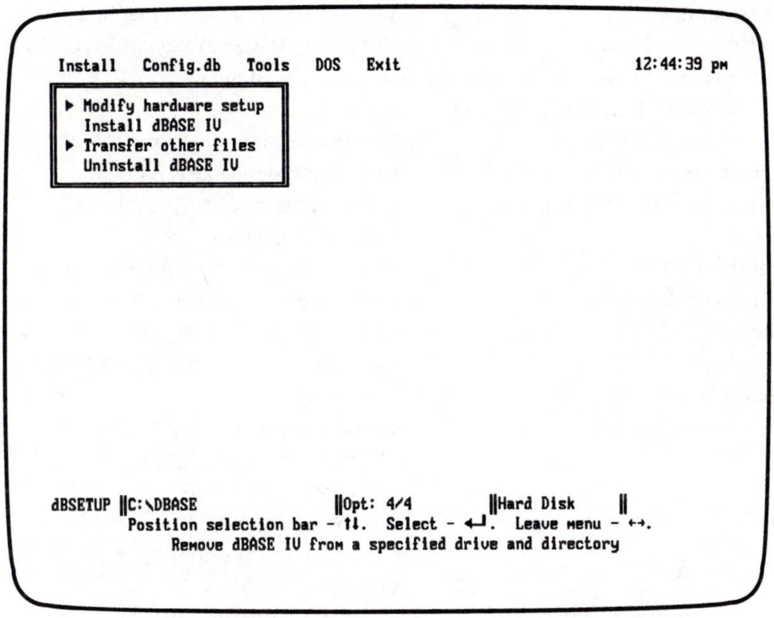

Fig. A.3. The Uninstall dBASE IV option in the DBSETUP program.

If you have any subdirectories within the \DBASE directory, you must erase all those files and subdirectories before you can remove the \DBASE directory. For example, if you have a DBDATA subdirectory within the \DBASE directory, you need to follow these steps before removing the directory from the hard disk:

C>CD \DBASE\DBDATA

C>ERASE *.*

Are you sure (Y/N)?Y

C>CD \DBASE

C>RD DBDATA

Index

A

B

C

Index

D

E

Index

G

Index

L

Index

M

N

Index

Index

P

Q

Index

R

S

Index

V

W

SELECT QUE BOOKS TO INCREASE YOUR PERSONAL COMPUTER PRODUCTIVITY

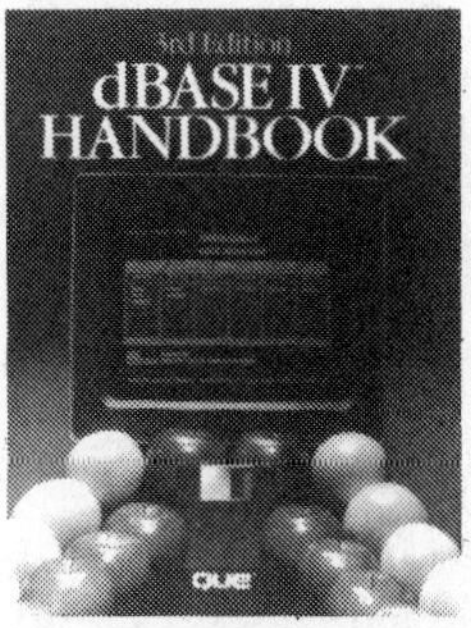

dBASE IV Handbook, 3rd Edition

by George T. Chou, Ph.D.

Learn dBASE IV quickly with Que's new *dBASE IV Handbook*, 3rd Edition! dBASE expert George Chou leads you step-by-step from basic database concepts to advanced dBASE features, using a series of Quick Start tutorials. Experienced dBASE users will appreciate the extensive information on the new features of dBASE IV, including the new user interface, the query-by-example mode, and the SQL module. Complete with comprehensive command and function reference sections, *dBASE IV Handbook*, 3rd Edition, is an exhaustive guide to dBASE IV!

dBASE IV QueCards

Developed by Que Corporation

dBASE IV QueCards—the easy-to-use reference to dBASE IV! QueCards are 5″ × 8″ cards, housed in a sturdy 3-ring binder. Convenient tabs help organize the cards into sections on functions, commands, and dBASE applications, with each card explaining proper command usage and offering helpful hints that improve your dBASE efficiency. The cards can be used with the built-in easel or removed and placed next to your computer keyboard. When you have difficulty remembering important commands or steps for developing and using dBASE applications, use *dBASE IV QueCards*—the fast and comprehensive dBASE IV reference!

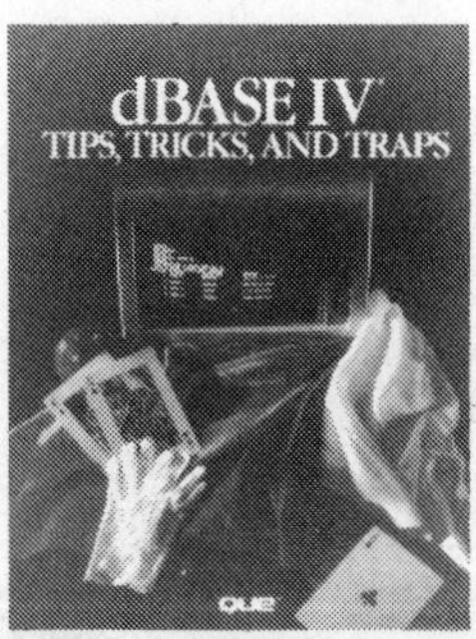

dBASE IV Tips, Tricks, and Traps, 2nd Edition

by George T. Chou, Ph.D.

Become a dBASE IV master with Que's informative *dBASE IV Tips, Tricks, and Traps*, 2nd Edition! This handy reference presents hundreds of hints and techniques that help you improve your dBASE IV efficiency. Organized by topic, this book will show you the best ways to use dBASE IV, from basic installation to advanced programming. Icons throughout the text highlight features new to dBASE IV, thus easing the transition to dBASE IV for previous dBASE users. Get more power from dBASE IV with *dBASE IV Tips, Tricks, and Traps*, 2nd Edition!

dBASE IV Quick Reference

Developed by Que Corporation

Put dBASE IV commands and functions at your fingertips with Que's *dBASE IV Quick Reference.* Whether you use a laptop or a desktop computer, this portable reference provides immediate access to information often buried in traditional text. This compact guide is an instant reference to often-used dBASE IV commands and functions!

ORDER FROM QUE TODAY

Item	Title	Price	Quantity	Extension
852	dBASE IV Handbook, 3rd Edition	$23.95		
854	dBASE IV Tips, Tricks, and Traps, 2nd Edition	21.95		
867	dBASE IV Quick Reference	6.95		
75	dBASE IV QueCards	21.95		

Book Subtotal ______

Shipping & Handling ($2.50 per item) ______

Indiana Residents Add 5% Sales Tax ______

GRAND TOTAL ______

Method of Payment

☐ Check ☐ VISA ☐ MasterCard ☐ American Express

Card Number ______________________ Exp. Date ______________________

Cardholder's Name ____

Ship to ____

Address ____

City ______________________ State ______________ ZIP ______________

If you can't wait, call **1-800-428-5331** and order TODAY.

All prices subject to change without notice.

FOLD HERE

Place
Stamp
Here

Que Corporation
P.O. Box 90
Carmel, IN 46032

R873—dBASE IV QuickStart

REGISTRATION CARD

Register your copy of *dBASE IV QuickStart*, and receive information about Que's newest products. Complete this registration card and return it to Que Corporation, P.O. Box 90, Carmel, IN 46032.

Name ____________________ Phone __________

Company ____________________ Title __________

Address ______________________________

City ____________ State ________ ZIP ________

Please check the appropriate answers:

Where did you buy *dBASE IV QuickStart*?

- ☐ Bookstore (name: ____________________)
- ☐ Computer store (name: ____________________)
- ☐ Catalog (name: ____________________)
- ☐ Direct from Que ____________________
- ☐ Other: ____________________

How many computer books do you buy a year?

- ☐ 1 or less
- ☐ 2–5
- ☐ 6–10
- ☐ More than 10

How many Que books do you own?

- ☐ 1
- ☐ 2–5
- ☐ 6–10
- ☐ More than 10

How long have you been using dBASE software?

- ☐ Less than 6 months
- ☐ 6 months to 1 year
- ☐ 1–3 years
- ☐ More than 3 years

What influenced your purchase of *dBASE IV QuickStart*?

- ☐ Personal recommendation
- ☐ Advertisement
- ☐ In-store display
- ☐ Price
- ☐ Que catalog
- ☐ Que mailing
- ☐ Que's reputation
- ☐ Other: ____________________

How would you rate the overall content of *dBASE IV QuickStart*?

- ☐ Very good
- ☐ Good
- ☐ Satisfactory
- ☐ Poor

How would you rate this book's graphics-based approach to learning dBASE IV?

- ☐ Very good
- ☐ Good
- ☐ Satisfactory
- ☐ Poor

How would you rate this book's organization of topics?

- ☐ Very good
- ☐ Good
- ☐ Satisfactory
- ☐ Poor

How would you rate the "pointer" method of referencing topics?

- ☐ Very good
- ☐ Good
- ☐ Satisfactory
- ☐ Poor

What do you like *best* about *dBASE IV QuickStart*?

What do you like *least* about *dBASE IV QuickStart*?

How do you use *dBASE IV QuickStart*?

What other Que products do you own?

For what other programs would a Que book be helpful?

Please feel free to list any other comments you may have about *dBASE IV QuickStart*.

____

____

____

____

____

____

FOLD HERE

Place
Stamp
Here

Que Corporation
P.O. Box 90
Carmel, IN 46032